India Studies in Business and Economics

Indian economy is one of the fastest growing economies of the world, entering the top 5 club in 2022. The country is an important G20 member and is also a founding member of BRICS. A significant player in the global market with a notable demographic advantage and an important geo-political and geo-trade position, India has a pivotal role to play in meeting global SDG goals. This makes research from the country of immense interest to the global community, especially to those trying to understand emerging developmental challenges through a developing economy and/or Global South perspective.

With this backdrop, this series aims to bring forth latest studies and research specific to India from all areas of economics, finance, business, trade, and management science, often with strong social science and political economy linkages. The titles featured in this series present rigorous research, both empirical and non-empirical in nature, usually accompanied by policy recommendations. They evoke and evaluate various aspects of the economical and/or the business and management landscape in India, with a special focus on India's relationship with the world. The series also tracks research on India's position on social issues, health, politics, agriculture, rights, and many such topics which directly or indirectly affect sustainable growth and SDG goals of the country.

Primarily publishing authored monographs and edited volumes, the series also considers collection of case studies, reports and proceedings of important national conferences. It welcomes contributions from the academic community, corporates, think tanks and/or non-governmental organizations, and also policymakers to publish their work. Proposals must contain a detailed concept note describing the book's content and its importance; academic CV of authors/editors; extended chapter abstracts that clearly define the chapter's content; and a sample chapter. Each proposal will undergo a double-blind peer review. Reviews can be more detailed if recommended by reviewers.

Guidelines for submission and our policies on ethics is found on the series homepage www.springer.com/series/11234.

Biswajit Chatterjee · Asim K. Karmakar
Editors

Analytical Issues in Growth & Structural Change, Macroeconomy, Security, and Sustainability of India's Economic Development

Springer

Editors
Biswajit Chatterjee
Department of Economics
Jadavpur University
Kolkata, West Bengal, India

Asim K. Karmakar
Department of Economics
Jadavpur University
Kolkata, West Bengal, India

ISSN 2198-0012 ISSN 2198-0020 (electronic)
India Studies in Business and Economics
ISBN 978-981-95-5241-2 ISBN 978-981-95-5242-9 (eBook)
https://doi.org/10.1007/978-981-95-5242-9

This Springer imprint is published by the registered company Springer Nature Singapore Pte Ltd.
The registered company address is: 152 Beach Road, #21-01/04 Gateway East, Singapore 189721, Singapore

Preface

The present volume was planned to reflect on the Indian Economy after 75 years of its existence. However, a plethora of books and edited volumes appeared covering a lot of issues experienced by the Indian economy. The present volume is a collection of essays written to reflect analytical understanding of contemporary Indian Economy. Issues chosen are *selective* and not *comprehensive.* The theoretical and empirical research on some aspect of India's economic development, and its development have been analysed by teachers and scholars to focus their attention to the following important aspects: growth and structural change, reforms and the macroeconomy, food and nutritional security, and sustainable development of our economy. This volume is being dedicated to the memory of Professor Dhiresh Chandra Bhattacharya, a legendary teacher of economics from West Bengal, an author of the pioneering analytical text book on the economy of divided India, and the Second President of the Bangiya Arthaniti Prishad. Some of the contributors, including myself, were direct student of Professor Bhattacharya, while others from different parts of Indian universities or research institutes were perhaps inspired by his analytical text book on the economy of independent India.

Getting so many papers and assessing and revising them in the forms of chapters as per the suggestions of the publishers, is not an easy task, which our editorial team has accomplished. I thank all the contributors and paper writers for their valuable contributions as well as the patience and endurance with which they have cooperated to make the volume truly important. I owe special thanks to Mr. Gowrishankar A and his team, and Ms. Nupoor Singh of the Springer Nature India for their kind help in making the volume ready for publication. A very special thanks are for the Co-editor of the volume, Dr. Asim Kumar Karmakar for his devoted and dedicated service in making the volume truly ready for seeing the light of the day (he passed away on 14.12.2024 after brief illness, leaving a void in the academic fraternity in India).

Thank you

Kolkata, India

Biswajit Chatterjee

About This Book (BARB)

Biswajit Chatterjee. Asim K. Karmakar editors

Analytical Issues in Growth & Structural Change, Macroeconomy, Security and Sustainability of India's Economic Development: Dedicated to Professor Dhiresh Chandra Bhattacharyya

This book is a collection of essays written to reflect analytical understanding of contemporary Indian Economy. The theoretical and empirical research on some aspect of India's economic development, and its development have been analysed by teachers and scholars to focus attention to the following important aspects: growth and structural change, political economy, and the macroeconomy, food and nutritional security, and sustainable development of our economy. All these issues are crucial for our understanding of the process of economic change and institutional reforms currently underway in India, and the need for policy initiatives to achieve the targets of our development. This selection gives focus on *analytical issues* as opposed to purely *descriptive narratives*, and shall be of interests to the researchers, teachers and policy thinkers on the domains of Indian economic development. Written by different scholars, the issues chosen are *selective*, and not *comprehensive,* but together the papers in the volume contain blend of theoretical and empirical methodologies to aptly portray the future issues of the economy. The book is dedicated to the memory of ***Professor Dhiresh Chandra Bhattacharyya***, a legendary teacher and scholar in Economics in the country The book is expected to have wide readership comprising advanced graduate students as well as researchers and policy thinkers on the Indian economy.

Introduction

The divided India's Economy is more than 75 years' old. During this period, the economy has not only grown, it has diversified the production base with implications for employment and output and the economy has been working with a globalized world for more than three decades now. In our search for analytical issues, we now-a-days ignore the economy of India under the colonial rule, relegating the discussions to the domain of economic history, which are beyond our cognition in this volume. The theoretical and empirical research on some aspect of India's economy, and its development have been contributed by teachers and scholars in this volume to pay tributes to ***Professor Dhiresh Chandra Bhattacharya***, a legendary teacher, an author of the pioneering text book entitled *Understanding India's Economy.*

Some of the analytical issues pertaining to Indian economic development since political independence for the long period have been picked up in this volume. It adopts a *selective* approach as opposed to a *comprehensive* one. Some such analytical issues are often theoretical or empirical in nature. While the theoretical issues reflect the lineage from the theoretical discourses on Development economics, the empirical issues are posed by the actual process of development experience and the data generated in the process. The analytical issues chosen in this volume differ from the discourses that were in vogue during the first four decades of India's economic development. The range of both theoretical and empirical issues have naturally undergone changes in their tenors and thrusts as the economy progressed towards more liberalized and globally integrated frame since the last three decades of economic reforms. The analytical themes chosen for the present volume are growth and structural change, political economy and the macroeconomy, food and nutritional security, and sustainable development of our economy.

Economic growth is a long-term process whereby the aggregate of domestic production undergoes changes over time. One crucial aspect of the issue of economic growth in a developing country like India happens to be the nature of market structure within which production can adjust and growth could occur. It is conceived that oligopolistic market structure typically prevails in India's corporate sector whereby contagion for networked oligopolies reduces the diversity of production and, consequently, the extensive margins of exports and imports shrink, and the effect is stronger in the presence of domestic and/or foreign networks than it would be without networks. This is important, in view of the prevailing market structure of our economy, which is far from the benchmark of perfect completion. The first paper of the volume provides a theoretical insight to capture the working of the oligopolistic corporate sector that evolved over the period. Secondly, in our rural economy, endowment differences, particularly land ownership pattern often govern the growth process which has deleterious effects on some social groups like child labour. While the prevalence of child labour in the Indian context, is noted in policy discussions in India and abroad, the moot question is whether economic growth, and its variants, are somewhat responsible for the emergence of this social evil. With the help of an overlapping generations household economy model in rural set up, the relationship between landholding and child labour as well as landholding and fertility in the presence of unemployment in the manufacturing sector, have been examined by the second chapter of the volume. If parents give more importance to expected earnings of children in their utility function rather than the quantity of children, the number of children is positive only if adult earnings exceed subsistence expenditure; time devoted to schooling by children increases as landholding increases, and the necessary condition of fertility increasing with increase in landholding in this case is adult earning being sufficiently lower than twice subsistence consumption expenditure.

Economic growth, in whatever form, however, cannot ensure automatic and quick trickle-down process through which the benefits of growth reach the lower strata of income and wealth, and we need alternative development paradigm which combines economic growth and income distribution within the same process as are outlined by the proponents of the Classical political economy. The inclusive growth paradigm in India has been examined in the volume in the context of rising inequality in income and wealth distribution in India, and it is argued that the tenets of long run behavior of the economy in the realm of growth of GDP need be juxtaposed against the imperatives of distributional challenges that the economy has been facing even now. There are several analytical issues involved: a. Would growth acceleration necessarily generates acceleration of inequality and wealth?; b. Would inequality reduction slower the rate of growth of the economy? And if so, what are the alternatives that are available to the policy maker, who may be interested in achieving inclusive growth in the economy? Usually, such issues are not put forward in the discussions on primacy of growth in the economy.

Structural Changes constitute an important element of modern development economics and in the Indian context, studies on structural changes tend to focus on changes in occupation that economic development and growth experienced. Modern approaches to structural change from primary to secondary to tertiary sectors' output composition is based on endogenous structural breaks tested by time series econometrics. In the present volume, there is a study which tries to explain the relationship between share of services and per capita state national product, in a quadratic as well as quartic form, for which there is an evidence of two waves of service sector growth, the second wave commencing after the 2000s. The structural change analysis shows that the share of services has been steadily increasing across all states. As per the quadratic form, the closed economy structural transformation model indicates that except for community, social and personal services, all other components of services, and services as a whole, show that share of services is negatively and significantly related to log of per capita, and is positively and significantly related to the square of per capita income. Therefore, as the economy develops, structural changes take place with the rise in the share of services. On the other hand, the population variable is positively and significantly related to service share, and it is negatively and significantly related to the square of the population variable.

Section II of the volume presents collections on Political economy and Macroeconomy.There is no denying the fact the experience of economic reforms in India is more than three decades old. During this period, the character of reform packages practiced have undergone changes, keeping however, the 'growth only' paradigm in the lead and market orientation and openness as concomitant strategies. The political economy questions about this paradigm shift in our reform process are to be viewed as the outcome of our macroeconomic behaviours. India's macroeconomy in recent years has experienced *two* types of shocks-Demonetization, and the Corona pandemic. When the government announced a major change in the indirect taxation system (implementation of Goods and Services Tax, GST) from July 2016 and an alternation of monetary environment by demonetizing the high value currency notes—of Rs 500 and Rs 1000—which ceased to be legal tender from the midnight of 8th of November 2016, the first wave of macroeconomic shocks to the economy occurred. Later, the world economy confronted the most serious challenge of mankind—"the Corona Pandemic" caused by the outbreak of (COVID-19) virus since March, 2020. It already brought considerable human suffering and major economic disruption. The devastation of this health pandemic made economists predict that the second innings of the battle would be even more severe and may take the world back to the days of "The Great Depression" of the 1930s. The present study (chapter "Impact of Demonetization Shock and Corona Pandemic on India") tries to analyze both the short and long run effects of demonetization and the corona pandemic. It attempts examine the long run impact on some macroeconomic variables-GDP, sectoral composition, industrial production, inflation, employment. Moreover, it tries to throw some light on the expected economic impact of the Corona pandemic on the world as well as on the Indian economy, with some policy measures. The whole analysis was based on secondary time series data from the RBI official statistics, Ministry of Statistics and Programme Implementation (MoSPI), Govt. of India, Centre for Monitoring Indian Economy (CMIE). International Labour Organization (ILO) and Organization for Economic Cooperation Development (OECD).

In the post-reform period, employment had been more or less stagnant in the organized sector even though average annual growth rates of both GDP and value added of the organized sector at constant prices were quite high. The stagnancy or deceleration in the level of employment in India in the post-pandemic era, may be explained with the help of a *structuralist* macroeconomic model (chapter "Generating Employment in India: A Suggestion"), whereby it can be shown that the larger the stock of infrastructure capital in the unorganized sector, the larger will be the levels of output and employment in both the sectors. If the government invests in infrastructure in the unorganized sector and finances it by taxing capitalists' income, employment will go up significantly. Further, it can be shown that, if the government invests in infrastructure in the unorganized sector and finances it by taxing capitalists' income, employment will go up significantly, but if the government finances its investment expenditure by imposing indirect taxes, employment and output levels are likely to contract in both the sectors.

Another important aspect of the reform process in the Indian economy has been the connect with the international economy, particularly during the globalization phase. Through such connectedness, there are international transmission of growth cycles across nations and that put a brake on the autonomy of domestic economic policies. Methods of investigating such connect between nations have been developed in recent years and Indian context such studies are emerging. As reported in the present volume (chapter "Dynamic Connectedness of Indian Business Cycle with G-7 Economies"), a study aims at exploring the business cycle connectedness among G7 countries and India using monthly industrial production data from April 1994 to December 2018. The variance decompostion method of generalized VAR model has been employed to estimate volatility spillover among all countries. Empirical findings suggest that US is net transmitter of volatility whereas Germany is the main recepient of spillover shocks. India is found to be weakly synchronized with G7 nations as far as industrial output based business cycle is concerned.

Also, it is relevant to examine the long run and causal relationship between financial development and economic growth with the help of new time series methodology for the period of 52 years (1971 to 2023) and we have included one such effort (in chapter "Financial Deepening—Growth Nexus in South Africa and India: An Evidence from Cointegration and Causality") for South Africa and India. The financial sector reforms adopted by the Indian economy since 1991 onwards and South African economy in 1985, were based on the theoretical backdrop of McKinnon–Shaw (1973) theory of Financial Liberalization. Further the chapter has analysed the trends of GDP growth rate and financial deepening in South Africa and India and that study infers that financial deepening is not co-integrated with economic growth in South Africa and shows no long run relationship, but in India, both the variables are co-integrated and the long run relationship is found significant at 5% level. Granger causality results also show the difference in the direction of causality. In South Africa, causality runs from growth to finance, which supports the hypothesis of Demand–Led Growth, while in India causality runs from finance to growth, which supports the hypothesis of Supply Led Growth. The above results were supported by the VECM, IRF, and VDC. The paper finds that the liberalized financial system has not been able to increase effective growth rates in South Africa, while it has succeeded in India. The Indian experience and India's appropriate regulatory and macroeconomic policies could be emulated by South Africa for the further improvement in its money and capital markets.

One important issue debated in the present context of India's economic development has been the Food and Nutritional Security of our population, which is the subject matter of section III. This is an important area where focus of contemporary research has come to the centre-stage. Elimination of hunger, chronic as well as transitory, food insecurity, and attainment of sustainable food security were projected goals of the international community. The main issue is that despite moving from a food deficit to food surplus and food exporting nation over the years, the problem of food and nutritional insecurity continues to haunt nation's economic policies. If food availability per capita in the aggregate is comfortable, why is the access to food poor and inadequate? In this context, we discuss the historical evolution of food security measures in India over time and their spatial and temporal behaviours and identify the policy dilemmas, and the present contextual domains. The macroeconomic implications of the link between marketable surplus, income distribution, industrial output and inter-sectoral terms of trade are also explored through an analytical model. Another serious area of concern in India in recent years is child under-nutrition. The extent of child under-nutrition in India is quite high, its prevalence and incidence require explanation. Using the unit-level information obtainable from NFHS-3, NFHS-4, & NFHS-5, a chapter in the present volume makes an attempt to identify the main social, demographic, and economic factors operating in India across the major states, which tend to determine the extent and prevalence of child under-nutrition in India.

One major issue in the contemporary discourses of the Indian economy is **Sustainability**. A study of inter-temporal behaviour of a less developed economy is presented in terms of a two-sector dynamic model consisting of an imported traded good sector and of a non-traded tourism service sector serving international tourists, is presented in the volume. Chapter "A Holistic and Concrete Approach to Sustainable Development" delineates the conceptual and analytical issues pertaining to sustainable development In the realm of irrigation in the country, an important issue has been whether adequate access to irrigation improves the Socio-Economic Status (SES) of poor and marginal rural farmers. Based on primary data from a sample of 440 rural farming households located in a saline zone, in the state of West Bengal, India, an attempt (chapter "Access to Irrigation and Socioeconomic Status of Farm Households: A Study in a Saline Zone in India") was made to derive the multi-dimensional index of SES for each household with the help of factor analysis. Then the relationship between the SES-index to various independent variables that affect livelihood, including access to irrigation,were discussed through quantile regression analysis. Quantile regression results show that while access to irrigation does improve SES, the marginal effects of access differ substantially between low-versus-high income quantiles, and that access to irrigation has larger marginal effects at lower end of the distribution. The results are useful for targeted irrigation-intervention policy programs.

While climate change is a major threat to our objective of sustainable development, an empirical enquiry based on primary surveys of a drought–prone area of Purulia district in West Bengal were undertaken in the last chapter (chapter "Measurement and Determinants of Climate Change Vulnerability: A Household-Level Study in the Drought-Prone District of West Bengal, India") of the volume. The resulting vulnerability index for the sampled households averaged at 0.6987, highlighting substantial variation in vulnerability across households: approximately half of the sample exhibited high vulnerability, 47% moderate and only 3% low. Using an ordered logit model, socio-economic and environmental factors were identified as significant contributors to household vulnerability. The study brings into focus the importance of devising strategies to mitigate the miseries of the people.

In all, the present volume presents an array of selected analytical issues that are debated in the contemporary discourse on Indian economic development. Each paper in the volume contains rigours of theoretical and empirical research and points to the required policy initiatives to address the problems posed during the course of India's economic development.

The editors of the volume are grateful to the contributors and paper writers for their valuable contributions as well as the patience and endurance with which they have cooperated to make the volume truly important. I owe special thanks to Mr. Gowrishankar A and his team, and Ms Nupoor Singh of the Springer Nature India and her teams for the kind help in making the volume ready for publication. A very special thanks are for the Co-editor of the volume, Dr. Asim Kumar Karmakar for his devoted and dedicated service in making the volume truly ready for seeing the light of the day (he passed away on 14.12.2024 after brief illness, leaving a void in the academic fraternity in India).

I hope the volume would be a valuable addition to the ever-growing literature on the analytical discourses on Indian Economic Development.

Biswajit Chatterjee

Contents

Food and Nutrition Security in India

India and Sustainable Development Goals

Editors and Contributors

About the Editors

Professor Biswajit Chatterjee (b.3.3.1954) is a leading development economist of the country. He is a Retired Professor of Economics, Jadavpur University, was the Head of Department of Economics, Jadavpur University, and was the Dean, Faculty of Arts, Jadavpur University, Kolkata from April 1, 2002 to 31.3.2010. The major areas of his teaching and research were: Macroeconomic Theory, International Trade Theory and Policy, Balance of Payments, Development Economics, & Indian Economic Development and Policies. He also taught at, Presidency College, Calcutta, Kalyani University before joining Jadavpur University in 1984, and he was Visiting Faculty at the Department of Economics, University of Calcutta, and the Rabindra Bharati University and also a Visiting Professor, CRRID, Chandigarh from June 2010 to June 2014.

He has published regularly in national and international journals of repute, contributed to edited volumes, and has published 8 books and 14 edited volumes on different branches of development economics. Professor Chatterjee also delivered lectures in various conferences throughout the globe. He was consultant to the World Bank, UNDP, and the Planning Commission.

Professor Chatterjee had the distinction of serving and leading various prestigious professional bodies of economics in the country. He was the President of The Indian Econometric Society for two consecutive years, 2011 and 2012, President Indian Society of Labour Economics, 2014, besides being the President of Bengal Economic Association for the period April 2005 to March 2014, and again from February 2017 to till date. He is the Conference President of the Indian Economic Association, 2023. He was also associated with various prestigious academic bodies in India in respect of promotion of social science research & education in the country.

Dr. Asim K. Karmakar (b.03.01.1956) was Assistant Professor in Economics, School of Professional Studies, Netaji Subhash Open University, Kalyani, West Bengal (*Till his untimely passing away on 14.12.2024, following critical illness*) and was formerly Assistant Professor, Department of Economics, Jadavpur University, Kolkata. He had contributed more than 150 research papers in reputed journals at home and abroad, and also co-edited and edited books published by leading national/international publishers like Springer, IGI Global, Emerald and Palgrave Macmillan. The present volume received his valuable help and advice till his last days.

Contributors

Zeeshan Nezami Ansari Department of Economics, GITAM (Deemed to be) University Bengaluru, Bengaluru, Karnataka, India

Supravat Bagli Presidency University, Kolkata, India

Aishwarya Basu Department of Economics, Sister Nivedita University (SNU), Newtown Kolkata, India

Jyotish Prakash Basu Department of Economics, West Bengal State University, Kolkata, India

Rajib Bhattacharyya Goenka College of Commerce and Business Administration, Kolkata, India

Avik Chakrabarti University of Wisconsin-Milwaukee (UWM), Milwaukee, WI, USA

Bidisha Chakraborty Jadavpur University, Kolkata, India

Kamalika Chakraborty Khatra Adibasi Mahavidyalaya (Affiliated to Bankura University), Makrara, India

Biswajit Chatterjee Economics, Jadavpur University, Kolkata, India

Purba Chattopadhyay Department of Home Science, University of Calcutta, Kolkata, India

Purba Roy Choudhury Department of Economics, The Bhawanipur Education Society College, Kolkata, India

Papita Dutta Gushkara Mahavidyalaya, Gushkara, India

Priya Brata Dutta Economics and Politics Department, Visva-Bharati University, Shantiniketan, West Bengal, India

Shailendra N. Gajanan Division of Business Management, University of Pittsburgh, Bradford, PA, USA

Ambar Nath Ghosh Department of Economics, Jadavpur University, Kolkata, India

Dipti Ghosh Department of Economics, Jadavpur University, Kolkata, India

Manash Ranjan Gupta Economic Research Unit, Indian Statistical Institute, Kolkata, India

Sebak Kumar Jana Department of Economics, Vidyasagar University, Midnapore, West Bengal, India

Siddhartha Mitra Department of Economics, Jadavpur University, Kolkata, India

Basudha Mukhopadhyay Department of Commerce, J D Birla Institute, Kolkata, West Bengal, India

Mahendra Pal Department of Commerce, Delhi School of Economics, University of Delhi, New Delhi, India

Rajendra Narayan Paramanik IIT Patna, Patna, Bihar, India

Sampriti Sarkar Michigan State University, East Lansing, MI, USA

Growth and Structural Change

Contagion, Production, and Trade with Networked Oligopolies: A General Equilibrium Model

Avik Chakrabarti

Abstract We study some unique implications of contagion for oligopolies with networks. In doing so, we build an attractable model of contagion with networked oligopolies in general equilibrium. We demonstrate that contagion reduces the diversity of production and, consequently, the extensive margins of exports and imports shrink. While contagion dampens the extensive margins of trade, the effect is stronger in the presence of domestic and/or foreign networks than it would be without networks. All else equal, the net effect of contagion on the extensive margins of trade depends on the relative economy of size of each network.

Keywords Network · Contagion · Oligopoly · General equilibrium

JEL Classification Codes L13 · L20 · F10 · F12

1 Introduction

Contagion, typically defined as the transmission of an influence from one individual unit to another, has gained significant attention since the recent pandemic. However, the absence of scientific inquiries into the role of contagion in strategic relationships between networked firms engaged in trade under oligopolistic competition is rather conspicuous. We demonstrate that an increase in contagion can reduce diversity of production and extensive margins of trade. We show that contagion dampens domestic (foreign) exports more, in the presence of a complete domestic (foreign) network, than it would have if domestic (foreign) networks were empty. We also show that an increase in contagion dampens domestic (foreign) imports more, in the presence of a complete foreign (domestic) network, than it would have if foreign

Note: This chapter draws heavily on Beladi and Chakrabarti (2020) with the consent of all authors.

A. Chakrabarti (✉)
University of Wisconsin-Milwaukee (UWM), Milwaukee, WI, USA
e-mail: chakra@uwm.edu

B. Chatterjee and A. K. Karmakar (eds.), *Analytical Issues in Growth & Structural Change, Macroeconomy, Security, and Sustainability of India's Economic Development*, India Studies in Business and Economics, https://doi.org/10.1007/978-981-95-5242-9_1

(domestic) networks were empty. In doing so, while we draw on a vast pool of relevant literature, our analytical construct is most closely related to Neary (2003, 2007), Jackson (2010), Beladi et al. (2013), Bonaccorsiet al. (2014), and Beladi and Chakrabarti (2019). Our model and insights are contained in the next section, and our observations are summarized in the concluding section.[1]

2 Model and Insights

Consider a stylized world consisting of two trading economies, home and foreign, with identical population (P) and a continuum of atomistic industries indexed by $\tilde{z} \in [0, 1]$ hosting firms that compete 'a la Cournot (1838). Let $\tilde{y}(z)$ and $\tilde{y}^*(z)$ be the industry outputs at home and abroad, respectively, with unit costs of production $c(z)$ and $c^*(z)$. Countries contain a set of networks for each industry z: $N(z)$ at home connecting $n_{1(z)}$ firms and $N^*(z)$ in the foreign country connecting $n_1^*(z)$ firms; $n_1(z) + n_{-1}(z) = n(z)$ and $n_1^*(z) + n_{-1}^*(z) = n^*(z)$ where $n_{-1}(z)$ and $n_{-1}^*(z)$ are the count of firms operating outside any network at home and in the foreign country, respectively. S is the segment of the global population susceptible to an infection such that $S'(t) = -\alpha_1 S(t)I(t)$ and $S(0) = S_0$; I is the infected segment of the population such that $I'(t) = \alpha_1 S(t)I(t) - \alpha_2 I(t)$; and $I(0) = I_0$; where $\alpha_1 \in (0, 1)$ is the transmission rate and $\alpha_2 \in (0, 1)$ is the recovery rate. Let M and M^* measure the mass action incidence at home and in the foreign country, respectively: $M + M^* \equiv S + I$ and an average member of the population makes contact, sufficient to transmit an infection, with $\alpha_1(M + M^*)$ others per unit of time while the rate of exit from the infective group is $\alpha_2 I$ per unit of time. Technology exhibits positive network externalities if:

$$\beta_i(z) = \begin{cases} \beta(z) - \left(\theta - \frac{M}{P}\right) n_i(\eta(z)) & \forall F_i \in N \\ \beta(z) & \text{otherwise} \end{cases} \tag{1a}$$

and/or

$$\beta_i^*(z) = \begin{cases} \beta^*(z) - \left(\theta^* - \frac{M^*}{P}\right) n_i^*(\eta^*(z)) & \forall F_i \in N \\ \beta^*(z) & \text{otherwise} \end{cases} \tag{1b}$$

where network $\eta = \left\{ (n_{ij}(z))_{F_i, F_j \in N(z)} \right\}$ and $\eta^* = \left\{ \left(n_{ij}^*(z)\right)_{F_i^*, F_j^* \in N^*(z)} \right\}$ define pair-wise relationships between firms at home and in the foreign country, respectively; $\beta(z) > 0$ and $\beta^*(z) > 0$ measure the unit labor requirements without any network externality, respectively, at home and in the foreign country; β_i measures the unit labor requirement for F_i; and β_i^* measures the unit labor requirement for F_i^*. Demand is characterized by quadratic utility functions

[1] This chapter draws heavily on Beladi and Chakrabarti (2020) with the consent of all authors.

$$U[\{x(z)\}] = \int_0^1 \left[\rho_1 x(z) - \frac{1}{2}\rho_2 x(z)^2\right] \mathrm{d}z \tag{2}$$

$$U[\{x^*(z)\}] = \int_0^1 \left[\rho_1 x^*(z) - \frac{1}{2}\rho_2 x^*(z)^2\right] \mathrm{d}z \tag{3}$$

where $x(z)$ and $x^*(z)$ measure the consumption of good z at the home and in the foreign country, respectively. A representative consumer in the home country maximizes (3) subject to the budget constraint

$$\int_0^1 p(z)x(z)\mathrm{d}z \leq Y \tag{4}$$

and, analogously, a representative consumer in the foreign country maximizes (4) subject to the budget constraint

$$\int_0^1 p(z)x^*(z)\mathrm{d}z \leq Y^* \tag{5}$$

where Y and Y^* measure the aggregate income at home and in the foreign country, respectively.

The first and second moments of the distribution of prices are

$$\mu_1^P \equiv \int_0^1 p(z)dz$$

$$\mu_2^P \equiv \int_0^1 p(z)^2 dz$$

The inverse demand function for each good, which is linear in its own price conditional on the marginal utility of income (λ), at home is

$$p(z) = \frac{1}{\lambda}[\rho_1 - \rho_2 x(z)]$$

where $\lambda = \frac{a\mu_1^P - bI}{\mu_2^P}$.

Analogously, in the foreign country, the inverse demand function for the same good is given by

$$p(z) = \frac{1}{\lambda^*}\left[\rho_1^* - \rho_2 x^*(z)\right]$$

where $\lambda^* = \frac{a\mu_1^p - bI^*}{\mu_2^p}$. The effects of prices on λ and λ^* are thus summarized by the first and second moments of the distribution of prices.

Therefore, the world inverse demand curve for each good is

$$p(z) = a - \frac{\alpha_1}{\alpha_2}S - s^{-1}\overline{x}(z) \tag{6}$$

where $\overline{x} = (x + x^*)$. We choose $\overline{\lambda} = (\lambda + \lambda^*)$, the world marginal utility of income, as the *numeraire* and normalize $W = \overline{\lambda}w$ and $W^* = \overline{\lambda}w^*$ where w and w^* are the hourly nominal wages at home and in the foreign country, respectively. Full employment requires

$$L = \int_{\tilde{z}}^{\tilde{z}^*} \begin{bmatrix} \beta_i(z)n_1 y_1\left(W, W^*, z, n_1, n_{-1}, n_1^*, n_{-1}^*\right) \\ +\beta(z)n_{-1}y_{-1}\left(W, W^*, z, n_1, n_{-1}, n_1^*, n_{-1}^*\right) \end{bmatrix} \mathrm{d}z$$

$$+ \int_{0}^{\tilde{z}^*} \begin{bmatrix} \beta_i(z)n_1 y_1\left(W, W^*, z, n_1, n_{-1}, 0, 0\right) \\ +\beta(z)n_{-1}y_{-1}\left(W, W^*, z, n_1, n_{-1}, 0, 0\right) \end{bmatrix} \mathrm{d}z \tag{7}$$

$$L^* = \int_{\tilde{z}^*}^{\tilde{z}} \begin{bmatrix} \beta_i^*(z)n_1^* y_1^*\left(W, W^*, z, n_1, n_{-1}, n_1^*, n_{-1}^*\right) \\ +\beta^*(z)n_{-1}^* y_{-1}^*\left(W, W^*, z, n_1, n_{-1}, n_1^*, n_{-1}^*\right) \end{bmatrix} \mathrm{d}z$$

$$+ \int_{0}^{\tilde{z}^*} \begin{bmatrix} \beta_i^*(z)n_1^* y_1^*\left(W, W^*, z, 0, 0, n_1^*, n_{-1}^*\right) \\ +\beta^*(z)n_{-1}^* y_{-1}^*\left(W, W^*, z, 0, 0, n_1^*, n_{-1}^*\right) \end{bmatrix} \mathrm{d}z \tag{8}$$

where L and L^* denote the supply of labor;y_1 and y_1^* measure the output of each networked firm at home and in the foreign country, respectively; y_{-1} and y_{-1}^* measure the output of each firm operating outside any network at home and in the foreign country, respectively; and $\tilde{z}$ and $\tilde{z}^*$ are the threshold sectors for the extensive margins of trade, at home and abroad respectively.

Case 1. $n_{ij} = 0 \, \forall F_i, F_j \in F$ and $n_{ij}^* = 0 \, \forall F_i^*, F_j^* \in F^*$.

In this case of empty networks, each domestic firm would

$$\underset{\{y_i\}}{\text{Maximize}} : \Pi_i = (p(z) - w\beta(z))y_i(z) \quad (i = 1, 2, \ldots, n)$$

Each foreign firm would

$$\underset{\{y_i^*\}}{\text{Maximize}} : \Pi_i^* = \left(p - w^*\beta^*(z)\right)y_i^*(z) \quad \left(i = 1, 2, \ldots, n^*\right)$$

Therefore, a necessary and sufficient condition for any domestic firm to produce is

$$c \leq \xi A_1 + (1-\xi)c^* \tag{9}$$

Where $A_1 = a - \frac{\alpha_1}{\alpha_2}S$; $c = w\beta(z)$; $c^* = w^*\beta^*(z)$; and $\xi = \left(\frac{1}{n^*+1}\right) \in (0, 1)$. Analogously, a necessary and sufficient condition for any foreign firm to produce is

$$c^* \leq \xi^* A_1 + \left(1-\xi^*\right)c \tag{10}$$

where $\xi^* = \left(\frac{1}{n+1}\right) \in (0, 1)$. The threshold sectors pinning down the extensive margins of trade are determined by

$$W\beta(\tilde{z}) - \xi A_1 - (1-\xi)W^*\beta^*\left(\tilde{z}^*\right) = 0$$

$$W^*\beta^*\left(\tilde{z}^*\right) - \xi^* A_1 - \left(1-\xi^*\right)W\beta(\tilde{z}) = 0$$

Case 2. $n_{ij} = 1\, \forall F_i, F_j \in F$ and $n^*_{ij} = 0\, \forall F^*_i, F^*_j \in F^*$.

Each domestic firm would

$$\underset{\{y_i\}}{\text{Maximize}}: \Pi_i = \left(p(z) - w\begin{pmatrix}\beta(z) \\ -(n-1)\left(\theta - \dfrac{M}{P}\right)\end{pmatrix}\right)y_i(z) - f(z) \quad (i = 1,\ 2,\ \ldots,\ n)$$

Each foreign firm would

$$\underset{\{y^*_i\}}{Maximize}: \Pi^*_i = \left(p(z) - w^*\beta^*(z)\right)y^*_i(z)\left(i = 1, 2, \ldots, n^*\right)$$

As $f(z) \to 0$, a necessary and sufficient condition for any domestic firm to produce is

$$c \leq \xi A_2 + (1-\xi)c^* \tag{11}$$

where $A_2 = \left(a - \frac{\alpha_1}{\alpha_2}S + (n^*+1)(n-1)w\left(\theta - \frac{M}{P}\right)\right)$. Analogously, a necessary and sufficient condition for any foreign firm to produce is

$$c^* \leq \xi^* A^*_2 + \left(1-\xi^*\right)c \tag{12}$$

where $A^*_2 = \left(a - \frac{\alpha_1}{\alpha_2}S + (n+1)(n^*-1)w^*\theta^*\right)$. The threshold sectors pinning down the extensive margins of trade are determined by

$$W\beta(\tilde{z}) - \xi A_2 - (1-\xi)W^*\beta^*\left(\tilde{z}^*\right) = 0$$

$$W^*\beta^*(\tilde{z}^*) - \xi^* A_2^* - (1-\xi^*)W\beta(\tilde{z}) = 0$$

Case 3. $n_{ij} = 0\ \forall F_i, F_j \in F$ and $n_{ij}^* = 1\ \forall F_i^*,\ F_j^* \in F^*$.
Each domestic firm would

$$\underset{\{y_i\}}{\text{Maximize}} : \Pi_i = (p(z) - w\beta(z))y_i(z) - f(z) \quad (i = 1, 2, \ldots, n)$$

Each foreign firm would

$$\underset{\{y_i^*\}}{\text{Maximize}} :\ \Pi_i^* = \left(\begin{array}{l} p(z) \\ -w^* \left(\begin{array}{l} \beta^*(z) - \\ (n^*-1) \\ \left(\theta^* - \dfrac{M^*}{P}\right) \end{array} \right) \end{array} \right) y_i^*(z) - f^*(z) \quad (i = 1,\ 2,\ \ldots,\ n^*)$$

As $f^*(z) \to 0$, for $z \in [\tilde{z}, z^*]$ i.e. the subset of sectors where all firms are active in equilibrium, therefore, a necessary and sufficient condition for any domestic firm to produce is

$$c \le \xi A_3 + (1-\xi)c^* \tag{13}$$

where $A_3 = \left(a - \frac{\alpha_1}{\alpha_2}S + (n^*+1)(n-1)w\theta\right)$.

Analogously, a necessary and sufficient condition for any foreign firm to produce is

$$c^* \le \xi^* A_3^* + (1-\xi^*)c \tag{14}$$

where $A_3^* = \left(a - \frac{\alpha_1}{\alpha_2}S + (n+1)(n^*-1)w^*\left(\theta^* - \frac{M^*}{P}\right)\right)$. The threshold sectors pinning down the extensive margins of trade are determined by

$$W\beta(\tilde{z}) - \xi A_3 - (1-\xi)W^*\beta^*(\tilde{z}^*) = 0$$

$$W^*\beta^*(\tilde{z}^*) - \xi^* A_3^* - (1-\xi^*)W\beta(\tilde{z}) = 0$$

Case 4. $n_{ij} = 1\ \forall F_i, F_j \in F$ and $n_{ij}^* = 1\ \forall F_i^*, F_j^* \in F^*$.
Each domestic firm would

$$\underset{\{y_i\}}{\text{Maximize}} :\ \Pi_i = \left(p(z) - w \left(\begin{array}{l} \beta(z) \\ -(n-1) \\ \left(\theta - \dfrac{M}{P}\right) \end{array} \right) \right) y_i(z) - f(z) \quad (i = 1,\ 2,\ \ldots,\ n)$$

Each foreign firm would

$$\underset{\{y_i^*\}}{Maximize}: \Pi_i^* = \left(p(z) - w^* \begin{pmatrix} \beta^*(z) \\ -(n^* - 1) \\ \left(\theta^* - \dfrac{M^*}{P}\right) \end{pmatrix}\right) y_i^*(z) - f^*(z) \quad \left(i = 1,\ 2,\ \ldots,\ n^*\right)$$

As and $f^*(z) \to 0$, for $z \in [\tilde{z}, z^*]$ i.e. the subset of sectors where all firms are active in equilibrium, a necessary and sufficient condition for any domestic firm to produce is

$$c \leq \xi A_4 + (1 - \xi)c^* \tag{15}$$

Where $A_4 = \left(a - \frac{\alpha_1}{\alpha_2} S + (n^* + 1)(n - 1)w\left(\theta - \frac{M}{P}\right) - n^*(n^* - 1)w^*\left(\theta^* - \frac{M^*}{P}\right)\right)$.

Analogously, a necessary and sufficient condition for any foreign firm to produce is

$$c^* \leq \xi^* A_3^* + \left(1 - \xi^*\right)c \tag{16}$$

where $A_4^* = \left(a - \frac{\alpha_1}{\alpha_2} S + (n + 1)(n^* - 1)w^*\left(\theta^* - \frac{M^*}{P}\right) - n(n - 1)w\left(\theta - \frac{M}{P}\right)\right)$.

The threshold sectors pinning down the extensive margins of trade are determined by

$$W\beta(\tilde{z}) - \xi A_4 - (1 - \xi)W^*\beta^*\left(\tilde{z}^*\right) = 0$$

$$W^*\beta^*\left(\tilde{z}^*\right) - \xi^* A_4^* - \left(1 - \xi^*\right)W\beta(\tilde{z}) = 0$$

To fix ideas, let us now split the time horizon $t \in [0, \infty)$ in two segments such that

$$S(t) = \begin{cases} 0 & \forall t \in [0, t_0] \\ S_0 & \forall t \in (t_0, \infty) \end{cases}$$

with identical mass action incidences across countries i.e.

$$M = \frac{S + I}{2} = M^*$$

Figure 1 below illustrates the effect that an increase in S_0 would have on production and trade when networks are empty both at home and in the foreign country. With empty networks, when S rises, region H (where exclusively home firms can compete) and region F (where exclusively foreign firms can compete) expand. This reduces the extensive margins of exports and imports. An increase in the susceptible population

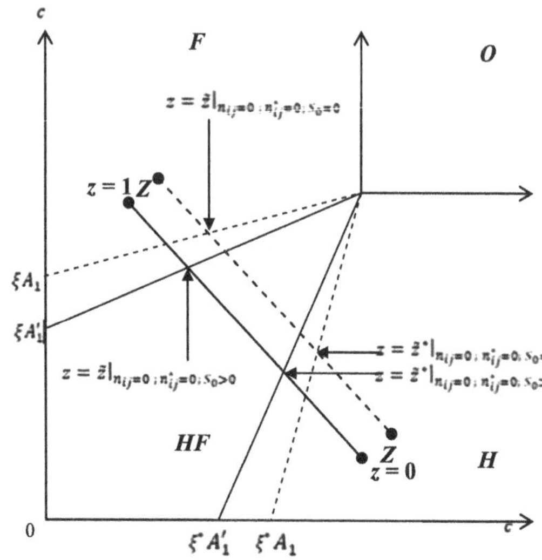

Fig. 1 Contagion, production, and trade with empty networks at home and abroad

leads to a reduction in demand for goods and services. At the initial wages, the demand for labor falls. This generates an excess supply of labor and wages fall to clear the labor market. A fall in wages causes the *ZZ* locus to shift toward the origin. This partially offsets the initial decline in the extensive margins of trade.

In comparison, Fig. 2 above illustrates the effect that contagion would have on production and trade when the foreign network is empty but the network at home is complete. With complete networks at home alone, when the susceptible population rises, region *H* (where exclusively home firms can compete) and region *F* (where exclusively foreign firms can compete) expand, with the latter expanding more than it would have if networks were empty at home. Consequently, the extensive margins of exports and imports shrink: domestic exports shrink more than they would have if networks were empty at home. An increase in the susceptible population leads to a reduction in demand for goods and services. At the initial wages, the demand for labor falls. This generates an excess supply of labor, and wages fall to clear the labor market. A fall in wages causes the *ZZ* locus to shift toward the origin. This partially offsets the initial decline in the extensive margins of trade.

Figure 3 above illustrates the effect that contagion would have on production and trade when the home network is empty but the foreign network is complete. With complete networks in the foreign country, when the susceptible population rises, region *H* (where exclusively home firms can compete) and region *F* (where exclusively foreign firms can compete) expand, with the former expanding more than it would have if foreign networks were empty. Consequently, the extensive margins of exports and imports shrink: domestic imports shrink more than they would have if foreign networks were empty. An increase in the susceptible population leads to a reduction in demand for goods and services. At the initial wages, the demand for labor falls. This generates an excess supply of labor, and wages fall to clear the labor

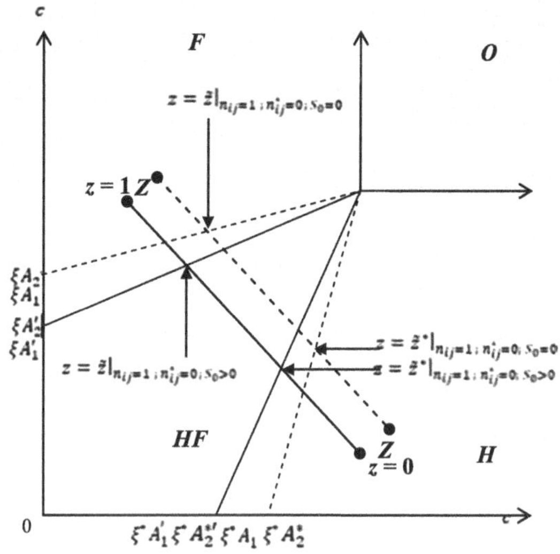

Fig. 2 Contagion, production, and trade with an empty foreign network and complete domestic network

market. A fall in wages causes the *ZZ* locus to shift toward the origin. This partially offsets the initial decline in the extensive margins of trade.

Figure 4 above illustrates the effect that contagion would have on production and trade when the home and foreign networks are complete. With complete networks at home and in the foreign country, when the susceptible population rises, region *H* (where exclusively home firms can compete) and region *F* (where exclusively foreign firms can compete) expand more than they would have if at least one of the two country's networks were empty. Consequently, the extensive margins of exports and imports shrink more than they would have if at least one of the two country's

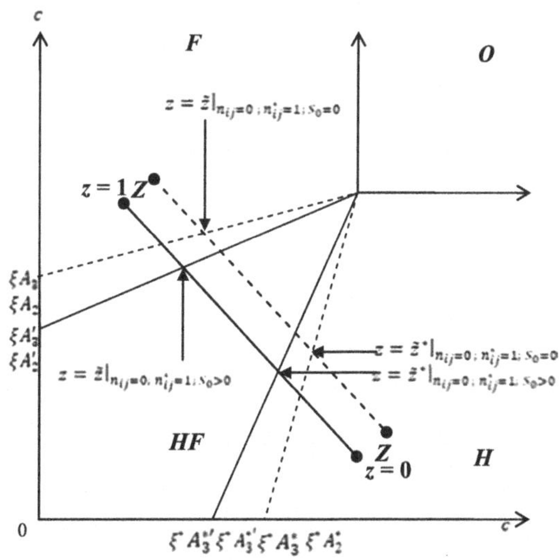

Fig. 3 Contagion, production, and trade with an empty domestic network and complete foreign network

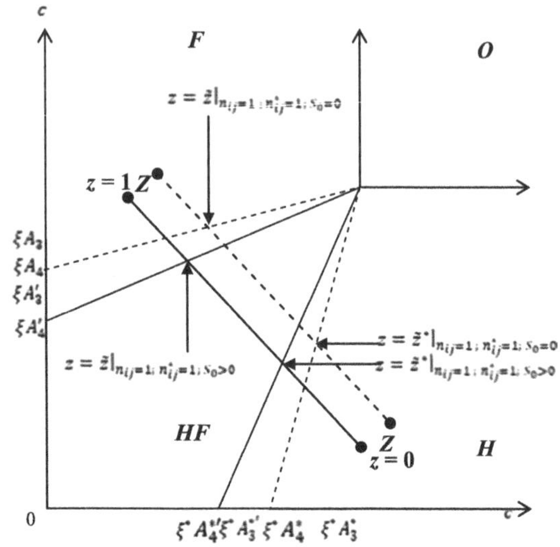

Fig. 4 Contagion, production, and trade with complete domestic and foreign networks

networks were empty. An increase in the susceptible population leads to a reduction in demand for goods and services. At the initial wages, the demand for labor falls. This generates an excess supply of labor and wages fall to clear the labor market. A fall in wages causes the *ZZ* locus to shift toward the origin. This partially offsets the initial decline in the extensive margins of trade.

3 Conclusion

We have developed a tractable general equilibrium model of networked oligopolies that allows us to analyze the role of contagion in specialization according to comparative advantage in the tradition of a typical neoclassical model of international trade. Embedding the possibility of networks, domestic and/or foreign, has non-trivial implications for contagion in general oligopolistic equilibrium. More specifically, our analysis highlights essential implications of contagion for production and trade in oligopolistic industries through interactions between network externalities, efficiency, and concentration. Contagion reduces the diversity of production and, consequently, the extensive margins of exports and imports shrink. We demonstrate that contagion dampens domestic (foreign) exports more, in the presence of a complete domestic (foreign) network, than it would have Contagion, Production, and Trade with Networked Oligopolies if domestic (foreign) networks were empty. By the same token, an increase in contagion dampens domestic (foreign) imports more, in the presence of a complete foreign (domestic) network, than it would have if foreign (domestic) networks were empty. All else equal, the net effect of contagion on the extensive margins of trade depends on the relative economy of size of each network.

A particularly challenging generalization of our model would allow for uncompensated technology transfers in NOGE. In a setting of Dornbusch, Fischer and Samuelson (DFS) that resembles Neary (2003, 2007) but for the strategic elements of oligopolistic competition, an adjustment in relative wages may not take place when the country with an advanced technology loses an export sector because of technology transfer without compensation. Not only can that country gain, such a possibility for paradoxical gains must occur in the neighborhood of what Jones and Ruffin (2008) call "turning points"—values of relative country size for which that country in the initial situation would be an incipient producer of an imported commodity, so that if its relative size were to increase, it would become a new producer of that commodity. An identification of such "turning points" in networked oligopolies is likely to further enrich our insights into the implications of contagion for production and trade.

References

Beladi, H., & Chakrabarti, A. (2019). Multidivisional firms, internal competition, and comparative advantage: Baye et al. Meet Neary. *Journal of International Economics, 116*, 50–57.

Beladi, H., & Chakrabarti, A. (2020). Standard setting organizations and networked oligopolies in general equilibrium. mimeo. https://wwws.law.northwestern.edu/research-faculty/clbe/events/innovation/documents/chakrabarti_2020.pdf

Beladi, H., Chakrabarti, A., & Marjit, S. (2013). Cross-border mergers in vertically related industries. *European Economic Review, 59*, 97–108.

Bonaccorsi, S., Ottaviano, S., De Pellegrini, F., & Socievole, A. (2014). Epidemic outbreaks in two-scale community networks. *Physical Review E, 90*(1), 012810.

Cournot, A. (1838). *Recherches sur les principesmathématiques de la théorie des richesses.* Hachette.

Dornbusch, R., Fischer, S., & Samuelson, P. A. (1977). Comparative advantage, trade, and payments in a Ricardian model with a continuum of goods. *The American Economic Review, 67*(5), 823–839.

Jackson, M. O. (2010). *Social and economic networks.* Princeton University Press.

Jones, R. W., & Ruffin, R. J. (2008). The technology transfer paradox. *Journal of International Economics, 75*(2), 321–328.

Neary, J. P. (2003). Globalization and market structure. *Journal of the European Economic Association, 1*(2–3), 245–271.

Neary, J. P. (2007). Cross-border mergers as instruments of comparative advantage. *Review of Economic Studies, 74*(4), 1229–1257.

Land Holding, Fertility, and Child Labour

Kamalika Chakraborty and Bidisha Chakraborty

Abstract This chapter constructs an economic model of a family economy with overlapping generations in rural settings and explores the correlation between land ownership and child labour as well as landholding and fertility, amidst the prevalence of manufacturing sector unemployment. If parents prefer quality of children proxied by expected earnings of children more to the quantity of children, then the number of children is positive only if adult earnings exceed subsistence expenditure. In this case, time devoted to schooling by children increases as landholding increases and fertility increases with increase in landholding only if subsistence consumption expenditure exceeds a critical level. However, if parents prefer quantity over quality of children, then fertility increases with increase in landholding even if subsistence consumption expenditure is less than the critical level. In this case, parents want to have more children just to add one earning member in the family.

Keywords Child labour · Land holding · Schooling · Fertility

JEL Classification Numbers E24 · I25 · J01 · J13 · J22 · Q15

1 Introduction

Land is regarded as a valuable asset. Hence, an augmentation in land ownership by rural households should reduce the prevalence of child labour (Luxury Axiom). However, many empirical studies and a few theoretical studies have obtained paradoxical results, i.e., the prevalence of child labour has been found to be higher in those households that possess more land (Wealth Paradox). One of the most notable theoretical investigations on the correlation between land ownership and child labour

K. Chakraborty
Khatra Adibasi Mahavidyalaya (Affiliated to Bankura University), Makrara, India

B. Chakraborty (✉)
Jadavpur University, Kolkata, India
e-mail: bidisha.chakraborty@jadavpuruniversity.in

B. Chatterjee and A. K. Karmakar (eds.), *Analytical Issues in Growth & Structural Change, Macroeconomy, Security, and Sustainability of India's Economic Development*, India Studies in Business and Economics, https://doi.org/10.1007/978-981-95-5242-9_2

was conducted by Basu et al. (2007). Their research article demonstrates a curvilinear association, namely an upside-down U-shaped pattern, between land ownership and the occurrence of child labour. Empirical testing of this outcome with data from India reveals that once the land holding exceeds 3.6 acres, the child labour decreases, notwithstanding an initial increase in child labour with larger land holdings. Bar and Basu (2008) demonstrate that a slight rise in land holdings increases child labour, both in the short term and the long term. Nevertheless, as the quantity of land exceeds a certain threshold, child labour decreases in the long run. However, neither of these studies addresses the issue of educating child labourers. Chakraborty and Chakraborty (2014) include the education of child labour as a key component in their paper on child labour, human capital, and landholding. This study shows that there is a positive correlation between land ownership and child labour in the short run. Over time, there exists a U-shaped correlation between the steady-state level of human capital and land ownership, as well as the growth rate of human capital and land ownership. In this paper it is assumed that adults exclusively participate in the manufacturing sector, while children exclusively work in agriculture.

Several empirical studies also examine the correlation between land ownership and child labour. Oryoie et al. (2017) draw the following conclusion based on data from three surveys performed in Zimbabwe in 2001, 2007–2008, and 2010–2011: child labour tends to decline as land holdings per capita increase. However, the authors note that there may be a slight upward trend in the correlation between child labour and landholdings near the midpoint of the land per capita range. The study conducted by Bhalotra and Heady (2003) focuses on Pakistan and Ghana, both of which are developing nations. Based on the findings of their research, they deduce that child labour rises in tandem with increase in ownership of land in these two nations. Boutin (2012) bases his empirical investigation on data collected in Mali. In Mali children assist their elders with family cultivation. The research findings indicate that as household land ownership increases, a greater proportion of minors participate in family farming as assistive members. Adults as well as children are commonly employed as substitutes of one another in the field of agriculture. However, the absence of employed adult labour sometimes motivates the greater use of juveniles for agricultural chores. Dumas (2007) shows that when there is no possibility to engage adult workers from outside the family, the use of child labour increases as land ownership grows. Rozenweig and Evenson (1977) analyse the correlation between child labour and land ownership in India by utilizing data from the 1961 Census. They demonstrate that the incremental value contributed by children becomes more significant as the extent of their property ownership expands. As land ownership expands, there is a corresponding drop in the schooling hours of children, and instead they are given the responsibility of agricultural labour. Moura (2009) studies the relationship between child labour and land tenure security using actual data from Brazil. This paper presents empirical evidence indicating that when the level of land tenure security rises, there is a discernible shift from child labour to adult labour. Therefore, there is a fall in child labour and a rise in adult labour.

The relationship between landholding and fertility is also an interesting one. There are two opposing views on this issue. According to one perspective, a rise in the landholding size leads to increased fertility, allowing greater family labour to contribute to higher land productivity. The term used to describe this perspective is the 'Land Labour Demand Hypothesis'. According to an alternative perspective, a growth in land ownership should serve as an extra means of family security in old age. As a result, this would reduce the significance of children as providers of support to parents in later life, leading to lower birth rates. Because cross-sectional data was employed instead of longitudinal data, the empirical data concerning the Land Labour Demand Hypothesis failed to determine the causal relationship between the variables. In his 1985 study, Cain posited that it was more rational to assume that the number of farm families remained relatively stable, but the size of operational holdings adapted to fluctuations in the labour availability of the farm family. Cain's 'Reverse Hypothesis' suggests that the data gathered from a rural hamlet in Bangladesh shows a correlation between each additional male aged 12–65 years in a home and an increase in the amount of land rented by the household, specifically by an additional 0.6 acres. Clay and Johnson (1992) examine the patterns of fertility and land ownership in the densely populated Republic of Rwanda. The results suggest that there is a direct correlation between the size of a farm and the fertility rate of couples who are employed in agricultural activities. Nevertheless, the results do not provide support for the idea that there is a reciprocal effect, in which fertility impacts farm size. Moreover, the relationship between the size of a farm and the number of children that survive does not appear to be caused by an increase in the demand for farm labour. This is due to the lack of correlation between the size of the farm and the number of household members within the working-age range (15–65 years) or the overall intended number of children by the husband. On the contrary, it appears that the rise in the number of offspring is attributable to the expansion of the farm, which enables a better provision of resources. Bhandari and Ghimire (2013) use longitudinal panel data from the Western Chitwan Valley of Nepal to explore the impact of contemporary agricultural technologies on change in the number of births in a household engaged in farming. The results suggest that implementing modern agricultural technologies, such as using a tractor and other advanced farming techniques, reduce the fertility rate in the farm households. James (2000) endeavours to comprehend the connection between land ownership and fertility in India by examining the existing research on this subject. The study concludes that the relationship between land and productivity may not always be consistent. It is influenced by various factors such as land quality, tenure status, climate, as well as fertility factors including the availability and use of contraception and child loss. Based on data collected in Uganda, Campenhout (2016) concludes that fertility exerts a significant adverse influence on the level of labour invested by individuals in subsistence farming within a family. However, there is a scarcity of scholarly research conducted on the correlation between land ownership and fertility. We aim to examine the correlation between land ownership and child labour, as well as the association between land ownership and fertility.

The "quantity-quality trade-off" refers to the inverse correlation between family size and children's education in the field of economics. This concept was initially formulated by Nobel Laureate Gary Becker (Becker & Lewis, 1973). The dilemma of balancing the level of excellence and the number of offspring has been captured well in Yakita (2010) and Croix and Doepke (2004). The aim of our study is to examine the correlation between children's education and fertility in a context where both the number of children and the expected income of children are factors that impact parents' welfare. It is presumed that the parents engage in agricultural cultivation on their personal property. Children, if they work, work on land only. Given that parents employed in the skilled sector typically do not allow their children to work, we will focus on the scenario where parents work in agriculture or on land. In this scenario, the issue of child labour is likely to emerge.

However, children, upon becoming adults, have the option of working either in the skilled sector or on land. We find that whether child schooling is positive or zero, i.e., whether child labour exists in the economy, is influenced by the comparative significance given by the parent to the number of children and expected earnings of children in her utility function. As landholding increases, time devoted to schooling increases if parent gives more importance to the expected earnings of children than the number of children. If parents give more importance to the expected earnings of children than the number of children, the necessary condition of fertility increasing with an increase in landholding is subsistence consumption expenditure is very high exceeding a critical level.

The remaining portion of the chapter is structured in the following manner. Section 2 presents an overview of the fundamental model, while Sect. 3 deals with the short-term equilibrium in which both parents and children work in the agricultural or farming sector, Sect. 4 explores the mechanisms involved in human capital development. Section 5 examines the impact on fertility rates. Section 6 delves into the practical consequences for policy-making. Section 7 contains the concluding remarks.

2 The Model

This research constructs an overlapping generations model to represent the family economy in a rural setting.[1] Each home has a single parent and a variable number of children, denoted as n_t. The economy comprises a manufacturing industry and an agricultural sector. In the manufacturing sector, an individual's wage is directly proportionate to their level of human capital. However, in the farming sector, the earning is constant regardless of the individual's human capital. The parental utility

[1] Additional publications that utilize the overlapping generations framework include Becker and Tomes (1979), Glomm (1997), Acemoglu and Pischke (2000), Glomm and Ravikumar (1998), Chakraborty and Chakraborty (2014), and Chakraborty and Chakraborty (2018).

function incorporates the anticipated future earnings of the child,[2] and the consideration of parental choice in selecting a school for their child in relation to child labour is being discussed. Since a massive portion of child labourers work in the agricultural sector, we follow the theoretical modelling of Chakraborty and Chakraborty (2014) and Glomm (1997) and examine the issue of parental selection of education for a farming family.

A representative adult's utility function is determined by the level of family consumption, the quantity of children in the family, and the anticipated future wages of the children. Adults are concerned with both the number of children and the anticipated income of those children. Upon reaching adulthood, there is a potential for the individual to be unable to secure employment as a skilled labourer in the manufacturing sector due to the uncertain job opportunities resulting from elevated levels of unemployment in that field. If she is unable to obtain a job in the manufacturing industry, she will shift her focus to the farm sector. An adult sets expectations regarding whether they anticipate the youngster will obtain a job in the industrial sector once they reach maturity. This forecast is based on the prevailing unemployment rate.

The degree to which a parent possesses human capital and the duration of time a child spends in school both impact the child's human capital development.

The function that represents the process of building human capital of a child is as follows:

$$h_{t+1} = bs_t h_t + \underline{\boldsymbol{h}}, \tag{1}$$

where 's_t' is denotes schooling hours of the child, and the variable 'h_t' indicates the human capital possessed by an adult. 'b' is a positive constant, while '$\underline{h}$' represents the minimum human capital achieved by children, even if they do not attend school (i.e., $s_t = 0$). Therefore, the value of h_{t+1} is greater than zero, even if the value of s_t is equal to zero.

The production function in the farming sector is given by $Y_{at} = A\{1 + \theta n_t(1 - s_t)\}T^{\alpha}$ where Y_{at} is the production in the farming sector, A is the indicator of technological advancements in agriculture, T represents the land which the household owns and which they utilize for farming practices, whereas θ represents the scaling factor for adult equivalents.

Aggregate yield obtained from land is by $P_a\ A\{(1 - \varphi n_t)\theta n_t(1 - s_t)\}T^{\alpha}$ where P_a represents the price of the good produced in the agricultural sector and φ denotes the cost of child rearing.

We assume $\theta > \varphi$ throughout our analysis, i.e., that the child wage exceeds the cost of child rearing.

[2] In the publication of Mukherjee and Sinha (2006) the parent's utility function incorporates the child's future earning potential. Genicot and Ray (2010) argue that individuals' motivation to invest is contingent upon their goals for their own and their offspring's future well-being. The utility of parents is contingent upon the expectations that parents have for their children. In the study conducted by Chakraborty and Chakraborty (2018), it was found that the anticipated earnings of a child are incorporated in the parental utility function.

Both parents and children contribute to the labour on land held by the household. The calculation for household income is as follows:

$$Y_t = P_a A\{(1 - \varphi n_t) + \theta n_t (1 - S_t)\} T^\alpha \tag{2}$$

The household's budget constraint is defined by:

$$P_a A\{(1 - \varphi n_t) + \theta n_t (1 - s_t)\} T^\alpha = p_c c_t \tag{3}$$

The following describes an adult's utility function from the sample household:

$$U_t = \begin{cases} \ln(c_t - \overline{c}) + \left[\begin{array}{l} (1-\gamma)\ln n_t \\ +\gamma \ln \left\{ \begin{array}{l} f\delta\left(bs_t h_t + \underline{h}\right) \\ +(1-f)P_a AT^\alpha \end{array} \right\} \end{array} \right] & \text{if } c_t \geq \overline{c}, \\ -\infty & \text{otherwise} \end{cases} \tag{4}$$

where c_t is the level of consumption, $\overline{c}$ indicates subsistence level of consumption expenditure, The variable $1-\gamma$ reflects the weight given to the number of children, whereas γ represents the weight given to the predicted income of a child in utility function of the adult. An adult feels that the probability of a child obtaining a job in the industry is represented by the variable f, which corresponds to the present rate of employment in the industrial sector. $\delta(bs_t h_t + \underline{h})$ is the possible return the child might get as an adult should they land a job in the manufacturing industry. The adult believes that there is $(1-f)$ chance that the child will not find job in the manufacturing industry. $P_a\ AT^\alpha$ is the return that a child might get for working on family property as an adult. The child's entire projected earnings are represented by $\left[f\delta\left(bs_t h_t + \underline{h}\right) + (1-f)P_a\ AT^\alpha\right]$. As children transition into adulthood, they opt to pursue employment in the skilled sector provided $\delta\left(bs_t h_t + \underline{h}\right) > P_a\ AT^\alpha$ or $\delta h_{t+1} > P_a\ AT^\alpha$ or $h_{t+1} > \frac{P_a\ AT^\alpha}{\delta}$. This suggests that children will only be inclined to enter the skilled workforce as adults if their degree of human capital surpasses a certain threshold.

3 Short-Run Equilibrium When Both Parents and Children Work in the Farming Sector

The adult in the representative home is responsible for solving Eq. (4)'s utility maximization problem. The budget provided in Eq. (3) limits the adult with reference to the choice variables (c_t, n_t, and s_t) of the household.

Based on the first-order conditions of[3] the above optimization problem, we obtain:

[3] Please refer to the Appendix for a comprehensive derivation.

$$s_t = \frac{\gamma f \delta b h_t(\theta - \varphi) + \theta(1-\gamma)\left[f\delta \underline{h} + (1-f)P_a\, AT^{\alpha}\right]}{f\delta b\theta h_t(2\gamma - 1)} \tag{5}$$

We assume $\theta > \varphi$. Therefore, if $\gamma > \frac{1}{2}$, s_t is always positive. This suggests that if a parent places a higher value on their child's potential earnings in their own satisfaction function, they will always ensure that their child receives at least some education. Regarding, this situation parent realizes that higher schooling increases the chance of higher expected earnings from child in future. Since child wage covers the cost of child rearing, she will send her child to school.

If $\gamma < \frac{1}{2}$, s_t is always zero. This implies that if a parent gives more importance to the number of children in her utility function, she only sends her child to work and not to school if the child's earnings are greater than the expenses of raising the child.

In this case, the parent assigns less weight to the child's future predicted income. Since the child's wage exceeds the cost of child rearing, she will not send her child to school. Instead, the child works full time as child labour.

$s_t = 1$ if $h_t \geq h_t \geq \frac{\theta(\gamma-1)\left[f\delta\underline{h}+(1-f)P_a\, T^{\alpha}\right]}{\theta-\gamma\theta-\gamma\varphi} \equiv \hat{h}$. This implies that only if parental human capital exceeds a critical level, then only schooling is equal to one.

Proposition 1 *If the relative importance given by the parent on the expected earning of* the *child in her utility function is higher than the quantity of children, then the child's schooling is always positive. Conversely, in those cases where the parent places greater significance on the quantity of children than on the expected income of each child, the educational attainment of the child is consistently rendered null. This implies that* the *child works full time as child labour. There will be full schooling of* the *child only if parental human capital exceeds a critical level.*

Incentive Compatibility Condition

As children transition into adulthood, they choose to seek employment in the skilled sector if the wages earned by them as adults are higher, i.e., $w_{t+1} = \delta\left(bs_t h_t + \underline{h}\right) > P_a AT^{\alpha}$ or $\delta h_{t+1} > P_a\, AT^{\alpha}$ or $h_{t+1} = \frac{P_a AT^{\alpha}}{\delta} = h_N$.

In our model we assume $h_N > \hat{h}$. This suggests that all children who have just partial education, as well as some children whose parents have a level of human capital between $\hat{h}$ and h_N, and who complete their education, would like to enter the sector which demands unskilled labour force once they become adults. Hence, we see that there is potential for educated individuals to be unemployed, which is a common characteristic in several developing nations. Furthermore, this demonstrates that the problem of child labour is limited to parents working in the unskilled industry. All those parents who are employed in specialized professions will enrol their children in full-time studies.

Next, we consider the relationship between landholding and schooling.

$$\frac{ds_t}{dT} = \frac{(1-\gamma)}{f\delta b h_t(2\gamma - 1)}\left[(1-f)P_a\, A\alpha T^{\alpha-1}\right]$$

$$\frac{ds_t}{dT} > 0 \text{ if } \gamma > \frac{1}{2}$$

Parents who prioritize their child's future earnings understand that more education enhances the likelihood of higher predicted earnings for their child. Consequently, they will enrol their children in school for longer periods of time, regardless of any rise in landholding.

Proposition 2 *If parents give higher importance to the expected earnings of children in their utility function than the quantity of children, then the amount of time that children spend on schooling grows as their landholding increases.*

4 Human Capital Formation Dynamics

$$h_{t+1} = bs_t h_t + \underline{h}$$

Substituting the value of s_t in the above equation, we get,

$$h_{t+1} = \frac{\gamma f \delta b h_t(\theta - \varphi) + (1-\gamma)\theta\left\{f\delta\underline{h} + (1-f)P_a\, AT^{\alpha}\right\}}{f\delta\theta(2\gamma - 1)} + \underline{h} \qquad (6)$$

$$\frac{dh_{t+1}}{dh_t} = \frac{\gamma b(\theta - \varphi)}{\theta(2\gamma - 1)}$$

We assume $\theta > \varphi$. If $\gamma > \frac{1}{2}$, $\frac{dh_{t+1}}{dh_t} > 0$. This implies that if parents give more importance to expected earnings from children in time to come, than to the number of children in their utility function, human capital of child increases with parental human capital.

If $\gamma < \frac{1}{2}$, $s_t = 0$. So, $h_{t+1} = \underline{h}$. Here $\frac{dh_{t+1}}{dh_t} = 0$. In this case, the dynamics of h_t are illustrated below.

Figure 1 displays a stable equilibrium at E_1. But human capital remains at the minimum level $(\underline{h})$ period after period.

Next, we concentrate on the case where $\gamma > \frac{1}{2}$ and $\frac{dh_{t+1}}{dh_t} > 0$.

If $\frac{dh_{t+1}}{dh_t} > 1$, then equilibrium does not exist. Thus, we presume $\frac{dh_{t+1}}{dh_t} < 1$ in our model.

$$\frac{d^2 h_{t+1}}{dh_t^2} = 0$$

Therefore, h_t will be an upward-sloping straight line.

The relationship between h_t and h_{t+1} when $\gamma > \frac{1}{2}$ (illustrated in Fig. 2).

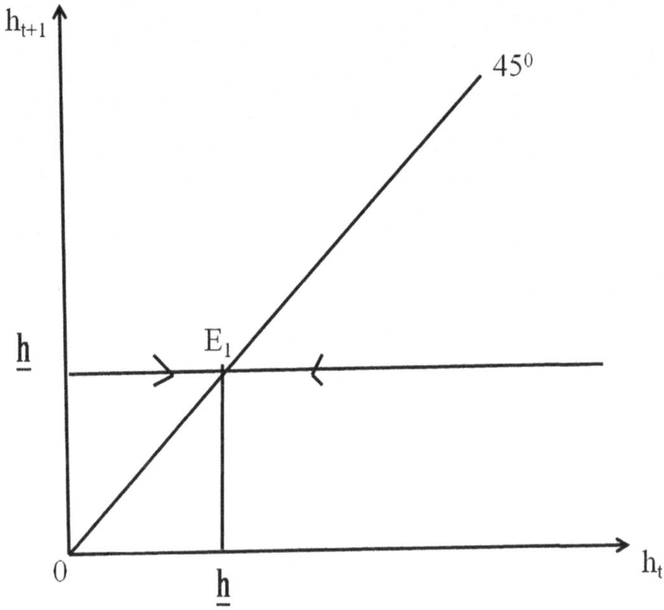

Fig. 1 The interrelation between the parental human capital and offspring's human capital when $\gamma < \frac{1}{2}$

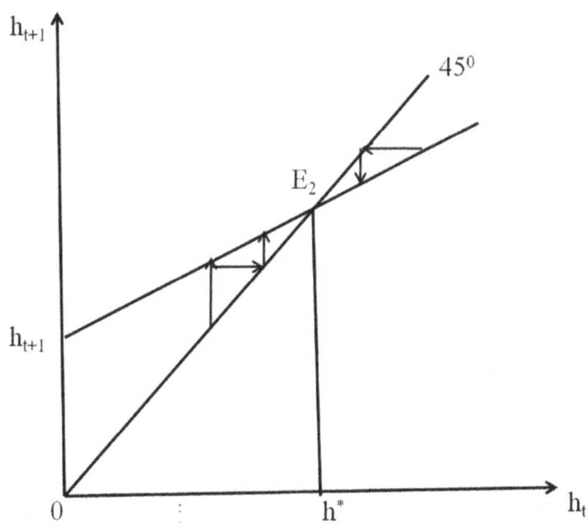

Fig. 2 The correlation between parental human capital and that of their offspring when $\gamma > \frac{1}{2}$

Denote h^* as the human capital at steady-state value. At equilibrium, h_t equals h_{t+1}. Consequently, the steady-state quantity of human capital can be calculated using Eq. (6):

$$h^* = \frac{(1-\gamma)\theta\{f\delta\underline{h} + (1-f)P_a\, AT^{\alpha}\} + f\delta\theta(2\gamma-1)\underline{h}}{f\delta\theta(2\gamma-1) - \gamma f\delta b(\theta-\varphi)} \tag{7}$$

In Fig. 2, we get a stable equilibrium at E_2. The human capital at steady state related to E_2 is h^*. Below E_2, human capital continues to increase until it reaches E_2, but beyond E_2, human capital continues to decline until it reaches E_2.

$$\frac{\mathrm{d}h^*}{\mathrm{d}T} = \frac{(1-\gamma)\theta(1-f)P_a\, A\alpha T^{\alpha-1}}{f\delta\theta(2\gamma-1) - \gamma f\delta b(\theta-\varphi)}$$

When $\gamma > \frac{1}{2}$, $\frac{\mathrm{d}h^*}{\mathrm{d}T} > 0$ if $f\delta\theta(2\gamma-1) - \gamma f\delta b(\theta-\varphi) > 0$. Lower is $(\theta-\varphi)$ and higher is $(2\gamma-1)$, higher is the chance of $\frac{\mathrm{d}h^*}{\mathrm{d}T} > 0$. This implies higher is φ, lower is θ and closer is γ to 1, higher is the chance of $\frac{\mathrm{d}h^*}{\mathrm{d}T} > 0$.

Proposition 3 *A rise in landholding increases the steady-state value of human capital if the cost of child upbringing is high, return from child work is low and if parents prioritize the expected earnings of their children over the quantity of children in their utility function.*

The expression for the rate of growth of human capital is

$$\Psi = \frac{h_{t+1} - h_t}{h_t} = \frac{\gamma f\delta b h_t(\theta-\varphi) + (1-\gamma)\theta\{f\delta\underline{h} + (1-f)P_a AT^{\alpha}\}}{f\delta\theta(2\gamma-1)h_t} + \frac{\underline{h}}{h_t} - 1 \tag{8}$$

$$\frac{\mathrm{d}\Psi}{\mathrm{d}T} = \frac{(1-\gamma)(1-f)P_a\, A\alpha T^{\alpha-1}}{f\delta(2\gamma-1)h_t}$$

$$\frac{\mathrm{d}\Psi}{\mathrm{d}T} > 0 \text{ if } \gamma > \frac{1}{2}$$

This suggests that when parents prioritize the anticipated earnings of their children over the quantity of children they have, the rate of augmentation of human capital will increase as the amount of land owned by the parents increases. Parents prioritize the anticipated financial gains from their children, leading them to enrol their children in school for longer durations as their land ownership increases. They are aware that pursuing a greater education raises the likelihood of better anticipated income for their children in the future. Consequently, the formation of human capital continues to grow. During the subsequent phase, as the children transition into the workforce as adults with enhanced human capital, their earnings increase, and, as parents, they enrol their children in school for an extended duration. Thus, the expansion rate of human capital is enhanced.

Proposition 4 *The rate of human capital growth is positively related to the expansion of landholdings if parents give more importance to the expected earnings of children than the quantity of children.*

5 Effects on Fertility

By applying the first-order requirements of the optimization problem,[4] we get,

$$n_t = \frac{(1-\gamma)\left[P_a\, AT^\alpha - p_c\overline{c}\right]}{P_a\, AT^\alpha(2-\gamma)\{\varphi - \theta(1-s_t)\}}$$

Substituting the value of s_t in the equation of n_t, we get,

$$n_t = \frac{(2\gamma - 1)f\delta bh_t\left[P_a AT^\alpha - p_c\overline{c}\right]}{P_a AT^\alpha(2-\gamma)\left[\theta\left\{f\delta\underline{h} + (1-f)P_a AT^\alpha\right\} - (\varphi-\theta)f\delta bh_t\right]}$$

If $\gamma > \frac{1}{2}$, $n_t > 0$ if $P_a\, AT^\alpha > p_c\overline{c}$. This implies that if parents give more importance to expected earnings from children in their utility function as compared to quantity of children, then fertility is positive if adult earning exceeds subsistence expenditure.

Fertility and landholding

Substituting the value of s_t in the equation of n_t, we get,

$$n_t = \frac{(2\gamma - 1)f\delta bh_t\left[P_a AT^\alpha - p_c\overline{c}\right]}{P_a AT^\alpha(2-\gamma)\left[\theta\left\{f\delta\underline{h} + (1-f)P_a AT^\alpha\right\} - (\varphi-\theta)f\delta bh_t\right]}$$

$$\frac{\mathrm{d}n_t}{\mathrm{d}T} = \frac{f\delta bh_t(2\gamma-1)}{P_a A(2-\gamma)}\left[\frac{-(1-f)A^2P_a^2\theta\alpha T^{3\alpha-1} + p_c\overline{c}\left\{\begin{array}{l}2(1-f)P_a A\theta\alpha T^{2\alpha-1}\\ +\theta f\delta\underline{h}\alpha T^{\alpha-1}\\ -\alpha T^{\alpha-1}(\varphi-\theta)f\delta bh_t\end{array}\right\}}{\left[T^\alpha\theta\left\{f\delta\underline{h} + (1-f)P_a AT^\alpha\right\} - T^\alpha(\varphi-\theta)f\delta bh_t\right]^2}\right].$$

We assume and θ > φ. If $\gamma > \frac{1}{2}$, then $\frac{\mathrm{d}n_t}{\mathrm{d}T} > 0$ if $p_c\overline{c} > \frac{-(1-f)A^2P_a^2\theta\alpha T^{3\alpha-1}}{2(1-f)P_a A\theta\alpha T^{2\alpha-1} + \theta f\delta\underline{h}\alpha T^{\alpha-1} - \alpha T^{\alpha-1}(\varphi-\theta)f\delta bh_t}$.

This implies that if parents give more importance to expected earnings of children rather than quantity of children, then fertility increases with increase in landholding only if subsistence consumption expenditure exceeds a critical level. Child's contribution to family farming is necessary to cover subsistence consumption expenditure of the household. Therefore, parents decide to have more children in spite of giving higher importance to expected earnings from children rather than quantity of children.

If $\gamma < \frac{1}{2}$, then $\frac{\mathrm{d}n_t}{\mathrm{d}T} > 0$ if $p_c\overline{c} < \frac{-(1-f)A^2P_a^2\theta\alpha T^{3\alpha-1}}{2(1-f)P_a A\theta\alpha T^{2\alpha-1} + \theta f\delta\underline{h}\alpha T^{\alpha-1} - \alpha T^{\alpha-1}(\varphi-\theta)f\delta bh_t}$.

This implies that if parents prefer quantity of children more to the quality of children measured by expected earnings of children, then fertility increases with

[4] Please see Appendix.

increase in landholding even if subsistence consumption expenditure is less than the critical level.

Proposition 5 *If parents prefer quality of children proxied by expected earnings of children more to the quantity of children, then fertility increases with increase in landholding only if subsistence consumption expenditure exceeds a critical level. However, if parents prefer quantity over quality of children, then fertility increases with increase in landholding even if subsistence consumption expenditure is less than the critical level.*

6 Policy Implications

Differentiating Eq. (5) with respect to θ, we get,

$$\frac{\mathrm{d}s_t}{\mathrm{d}\theta} = \frac{\varphi\gamma}{(2\gamma - 1)\theta^2}$$

If $\gamma > \frac{1}{2}$, $\frac{\mathrm{d}s_t}{\mathrm{d}\theta} > 0$. Now, inadequately implemented prohibition on child labour results in a decrease in wages for children. If parents prioritize the anticipated income generated by their child over the number of children in their overall satisfaction, prohibiting child labour will negatively impact the household. This is because a decrease in child wages results in a decline in the child's access to education. Therefore, prohibiting child work in this particular situation is not a favourable proposal.

Differentiating Eq. (5) with respect to φ, we get,

$$\frac{\mathrm{d}s_t}{\mathrm{d}\varphi} = \frac{-\gamma}{\theta(2\gamma - 1)h_t}$$

If $\gamma > \frac{1}{2}$, $\frac{\mathrm{d}s_t}{\mathrm{d}\varphi} < 0$. This suggests that a decrease in the cost of raising children always results in an increase in the cost of education. A subsidy provided for child raising will inevitably have a beneficial effect on schooling if parents prioritize the anticipated financial gains from having a child above the number of children in their utility function.

Proposition 6 *If parents prioritize the anticipated financial gains from their children over the number of children they have, then providing subsidy for raising children is a more effective governmental approach than prohibiting child labour in promoting education.*

7 Conclusion

This research paper presents a household model of overlapping generations situated in a rural region. Its primary objective is to investigate the impact of expanding land ownership on the academic attendance of child labourers, the child's human capital development, and overall growth. To achieve this, the study incorporates the concern of unemployment. An additional focal point of this paper is the impact of land ownership growth on fertility. Assumed within this model is that every household consists of a solitary adult and an arbitrary quantity of children, represented as 'n'. Household expenditures, the number of children, and the projected income of each child provide adults with pleasure. Preconceived notions are developed concerning her faith in the child's prospective employment opportunities in the manufacturing sector, in light of the industry's unemployment rate. The progression of a child's human assets is reliant on two factors: the child's educational commitment and the parental human capital. Utility is maximized by the adult through decision-making concerning consumption, the number of children to be raised, and the child's time distribution between school and employment.

A scenario is under investigation wherein children and their guardians are engaged in agricultural labour. We have obtained noteworthy discoveries. It is evident that parental prioritization of child labour in the economy is determined by the anticipated earnings of children or the quantity of children in their utility function. When parents place greater importance on the expected financial gains of their children as a measure of overall satisfaction rather than the quantity of offspring, they will exclusively decide to have children if their income surpasses the bare minimum required for daily necessities. An increase in ownership of land is associated with a corresponding rise in the amount of time parents devote to education, provided that the anticipated incomes of their children take precedence over the quantity of children in their utility function. The child earns a smaller percentage of the adult wage as the cost of rearing the child increases. Furthermore, where parents prioritize the anticipated earnings of their children over the quantity of children in their utility function, an increase in landholding is linked with a greater chance of steady-state human capital growth. A positive correlation exists between the extent of landholdings and the rate of growth of human assets when parents place a higher value on the anticipated incomes of their children rather than the quantity of offspring. When parents place greater importance on the anticipated earnings of their children rather than the quantity of offspring, if the subsistence consumption expenditure is very high and exceeds a critical level, then an increase in landholding results in higher fertility. It has been observed that educated parents tend to place a higher value on the education of their children, ensuring that they attend full-time study programmes instead of working. In the event that parents place greater importance on the expected financial benefits derived from their children rather than the quantity of offspring, then governmental support for child-rearing would be a more efficacious measure to advance education than the prohibition of child labour. When the expected earnings of children (quality) take precedence over the quantity of children, there is a tendency for educational attainment to increase in tandem with the expansion of the parental landholding. Additionally, an increase in the size of landholding corresponds to a steady-state increase in human capital. Hence, it is recommended that the government ensures that poor farmers get entitlement of larger landholding. However, we consider γ (the weight attributed to expected earnings to be obtained from children in the parent's utility function) to be exogenously determined in our model. Conducting further research on the endogeneity of γ would be an intriguing avenue to pursue.

Appendix

The objective of the household is to maximize

$Z = \ln(c_t - \bar{c}) + \left[(1-\gamma)\ln \boldsymbol{n_t} + \gamma \ln\left\{f\delta\left(bs_t h_t + \underline{h}\right) + (1-f)P_a AT^\alpha\right\}\right] + \lambda \left[P_a A\{(1-\varphi n_t) + \theta n_t(1-s_t)\}T^\alpha - p_c c_t\right]$. Here, λ is the Lagrange multiplier. The decision variables pertaining to the household are c_t, $s_{t,}$ and $n_{t.}$

The necessary criteria for maximizing utility are expressed by the first-order conditions:

$$\frac{\delta Z}{\delta c_t} = \frac{1}{c_t - \bar{c}} - \lambda p_c = 0 \tag{9}$$

$$\frac{\delta Z}{\delta s_t} = \frac{\gamma f \delta b h_t}{f\delta\left(bs_t h_t + \underline{h}\right) + (1-f)P_a\, AT^\alpha} - \lambda P_a\, AT^\alpha n_t \theta = 0 \tag{10}$$

$$\frac{\delta Z}{\delta n_t} = \frac{(1-\gamma)}{n_t} = \lambda\left[P_a A\varphi T^\alpha - P_a A\theta T^\alpha(1-s_t)\right] \tag{11}$$

Based on Eq. (9) and the constraint imposed by the budget.
$P_a A\{(1-\varphi n_t) + \theta n_t(1-s_t)\}T^\alpha - p_c c_t$, we get

$$\frac{1}{P_a A\{(1-\varphi n_t) + \theta n_t(1-s_t)\}T^\alpha - p_c c_t} = \lambda \tag{12}$$

From (12) and (13) we get,

$$n_t = \frac{(1-\gamma)\left[P_a AT^\alpha - p_c\bar{c}\right]}{P_a AT^\alpha(2-\gamma)\{\varphi - \theta(1-s_t)\}} \tag{13}$$

From (10), (12) and (13W) we get,

$$s_t = \frac{\gamma f\delta b h_t(\theta - \varphi) + \theta(1-\gamma)\left[f\delta\underline{h} + (1-f)P_a AT^\alpha\right]}{f\delta b\theta h_t(2\gamma - 1)} \tag{14}$$

References

Acemoglu D., & Pischke, J. S. (2000). *Changes in the wage structure, family income, and children's education* (NBER Working Paper Number 7986).

Bar, T., & Basu, K. (2008). *Children, education, labour and land: In the long run and short* (CAE Working Paper # 08-06).

Basu K., Das, S., & Dutta, B. (2007). *Child labour and household wealth: Theory and empirical evidence of an inverted-U* (IZA Discussion Paper No. 2736).

Becker, G. S., & Lewis, H. G. (1973). On the interaction between the quantity and quality of children. *Journal of Political Economy, 81*(2), S279–S288.

Becker, G. S., & Tomes, N. (1979). An equilibrium theory of the distribution of income and intergenerational mobility. *Journal of Political Economy, 87*(6).

Bhalotra, S., & Heady, C. (2003). Child farm labour-the wealth paradox. *The World Bank Economic Review, 17*(2), 197–227.

Bhandari, M., & Ghimire, D. (2013). Rural agricultural change and fertility transition in Nepal. *Rural Sociology, 78*(2), 229–252.

Boutin, D. (2012). Family Farming, child labour and the wealth paradox: Evidence from Mali. *Economics Bulletin, 32*, 3471–3479.

Cain, M. (1985). On the relationship between landholding and fertility. *Population Studies, 39*, 5–15.

Campenhout, B. V. (2016). Fertility, agricultural labor supply, and production: Instrumental variable evidence from Uganda. *Agricultural and Resource Economics Review, 45*(3), 581–607.

Chakraborty, B., & Chakraborty, K. (2014). Child labour, human capital formation and size of landholding: Short run and long run analysis. *Economics Bulletin, 34*(3), 2024–2037.

Chakraborty, K., & Chakraborty, B. (2018). Low level equilibrium trap, unemployment, efficiency of education system, child labour and human capital formation. *Journal of Economics, 125*(1), 69–95.

Clay, D. C., & Johnson, N. E. (1992). Size of farm or size of family: Which comes first? *Population Studies, 46*(3), 491–505.

Contreras, S. (2008). Child labor participation, human capital accumulation, and economic development. *Journal of Macroeconomics, 30*, 499–512.

Croix, D., & Doepke, M. (2004). Public versus private education when differential fertility matters. *Journal of Development Economics, 73*, 607–629.

Dumas, A. (2007). Why do parents make their children work? A test of the poverty hypothesis in rural area of Burkina Faso. *Oxford Economic Papers, 59*, 301–329.

Emerson, P. M., & Knabb, S. D. (2006). Opportunity, inequality and the intergenerational transmission of child labour. *Economica, New Series, 73*(291), 413–434.

Emerson, P. M., & Souza, A. (2003). Is there a child labour trap? Intergenerational persistence of child labour in Brazil. *Economic Development and Cultural Change, 51*(2), 376–397.

Galor, O., & Tsiddon, D. (1997). The distribution of human capital and economic growth. *Journal of Economic Growth, 2*, 93–124.

Genicot, G., & Ray, D. (2010). *Aspirations and inequality* (NBER Working Paper No. 19976).

Glomm, G. (1997). Parental choice of human capital investment. *Journal of Development Economics, 53*, 99–114.

Glomm, G., & Ravikumar, B. (1998). Increasing returns, human capital, and the Kuznets curve. *Journal of Development Economics, 55*, 353–367.

James, K. S. (2000). Landholding and fertility in India: A review of theoretical and empirical evidence, *56*(3/4), 61–79.

Khan, R. E. A. (2003). Children in different activities: Child schooling and child labour. *The Pakistan Development Review, 42*(2), 137–160.

Moura, M. (2009). *How land title affects child labour?* (World Bank Policy Research Working Paper 5010).

Mukherjee, D., & Sinha, U. B. (2006). Schooling, job prospect and child labour in a developing economy. *mimeo*. Indian Statistical Institute, Kolkata.
Oreopoulos, P., Page, M. E., & Stevens, A. H. (2003). *Does human capital transfer from parent to child? The intergenerational effects of compulsory schooling* (NBER Working Paper No. 10164).
Oryoie, A. R., Jeffrey, A., & Tideman, N. (2017). Child labor and household land holding: Theory and empirical evidence from Zimbabwe. *World Development, 20*, 45–58.
Ray, R. (2000). Analysis of child labour in Peru and Pakistan: A comparative study. *Journal of Population Economics, 13*(1), 3–19.
Rosenzweig, M. R., & Evenson, R. (1977). Fertility, schooling, and the economic contribution of children in rural India: An econometric analysis. *Econometrica, 45*(5), 1065–1079.
Wahba, J. (2005). *The influence of market wages and parental history on child labour and schooling in Egypt* (IZA Discussion Paper No. 1771).
Yakita, A. (2010). Human capital accumulation, fertility and economic development. *Journal of Economics, 99*, 97–116.

Inequality, Inclusive Growth, and Reflections on the Indian Economy

Biswajit Chatterjee

Abstract Increase in income and wealth inequality across individuals and also in the levels of human development and deprivations in many parts of the world have received increasing attention among researchers and policy designers in recent years, and India is no exception to this tendency. Growth distribution linkage has been reflected upon by the Classical and Neo-classical economists, and a synoptic review of the issues related to inequality and economic development, including the theoretical and empirical validity of the inverted U hypothesis, have been made in Sect. 2 of the paper. In Sect. 2, we review the inequality development linkage in terms of the selected theoretical and empirical literature since the days of Classical economists, and explicate the analytical issues involved, including the important contributions of Thomas Piketty and his team at the World Inequality Lab. Sect. 3 examines critically the analytical frame of the inclusive growth paradigm of development and its implications for inequality mitigation, followed by Sect. 4 reflecting on the trends in inequality in India and the possible policy interventions to mitigate inequality and promote inclusivity in the growth process of the Indian economy. Section 5 concludes.

JEL Classification Codes I32 · O15 · R10

1 Introduction

An imbalance between rich and poor is perhaps the oldest and most fatal ailment of all nations. The Sustainable Development Goal (SDG 10) of the United Nations has set the reduction of inequality within and among nations as the target for improving human livelihood through the adoption of policies to create equal opportunity for everyone, regulate markets and institutions, and initiate development for mitigating inequalities of various forms. Inequality persists across the globe and is on the rise.

B. Chatterjee (✉)
Economics, Jadavpur University, Kolkata, India
e-mail: chatterjeeb3354@gmail.com

B. Chatterjee and A. K. Karmakar (eds.), *Analytical Issues in Growth & Structural Change, Macroeconomy, Security, and Sustainability of India's Economic Development*, India Studies in Business and Economics, https://doi.org/10.1007/978-981-95-5242-9_3

Impressive economic growth notwithstanding, many countries in the world have experienced a sharp rise in income inequality across individuals, which has aggravated social tensions and political turmoil in different parts of the world. Notwithstanding impressive economic growth, many countries in the world have experienced a sharp rise in income inequality across individuals, which has aggravated social tensions and political turmoil in different parts of the world. Inequality has many dimensions—income inequality between nations, income and asset inequality between persons within a nation, and in dimensions of human development and deprivations, and in government programs aimed to ameliorate poverty, or to usher in inclusive growth.

The accentuation of inequality in all dimensions has important bearings on social, economic, and political conflicts, which runs counter to the UN Goals of Sustainable Development Goals (SDGs). The statistical update of the UNDP's Human Development Indices and Indicators 2018 (2018) reports overall improvements across the globe in health, education, and income levels over the last thirty years, yet "wide inequalities" both among and within countries, which cast a shadow on sustained human development. Achim Steiner (UNDP Report, 2018) reports, "While these statistics present a stark picture in themselves, they also speak to the tragedy of millions of individuals whose lives are affected by inequity and lost opportunities, neither of which are inevitable", Recent Oxfam International reports also show that "eight men own the same wealth as the 3.6 billion people who make up the poorest half of humanity" (2017, p. 1) and that "82% of all global wealth in the last year went to the top 1%, while the bottom half of humanity saw no increase at all" (2018, p. 10). While the share of the richest 1% and 0.1% are exceedingly high, focusing on these groups' risks obscuring another growing concern in inequality—the decline and stagnation in the livelihood conditions of middle-income households. Thus, not only perpetuation, persistence, but also upward tendency of inequality in different forms across the globe have raised concerns among economists and policy makers. In this paper, we reflect on these issues in detail.

The main questions that are addressed in the literature are why inequality in income and wealth distribution is generated and remains persistent in the process of capitalist development. In the context of developing nations, where the bulk of the world's poor people are located, the issue of inequality development linkage has remained the center stage of discussions. From the perspectives of Classical Political Economy—Smith, Ricardo, Marx—to the Inverted U hypothesis of Kuznets in the context of development in the early post-War days to the recent upsurge of interest following the seminal works of Thomas Piketty (2014, 2015), we have experienced growth inequality interdependence in the world capitalist economies. The focus on "Inclusive Growth" paradigm in India's development discourse in recent decades has received renewed attention due to the policy rhetoric of *Sab Ka Sath Sab Ka Bikas, and so on.*

The plan of the present paper is as follows. In Sect. 2, we review the inequality development linkage in terms of the selected theoretical and empirical literature since the days of Classical economists, and explicate the analytical issues involved, including the important contributions of Thomas Piketty and his team at the World

Inequality Lab. In Sect. 3, we reflect on the analytical structure of the Inclusive Development paradigm, and the implications for the mitigation of inequality in income distribution during the process of development. Section 4 reflects on the Indian scenario and the implications of various policy initiatives for mitigation of inequality to achieve the sustainable goal of inclusivity in development. Section 5 concludes.

Sections 2 and 3 are borrowed substantially from my own paper Chatterjee (2023a), and Section 4 bears strong similarity with Chatterjee (2023b).

2 Growth, Inequality and Development Linkage—A Relook

The Classical economists, writing in the background of rising industrial capitalism in England, were primarily concerned with economic growth as it suited the notion of material progress of mankind. The link between economic growth and income distribution had been at the core of Classical Political Economy a la Adam Smith, David Ricardo, and Karl Marx. Chatterjee (2023a) argued that "the main impetus of growth comes through capital accumulation and innovation and the relationship between growth and distribution is interdependent-while the growth process and the stages of development affect the distribution of wealth in a society, the pattern of income distribution in turn determines the possibilities of growth"[1] The argument goes on as the following: "in a capitalist system, capitalists as owners of capital, hires labor at wages determined in the market, and land rent is similarly determined and accrues to the owners of land. The surplus of output that remains after payment of wages and rent accrues to the capitalist as profit, which he retains for self-consumption as well as for accumulation. It is the accumulation of surplus through investment that propels the dynamics of the capitalist system. As growth through capital accumulation generates land rent, the size of profit dwindles and in the long run, the rate of profit shows a tendency to fall to zero and when it does, there is arrival of the stationary state with zero rate of growth. Thus, there exists an intimate relationship between economic growth and income distribution among factor shares (labor, land, and capital) and the relation can be affected by technological innovation which might postpone and delay the arrival of stationary state in a capitalist economy. While Smith, Ricardo and Mill predicted long run convergence to stationary state as the outcome of accumulation, Marx linked it with the withering away of the capitalist system".

The neoclassical marginal productivity theory, on the other hand, deviated from distribution based on conflict of interests to factor pricing under a perfectly competitive market mechanism which is supposed to generate efficient allocation of productive resources and payment to factors on the basis of their individual contribution to the production process, even at a macroeconomic level. According to this view, in the long run, market forces, individual initiatives, and productivity growth are the

[1] Since I was the Editor in Chief of that journal during the period when the present paper was drafted, separate permission letter would be superfluous at this stage.

principal determinants of income distribution and standard of living, in particular of the least well-off members of the society. Government's efforts to redistribute wealth, according to this view, should be limited to a minimum and reliance should be on the equitable distribution in the long run achievable through the efficient working of the market mechanisms.

The second half of the twentieth century witnessed a significant surge in the literature on development economics. The issues of distribution of income and inequality thereof have been extensively discussed in the modern theories of economic development. In the immediate post-war period, the focus was on rapid growth and industrialization (Mahalanobis, 1963; Rosenstein-Rodan, 1943). Simon Kuznets (1955) put forward his "inverted U hypothesis", that inequality first increases and then decreases as per capita income rises. According to him, during the process of development, population shifts from rural to non-agricultural sectors, such that, under certain assumptions, it would lead to a temporary rise in overall inequality. His famous conjecture about the (curvilinear) relationship between inequality and development spurred an extraordinary amount of empirical research, but Kuznets never intended to assert that inequality was a necessary condition of economic takeoff. The 1960s and 1970s saw the culmination of concerns on the distributional consequences of fast growth, led by the experiences of such countries as Brazil, where worsening of distribution might even have been such as to increase poverty despite rapid growth (Fishlow (1972)). The Indian Third Five Year Plan also explicitly mentioned distributional objectives. The World Bank's (1990) World Development Report (WDR) and the UNDP's (1990) Human Development Report captured the consensus that not only is growth necessary for poverty reduction but that growth and equitable distribution of growth can indeed go hand in hand—all that is needed are the right policies. The WDR 1990, in particular, put forward a two-pronged strategy which seemed to resolve the conflicts highlighted in the earlier literature—the two prongs being labor-demanding growth based on private sector incentives, and public investment in basic education, health, and infrastructure, these two prongs to be supported by social safety nets to protect the very poor and vulnerable.

The "inverted U hypothesis" of Simon Kuznets (1955) suggests that inequality first increases and then decreases as per capita income rises. He argued that as countries developed, income inequality first increased, peaked, and then decreased, and documented this using both cross-country and time-series data. The inverted U arises in his model due to the fact that the sector (non-agriculture) to which people migrate in the process of development is the sector with the higher mean income as well as with higher internal inequality. It may be noted that the empirical validity of this "Kuznets curve" has been intensively investigated, but the evidence is mixed.

Historical investigations of Western European countries, e.g., England, France, Sweden, and Germany tend to support Kuznets' conjecture, while evidence from Norway and the Netherlands suggested monotonically declining inequality from the mid-nineteenth century. Adelman and Morris (1973) used analysis of variance with data on the size distribution of income by quantiles for 44 less developed countries. They found that all the less developed countries in the sample experienced significant decline in the share of income that accrues to the poorest, as the process of development started, although the share of income accruing to the poorest 60% of the population declined at a slower rate. "For about one-third of the developing countries in the sample of their study, the policy choices actually determined whether the share of income accruing to the poorest improved or not. Thus we see that cross-country relationship could be either inverted U shaped or J-shaped. Studies on inequality-development nexus based on cross country regressions that followed were many, mostly based on heterogeneous data and varied samples, often inclusive of developed countries, and the results were also mixed. While data from some Latin American countries, such as Colombia and Brazil, seem consistent with the hypothesis, Asian countries such as South Korea, Japan, and Taiwan have experienced monotonically falling inequality (Chatterjee, 2023a, op cit.)".

It may be recognized that although the relationship examined is essentially an inter-temporal one, the above studies relied on cross-section data because time series information were not ready at that time. These cross-section studies therefore examined patterns of income distribution and economic growth in a correlative sense and examined, for example, whether the middle-income countries have higher inequality than lower-income or higher-income countries, with no causality implied. The examples include Paukert (1973), Cline (1972), and Ahluwalia (1976). Usually, two functional forms were used. One is to include per capita national income and its square (or logarithms thereof) as explanatory variable. To test for inverted U hypothesis, one expects a positive slope to per capita national income and a negative coefficient of its square, and the derivatives must alternate signs within the range of the data. The other form is to take per capita national income, and its inverse with negative slopes for both explanatory variables to generate an inverted U by OLS estimates. The inverted U pattern is confirmed for both top 20% income share, and bottom 40% of income share. The most cross-section studies confirm inverted U pattern of relationship, but with very poor $\mathbf{R}^2$ (0.2), or less. Since inverted U is weakly supported by cross-section regressions, and since the temporal effects are likely to stronger, the focus seems to have shifted from various cross-sectional studies to time-series panel data estimation methods.

There have been spurts in empirical work on inequality–growth relationship since the 1990s. A number of authors have tried to analyze the inequality–growth linkage by examining the cross-country relation between inequality and growth. A long literature (see Benabou, 1996a, 1996b for a survey) estimated a long-run equation with growth between 1960 and 1990 regressed on income in 1960, a set of control variables, and inequality in 1960. Estimates of such equations generate negative coefficients for inequality, but many such relations are caused entirely by omitted variables. Until the late 1990s, results from the empirical literature in general indicated that more inequality acts as a deterrent to future growth prospects of nations. The negative effect of inequality is obtained from cross-sectional OLS estimation of growth rates, measured over a single interval of 20–30 years as a function of several variables, including a measure of inequality. Furthermore, the negative effect of land inequality on growth turned out to be more robust than income inequality, that is, it remained statistically significant after the introduction of regional dummies for

Latin America, Africa, and Asia (Deininger & Squire, 1998). With the availability of larger and better quality data set of Deininger and Squire, empirical research had evolved to include the panel estimation methods—like fixed effects (FE) and first-difference GMM panel estimators. The panel approach estimated a set of repeated growth observations in several countries as a function of time-varying variables, after controlling for unobserved time-invariant country-specific characteristics, and reported a positive effect of inequality on growth (vide Banerjee–Duflo, 2003, for similar conclusion). Currently, there exist several concurring explanations for the commonly observed split between the negative and positive effects of inequality and growth. One argument is that the neglect of time-invariant omitted variables in cross-sectional studies biases the estimated coefficients on inequality downwards. These omitted time-invariant variables are simultaneously associated with growth and inequality in the opposite direction, due to, e.g., corruption, fertility rates, or the quality of government policies on health and education (Forbes, 2000). The negative effect reported in cross-sectional studies is usually found to be sensitive to the inclusion of regional dummies or other explanatory variables or to sample composition (Deininger & Squire, 1998). There is also the impact of measurement errors on estimation results—studies which report a positive effect of inequality on growth using panel methods also rely on more limited time-series variation in the data, particularly when the variable is persistent and the time structure is short. On the other hand, negative effect reported in cross-sectional studies often results from country or region-specific measurement errors in inequality data. Banerjee and Duflo (2003) argued that this sign pattern could be explained by the misspecification of the linear effect of inequality that is commonly estimated. If the real effect of inequality on growth is non-linear, a linear specification is likely to yield a negative effect of inequality with a cross-sectional estimation method, and a positive effect in a fixed-effects analysis. Banerjee and Duflo (2003) regressed growth (or changes in growth) non-parametrically on changes in inequality and found the relationship to be an inverted U shape. In other words, both reductions and increases in inequality seem to be accompanied by a fall in growth—this result may either be due to omitted variables or by the poor measurement of inequality.

2.1 Piketty and Beyond

Thomas Piketty's epoch-making book *Capital in the Twenty-First Century* (2014) documented the long period trends in the top income and wealth shares for the last two centuries, and estimated time series for the top 10% and the top 1% of the two distributions. He argues that as long as the rate of return to capital is higher than the rate of growth in the economy ($r > g$), the owners of capital will accrue an ever larger share of the economic pie. Thus, inter-temporal rise in inequality in the distribution of income is due to the uneven distribution of wealth and inherited capital which has propelled the forces of generation and augmentation of income inequality between persons, and even between nations. In his own words, "*the fundamental source of inequality is the unequal ownership of capital, more so of human capital between persons and nations*" Piketty (2015). Piketty predicted, "*It is almost inevitable that inherited wealth will dominate wealth amassed from a lifetime's labor by a wide margin, and the concentration of [wealth] will attain extremely high levels—levels potentially incompatible with the meritocratic values and principles of social justice fundamental to modern democratic societies*" (Piketty 2014, p. 26).

According to Piketty (2014), the debate on capital—labor split and more so on the unequal distribution of capital ownership prompts discussions on how to tackle such inequality in income and wealth distribution. He favored the imposition of a global tax on wealth that might at least reduce net differences in the returns to labor and capital. Since such progressive redistribution mechanism would benefit *some* and hurt *some others* at least in the short run, there are debates regarding his recommended redistribution mechanism. The first set of criticisms points to within-factor inequality, i.e., inequalities in the distribution of wage income across individuals, whereas his book for most part is really about the relative returns to capital vis-à-vis labor, i.e., between-factor inequality. It is also not clear how wealth inequality across people in society could be tackled by a tax on income from capital alone. Indeed, there is ample inequality in the asset holdings among those people that do possess wealth—indeed most measures of wealth inequality, be it land inequality or housing inequality, show higher rates of wealth inequality (by, say, the Gini measure) than hold for income inequality. The political economy of asset redistribution appears to be much more difficult than redistribution of income via taxation.

Piketty's influential narrative of the dynamics of wealth inequality in capitalist economies and the distribution of income between capital and labor poses important challenges to the researchers on inequality and well-being. It may be argued that capitalism in the contemporary world had long deviated from the idealized vision of perfect competition—there are imperfections in markets of commodities, factors, as well as financial instruments, and there were significant technological progresses in different sectors within a nation and between nations, with varying effectiveness, such that it is meaningless to rely on dynamic general equilibrium version of neoclassical economics, as has been attempted by Piketty and his followers. Perhaps one could go back to the analysis of Michael Kalecki on the dynamics of capital accumulation and income distribution in an imperfectly competitive capitalist economy, which is integrated to the working of the world economy in an era of globalization.

It is clear from the above discussion that whether economic growth in poor underdeveloped nations would exhibit a pattern depicted by Kuznets curve or not depends crucially on initial conditions of distribution prevalent in a given country. If the path of growth-inequality relationship is uniformly negatively sloped, then growth process directly trickles down and there is spread of the benefits of growth to the lower end of the income distribution. If, however, economic growth is accompanied by rising income inequality and then followed by falling inequality, trickle down operates only in the long run. The path, therefore, becomes circuitous and often long-drawn, and how long is the period required for inequality to diminish in a growing economy depends on the initial distribution of wealth and income in a given country and the speed of growth, which is likely to exhibit a nonlinear path and is unlikely to be uniform for all developing countries.

Section 3 depends on and borrows largely from the narratives of my own paper, Chatterjee (2023a).

3 Paradigm of Inclusive Growth

A new paradigm of development, called the ***inclusive growth paradigm***, has surfaced in contemporary discussions on development policies according to which the primary focus of development has to be faster economic growth generated from the productive use of inputs and total factor productivity growth in an environment of not controlled but judicially regulated markets, while at the same time including in the growth process those who were left out by the hitherto initiated growth programs. Dr Manmohan Singh, as Prime Minister, introduced this inclusive growth paradigm in India's XI and XII plan document to highlight the importance of development programs that seek to include those who were hitherto neglected or not included in the distribution of fruits of development over the years. As per this paradigm of development, argues Chatterjee (2023b), removal of inequality of distribution in income and wealth across persons has become the top agenda for development policy, such that instead of relying on the trickle-down mechanism, there is spread of the fruits of development from the bottom layers itself, without sacrificing macroeconomic stability, but may be at the cost of slower yet sustained rate of economic growth in developing nations.

The principal characteristics of the inclusive growth (IG) strategy of the development process focus on sustained economic growth in the long run and be broad-based across sectors, and be inclusive of the large part of the country's labor force. In other words, both the pace and pattern of growth (i.e., not only employment growth but also productivity growth), as well as the equality of opportunity in terms of access to markets, resources, and unbiased regulatory environment for businesses and individuals, must be considered in devising the proper IG strategy for a developing economy.

A plausible way of judging inclusiveness of the growth process may be to consider the distribution of income/expenditure across the quintile classes. Analytically, the simple test of IG is to check whether the inequality in the distribution has *remained invariant over time or has diminished.* In terms of the relative view of inequality, we could say that inequality over time, in the presence of growth in per capita income, has remained unchanged when each person's income has increased by the same proportion. In terms of a wholly absolute view of inequality, however, we would expect over-time invariance in inequality when each person's income has increased by the same amount.

One may consider *three* important ways of achieving inclusive development. The *first* one is expansion of employment, which is connected with the nature of economic growth. The rationale is that productive job creation will be associated with income generation at the lower stratum of income distribution and will directly transfer the benefits of growth to those who are hitherto bypassed because of a variety of reasons. The *second* alternative channel of inequality mitigation is through direct and redistributive taxation, which in principle can reduce the incidence of inequality and poverty in a growing economy. As most of the existing transfer mechanisms in India are either inefficient or mis-targeted, the effects of such redistributive tax-transfer schemes on income and wealth redistribution would in all probability fail. A *third* important step could be expansion of public spending on the social sector of the economy, viz., education and health. It is expected that public expenditure on social services would help in redistribution of income, as these services tend to provide "virtual income" to the poor by freeing up resources spent on privately provided services. Per capita real expenditure on education and health could provide the poor an opportunity to invest in human capital and augment their future income potentials. If education and health are made public goods for all with no exclusion clause, and if care and efficiency are forthcoming, then such spending would definitely strengthen the other redistributive mechanisms, like transfer and employment-generating schemes, and if sustained for a long period, the inequality-breeding effects of capitalist accumulation could be minimized. Otherwise, the call for *Sab Ka Sath Sab ka Vikas* would simply remain illusory.

4 Implications for India

Most of the studies on poverty and inequality in India focused on how overall inequality in income distribution undermined the 'trickle down' effect, i.e., higher is the inequality in the income distribution, the lower is the growth elasticity of poverty. Banerjee and Piketty (2005) pointed out that because of unequal growth across sectors, the income of a few had grown, but the majority did not benefit much, resulting in rise in income inequality. This rise of inequality in income and wealth distribution was accompanied by augmentation of social and religious inequalities in India over the ages. Available statistics indicate that most of the Indian states had become unequal over time, consistent with the national trend. Inequality had increased the most in faster-growing states, implying worsening of relative economic outcomes with growth. Again, even though the incidence of poverty had been reduced in faster-growing states, the intensity of poverty as indicated by the PGI did not change much, suggesting that the reduction in poverty in the periods of growth was brought about by improvement in outcomes for households very close to the poverty line.

The India Human Development Survey (IHDS) (University of Maryland and NCAER, 2015) data covering the period 2005–2012 examined the effects of income (measured as per capita income of a state), ratio of income share of the top 1% to that of the bottom 50%, and their interaction or joint effect on the Foster–Greer–Thorbecke (FGT) class of poverty indices. Their study further disaggregates the results of Chancel and Piketty (2019) showing that the ratios of shares of the top 1% and

0.05% to that of the bottom 50% of the income distribution have a robust relationship to poverty during this period.

Narayan and Murgai (2016) [also see Kulkarni and Gaiha (2018), *op cit* for such exercises] have reviewed India's poverty reduction in the context of the global experience, and argued that India accounted for 26% of the global poor at the poverty cut-off of $1.90 a day (2011 PPP). Their findings reveal that between 1993–1994 and 2011–2012, the percentage of poor people as per the official poverty line had actually diminished from 45 to 22%—of which, the rural poverty rate reduced from 50 to 26%, and urban poverty declined from 32 to 14%. However, relative to 1994–2005, poverty reduction in India had become more responsive to growth of income/consumption during 2005–2012. Chancel and Piketty (2017) offered a description of the evolution of income inequality in India since 1922, combining household survey data, tax returns data and other specialized surveys, and their major findings are: (a) the share of national income accruing to the top 1% income earners is now at its highest level since the launch of the Indian Income Tax Act in 1922. The top 1% of income earners in India captured less than 21% of total income in the late 1930s, which dropped to 6% in the early 1980s, but rose to 22% in 2015; (b) between 1951 and 1980, the bottom 50% captured 28% of total growth and this group's income group grew faster than the average, while the incomes of the top 0.1% decreased; (c) between 1980 and 2014, the situation was reversed; the top 0.1% of earners captured a higher share of total growth than the bottom 50% (12% versus 11%), while the top 1% received a higher share of total growth than the middle 40% (29% versus 23%) [One may see, Chatterjee, 2023b for details].

N. K. Bharti et al. (2024) argued that post-independence inequality in India declined till the early 1980s, and it showed an upward trend which has sharpened since the early 2000s. Between 1960 and 2022, India's average income grew at 2.6% per year in real terms, but till the middle of the 1970s, this growth became sluggish and fluctuating in nature. Growth picked up in the 1980s and accelerated during the 1990s and 2000s. On a comparative note, there emerged extreme levels of inequality in India compared to international standards. While in China and Vietnam, the average income levels were similar to those in India till 1975, by the turn of the century, growth in China and Vietnam accelerated much such that the Chinese average incomes exceeded those of India's by 35 to 50%, and Vietnam's by more than 33% during the period. By 2022–2023 (and this includes the Covid-19 period), on the other hand, India's top 1% income and wealth shares (22.6% and 40.1%) are at their highest historical levels, and India's top 1% income share is among the very highest in the world. "In 2022–2023, 22.6% of India's national income went to just the top 1%", argues the paper (Bharti et al. 2024 and the World Inequality Report 2022), "the highest level recorded in our series since 1922, higher than even during the inter-war colonial period. The top 1% wealth share stood at 40.1% in 2022–2023, also at its highest level since 1961 when our wealth series begins. In other words, the 'Billionaire Raj' headed by India's modern bourgeoisie is now more unequal than the British Raj headed by the colonialist forces". According to data from Forbes billionaire rankings, "the number of Indians with net wealth exceeding 1 billion USD at market exchange rate (MER) increased from 1 to 52 to 162 in 1991, 2011 and 2022 respectively". During this period, "the total net wealth of these individuals as a share of India's net national income boomed from under 1% in 1991 to a very high 25% in 2022. Perhaps not surprisingly, the share of adult population that filed an income tax return, which had remained under 1% till the 1990s, also grew significantly in the three decades post the economic reforms of 1991. By 2011, the share had crossed 5% and the last decade too saw sustained growth with around 9% of adults filing a return in the years 2017–2020" (Bharti et al., 2024).

5 Concluding Observations

Inequality has many dimensions and the connect between economic growth and income or wealth inequality has been reviewed in the present paper in terms of the evolving literature, and references thereof. Discussions regarding Kuznets' inverted U hypothesis, and its theoretical and analytical foundations, point to the need to look at the linkage between economic growth and income distribution, and the growth-inequality connect from the perspective of classical political economy and Kalecki's (1971) macroeconomic framework for a structurally differentiated less developed economy. The much publicized paradigm of inclusive growth in India and the declared objective of poverty eradication call for coordination and complementarity among alternative policy interventions to bring about an equitable social and economic order. The process of inclusive growth would entail *if and only* if the planners set out a growth process in those lines of productive activities for which the weak, marginalized, and so-called inefficient or low-skill workers are capable of participating. The essence of achieving inclusive growth lies in reducing inequalities in the bottom layers of income distribution, but India's record of achieving inclusiveness is rather poor across the states. Policy complementarity, efficiency, and macroeconomic stabilization are essential ingredients of achieving equitable and accelerating growth process in the Indian economy. The sharp acceleration of income and wealth inequality in India, particularly during the Covid-19, point to the need to probe deeply into the causes of such disarray and deprivation, and devise policies at both micro and macro levels to address the goals of sustainable and equitable growth in the Indian economy.

References

Adelman, I., & Morris, C. T. (1973). *Economic growth and social equity in developing countries*. Stanford University Press.

Aghion, P., & Bolton, P. (1997, April). A theory of trickle-down growth and development. *The Review of Economic Studies, 64*(2), 151–172.

Ahluwalia, M. S. (1976). Inequality, poverty and development. *Journal of Development Economics, 3*, 307–342.

Anand, R., Mishra, S., & Peiris, S. J. (2013). *Inclusive growth: Measurement and determinants* (IMF Working Paper WP/13/135).
Anand, S., & Kanbur, R. (1985). Poverty under the Kuznets process. *Economic Journal (Supplement), 95*, 42–50.
Anand, S., & Kanbur, R. (1993). The Kuznets process and the inequality-development relationship. *Journal of Development Economics, 40*, 25–52.
Anand, S., & Kanbur, R. (1993). Inequality and development: A critique. *Journal of Development Economics, 41*, 19–43.
Banerjee, A. V., & Duflo, E. (2003). Inequality and growth: What can the data say? *Journal of Economic Growth, 8*, Article 267299.
Banerjee, A., & Piketty, T. (2005). Top Indian incomes, 1922–2000. *The World Bank Economic Review, 19*(1), 1–20.
Benabou, R. (1996a). Inequality and growth. In B. Bernanke & J. J. Rotemberg (Eds.), *NBER macroeconomics annual 1996* (p. 1173). MITPress.
Benabou, R. (1996). Equity and efficiency in human capital investment: The local connection. *Review of Economic Studies, 63*, 237–264.
Bharti, N. K. (2018). *Wealth inequality, class and caste in India, 1961–2012* (WID.world Working Paper No. 2018/14). https://wid.world/wp-content/uploads/2018/11/WID_WORKING_PAPER_2018_14_India_wealth-3.pdf
Bharti, N. K., & Yang, L. (2024). *The making of China and India in 21st century: Long Run human capital accumulation from 1900 to 2020* (WIL Working Paper).
Bharti, N. K., Chancel, L., Piketty, T., & Somanchi, A. (2024, March). *Income and wealth inequality in India, 1922–2023: The rise of the Billionaire Raj* (Working Paper No. 2024/ 09). World Inequality Lab.
Chancel, L., & Piketty, T. (2017). Indian income inequality, 1922–2014: From British Raj to Billionaire Raj? (WID.world Working Paper Series No. 2017/11).
Chancel, L., & Piketty, T. (2019). Indian income inequality, 1992–2015: From British Raj to Billionaire Raj? *Review of Income and Wealth, 65*(S1), S33–S62. http://piketty.pse.ens.fr/files/ChancelPiketty2019RIW.pdf
Chatterjee, B. (2013, January 9–11). *Economic growth and income distribution*. 49th Annual Conference of The Indian Econometric Society (TIES), Patna University, Patna, mimeo.
Chatterjee, B. (2023a, June–September). Growth, distribution and development. *Artha Beekshan, 32*(1 & 2). ISSN No. 0972-1185.
Chatterjee, B. (2023b, December 28–30). *Political economy of India's development paradigm*. 106th Annual Conference of The Indian Economic Association (IEA), KIIT University, Bhubaneswar, mimeo.
Chenery, H., Ahluwalia, M., Bell, C., Duloy, J., & Jolly, R. (1974). *Redistribution with growth*. Oxford University Press.
Cline, W. (1972). *Potential effects of income distribution on economic growth: Latin American Cases*. Prager.
Datt, G., & Ravallion, M. (2002). Is India's economic growth leaving the poor behind? *The Journal of Economic Perspectives, 16*(3), 89–108.
Deininger, K., & Squire, L. (1998). New ways of looking at old issues: Inequality and growth. *Journal of Development Economics, 57*(2), 259–287.
Deininger, K., & Squire, L. (1996). A new data set for measuring income inequality. *World Bank Economic Review, 10*, 565–591.
Deininger, K., & Squire, L. (1996b). Does inequality matter? Reexamining the links between growth and inequality. *Mimeo*. World Bank, Washington, DC.
Deininger, K., & Squire, L. (1996c). New ways of looking at old issues: Inequality and growth. *Mimeo*. World Bank, Washington DC.
Deininger, K., & Squire, L. (1996). A new data set measuring income inequality. *World Bank Economic Review, 10*, 565–591.
Fishlow, A. (1972). Brazilian size distribution of income. *American Economic Review, 62*, 391–402.

Fishlow, A. (1996). Inequality, poverty and growth: Where do we stand? In M. Bruno & B. Pleskovic (Eds.), *Annual World Bank Conference on Development Economics, 1995* (pp 25–39). World Bank.
Forbes, K. J. (2000). A reassessment of the relationship between inequality and growth. *American Economic Review, 90*, 869–887.
Ghosh, A. K. (2012, January–March). The growth employment interaction in a developing economy. *The Indian Journal of Labour economics, 55*(1).
Jayaraj, D., & Subramanian, S. (2018). The distribution of household assets in India: 1991–1992 to 2012–2013. *Indian Journal of Human Development, 12*(2), 181–203. https://doi.org/10.1177/0973703018789244
Kalecki, M. (1971). *Selected essays on the dynamics of the capitalist economy*. Cambridge University Press.
Kulkarni, V. S., & Gaiha, R. (2018). *Beyond Piketty: A new perspective on poverty and inequality in India* (GDI Working Paper 2018-033). The University of Manchester, Manchester (which noted, among others, the paper by Narayan, A. and Murgai, R. (2016)).
Kuznets, S. (1955). Economic growth and income inequality. *American Economic Review, 45*, 1–28.
Mahalanobis, P. (1963). *The approach of operational research to planning in India (Asia, Bombay).*
National Sample Survey Office. (2024). *Household consumption expenditure survey: 2022–23 fact sheet*. Ministry of Statistics and Programme Implementation, Government of India, New Delhi. https://www.mospi.gov.in/sites/default/files/publication_reports/Factsheet_HCES_2022-23.pdf
Press Information Bureau. (2024). *Percapita monthly household consumption expenditure more than doubled during 2011–12 to 2022–23*. Ministry of Statistics and Programme Implementation, Government of India, New Delhi. https://pib.gov.in/PressReleseDetailm.aspx?PRID=2008737
Narayan, A., & Murgai, R. (2016). *Looking back on two decades of poverty and well-being in India* (Policy Research Working Paper 7626). World Bank, Washington DC.
Paukert, F. (1973). Income distribution at different levels of development: A survey of the evidence. *International Labor Review, 108*, 97–125.
Piketty, T. (2014). *Capital in the twenty-first century* (A. Goldhammer, Trans.). Belknap Press.
Piketty, T. (2015). *The economics of inequality*. Belknap/Harvard University Press.
Ravallion, M., & Chen, S. (2003). Measuring pro-poor growth. *Economics Letters, 78*, 93–99.
Subramanian, S., & Jayaraj, D. (2015). *Growth and inequality in the distribution of India's consumption expenditure 1983 to 2009–10* (WIDER Working Paper No. 2015/025).
Rosenstein-Rodan, P. (1943). Problems of industrialization in Southern and Eastern Europe. *Economic Journal, 53*, 202–211.
UNDP. (2018). *Human development indices and indicators: 2018 statistical update*. NY.
World Bank. (2013). World*development report.*
World Bank. (2006). *World development report: Equity and development*. World Bank.
World Inequality Lab. (2018). *The world inequality report 2018.*
World Inequality Lab. (2022/2023). *The world inequality report 2022.*

Structural Change and Economic Development in India's Service Sector: A State Level Study

Purba Roy Choudhury

Abstract According to the conventional wisdom of development, there may be a positive association between the service sector share of GDP and per capita income. The paper explores the relationship between the service sector share of GDP and per capita income, proposing a quadratic and quartic model to understand how this relationship evolves over time. It finds evidence of two distinct waves of service sector growth. The first wave, beginning at relatively low income levels, shows an increase in the service sector share at a decelerating rate as income rises. The second wave, starting after 2001, demonstrates an upward shift in service sector growth, though the patterns vary across different specialized services. In the quadratic model, based on Chenery and Syrquin's (1975) structural transformation theory, it is found that, except for community, social and personal services, the share of services is negatively related to per capita income but positively related to the square of per capita income. This suggests that, as an economy develops, structural changes occur, with the service sector growing as per capita income increases. Population size is positively related to the service share, but its squared term shows a negative relationship. These findings align with typical cross-country results, suggesting that the rise of services is a part of a standard development process. The quartic form analysis as envisaged by Eichengreen and Gupta (2013) further supports the existence of two waves of service sector growth. It shows that as economies grow, the service sector expands initially at a slower rate, then experiences an accelerated growth in the second wave after 2001. Specialized services like trade, transportation, financial services, and others show a quartic relationship with per capita income, indicating that the evolution of the service sector's relative size is complex and varies across different types of services. In conclusion, the paper suggests that there are two waves of service sector growth, with different patterns emerging for various service sectors.

Keywords Share of services · Per capita income · Fixed effects · Structural change · Economic development

---

P. R. Choudhury (✉)
Department of Economics, The Bhawanipur Education Society College, Kolkata, India
e-mail: purbarc@gmail.com; roychoudhury@thebges.edu.in

B. Chatterjee and A. K. Karmakar (eds.), *Analytical Issues in Growth & Structural Change, Macroeconomy, Security, and Sustainability of India's Economic Development*, India Studies in Business and Economics, https://doi.org/10.1007/978-981-95-5242-9_4

JEL Classification O10 · C23

1 Introduction

1.1 The paper highlights India's impressive economic growth since the 1990s, driven largely by the service sector, which has become a key engine in the country's structural transformation. This growth, however, does not necessarily translate into improved well-being for the population. Issues like insufficient employment opportunities and rising regional disparities are pointed out as negative consequences of focusing solely on growth. The paper aims to provide simple insights into the relationship between economic development and economic structure, using data from 16 major Indian states between 1970 and 2010. While similar cross-country analyses exist, there is limited research at the sectoral level within Indian states.

1.2 The paper tries to explain the relationship between share of services and per capita state domestic product, in a *quadratic* as well as *quartic* form, for which there is evidence of two waves of service sector growth, the second wave commencing after the 1990s. The structural change analysis shows that the share of services has been steadily increasing across all states. The paper therefore is organized as follows: Sect. 2 describes the selective survey of literature regarding the relationship between the service-share of output and per capita income. Section 3 describes the data and the methodology of panel fixed effects model used in this analysis. Section 4 forms the overview of the share of services and per capita income in a cross section of 16 major States of India, for the period 1970–2010. Section 5 examines what these economic variables explain, regarding the service share of output and per capita income along with specific specialized service sector experiences. Section 6 concludes the study.

2 Selective Survey of Literature

2.1 The World Development Report (2004) highlights that over 60% of global output and a significant portion of employment in many countries come from the service sector. There has been a shift in foreign direct investment (FDI) from manufacturing to services. The internationalization of services is central to globalization, as service industries create essential links between geographically dispersed economic activities, fostering market and production interdependence across countries. Advances in information technology have also reduced communication costs, fuelling the growth of services. As a result, the service sector has become the largest and fastest-growing sector in the world economy over the past two decades.

2.2 High-income countries, which are post-industrial, have become less dependent on industry, while low-income countries, still in the process of industrializing, have become more reliant on industry. However, even in industrializing countries, the service sector is growing relative to other sectors of the economy. This trend represents a departure from traditional growth theory, which typically expects a gradual transition from agriculture to industry before moving to services. Between 1990 and 2000, the growth of world services output was 2.9%, twice the growth rate of agriculture at 1.4%. Consequently, the service sector's contribution to world GDP increased from 57% in 1990 to 64% in 2000. This shift marks a new phase in the growth paradigm. (World Bank- World Development Indicators, 2001).

2.3 According to conventional theory of development, there is often a positive relationship between the share of the service sector in GDP and per capita income, though there is debate over the exact nature of this relationship. Early scholars like Fisher (1939) and Clark (1940) focused on the transition from agriculture to industry as central to economic growth, with little attention to services. Modern development theory, as described by Solow (1956) and Syrquin (1988), views economic growth as a long-term process of structural transformation. Kuznets (1966) emphasized the shift from agriculture to industry, driven by higher income elasticity for industrial goods compared to agricultural products, which helped sustain industrial growth. This process was further facilitated by productivity increases that led to lower industrial goods prices relative to agriculture (Kaldor, 1950) and greater demand for industrial goods (Chenery & Syrquin, 1977). According to Engel's law, as income rises, the share of food in consumption declines, necessitating industrialization unless export growth or service exports can offset the effects of rising demand for industrial goods. Chenery and his colleagues explored these patterns through empirical studies using cross-country data, culminating in their publication *Patterns of Development 1950–1970* (Chenery & Syrquin, 1975).

2.4 There are various studies examining the relationship between per capita income and the share of services in national output. Kuznets (1973) found that the share of services did not significantly change with per capita income. Chenery (1960) also found no significant relationship between services and per capita income across countries. Chenery and Syrquin (1975) showed that the relationship between the share of services and per capita income was concave, meaning it increased but at a decreasing rate as per capita income rose. Kongsamut et al. (2001) found a linear relationship between the share of services and per capita income. Syrquin (1988) argued that development patterns can be defined by systematic changes in economic and social structure associated with a rising level of per capita income. Analyses of inter-regional and inter-country differences in growth and level of income are largely based on neo-classical growth paradigms (Baumol, 1986; Barro & Sala-i-Martin, 1990).

2.5 There have been few studies regarding growth and interstate disparities in India, but mostly of convergence or divergence of state-wise per capita SDP. Dasgupta et al. (2000) in their study revealed that there was a clear tendency for Indian states to diverge in per capita SDP, but converge in shares of different sectors in the SDP for the period 1960–61 to 1995–96. However, a relatively new paper in the similar lines of this paper has been done by Singariya (2015). Using panel data for thirty-two states and UTs of India for the period of 2004–05 to 2013–14, the present paper examines the effect of structural change on economic growth with an augmented Chenery-Syrquin Model. Our results show any increases in the shares of manufacturing sector and industrial sectors have significant positive effect on economic growth, while the patterns of industrial sector have significant positive effects on population density.

2.6 The novelty of the present paper is envisaged by extending the Chenery-Syrquin model to a quartic form, which enables the analysis of two distinct waves of service sector growth across Indian states using a larger dataset from 1970 to 2010. Unlike the ***cross-country*** analysis of Eichengreen and Gupta (2013), which includes international trade and other geographical factors as well as exogenous year dummies to highlight service sector growth waves, the present study focuses on ***inter-state*** investigation within a closed economy framework. Additionally, it introduces endogenously determined structural breakpoints, identified using Bai and Perron's (1998, 2003) methodology, and incorporates them as year dummies derived from an earlier study by Roy Choudhury and Chatterjee (2016). In essence, while previous literature has primarily analysed convergence or divergence at the national or cross-country level, this paper offers a more detailed and localized perspective on how the service sector has evolved within Indian states, taking into account endogenous structural changes and providing insights into two waves of service sector growth.

3 Data and Methodology

3.1 In analysing the regional growth pattern, state level data on domestic product and its sectoral components are required. The National Accounts division of the Central Statistical Organisation (CSO), under the Ministry of Statistics and Programme Implementation, Government of India, has been compiling the data base after receiving from the state agencies. This study analyzes the data on state domestic product published by Economic and Political Weekly Research Foundation (EPWRF) in 2011. The electronic version of the data base of EPWRF (2012) covers the period from 1960–61 to 2009–10. As different series based on different base years are not comparable and the data for all the States are not available from the 1960s, the paper has constructed a consistent chain linked time series of NSDP by extending the 2004–05 series backwards to convert the old series to the series based on the new base year (2004–05) following the splicing method recommended by the CSO (2001).The method reduces the data set into a balanced panel of sixteen major states for forty years with Bihar including Jharkhand, Madhya Pradesh including Chattisgarh, and Uttar Pradesh including Uttaranchal. (Das, 2012).

3.2 To estimate the relationship between share of services and log of per capita income, the fixed effects panel regression is applied. The Breusch Pagan LM test is used to indicate the presence of individual heterogeneity across the region and so that panel data analysis is conducted instead of pooled OLS. However, the Hausman specification test is used to check for the fixed effects versus random effects and the test indicated the presence of heterogeneity and therefore the fixed effects model is presented as against the random effects model.

4 Macroeconomic View

4.1 In this section, a ***state wise*** analysis of the service sector share in aggregate NSDP in sixteen states of India are taken into consideration. Table 1 gives us a comparative study of the share of agriculture, industry and services at a percentage proportion of GDP at factor cost of India as a whole at 2004–05 prices along with the same at the percentage share of NSDP at factor cost at 2004–05 prices of sixteen major states of India. In India, the share of the service sector in GDP has been more than 50% since 2000–01. Most of the states have shown around 50% share of services as a proportion of NSDP coming from the services sector since 2000–01. The state with the highest services share (above 60%) in 2009–10 is Kerala (69%) followed by Maharashtra, Tamil Nadu and West Bengal. The states like Andhra Pradesh, Assam, Bihar, Haryana, Karnataka, Orissa and Uttar Pradesh have more than 50% services share in NSDP. However, states like Rajasthan, Punjab, Madhya Pradesh, Himachal Pradesh and Gujarat have a less than 50% share in services in NSDP in 2009–10.

4.2 A comparison of the rising rates of share of services as a percentage of NSDP in different states may help the analysis at a later stage. There has been a fall in agricultural share in NSDP in all the states and this has been compensated largely by the increase in services share in most of the states. For states like West Bengal and Maharashtra, the fall in the share of both agriculture and industry has been mirrored by a commensurate rise in services share from 1970–71 to 2009–10. Again, for example, in Gujarat, decline in agricultural share is compensated equally by the equal rise in industrial and services share, where services share has been only around 48% in 2009–10.

4.3 Table 2 shows the state-wise percentage distribution of different subsectors of services namely, transport, storage and communication (TSC), trade, hotels and restaurants (THR), banking and insurance, real estate and ownership of dwelling and business services (FIRB), and community, social and personal services (CSP).As a share of NSDP, there seems to be a clear demarcation, transport services especially railways have been driving demand in low income states, while higher income states have been focusing on communication, financial and other business services. Trade, hotels and restaurant services have been important in both low- and high-income states. When it comes to growth rates, one or the other low-income states seem to be "catching-up" with the high-income states across sub-sectors. One may also refer to World Bank Institute's working paper February (1998) (No 19670, titled **Patterns of WORLD Development 1970–1994**) for sectoral patters across these countries.

Table 1 Share of broad sectors of NSDP in India and major Indian states (%)

States	Activity	1970–71	1980–81	1990–91	2000–01	2009–10
AP	AGR	56.67	46.91	35.57	29.53	21.14
	IND	11.35	13.63	18.30	18.79	20.63
	SER	*31.98*	*39.46*	*46.13*	*51.68*	*58.23*
Assam	AGR	52.95	50.59	43.24	37.59	24.26
	IND	20.48	19.42	25.73	24.36	21.48
	SER	*26.57*	*29.98*	*31.03*	*38.06*	*54.27*
Bihar	AGR	62.88	54.74	46.45	30.38	20.56
	IND	7.30	8.68	11.55	24.42	25.27
	SER	*29.82*	*36.58*	*42.00*	*45.20*	*54.18*
Gujarat	AGR	50.63	41.10	28.09	15.79	12.46
	IND	21.43	25.94	32.90	35.19	39.97
	SER	*27.94*	*32.96*	*39.01*	*49.02*	*47.57*
Haryana	AGR	61.66	49.27	40.79	30.55	17.88
	IND	18.78	24.30	29.19	28.10	27.14
	SER	*19.56*	*26.42*	*30.02*	*41.35*	*54.98*
HP	AGR	59.91	53.97	44.03	28.72	18.24
	IND	19.72	19.59	24.70	34.97	39.31
	SER	*20.37*	*26.44*	*31.27*	*36.31*	*42.44*
Karnataka	AGR	52.68	42.96	32.89	27.17	16.89
	IND	19.02	23.92	26.98	24.49	25.91
	SER	*28.29*	*33.11*	*40.13*	*48.35*	*57.20*
Kerala	AGR	37.51	30.55	27.95	19.85	10.70
	IND	15.82	19.94	19.71	19.63	20.05
	SER	*46.66*	*49.51*	*52.34*	*60.52*	*69.25*
MP	AGR	55.27	46.74	39.84	25.45	23.54
	IND	13.96	18.16	19.57	28.70	31.23
	SER	*30.76*	*35.10*	*40.59*	*45.85*	*45.23*
Maharashtra	AGR	24.28	22.43	17.68	13.08	8.46
	IND	33.87	35.39	34.74	27.53	28.01
	SER	*41.85*	*42.17*	*47.58*	*59.39*	*63.53*
Orissa	AGR	56.52	52.41	37.47	28.43	21.91
	IND	18.95	19.01	24.38	27.16	25.10
	SER	*24.53*	*28.58*	*38.15*	*44.41*	*52.99*
Punjab	AGR	51.88	43.62	43.17	37.19	26.35
	IND	14.75	15.74	19.47	22.33	29.79
	SER	*33.36*	*40.65*	*37.35*	*40.48*	*43.86*
Rajasthan	AGR	54.30	43.01	40.14	25.98	20.64

(continued)

Table 1 (continued)

States	Activity	1970–71	1980–81	1990–91	2000–01	2009–10
	IND	17.51	21.13	20.89	27.39	30.21
	SER	*28.19*	*35.86*	*38.97*	*46.63*	*49.15*
Tamil Nadu	AGR	32.91	23.17	20.64	15.63	9.03
	IND	29.42	35.22	34.52	29.14	28.28
	SER	*37.68*	*41.61*	*44.84*	*55.23*	*62.69*
Uttar Pradesh	AGR	55.27	46.74	39.84	25.45	23.54
	IND	12.23	15.46	19.76	18.89	23.92
	SER	*36.64*	*38.38*	*43.02*	*46.77*	*53.01*
West Bengal	AGR	35.20	34.37	32.99	27.63	20.51
	IND	22.68	19.98	17.97	17.18	17.24
	SER	*42.12*	*45.65*	*49.04*	*55.20*	*62.25*
India	AGR	44.31	37.92	31.37	23.89	15.68
	IND	22.10	24.04	25.92	25.80	26.78
	SER	*33.59*	*38.04*	*42.71*	*50.31*	*57.53*

Note Bihar includes Jharkhand, Madhya Pradesh includes Chhattisgarh, and Uttar Pradesh includes Uttaranchal
Source National Accounts Statistics, Central Statistical Organistaion (2011), Economic and Political Weekly Research Foundation (2011): Domestic products of states of India
Reserve Bank of India (2011): Handbook of Statistics on Indian Economy

5 Empirical Results: Structural Change and Rising Regional Disparity

5.1 The objective of this paper is to establish the stylized facts on relationships between development and economic structure based on the experience of sixteen states for which a data are available from 1970 to 2010. Chenery and Syrquin (1975) pointed out, "a development pattern may be defined as a systematic variation in any significant aspect of the economic or social structure associated with a rising level of income or other index of development." This section examines simple development patterns along the definition of Chenery and Syrquin (1975).

5.2 There are many problems in analysing the relationships between the level of development and economic structure. An initial problem is related to the definitions of development and economic structure, as there is no unanimity among the users regarding the exact definition of either development or economic structure. The usual measure in the patterns of development literature is either real GDP per capita or real GNP per capita. Income per capita has well-known limitations as a measure of development. The term "economic structure" is generally used for a wide variety of characteristics of an economy. The variable characterising economic structure is usually the sectoral composition of output.

Table 2 State-wise share of different subsectors of Services in India (%)

India/States		1970–71 Share in services GDP (Share in GDP)	1980–81 Share in services GDP (Share in GDP)	1990–91 Share in services GDP (Share in GDP)	2000–01 Share in services GDP (Share in GDP)	2009–10 Share in services GDP (Share in GDP)
Andhra Pradesh	THR	30.0 (9.6)	25.3 (10.0)	28.0 (12.9)	26.6 (13.7)	24.8 (14.4)
	TSC	23.9 (7.7)	22.8 (9.0)	17.7 (8.1)	19.5 (10.1)	24.8 (14.4)
	FIRB	19.7 (6.3)	25.5 (10.1)	30.0 (13.8)	28.3 (14.6)	30.7 (17.8)
	CSP	26.4 (8.4)	26.4 (10.4)	24.3 (11.2)	25.6 (13.2)	19.8 (11.5)
Assam	THR	55.4 (14.7)	51.9 (15.6)	46.9 (14.6)	42.3 (16.1)	30.8 16.7
	TSC	20.0 (5.3)	20.6 (6.2)	21.7 (6.7)	12.9 (4.9)	15.2 (8.2)
	FIRB	11.7 (3.1)	11.1 (3.3)	13.4 (4.2)	18.5 (7.0)	13.0 (7.0)
	CSP	12.9 (3.4)	16.4 (4.9)	17.9 (5.6)	26.4 (10.0)	41.1 (22.3)
Bihar	THR	23.5 (7.0)	35.2 (12.9)	35.6 (15.0)	30.4 (13.7)	37.4 (20.3)
	TSC	19.2 (5.7)	15.0 (5.5)	11.7 (4.9)	12.6 (5.7)	15.1 (8.2)
	FIRB	18.1 (5.4)	16.2 (5.9)	14.1 (5.9)	15.6 (7.1)	15.7 (8.5)
	CSP	39.2 (11.7)	33.6 (12.3)	38.5 (16.2)	41.4 (18.7)	31.8 (17.2)
Gujarat	THR	38.7 (10.8)	39.6 (13.0)	37.1 (14.5)	32.8 (16.1)	42.4 (20.2)
	TSC	7.3 (2.0)	9.0 (3.0)	10.8 (4.2)	16.2 (8.0)	17.1 (8.1)
	FIRB	27.2 (7.6)	27.7 (9.1)	31.0 (12.1)	28.0 (13.7)	25.1 (11.9)
	CSP	26.8 (7.5)	23.7 (7.8)	21.0 (8.2)	23.0 (11.3)	15.4 (7.3)
Haryana	THR	27.9 (5.5)	35.1 (9.3)	36.7 (11.0)	40.1 (16.6)	41.2 (22.6)
	TSC	12.9 (2.5)	13.3 (3.5)	13.7 (4.1)	14.6 (6.0)	15.7 (8.6)
	FIRB	19.5 (3.8)	20.3 (5.4)	21.9 (6.6)	24.3 (10.1)	26.4 (14.5)

(continued)

Table 2 (continued)

India/States		1970–71 Share in services GDP (Share in GDP)	1980–81 Share in services GDP (Share in GDP)	1990–91 Share in services GDP (Share in GDP)	2000–01 Share in services GDP (Share in GDP)	2009–10 Share in services GDP (Share in GDP)
	CSP	39.6 (7.8)	31.3 (8.3)	27.6 (8.3)	21.1 (8.7)	16.7 (9.2)
Himachal Pradesh	THR	17.3 (3.5)	24.1 (6.4)	23.3 (7.3)	27.9 (10.1)	27.2 (11.5)
	TSC	9.6 (2.0)	7.5 (2.0)	5.0 (1.6)	8.5 (3.1)	14.4 (6.1)
	FIRB	24.3 (5.0)	25.0 (6.6)	26.2 (8.2)	19.8 (7.2)	20.1 (8.5)
	CSP	48.8 (9.9)	43.4 (11.5)	45.5 (14.2)	43.7 (15.9)	38.4 (16.3)
Karnataka	THR	29.5 (8.3)	26.5 (8.8)	28.0 (11.2)	28.7 (13.9)	26.6 (15.2)
	TSC	5.7 (1.6)	6.2 (2.1)	5.5 (2.2)	10.6 (5.10	13.3 (7.6)
	FIRB	31.4 (8.9)	34.6 (11.5)	38.2 (15.3)	35.9 (17.3)	41.7 (23.9)
	CSP	33.3 (9.4)	32.7 (10.8)	28.3 (11.4)	24.8 (12.0)	18.3 (10.5)
Kerala	THR	60.9 (28.4)	52.0 (25.7)	45.0 (23.5)	37.9 (22.9)	32.7 (22.6)
	TSC	3.2 (1.5)	4.1 (2.0)	6.2 (3.2)	12.5 (7.5)	20.1 (13.9)
	FIRB	13.5 (6.3)	18.0 (8.9)	21.6 (11.3)	25.2 (15.2)	26.5 (18.3)
	CSP	22.3 (10.4)	25.9 (12.8)	27.3 (14.3)	24.5 (14.8)	20.7 (14.4)
Madhya Pradesh	THR	55.2 (17.0)	43.1 (15.1)	35.5 (14.4)	32.3 (14.8)	28.6 (12.9)
	TSC	6.7 (2.1)	8.3 (2.9)	7.4 (3.0)	10.2 (4.7)	15.1 (6.8)
	FIRB	18.5 (5.7)	21.1 (7.4)	27.3 (11.1)	24.9 (11.4)	26.2 (11.9)
	CSP	35.1 (14.7)	36.9 (15.6)	33.0 (15.7)	25.8 (15.3)	25.6 (16.3)
Maharashtra	THR	35.1 (14.7)	36.9 (15.6)	33.0 (15.7)	25.8 (15.3)	25.6 (16.3)
	TSC	12.0 (5.0)	12.0 (5.1)	11.9 (5.7)	13.3 (7.9)	14.0 (8.9)

(continued)

Table 2 (continued)

India/States		1970–71 Share in services GDP (Share in GDP)	1980–81 Share in services GDP (Share in GDP)	1990–91 Share in services GDP (Share in GDP)	2000–01 Share in services GDP (Share in GDP)	2009–10 Share in services GDP (Share in GDP)
	FIRB	28.9 (12.1)	27.6 (11.6)	30.7 (14.6)	39.1 (23.2)	45.0 (28.6)
	CSP	24.1 (10.1)	23.5 (9.9)	24.4 (11.6)	21.8 (13.0)	15.4 (9.8)
Orissa	THR	33.4 (8.2)	26.3 (7.5)	20.5 (7.8)	23.4 (10.4)	29.3 (15.5)
	TSC	7.6 (1.9)	7.7 (2.2)	10.1 (3.8)	12.0 (5.3)	18.2 (9.6)
	FIRB	20.8 (5.1)	25.0 (7.2)	26.3 (10.0)	25.6 (11.4)	22.5 (11.9)
	CSP	38.3 (9.4)	41.0 (11.7)	43.1 (16.4)	39.0 (17.3)	30.1 (15.9)
Punjab	THR	35.0 (11.7)	37.8 (15.4)	32.4 (12.1)	31.3 (12.7)	27.3 (12.0)
	TSC	4.2 (1.4)	4.0 (1.6)	5.0 (1.9)	10.1 (4.1)	14.4 (6.3)
	FIRB	20.4 (6.8)	19.1 (7.8)	24.4 (9.1)	23.8 (9.6)	26.1 (11.5)
	CSP	40.4 (13.5)	39.0 (15.8)	38.1 (14.2)	34.8 (14.1)	32.3 (14.2)
Rajasthan	THR	44.1 (12.4)	34.7 (12.4)	39.9 (15.6)	33.1 (15.4)	31.3 (15.4)
	TSC	8.7 (2.5)	9.2 (3.3)	6.8 (2.7)	8.6 (4.0)	12.3 (6.1)
	FIRB	19.7 (5.5)	25.7 (9.2)	22.8 (8.9)	24.7 (11.5)	26.7 (13.1)
	CSP	27.5 (7.8)	30.4 (10.9)	30.4 (11.9)	33.6 (15.7)	29.7 (14.6)
Tamil Nadu	THR	34.0 (12.8)	30.6 (12.8)	27.6 (12.4)	30.3 (16.8)	29.0 (18.2)
	TSC	13.0 (4.9)	13.3 (5.5)	11.9 (5.3)	13.5 (7.5)	15.1 (9.5)
	FIRB	20.5 (7.7)	23.5 (9.8)	29.6 (13.3)	30.6 (16.9)	35.0 (22.0)
	CSP	32.6 (12.3)	32.5 (13.5)	31.0 (13.9)	25.5 (14.1)	20.9 (13.1)
Uttar Pradesh	THR	44.9 (16.4)	41.7 (16.0)	33.2 (14.3)	33.1 (15.5)	29.1 (15.4)

(continued)

Table 2 (continued)

India/States		1970–71 Share in services GDP (Share in GDP)	1980–81 Share in services GDP (Share in GDP)	1990–91 Share in services GDP (Share in GDP)	2000–01 Share in services GDP (Share in GDP)	2009–10 Share in services GDP (Share in GDP)
	TSC	10.0 (3.6)	12.1 (4.7)	10.8 (4.6)	13.1 (6.1)	15.9 (8.4)
	FIRB	18.9 (6.9)	22.5 (8.6)	28.0 (12.0)	26.4 (12.3)	27.7 (14.7)
	CSP	26.3 (9.7)	23.6 (9.1)	28.0 (12.0)	27.4 (12.8)	27.3 (14.5)
West Bengal	THR	37.6 (15.8)	31.6 (14.4)	28.9 (14.2)	29.7 (16.4)	28.4 (17.7)
	TSC	10.5 (4.4)	9.5 (4.3)	13.5 (6.6)	13.1 (7.2)	15.4 (9.6)
	FIRB	19.1 (8.0)	21.2 (9.7)	20.1 (9.9)	26.9 (14.9)	29.4 (18.3)
	CSP	32.9 (13.8)	37.8 (17.3)	37.5 (18.4)	30.3 (16.7)	26.9 (16.7)
All-India	THR	31.84 (10.5)	31.42 (11.89)	29.29 (12.4)	29.19 (14.55)	28.60 (16.39)
	TSC	11.08 (3.6)	13.12 (4.93)	12.17 (5.18)	13.32 (6.64)	17.73 (10.16)
	FIRB	22.29 (7.41)	21.6 (8.1)	26.79 (11.41)	28.12 (14.02)	29.97 (17.17)
	CSP	34.77 (11.56)	33.81 (12.73)	31.73 (13.51)	29.35 (14.63)	23.68 (13.56)

Note Bihar includes Jharkhand, Madhya Pradesh includes Chhattisgarh, and Uttar Pradesh includes Uttaranchal

Source National Accounts Statistics, Central Statistical Organistaion (2011), Economic and Political Weekly Research Foundation (2011): Domestic products of States of India, Reserve Bank of India (2011): Handbook of Statistics on Indian Economy

5.3 In this paper, the systematic relationship between development and economic structure are examined as done in a cross-state analysis of structural evolution of an economy by Chenery and Syrquin (1975).The model provides the basic structuralist view on economic growth. The model broadly uses a linear logarithmic regression equation to explore the effects of income (GDP per capita) and population size on the sectoral shares of GDP. In our analysis, for state-wise analysis, NSDP per capita is used as the explanatory variable in determining the sectoral shares of services. Thus, if in the process of economic growth there are concentration of service activities in a few regions, then it would lead to divergences in regional growth rates which eventually would be reflected in rising interregional growth rates which eventually would be reflected in rising regional disparity in the country.

5.4 The regression equation for estimation with cross states data is given by the equation, is adapted from the principal specification of Chenery and Syrquin (1975) and Chenery and Syrquin (1979):

$$x = \alpha + \beta 1 \ln Y + \beta 2(\ln Y)^2 + \gamma 1 \ln N + \gamma 2(\ln N)^2 + \varepsilon F + u \quad (1)$$

where x stands for a structural variable as a percent of GDP, Y is the per capita income or GDP per capita, N is the population size, and F is the trade balance. Although N was supposed "to allow for effects of economies of scale and transport costs on patterns of trade and production" N is defined as the country's population but not as the country's size in terms of land area or as a country's population density. Though this equation was usually used to analyse the cross-states patterns of structural changes, this structural framework is applied to examine the patterns of evolution of the regions with the help of cross state data for the Indian economy for the period 1970–2010. In this analysis, the trade variable is dropped and a closed economy framework is considered. The regression equation is supposed to explain that the structural variable output share depends on per capita income as well as the size of the population. Since income and size of the population appear as explanatory variables in equation, deviations from predicted values reflect variations in resource endowments, other initial conditions, and policy. It is assumed that all states follow a common time tend of economic growth over time, maintaining similar relationships between share of services and per capita GDP/NSDP.

5.5 The estimated equation for elasticity can be written as:

$$(Y/x)(dx/dY) = [\beta_1 + 2\beta_2 \ln Y]/x$$

Putting the values of β_1 and β_2 into the above equation, the elasticity is coming significantly positive. This implies that the graph (Fig. 1) depicting the relationship between services share and per capita income has to be a positively sloped curve. Explore the relationship between log of per capita income and share of services in GDP, the lowess plots are estimated. These locally-weighted regressions use a function that attaches less weight to points far from the mean. Thus, the relation between per capita income and estimated services share, as shown in Fig. 1, is quite consistent with the standard cross-country results.

5.6 In order to find the relationship between services share and log per capita income, the elasticity of services share with per capita income is calculated, which is found to be positive. To estimate the relationship between share of services and log of per capita income, as envisaged by Chenery and Syrquin (1975), the fixed effects panel regression is applied. The Breusch Pagan LM test indicated presence of individual heterogeneity across the region and so panel data analysis is conducted instead of pooled OLS. However, the Hausman specification test for the fixed effects versus random effects have been considered and the test indicated the presence of

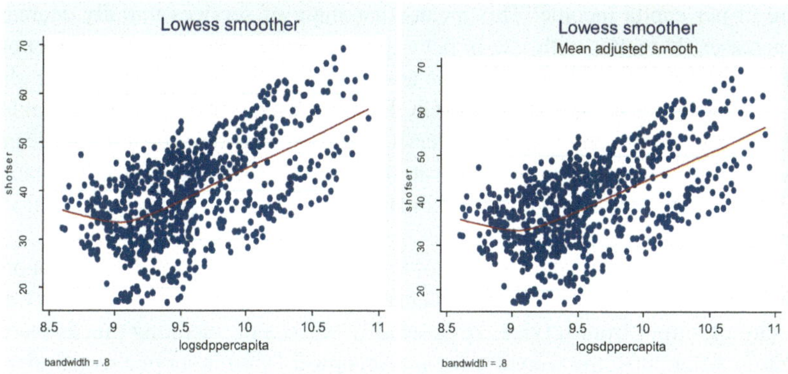

Fig. 1 Lowess Plot of the Relationship between log per capita income and services/NSDP. Figure 1 shows the Lowess plot for the default options in STATA 12.0 which include a bandwidth of 0.8 (which means that in each regression 80 percent of the observations are included) and a Tricube Weighting scheme (which means that the observations farther away from the mean get a lower weight). Results are robust to changing the weighing scheme including to a rectangular weighting scheme (in which all observations get equal weights) and to changing the band width

heterogeneity and therefore the fixed effects model is presented as against the random effects model in Table 3.

5.7 Table 3 therefore determines the closed economy structural transformation model as suggested by Chenery-Syrquin (1975). This table suggests that except for community, social and personal services, all other components of services and services as a whole show that share of services is negatively and significantly related to log of per capita income and is also positively and significantly related to the

Table 3 Structural change equations (closed economy Chenery Syrquin model)

Share of	Constant	lnY	$(\ln Y)^2$	lnN	$(\ln N)^2$	Adj- R^2(Overall)
SER	−179.14*** (−4.11)	−78.97*** (10.78)	2.57*** (7.82)	132.06*** (8.19)	−5.10*** (−7.18)	0.29
THR	161.90*** (3.55)	−53.18*** (−7.91)	2.67*** (7.95)	14.59*** (3.27)	−0.34* (−1.66)	0.13
TSC	160.01*** (6.36)	−27.23*** (−7.34)	1.56*** (8.37)	−8.41*** (−3.42)	0.46*** (3.97)	0.36
FIRB	383.33*** (10.06)	−50.21*** (−8.94)	2.79*** (9.92)	−32.61*** (−8.74)	1.74*** (9.93)	0.51
CSP	−117.59** (−2.70)	0.021 (0.00)	−0.22 (−0.70)	16.92*** (3.97)	−0.25 (−1.27)	0.02

Notes Figures in parentheses are t- values
*** significant at 1% level of significance;
** significant at 5% level of significance;
* significant at 10% level of significance

square of per capita income. This means that share of services initially decreases but increases thereafter with rise in per capita income. Therefore, as the economy develops with rise in per capita income across states, structural changes take place with the rise in the share of services. On the other hand, the population variable is positively and significantly related to service share, it is negatively and significantly related to the square of the population variable. These results imply that the relationship between per capita income and estimated services share is quite consistent with standard cross-country results.

5.8 The paper explores how the size of the service sector evolves during economic growth, focusing on two distinct waves of service sector expansion. In the first wave, the share of output from services rises steadily but at a decelerating rate as income increases. After 2001, the second wave sees an upward shift in service sector growth, though the patterns differ for specialized services and aggregate services as a whole. The relationship between income and service sector share appears to follow a cubic or quartic curve. While the quartic term is not immediately obvious in visual data, the paper argues that assuming an accelerating growth in the service sector (as suggested by the cubic model) is problematic because it cannot exceed 100%. The statistical evidence supports the quartic model, which shows that service sector growth slows at higher income levels, even if this is less visually apparent (Fig. 1).

5.9 Finally, a quartic relationship between the share of services in GDP and per capita income, similar to the model developed by Eichengreen and Gupta (2013), is estimated. If the cubic (or logistic) fits the data better, it could be expected that the coefficient on per capita value added raised to the fourth power to go to zero. The regression framework is given by Eq. 2. The dependent variable is service sector as a percentage of GDP, where (as throughout) i refers to State and t to year. The independent variables include the four powers of log per capita income. All regressions include state fixed effects. In subsequent regressions, different intercepts for different time periods, different slopes of per capita income terms in different time periods; based on the different breakpoints in per-capita GDP as estimated by Roy Choudhury and Chatterjee (2016).

$$\frac{Serit}{SDPit} = Consant + \sum\nolimits_{i} \theta iDi + \alpha 1Yit + \alpha 2Yit^2 + \alpha 3Yit^3 + \alpha 4Yit^4 + \varepsilon it \quad (2)$$

It needs to be mentioned that the breakpoints in GDP for the period from 1950–2010 is 1978, 1991, 2001, as found applying the Bai and Perron (1998, 2003) method of multiple structural breaks in Roy Choudhury and Chatterjee (2016). The novelty of this paper lies in the fact that while the paper by Eichengreen and Gupta (2013) takes exogenously chosen years as dummies, in our exercise, the breakpoint dummies are endogenously chosen multiple breakpoints. The results are in Table 4. In all cases, the hypothesis of a quartic relationship similar to the model by Eichengreen and Gupta (2013) is established. In our Model I, a quartic relationship is estimated with a common intercept for all years. In Model II, however, the intercept varied to differ in 1978–1990, 1991–2001and 2002–2010, the breakpoint dummies being established in the paper by Roy Choudhury and Chatterjee (2016). In Model III, the intercepts as well as the coefficients on log per capita income (PCY) terms are allowed to differ in the different periods. In Model IV the same is done but the 1970–78 and 1979–90 sub-periods are combined. Finally, in Model V, the periods 1970–78, 1979–90 and 1991–2000 are combined. The reason for doing so is that the coefficients on the per capita income variables in 1978–1990 are statistically indistinguishable from those for 1950–1978. There, the dummy variable for 1978–1990 is insignificant, but the dummy variable for the 1991–2001 and 2002–2010 sub-period (not interacted) is significant, while the big and statistically significant coefficients on the post-2000 shifters are on the cubic and quartic terms. The coefficient on per capita income squared after 1990 is also statistically significant, but it is small relative to that on per capita income squared over the entire period.

5.10 This pattern is robust to changes in sample and specification and using individual year fixed effects rather than just distinguishing two or three time periods, the quartic relationship between log per capita income and the share of the service sector continues to hold in all the cases, providing evidence of a more pronounced second wave (larger cubic and quartic terms) after 2001. The first wave appears to be made up primarily of traditional services, the second wave of modern (financial, communication, computer, technical, advertising and business) services that are receptive to the application of information technologies.

5.11 The paper further extends the earlier empirical results where the quartic relation between the specialised share of services, like trade hotel restaurants, transport storage and communication, banking insurance and financial services and community social and personal services are considered. The results of Model I and Model II, as envisaged in Table 4 is reported in Tables 5 and 6.

5.12 The results in Table 5 establishes that except for community, social and personal services, all other services, like trade, hotel restaurants, transport, storage and communication, and financial services, establishes that the relationship between share of services and log per capita income is quartic holds.

5.13 The estimations reported in Table 6 establishes the fact that for the services like trade, hotels and restaurants and transport storage and communication and also financial services not only establishes a quartic relationship but also shows that the breakpoint of GDP dummies is also highly significant. This establishes a two-wave relationship in service sector growth. However, for sectors like community, social and personal services, the quartic relationship between share of services and log per capita income is non-significant.

6 Conclusion

6.1 The paper analyses the evolution of the regional disparity in India for the period 1970–2010 with special reference to the service sector. It has been observed that regional disparity in India has been steadily increasing over time. Regional disparity among the states has been rising and this growing divide between the richer states and the poorer states deserve immediate attention of policy makers and economists.

Table 4 Quartic relationship between log per capita and share of services in GDP. [Dependent variable: services/GDP (in percent)]

	Model I	Model II	Model III	Model IV	Model V
Log per capita Income	75.26 (1.25)	81.37 (1.67)	79.86 (0.81)	142.67** (2.17)	96.75* (1.80)
Log per capita income-squared	−94.11*** (−2.43)	−51.04*** (−2.19)	−30.47 (−0.72)	−96.51*** (−2.87)	−122.6*** (−4.33)
Log per capita Income-cube	12.12** (2.30)	5.86* (1.80)	0.78 (0.13)	10.88** (2.31)	15.66*** (4.05)
Log per capita Income-quartic	−0.45** (−2.23)	−0.20 (−1.60)	0.09 (0.37)	−0.36* (−1.93)	−0.58*** (−3.86)
Dummy for the year 1978–1990		5.91*** (4.83)	469.12 (0.47)	4.98*** (12.28)	5.62*** (13.64)
Dummy for the year 1991–2001		11.11*** (3.79)	−194.60 (0.42)	425.08 (1.11)	10.37*** (16.46)
Dummy for the year 2002–2010		17.37*** (4.15)	−118.55 (−0.12)	−634.48 (−0.75)	−1498.15** (−1.81)
Log per capita Income *dummy 1978–1990			65.15 (0.50)		
Log per capita Income squared*dummy 1978–1990			−68.15 (−1.09)		
Log per capita Income cubic*dummy 1978–1990			10.19 (1.16)		
Log per capita Income quartic*dummy 1978–1990			−0.45 (−1.27)		
Log per capita Income *dummy 1991–2001			−69.01 (−0.54)	−114.73 (1.08)	
Log per capita Income squared*dummy 1991–2001			16.88 (1.56)	9.46 (1.10)	
Log per capita Income cubic*dummy 1991–2001			−0.08*** (−2.99)	−0.02 (−1.24)	
Log per capita Income quartic*dummy 1991–2001					
Log per capita Income *dummy 2001–2010			−86.50 (−0.65)	146.31 (−1.29)	−84.83 (−0.77)
Log per capita Income, squared*dummy 2001–2010			13.25 (0.24)	84.66* (1.69)	126.71*** (2.60)
Log per capita Income, cubic*dummy 2001–2010			1.04 (0.14)	−9.77 (−1.47)	−16.71*** (−2.62)
Log per capita Income, quartic*dummy 2001–2010			−0.139 (−0.46)	0.34 (1.33)	0.64*** (2.65)
State fixed effects	Yes	Yes	Yes	Yes	Yes
Observations	640	640	640	640	640

(continued)

Table 4 (continued)

	Model I	Model II	Model III	Model IV	Model V
Number of States	16	16	16	16	16
R-squared (Overall)	0.34	0.53	0.27	0.50	0.53

Note: Robust t statistics are in parenthesis. *, **, *** indicate coefficient is significant 10, 5 and 1 percent levels respectively. Column I shows the quartic relation with a common intercept for all years. Column II allows intercepts to differ in 1978–1990, 1991–2001, 2002–2010. Column III allows the coefficients on log per capita income terms to differ in 1970–1978, 1979–1990, 1991–2001and 2002–2010 subperiods. Column IV allows for the coefficients on log per capita terms to differ in 1970–1990 and 1991–2001 and 2002–2010. Column V allows the coefficient on log per capita terms to vary in 1970–2001 and 2001–2010

Table 5 Quadatic relationship between share of specialised services and per capita income

[Dependent variable: $services_i$/ GDP (in percent)]

	THR	TSC	FIRB	CSP
Log per capita Income	36.80 (1.31)	24.78* (1.75)	24.77 (1.04)	−8.15 (−0.26)
Log per capita income-squared	−35.29*** (−4.13)	−20.56*** (−4.76)	−13.94** (−1.91)	−10.08 (−1.06)
Log per capita Income-cube	4.35*** (4.12)	2.51*** (4.71)	1.63* (1.82)	1.64 (1.40)
Log per capita Income-quartic	−0.16*** (−3.98)	−0.09*** (−4.52)	−0.057* (−1.70)	−0.07 (1.59)
Adjusted R^2(Overall)	0.06	0.18	0.34	0.01

Note Robust t statistics are in parenthesis. *, **, *** indicate coefficient is significant 10, 5 and 1 percent levels respectively. This shows the quartic relation with a common intercept for all years for all the specialized services

Keeping the negative influences of regional disparity in mind, it becomes necessary to analyse whether service sector growth has actually accentuated regional disparities in India or not, especially after India's policy of economic liberalisation, which is presumed to have aggravated regional disparity in India.

6.2 The structural change analysis shows that the share of services has been steadily increasing across all states. The closed economy structural transformation model proposed by Chenery-Syrquin (1975) indicates that except for community, social and personal services, all other components of services and services as a whole show that share of services is negatively and significantly related to log of per capita income, and is also positively and significantly related to the square of per capita income. The service share variable, though significant and negatively related to per capita income, is also significant and positively related to the square of per capita income. Therefore, as the economy develops, structural changes take place with the rise in the share of services. On the other hand, the population variable is positively and significantly related to service share, it is negatively and significantly related

Table 6 Quartic relationship between share of specialised services and per capita income

[Dependent Variable: $Services_i$/ GDP (in percent)]	THR	TSC	FIRB	CSP
Log per capita Income	37.39 (1.39)	19.30 (1.52)	30.67 (1.39)	−2.85 (−0.11)
Log per capita income- squared	−27.13*** (−3.27)	−19.60*** (−4.99)	−3.62 (−0.53)	10.19 (1.27)
Log per capita Income-cube	3.17*** (3.07)	2.43*** (4.99)	0.08 (0.10)	−1.33 (−1.34)
Log per capita Income-quartic	−0.11*** (−2.85)	−0.088*** (−4.82)	0.005 (0.17)	0.048 (1.29)
Dummy for the year 1978–1990	1.25*** (5.40)	0.481*** (4.37)	1.68*** (8.79)	2.28*** (10.13)
Dummy for the year 1991–2001	2.19*** (6.32)	0.416** (2.53)	2.75*** (9.60)	5.17*** (15.34)
Dummy for the year 2002–2010	3.68*** (7.58)	2.055*** (8.94)	3.39*** (8.46)	7.68*** (16.29)
Adjusted R^2(Overall)	0.10	0.28	0.39	0.19

Note Robust t statistics are in parenthesis. *, **, *** indicate coefficient is significant 10, 5 and 1 percent levels respectively. This shows the quartic relation with intercepts to differ in 1978–1990, 1991–2001, 2002–2010 for specialized services

to the square of the population variable. These results imply that the relationship between per capita income and estimated services share is quite consistent with standard cross-country results.

6.3 The paper further, in its quartic form, seeks to provide new evidence about how the relative size of the service sector evolves over the growth process. The paper identifies two distinct phases or "waves" of growth in the service sector's share of value added to the economy. The first wave occurs at relatively modest income levels, where the service sector begins to grow, but at a decelerating rate as the economy expands. This phase is mainly driven by traditional services. The second wave happens after 2001 when there is an upward shift in service sector growth, but with noticeable differences in patterns for different specialised services. The second wave is dominated by modern services—those related to financial services, communication, technology, and business services—which benefit from the increased use of information technologies.

6.4 The paper highlights that, with the exception of community, social, and personal services, specialized services like trade, hotels and restaurants, transport, storage and communication, and financial services exhibit a quartic relationship between the share of services and log per capita income. This supports the conclusion that there are two distinct waves of service sector growth. Additionally, these results from the cross-state analysis in India are consistent with the findings from cross-country studies, reinforcing the broader trends in service sector development.

References

Bai, J., & Perron, P. (2003). Computation and analysis of multiple structural change models. *Journal of Applied Econometrics, 18*(1).

Bai, J., & Perron, P. (1998). Estimating and testing linear models with multiple structural changes. *Econometrica, 66*(1).

Barro, R. J. & Sala-i-Martin, X. (1990). *Economic growth and convergence across the United States*. (Working Paper 3419). National Bureau of Economic Research.

Baumol, W. J. (1986). Productivity growth, convergence, and welfare: What the long-run data show? *The American Economic Review*, 1072–1085.

Clark, C. (1940, revised and reprinted in 1951). *The conditions of economic progress*. MacMillan & Co.Ltd.

Chenery, H. B. (1960). Patterns of industrial growth. *The American Economic Review, 50*(4), 624–654.

Chenery, H. B., & Syrquin, M. (1975). *Patterns of development, 1950–1970*. Oxford University Press.

Chenery, H. B., & Syrquin, M. (1979). *Structural change and development policy*. Oxford University Press.

CSO. (2011). *National accounts statistics: Back series 1950–51 to 2004–05*. Central Statistical Organisation, Ministry of Statistics and Programme Implementation.

Das, P. (2012). Structural dynamics, growth and regional inequality: Incidence of industrial development in India. In *Paper Prepared for the 32nd General Conference of the International Association for Research in Income and Wealth, Boston, USA, August 5–11, 2012*.

Dasgupta, D., Maiti, P., Mukherjee, R., Chakravarti, S., & Sarkar, S.(2000, July 1). Growth and interstate disparities in India. *Economic and Political Weekly, 35*(27).

Eichengreen, B., & Gupta, P. (2013). The two waves of service-sector growth. *Oxford Economic Papers, Oxford University Press, 65*(1), 96–123.

EPWRF. (2012). State domestic products of India. *Economic and Political Weekly Research Foundation*.

Fisher, A. G. B. (1939). Primary, secondary and tertiary production. *Economic Record, 15*, 24–38.

Kaldor, N. (1950). *A contribution to the theory of the trade cycle*. Oxford University Press.

Kaldor, N. (1957). A model of economic growth. *The Economic Journal, 67*(268), 591–624.

Kaldor, N. (1966). *Causes of the slow rate of economic growth of the United Kingdom*. Cambridge University Press.

Kaldor, N. (1967). *Strategic factors in economic development*. Cornell University.

Kaldor, N. (1975). What is wrong with economic theory. *Quarterly Journal of Economics, 89*, 347–357.

Kongsamut, P., Rebelo, S., & Xie, D. (2001). Beyond balanced growth. *Review of Economic Studies, LXVII*, 869–882.

Kuznets, S. (1966). *Modern economic growth*. Yale University Press.

Kuznets, S. (1973). Modern economic growth: Findings and reflections. *American Economic Review, 63*, 247–258.

Roy Choudhury, P., & Chatterjee, B. (2016). Growth in India's service sector: Implications of structural breaks. *Journal of Quantitative Economics, 15*(1).

Singariya, M. R. (2015). Dynamic patterns of structural change and economic growth during the high growth regime in India: A panel data analysis. *Journal of Econometrics and Financial Management, 3*(2), 76–83.

Solow, R. (1956). A contribution to the theory of economic growth. *Quarterly Journal of Economics, 70*(1), 65–94.

Syrquin, M. (1988). Patterns of structural change. In C. Hollis & T. N. Srinivasan (Eds.), *Handbook of development economics* (1 ed., Vol. 1, pp. 203–273). Elsevier.

World Bank. (2004). *Sustaining India's services revolution: Access to foreign markets, domestic reform and international negotiations*. South Asia Region.

World Bank. (1995). India: Recent economic developments and prospects.
World Bank Institute. (1998). Working paper No 19670, February1998 titled Patterns of World Development 1970–1994.
World Bank. (2011). *World development indicators*. World Bank.

Reforms and Macroeconomy

Impact of Demonetization Shock and Corona Pandemic on India

Rajib Bhattacharyya

Abstract Though each shock, may it be external or internal, has its own distinguishing characteristics, but the common thing about them is they tend to destabilize an economy which is hit by that shock. Due to the strong governance and supervision of RBI, the Indian economy successfully managed in mitigating the adverse effect of the Global Financial Crisis (GFC) in 2008 and also showed positive signs of progress in the post crisis era. But this recovery was short lived as the economy had to face two internally self-inflicted shocks in the form of—(a) shift in indirect tax regime with the implementation of Goods and Services Tax, GST) from July 2016 and (b) major change in the currency system in the form of "Demonetization" by replacing higher value denomination from the midnight of 8th of November 2016. But the greatest human suffering and major economic disruption was caused by the outbreak of (COVID-19) virus since beginning of 2020, which started as a health shock but later on turned into a severe economic crisis. The present study attempts to analyze both the short and long run impact of demonetization and the corona pandemic. It also tries to examine whether there is any further possibility of recessionary situation which can again disrupt and destabilize the macroeconomic growth and progress in future. The whole analysis is based on secondary time series data available from various government websites and national and international official statistical agencies of repute.

Keywords Demonetization · Corona Pandemic · Recession · GST · Unemployment Rate · Time-series analysis

---

R. Bhattacharyya (✉)
Goenka College of Commerce and Business Administration, Kolkata, India
e-mail: rajib2014hmc@gmail.com

B. Chatterjee and A. K. Karmakar (eds.), *Analytical Issues in Growth & Structural Change, Macroeconomy, Security, and Sustainability of India's Economic Development*, India Studies in Business and Economics, https://doi.org/10.1007/978-981-95-5242-9_5

1 Introduction

The history of global downturn or recession since 1970s reveals that slowing down of economic growth has been coupled with stagflation in most cases. Supply bottlenecks and product market volatility casts deep shadows on growth prospects resulting in weaking of major macroeconomic indicators in majority of nations. In some cases, major change in economic policies (such as shifting of tax regime to GST, demonetization in case of India), or sometimes it is the oil price shock (like in 1975 and 1982) or in others it is the deregulation in financial markets creating stress and volatility. According to Kose and Terrones (2015), a contraction in the annual global real per capita GDP characterizes a global recession.

During the five major global recessions in the span of 1970–2021, (1975, 1982, 1991, 2009, and 2020) the sharp fall in per capita GDP was supplemented by rapid decline in world industrial output, global trade, international capital flows, global employment (Guénette et al., 2022). Figure 1 shows the comparative positions of GDP and per capita GDP in the five recessionary periods. It clearly demonstrates that both GDP and per capita GDP suffered stronger blows in the recessions of 2009 and 2020 as compared to others. Also, in almost all the recessions (excepting 1982), Emerging Market and Developing Economies (EMDEs) were better performers than the Advanced Economies (AEs).

Now let us try to analyze the shocks which Indian economy faced since Global Financial Crisis (GFC) in 2008. Though the Indian economy quickly recovered from the GFC and registered a growth rate of 8.4 percent in 2009–10, but it fell abruptly in 2011, and finally reaching to about 5.3 percent in last half of 2012 due to the Euro-zone crisis which surfaced in 2011–12. There was a sharp fall in exports and foreign institutional investment. Rise in inflation and poverty rates was supplemented by insufficient infrastructure, high corruption and poor governance (Sengupta, 2013). But one interesting point to note is that throughout the entire period 2009 to 2014 the

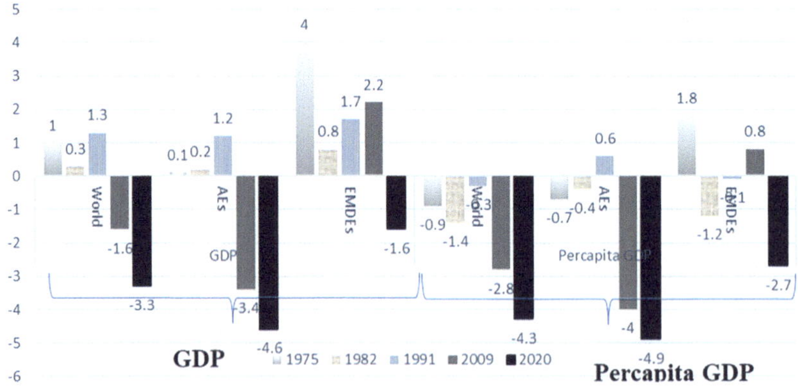

Fig. 1 Performance of GDP and Per capita GDP during the Recessions (1970–2021). *Source* Author's construction based on Kose et al. (2020); World Bank

government attempted to sustain the high growth rates by incurring high fiscal deficits (in fact both fiscal and current account deficits were about 4.8 percent of GDP in 2013). The was coupled with inflation in double digits between 2009 to 2014. There was a depreciation of Indian rupee and growth was stalled. But proper macroeconomic management helped India to recover from the Eurozone crisis after 2013–14 the growth rate accelerated to 6.4 percent. The pace of acceleration continued for the two consecutive years 2014–15 and 2015–16 where the figures for growth rates were 7.5 and 8.0 percent respectively. So, the period 2014 to 2016 may be identified as robust transformative growth.

But two major internal shocks—demonetization shock (8th of November 2016) and Goods and Services Tax (GST) implementation effect (1st July 2017) marks two historically significant milestone in the path of economic reforms in India. The internal demonetization shock was a miserable, destabilizing, critical macroeconomic disaster on the Indian economy which took place and the government decided to declare a fundamental change in the monetary system by demonetizing the high value currency notes—of Rs 500 and Rs 1000 (as these notes were declared obsolete from the 8th of November, 2016). In case of GST, the last two decades has witnessed major tax reforms starting from the Chelliah Committee recommendation in 1991 and a gradual shift of indirect taxes to a genuine value added tax (VAT). But finally, the GST was implemented on 1st July 2017 (though Constitutional Amendment Act was passed in September 2016). Though the main objective was to minimize the adverse impact of indirect taxes through the creation of input tax credit, but burden of tax at the beginning on business or SMEs and deficiency of working capital for the exporters were considered to be its major drawbacks.

After these internal shocks, the severest human suffering and major macroeconomic set back took place with the outbreak of corona virus (COVID-19) from the beginning of the year 2020. It started as a health pandemic but gradually took the shape of global economic slowdown. On the one hand it resulted in loss of lives of millions and on the other hand created disruption of global production network and value chain, bringing life to a standstill situation. After the "Great Depression" of 1930s, it was probably the biggest external shock with devastating impact on human life and its various macroeconomic indicators (Bhattacharyya et al., 2021). In fact, lockdowns and movement restrictions were announced both within and outside nations to arrest the high death tolls due to the pandemic. The need huge finance for upgrading public health infrastructure in order to combat this kind of pandemic in both developed and developing nation was reemphasized. So fiscal and monetary support packages were launched by all governments to restore basic necessities and amend job loss.

2 Literature Survey

Nataraj (2017) in her study on the impact of demonetization, explains the rational for it, the procedures, effect on the financial sector, growth, inflation, industry, manufacturing trade and external sector. Kose et al. (2020) clearly portrayed the performance of various nations of AEs and EMDEs during five major episodes of global recessions in the span of 1970–2021, (1975, 1982, 1991, 2009, and 2020). Their study shows that most of EMDEs and developing economies of the world had exhibited strong recovery from the 2009 GFC in compared to the previous global recessions. Guénette et al. (2022) in their study had demonstrated that GDP and per capita GDP suffered stronger blows in the recessions of 2009 and 2020 as compared to others periods of recessions. We come across a huge literature on the various issues in the context of demonetization in India since the time it was announced. Some of the important contributions in this field are discussed below. Chanda and Cook (2019) in their study attempted to show the huge extent region-wide differences in the growth of deposit due of demonetization in order to analyze the effects of the policy in the medium run. Their study found that areas where the growth of deposit was high, had shown enhanced levels of economic activity in the following years. Bhavnani, and Copelovitch (2018) use the number of bank branches as a measure of exposure to demonetization at the district level and show that while economic activity, as captured by new investment projects, was lower during that quarter, political support for the government actually increased in the first half of 2017. Vyas (2017) tried to explore the impact of demonetization (if any) on jobs with the help of the data available from the Consumer Pyramids Household Survey (CPHS). He considered data on two consecutive phases preceding demonetization and two phases after demonetization. Additionally, he tried to estimate the effect of demonetization using both monthly and weekly data. Dash (2017) attempts to examine both the social and economic impacts of demonetization. Rasel et al. (2019) focuses on the major motivations behind the decision for demonetization in India in 2016 and also discusses the effects of demonetization. Shirley (2017) aims to examine the impact of demonetization on households, farming and fishing industry, jewellery and real estate and on IT sector. Rao et al. (2016) tried to evaluate the short run and medium-term impacts that such a shock is expected to have on the economy. The study by ILO (March, 2020) and ILOSTAT (2023) enlightens us with the advance estimates of the possible devastating effects of corona pandemic on the world employment structure and suggests an array of policy measures to minimize the impacts and enhance strong and quick recovery. Deloitte (March, 2020) report presents four different probable scenarios of the severity of the disease outbreak and tried to assess its impact upon various sectors. Abiad et al. (2020), Surico and Galeotti (2020), Dev and Sengupta (2020) tried to estimate the initial impact of Covid-19 virus on different segments of the economy and discusses the effectiveness of the policies which have been declared by the government and the RBI. OECD report, March, 2020 also provides a wide view of the risk from the outbreak of Corona throughout the world and points out the possible measures to be taken by the government. The edited book by Bhattacharyya et al. (2021) is a comprehensive collection of 24 original essays on a wide range of economic and social issues that have acquired prominence in the wake of the pandemic.

3 Objective of the Study and Methodology

The present seeks to analyze the impacts of demonetization as well as the corona pandemic for both the short and long term. It attempts to explore the immediate effect of expunging of cash on both consumers and business system. The effect in the short-term may be assessed in terms of the time interval between withdrawal of old currency and replacing it by new ones. In the medium term, the study tries to examine the extent and depth of the impact on banking system and switch to a new mode of payment and tax system. Finally attempts have been made to assess the impact of some fundamental macroeconomic variables- GDP, sectoral composition, industrial output, inflation, employment, using secondary time-series data published by the government and official agencies.

4 Impact of Internal and External Shock

One may identify three types of impact- (a) short term effect- which takes place immediately after any shock. In case of demonetization in 2016, this resulted in immediate deficiency of cash in the hands of consumers and businessmen. In case of Corona pandemic, it was the high percentage of death with the rapid spread of pandemic creating a health panic. (b) medium term effect- which normally starts at a gap from the date of its first impact where the initial period provides some indication towards the future trend. The medium-term impact of demonetization was the effect on the banking structure, which had to take back the old currency and substitute it by new one. In the case of pandemic, it resulted it containment zones and lock downs lockdown and disruptions in the movements of goods and services. (c) long-term impact refers to the depth and magnitude of the shock on major macroeconomic variables like output, employment, inflation, sectoral composition, investment, changes in the and tax structures, fiscal and monetary policy changes.

If we analyse the sectoral impact of both the demonetisation and the Covid 19 pandemic we will observe that in case of demonetisation it primarily affected the banking industry within the services and then its secondary impact fell via banking to the entire goods and services industry which was badly crippled due to short term fund crunch. But later on, the restriction on the money transfer was relaxed and problems was minimized. But there was a clear emphasis of a shift from cash exchange to digital transaction or online money transfer which induced increased usage of plastic money, cards, wallets, UPI etc. In case of Covid 19, it primarily affected the health sector but later on its impact was felt in all sectors and pockets of the economy. Within the services sector, the economic activities that was affected primarily are the retail- and tourism-related, entertainment, education and transport sectors. There was tremendous disruption of movements of goods causing direct adverse impact on employment and earning and hence on investment and business expectations. Consumer sentiments were also depressed due to various restrictions and containment measures. The already created the US-China trade and tariff war was further aggravated by the disruptions in the global supply chains, resulting in deep repercussion on the rest of Asia and the world. Foreign direct investment flows also suffered heavy blows due to travel restrictions and delays in normal business operations.

5 Assessment of the Impact of Demonetization

Demonetization has been analyzed by different economists from different angles using different dimensions, like effect on economic growth, agriculture, business (including small and medium enterprises) real estate, informal sector. wage movement, employment trends and digital economy. There are two opposing views: some researchers have found it as a positive move while there are others who cautioned against this change (economists like Prof. A. K. Sen, K. Basu, Manmohan Singh, Raghuram Rajan, Paul Krugman falls in this category). Though there was a initial transitory shock when the demonetization was declared, but the RBI has argued that the economy managed to sustain itself to its earlier level by mid-February of 2017. Bryson and Pershing (2017) were of the opinion that the negative temporary effects of demonetization gradually dissipated, however, the key driver for sustainable long-term growth was the ongoing reform process.

a. **Short run and medium term economic and social impacts**

NITI Aayog, identified the positive impacts of demonetization:

i. Sweeping away of already piled up illegal cash from the monetary system is expected to have direct impact on the inflation rate.
ii. Ceasing of counterfeit currency from circulation.
iii. Checking corruption and arresting terrorism by ceasing black money transaction.
iv. Recovery of bad and outstanding loans and improvement in Bank's Non-Performing Assets (NPA) position.
v. Escalation in tax revenue collection by implementing greater transparency in operation.
vi. Providing impetus to the housing market through a fall in the price of assets.
vii. Sterilization policy for building confidence in the global front.

Apart from these it created a lot of negative distortions. As a sudden liquidity shock, it created currency crisis in the lower end of the income profile who depend on daily earning in cash. Small retailers, traders were faced with tremendous cash stringency which reduced their earning. Hence, a short-term shock held back the demand for mass consumption goods. So, investment, output, employment and tax revenue all dropped in a series. Small farmers had a difficult time to buy seeds, fertilizers and so were compelled to sell products (mainly perishable items) at low prices. Medical emergencies and social commitments (like marriage, funeral) had to bear huge tolls. Severe shortage of cash and its withdrawal restrictions developed panic in common man, standing in long queues in front of counters. This created opportunity for unscrupulous money traders for money hoarding and charging high lending price.

Figure 2 shows the short run impact of demonetization on the M1 components of money aggregates viz currency with the public and Deposit money of the public. It demonstrates that prior to demonetization people held a high percentage of money in cash. But the ratio of currency with the public to M1 declined abruptly after demonetization. Hence it provides some clue that demonetization has developed the inclination of people towards digital transaction. This change in the usage of debit and credit cards and the use of debit card for ATM and POS reflects the gradual movement towards digital transaction.

Due to various restrictions on money withdrawal the credit card transaction amount (both ATM and POS) and debit card (ATM) declined, but Debit card (POS) increased due to online purchase. National Electronic Fund Transfer (NEFT) and mobile banking jumped from Nov. 16 to Dec. 16, revealing an increase in digital transactions (Table 1).

b. **Long run Impact of Demonetization on some Major Macro Variables**

1. **Output growth**

The long run effect of demonetization can be seen from the sudden drop in GDP from the fourth quarter of 2016–17 financial year (fall in GDP from 8.6 percent in Q3 to 6.3 percent in Q4). This falling trend was reversed from Q2 in 2017–18. But following the global recessionary trend, the GDP growth started to fall from Q2 in 2018–19.

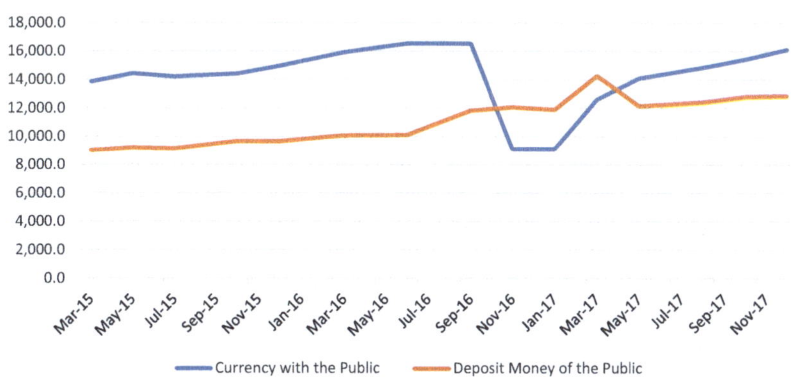

Fig. 2 Change in M1 Components of Money aggregates. *Source* Author's construction based on RBI monthly data for the period 2015 to 2017 (Reserve Bank of India, 2017)

Table 1 Impact on digital transactions

			Credit Card		Debit Card	
	NEFT (amt. in billion)	Mobile Banking (value in billion)	ATM amt. (in million)	POS amt. in million	ATM amt. (in million)	POS amt. in million
Sep-16	9880.17	1042.6	2852.51	241,977.1	2,219,762	159,321
Oct-16	9504.5	1139.41	2996.8	299,424.01	2,547,814	219,413
Nov-16	8807.88	1365.7	1393	265,594.01	1,234,516	321,743
Dec-16	11,537.63	1498.18	880.9	311,491.2	849,341	580,313
Jan-17	11,355.08	1383.01	1539.2	327,082.5	1,516,437	490,042
Feb-17	10,877.91	1279.93	1883.7	284,426.7	1,928,381	358,434

Source Constructed using data available from RBI Website: https://rbi.org.in/scripts/NEFTView.aspx; https://rbi.org.in/scripts/ATMView.aspx

Hence, the empirical data clearly supports the adverse effect of demonetization on output growth in India (Table 2).

2. **Sector-wise impact of demonetization**

Except public administration, defense and other services, all the other sub-sectors had shown a downward trend in their performance. After the implementation of the demonetization, rapid decline was observed in sectors like agriculture, forestry and fishing', 'mining & quarrying', 'manufacturing', 'construction', and Electricity, gas, water supply & other utility services (Table 3).

3. **Movements in Index of Industrial Production (IIP)**

According to the press release of MoSPI, Govt. of India on 12th of May 2017, we find that except for mining, the IIP has been severely hit in all other sectors viz. manufacturing, electricity and general. The fall in the overall IIP clearly indicates negative impact of demonetization on industrial production (Table 4).

4. **Inflation**

The downward inflationary movements in food items were the key factor responsible for the fluctuations in prices in the post demonetization period. This was because prices non-food and non-fuel items remained more or less stable or was least affected. Due to disruptions in supply chains on account of demonetization, prices, instead of pushing up, displayed a downward trend as a result of contraction of demand and sales of perishable vegetables in distress. There was a decline in the level of food inflation declined from 3.7 per cent (October 16) to 2.6 per cent (November 16), to 2.0 per cent (December 16) and further to 1.3 per cent January 2017. A fall in prices of vegetables and pulses was the major factor behind this.

Though there may had been some impact of consumer expenditure on items like clothing and footwear, household goods and services, and personal care and effects

Table 2 Estimates of GDP growth (for each quarter) at Constant Prices, 2011–12

Pre- Demonetization		2015–16	Q1 (April–June)	7.6
			Q2 (July–September)	8.0
			Q3 (October–December)	7.2
			Q4 (January–March)	9.1
		2016–17	Q1 (April–June)	8.7
			Q2 (July–September)	9.7
Post Demonetization			Q3 (October–December)	8.6
			Q4 (January–March)	6.3
		2017–18	Q1 (April–June)	5.8
			Q2 (July–September)	6.5
			Q3 (October–December)	7.6
			Q4 (January–March)	8.2
		2018–19	Q1 (April–June)	7.1
			Q2 (July–September)	6.2
			Q3 (October–December)	5.6
			Q4 (January–March)	5.7
		2019–20	Q1 (April–June)	5.6
			Q2 (July–September)	5.1
			Q3 (October–December)	4.7
			Q4 (January–March)	4.6

Source Author's construction based on data from MoSPI, Govt. of India (as on March, 2020)

Table 3 Sector-wise impact of demonetization

Sectors	2015–16	2016–17	2017–18	2018–19	2019–20
1. Agriculture, forestry and fishing	0.6	6.8	5.9	2.4	3.7
2. Mining and quarrying	10.1	9.8	4.9	−5.8	2.8
3. Manufacturing	13.1	7.9	6.6	5.7	0.9
4. Utility services, electricity, gas, water supply	4.7	10.0	11.2	8.2	4.6
5. Construction	3.6	5.9	5.0	6.1	3.0
6. Trade, transport, communication and broadcasting services	10.2	7.7	7.6	7.7	5.6
7. Financial, real estate and professional services	10.7	8.6	4.7	6.8	7.3
8. Public Administration, defense and other services	6.1	9.3	9.9	9.4	8.8
9. GVA at basic prices	8.0	8.0	6.6	6.0	4.9

Source Author's construction based on data from MoSPI, Govt. of India (as on March 2020)

Table 4 Performance of IIP during demonetization

Period	Mining	Manufacturing	Electricity	General
Jun-16	98.4	122.4	144.3	120.7
Jul-16	88.4	120.6	142.5	117.7
Aug-16	84.7	120.9	143.5	117.5
Sep-16	87.7	122.1	145.6	119.0
Oct-16	101.0	122.5	145.1	121.2
Nov-16	106.2	116.6	134.9	116.6
Dec-16	114.1	122.5	137.8	122.5
Jan-17	114.4	124.4	138.9	124.1
Feb-17	110.5	121.3	130.2	120.5
Mar-17	127.2	130.6	147.9	131.5

Source Author's compilation based on Press Release, MoSPI, Govt. of India (Press Release-12th May, 2017)

but housing, health, transport and communication basket were held more or less constant due to restrictions of fund (Table 5).

5. Impact on employment

Figure 3 demonstrates the fluctuations in the unemployment rate in general and also separately for male and female during the pre and post demonetization period in India. Prior to demonetization the unemployment rate was as high as 9.24 percent (May-Aug, 2016). This sharply declined to about 6.68 percent during Sept- Dec 2016, and further to 3.81 (May-Aug, 2017) but thereafter there has been a steady

Table 5 Effect on INFLATION

Period	Fuel and light	Clothing and footwear	Housing	Miscellaneous*	CPI-excluding food-fuel
Nov-15	5.3	5.8	5	3.8	4.7
Dec-15	5.4	5.7	5.1	4	4.9
Jan-16	5.3	5.7	5.2	3.9	4.7
Oct-16	2.9	5.2	5.1	4.7	4.9
Nov-16	2.8	5	5	4.8	4.9
Dec-16	3.8	5	5	4.7	4.9
Jan-17	3.4	4.7	5	5.1	5.1

Note *Includes household goods and services; health; transport and communication; recreation and amusement; education; and personal care and effects
Source Author's construction based on RBI Report on Demonetization, March 10, 2017

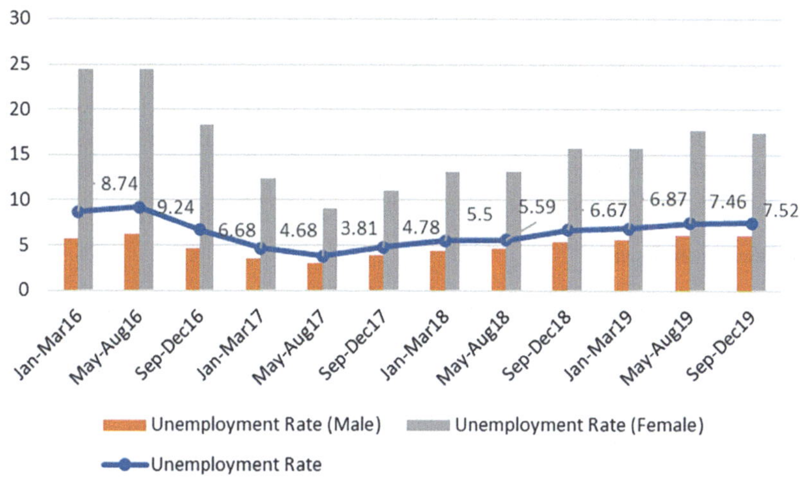

Fig. 3 Changes in unemployment rate during pre and post demonetization. *Source* Author's compilation based on various CMIE Reports, Jan2016- Dec-2019; Mehrotra and Parida (2019)

upsurge in the unemployment rate. Moreover, throughout the entire period under consideration, the unemployment rate for female was higher than that of male.

6 Economic and Social Impact Corona Pandemic

a. Effect across the Globe

There is no doubt that the Covid-19 pandemic was once of the biggest devastating attack to mankind (McKibbin & Fernando, 2020) since the Great Depression of

1930s. But the Covid-19 pandemic had to fight two great battles—the first was the health pandemic, which was immediately followed by the second battle called the economic pandemic. The very high rate of geographical spreading and the consequent death rates created a panic throughout the entire globe.

Economists and social thinkers are of the consensus that if proper action for recovery are not implemented the economic battle would be much more difficult in future than those days of "The Great Depression" of the 1930s. Besides this the growing inequality and unemployment scenario is deteriorating with more informal sector jobs and the already existing recessionary trend. This may create huge social unrest and instability in the long run.

i. **Real GDP growth**

According to the published report of the World Bank (Global Economic Prospects, January 2023), except China (2.2 per cent) all countries of the world registered a negative growth rate of GDP in the year 2020. However, the real GDP growth in 2021 and 2022 are positive, but with varying degrees depending on the post-Covid recovery situation. But it is interesting to note that among all such facts, the growth rate in 2021 was highest in Turkey (11.4 per cent), Argentina (10.4 per cent) and India (8.7 per cent) and in 2022 it was Saudia Arabia (8.3 per cent), Bangladesh (7.2 per cent) and India (6.6 per cent). So, not only has India performed more consistently than other nations, but its growth rate has been higher compared to China and other advanced and other emerging economies for both years (Table 6).

ii. **International trade**

In line with the slowdown of activity in major economies global trade growth weakened in the second half of 2022. Decelerating trade mirrored the downfall in global industrial production as demand shifted toward its pre-pandemic composition. Services trade continued to recover, supported by the gradual shift in demand toward services, but despite moderation, goods trade surpassed pre-pandemic levels last year. As travel restrictions eased in many countries, tourism flows rebounded but remained well below pre-pandemic levels and uneven across regions (WTO 2022). Lower transportation costs and normalisation of inventories reflect that global supply chain pressures have eased since mid-2022, although they are still above pre-pandemic levels. Trade activity remained subdued in EMDEs due to strong trade linkages with developed economies where demand is expected to slow sharply.

The WTO's trade projections, set out in the new Global Trade Outlook and Statistics (2023) Report, estimate real global GDP growth at market exchange rates of 2.4% for 2023. Projections for both trade and output growth are below the averages for the past 12 years of 2.6% and 2.7% respectively (Fig. 4).

iii. **Inflation**

According to the report of the IMF, world inflation was expected to fall to 5.2 per cent (yearly average) in 2024 from 6.8 per cent in 2023 from 8.7 per cent in 2022. But still it is much above the pre-pandemic (2017–19) levels of about 3.5 per cent.

Table 6 Real GDP growth across the world

	2020	2021	2022e	2023f	2024f
World	−3.2	5.9	2.9	1.7	2.7
Advanced economies	−4.3	5.3	2.5	0.5	1.6
United States	−2.8	5.9	1.9	0.5	1.6
Euro area	−6.1	5.3	3.3	0.0	1.6
Japan	−4.3	2.2	1.2	1.0	0.7
Emerging market and developing economies	−1.5	6.7	3.4	3.4	4.1
East Asia and Pacific	1.2	7.2	3.2	4.3	4.9
China	2.2	8.1	2.7	4.3	5.0
Indonesia	−2.1	3.7	5.2	4.8	4.9
Thailand	−6.2	1.5	3.4	3.6	3.7
Europe and Central Asia	−1.7	6.7	0.2	0.1	2.8
Russian Federation	−2.7	4.8	-3.5	-3.3	1.6
Turkey	1.9	11.4	4.7	2.7	4.0
Poland	−2.0	6.8	4.4	0.7	2.2
Latin America and the Caribbean	−6.2	6.8	3.6	1.3	2.4
Brazil	−3.3	5.0	3.0	0.8	2.0
Mexico	−8.0	4.7	2.6	0.9	2.3
Argentina	−9.9	10.4	5.2	2.0	2.0
Middle East and North Africa	−3.6	3.7	5.7	3.5	2.7
Saudi Arabia	−4.1	3.2	8.3	3.7	2.3
Iran, Islamic Rep	1.9	4.7	2.9	2.2	1.9
Egypt, Arab Rep	3.6	3.3	6.6	4.5	4.8
South Asia	−4.5	7.9	6.1	5.5	5.8
India	−6.6	8.7	6.9	6.6	6.1
Pakistan	−0.9	5.7	6.0	2.0	3.2
Bangladesh	3.4	6.9	7.2	5.2	6.2
Sub-Saharan Africa	−2.0	4.3	3.4	3.6	3.9
High-income countries	−4.3	5.3	2.7	0.6	1.6
Middle-income countries	−1.2	6.9	3.2	3.4	4.3
Low-income countries	1.6	3.9	4.0	5.1	5.6
EMDEs excl. China	−3.9	5.7	3.8	2.7	3.6

Source Author's compilation based on World Bank: Global Economic Prospects, January, 2023, *Note*: 'e' stands for estimate; 'f' stands for forecast

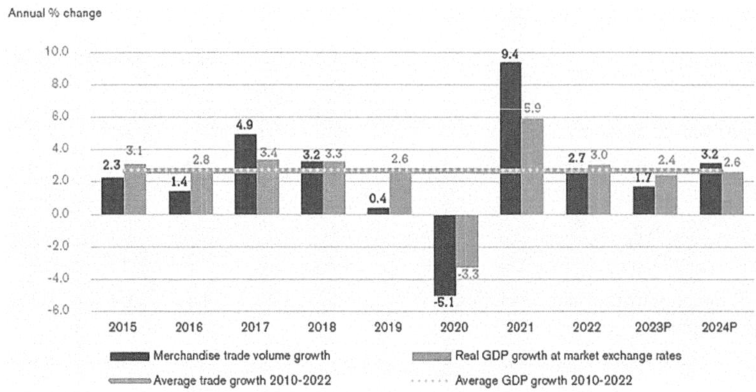

Fig. 4 World GDP growth and merchandise trade volume (2015–2024). *Note* 2023 and 2024 are projections only. April, 2023 *Source* Author's construction based on Global Trade Outlook and Statistics,

Core inflation is generally declining more gradually. Globally, it is set to decline from an annual average of 6.5 per cent in 2022 to 6.0 per cent in 2023 and 4.7 per cent in 2024. Monetary policy tightening is expected to gradually dampen inflation, but a central driver of the disinflation projected for 2023 is declining international commodity prices (WEO, IMF, July 2023).

iv. **Employment Scenario**

The most devastating impact of the covid-19 was witnessed when the world youth employment dropped by 34 million between the period 2019 and 2020. About 75 million young people were unemployed, 408 million were in employment, and 732 million were out of the labour force globally in 2021. The Employment-to-Population ratio (EPR) showed a strong downward trend in in the years before the COVID-19 pandemic. In Eastern and Southern Asia, the decline was strongest, and in sub-Saharan Africa, it was relatively weak. The adverse impact on employment has been strongly felt by nations which belong to upper middle-income category while it has been weakly experienced by countries belonging in the low- and high-income category (Table 7).

Manufacturing, retail, wholesale, real estate, food and accommodation were the sectors which were the most affected ones. The least affected sectors were public administration and defense, human health, education, utilities (Table 8).

b. **Impact on the Indian Economy**

i. **Quarterly growth rates of GDP**

The real GDP and its growth rate had already been falling since 2019–20 (Q1), but due to the Covid-19 pandemic there was a drastic fall by -23.4 percent in 2020–21 (Q1) (Fig. 5). Then it started rising up to 9.1in Q2 of 2021–22. The rates were above

Table 7 World unemployment and unemployment rate by sex and across regions (2019–24)

Country	Sex	Unemployment rate (Percentage)					
		2019	2020	2021	2022	2023	2024
World	Total	5.5	6.9	6.2	5.8	5.8	5.8
	Women	5.6	6.7	6.2	5.8	5.8	5.9
	Men	5.5	7.0	6.1	5.7	5.7	5.7
Low-income countries	Total	5.2	5.9	5.8	5.8	5.7	5.7
	Women	5.4	6.1	6.1	6.0	6.0	6.0
	Men	5.0	5.7	5.6	5.5	5.5	5.4
Lower-middle income countries	Total	5.5	7.4	6.4	6.2	6.1	6.2
	Women	5.6	6.8	6.3	6.2	6.2	6.2
	Men	5.5	7.7	6.4	6.2	6.1	6.1
Upper-middle income countries	Total	6.0	6.8	6.3	6.0	5.8	5.8
	Women	6.0	6.6	6.4	5.9	5.8	5.8
	Men	6.1	6.9	6.3	6.0	5.9	5.8
High income countries	Total	4.8	6.5	5.6	4.5	4.9	5.0
	Women	5.0	6.9	5.9	4.8	5.2	5.3
	Men	4.5	6.2	5.4	4.3	4.7	4.7

Source Author's compilation based on ILO modelled estimate, November, 2022; World Employment and Social Outlook (WESO) (2023)

8 percent for three consecutive quarters of 2023–24. Again, from the end of the last quarter of 2023–24 its growth rate has started to decline.

ii. **Inflation Predictions (CPI)**

In contrast to the impact of corona pandemic on economic growth, the effect on CPI is ambiguous. Probably the explanation lies in the fact that the decline in the prices of food items is being offset by the rise in prices of non-food items as a result of disruptions in the global supply chain (Fig. 6). The figure clearly demonstrates the variations in movements of CPI between the rural and urban customers.

iii. **Extent of Job Losses in India**

As majority of the jobs are informal (about 90 percent), which are highly volatile, insecure and poorly paid, hence the corona pandemic severely impacted the poverty and unemployment of this informal sector works. Compared to formal jobs, these informal works lack basic social protection coverage and are devoid of proper health care access. They suffered the most as they had no alternative sources of earnings during their illness.

Big job absorbing sectors failed to employ to their full capacity. This was particularly true for industries like food and accommodation industry, tourism, aviation, real estate, automobile (for e.g. companies like Maruti, Hundai, Honda closed down

Table 8 Sector-wise adverse impact on workers

Economic sector	Impact on output	Share in global employment (%)
Manufacturing	High	13.9
Wholesale and retail trade; repair of motor vehicles and motorcycles	High	14.5
Real estate; business and administrative activities	High	4.7
Accommodation and food services	High	4.3
Arts, entertainment and recreation, and other services	Medium High	5.4
Transport; storage and communication	Medium High	6.1
Construction	Medium	7.7
Financial and insurance activities	Medium	1.6
Mining and quarrying	Medium	0.7
Agriculture; forestry and fishing	Low- Medium	26.5
Education	Low	5.3
Human health and social work activities	Low	4.1
Public administration and defense; compulsory social security	Low	4.3
Utilities	Low	0.8

Source Author's Compilation based on the ILO Estimates 7th April, 2020

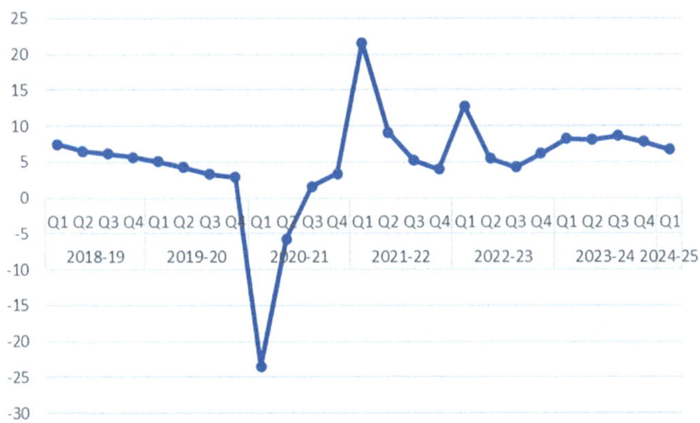

Fig. 5 Growth rates of real GDP (percentage, quarterly) between FY 2018–19 and FY 2024–25 at constant Prices with base period 2011–12. *Source* Author's Construction based on MoSPI, India [https://www.mospi.gov.in/dataviz-quarterly-gdp-growth-rates]. *Note* Growth rates Calculated with respect to previous year]

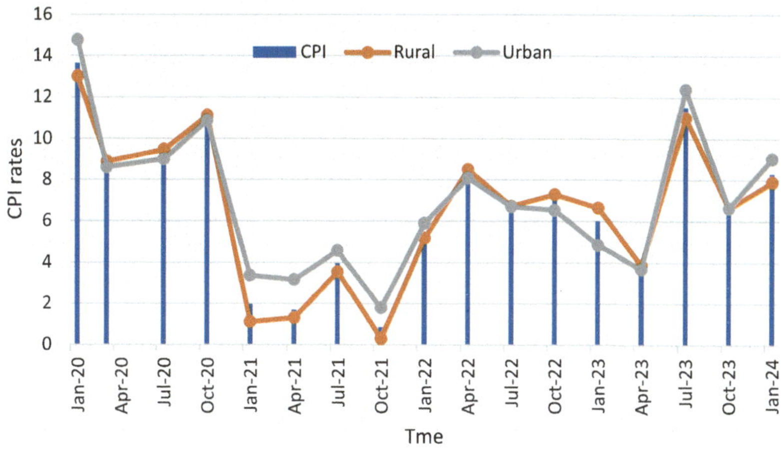

Fig. 6 Movement of CPI during and after Covid-19 Pandemic. *Source* Author's Constrction based on MoSPI; [https://cpi.mospi.gov.in/Inflation_CurrentSeries_2012.aspx]

their production temporarily, resulting in an increase the lay-offs). About 50 million workers were at temporary layoff as per the records of "The World Travel and Tourism Council". According to 'The Consumer Pyramids Household Survey estimates (CMIE) the job loss was approximately 114 million. Within this category, the worst hit was the small and retail traders and wage earners (including hawkers and daily wage-earning labourers who earn income by working on a daily "no-work, no-pay" basis. Also, there was drop in employment for entrepreneurs (18.2 percent) and salaried employees (17.8 percent) (Fig. 7).

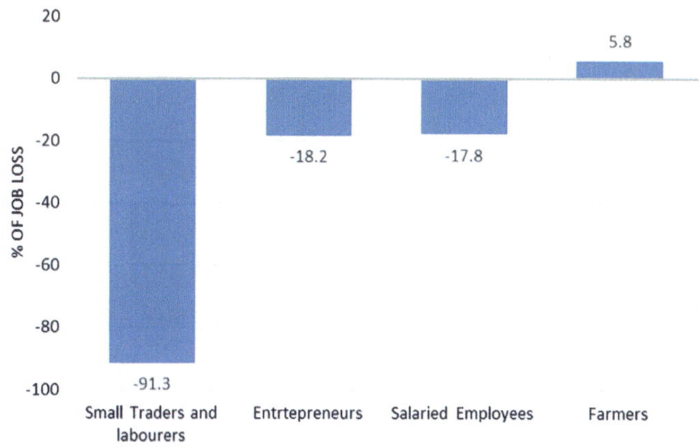

Fig. 7 Extent of job Los (April 2020). *Source* Author's construction based on CMIE report, May, 2020

The MoSPI estimates Periodic Labour Force Survey (PLFS), Annual Report (July 2023–June 2024) depicts that the unemployment rates have sequentially fallen for both male and female across both the rural and urban areas (Fig. 8). But as per the figures of unemployment rates provided by CMIE the unemployment rates rose to an all-time high 23.4 percent in April 2020. It has also been found from the Consumer Pyramids Household Survey that nearly 20 million jobs were lost in travel and tourism accounts, 4 million jobs. hotels and restaurants account. An interesting point to note is that young people (20–24 years) account for 11 per cent of the total job loss which amounts to over 13 million; for age group (25–29 years) the job loss was about 14 million 11.1 per cent); in the age group (40 years) 52 per cent jobs were lost. The loss of jobs among younger generation has significant impact on consumer demand and savings.

iv. **Components of Aggregate demand and Supply**

The containment measures and lockdowns had created disruption on the supply of raw materials and final products. This had imposed downward pressure on all the three components on aggregate demand viz, consumption, investment and government expenditure. This had a negative impact on the output of almost all industries. Moreover, as migrant workers returned to their native places, were out of jobs, demand for goods and services were depressed. The hospitality, tourism and aviation sectors suffered heavy losses and huge proportions of employees were thrown out of their jobs. The National Stock Exchange (NSE) suffered as panic had shaved almost 23 percent market capitalization of companies (CMIE, Economic Outlook (2020)).

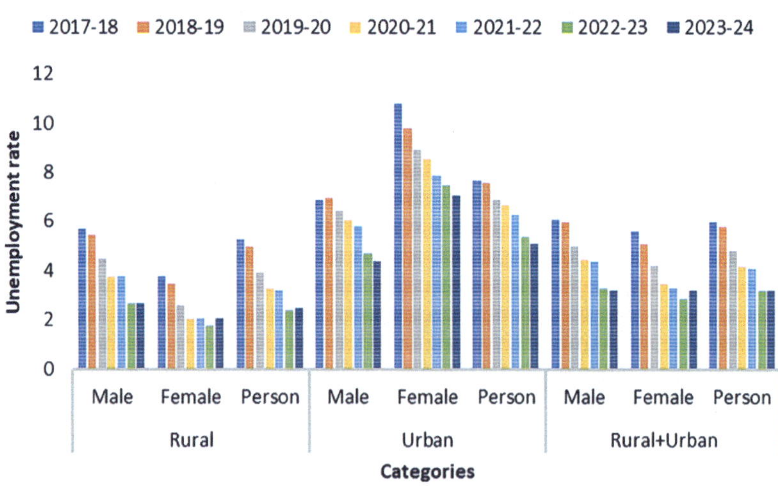

Fig. 8 Annual unemployment rates in India (2017–18 to 2023–24). *Source* Author's construction based on Press Note on Periodic Labour Force Survey (PLFS), annual report (July 2023–June 2024)]. *Note* Here unemployment rate (UR) refers to usual status unemployment for people in the age group of 15 years and more

But external shocks of this form or other may have serious repercussion on Indian economy. Firstly, it can reduce export demand, shrinking of market and growth. Secondly, as prices of crude oil and natural gas had softened within the high volatility situation, India may benefit as a net importer of these products. Thirdly, the global financial market volatility may in turn impact the domestic financial market stability which may affect growth and inflation.

Policy Suggestions

As the global economy recovers from the devastations of corona pandemic, it calls for comprehensive policy actions to combat these kinds of health pandemic by developing strong health care system, boosting consumer demand and remove the supply bottlenecks. Governments of various countries had announced multiple policy packages to restrain the spread and restore normalcy. Initially the Finance Minister of India declared a Rs. 1.7 lakh crore package particularly for the unorganized sector workers and daily wage labourers. Later on a 20 lakh crore mega stimulus package was launched by the government to mitigate the negative impact of the pandemic.

In future these kinds of pandemic may not only create health disaster but may result in economic recessions. So, workers and companies need to be protected from temporary income down fall and save economy from catastrophic damage. For these the following policy suggestions are essential:

1. Firstly, it is essential to have sufficient flow of funds to the health care sector as a priority and this automatically requires increase in social sector spending at to 10 percent of GDP. Moreover, additional fiscal support for health services is required, including sufficient resources to ensure adequate staffing and testing facilities, and all necessary prevention, containment and mitigation measures.
2. Schemes like cash transfers or unemployment insurance, may be introduced to provide workers social security during no pay. Also, free health checkup during pandemic period for workers temporarily thrown out jobs may be a good measure.
3. The Government may urge the companies in the private sector not reduce salary or go for wage cuts during this period of emergency and provide them alternative working hours or facilities or work-from-home (as in case of IT jobs) options.
4. Government may provide temporary tax benefit by relaxing tax laws or allowing delayed payment of tax or debt, or lower the costs of inputs such as energy, particularly for companies and sectors which are more severely affected by the shocks. All forms of rebates or concessions should be allowed to the distressed people, including free food packages needed to support their lives are essential.
5. Automatic fiscal stabilizers and expanding spending on health services, targeted and temporary fiscal measures could also be implemented to support businesses in sectors particularly exposed to a sharp downturn in travel and tourism.

7 Concluding Remarks

The above analysis clearly points out the there are possibilities of economy moving towards a recession due to the twin impact of demonetization and corona pandemic. It all depends on how the policy makers are able to combat both the health emergency as well as the economic crisis. There are concerns and challenges of saving both life and livelihood. Both the demand and supply shocks on output and employment needs to be tackled with appropriate policy measures not only at the national, but also at international level. It may also be thought of as "**C**ooperation for **O**ptimal **R**estructuring for **O**rganized **N**ew **A**lliance (CORONA)". Fiscal stimulus as well as providing basic necessities to those who have lost jobs and also the poor and needy, through the public distribution system, free of cost can boost demand and help the economy come out of the crisis.

There are opportunities, which if grabbed, could provide new sources of earning dividends and could boost the economy from the possibility of a recession. Since independence India has suffered heavily due to the lack of proper industrialization policy. The situation has given immense opportunity to capitalize on the "Make-in-India" strategy and develop a comprehensive plan for manufacturing for the world market as large firms from Japan, USA, Korea has decided to relocate production process from China. But it requires government initiatives to formulate strategic plans for industrializations coupled with massive investments in infrastructure, like power, communication, transport etc. This will not only create employment opportunity and boost effective demand in the short run but will also ease supply constraints and through multiplier effects revive economic growth in the long run. It has also pointed out to the need for the development of social infrastructure on public health to reduce issues like child mortality.

References

Abiad, A., Arao, M., Dagli, S., Ferrarini, B., Noy, I., Osewe, P., Pagaduan, J., Park, D., & Platitas, R. (2020). The economic impact of the COVID-19 outbreak on developing Asia. Asian Development Bank (ADB) Brief, No. 128 [Available at: https://doi.org/10.22617/BRF200096]

Bhavnani, R. R., & Copelovitch, M. (2018). The political impact of monetary shocks: Evidence from India's 2016 demonetization, January. [Available at SSRN: https://ssrn.com/abstract=3095228]

Bhattacharyya, R., Dastidar, A., & Sikdar, S. (2021). The Covid-19 Pandemic, India and the world-economic and social policy perspective, Edited Book, Routledge London and New York.

Bryson, J. H., & Pershing, H. E. (2017). Economic analysis, Indian GDP Growth Depressed by Demonetisation, special commentary, economics group. [Available at https://wellsfargo.com/economics and on Bloomberg WFRE]

Chanda, A., & Cook, C. J. (2019). *Who gained from India's demonetization? Insights from satellites and surveys*. (Working Paper 2019–06). Department of Economics, Louisiana State University [Available at https://www.lsu.edu/business/economics/files/working papers /pap19_06.pdf]

CMIE, Economic Outlook (2020)

Dash, A. (2017). A study on socio economic effect of demonetization in India. *International Journal of Management and Applied Science, 3*(3). ISSN: 2394-7926.

Dev, S. M., & Sengupta, R. (2020). *Covid-19: Impact on the Indian economy*. (Working paper, WP-2020-013). Indira Gandhi Institute of Development Research, Mumbai.

Global Trade Outlook and Statistics. (2023, April).

Guénette, J. D., Kose, M. A., & Sugawara. N. (2022, September). Is a global recession imminent? Equitable growth, finance and institutions policy note, World Bank Group.

International Labour Organization (ILO) Note, COVID-19 and the World of Work: Impact and Policy Responses, 18th March, 2020.

ILO Estimates 7th April, 2020.

ILOSTAT. (2023). ILO modelled estimate: World employment and social outlook, November, 2022.

Kose, M. A., & Terrones, M. E. (2015). *Collapse and revival: Understanding global recessions and recoveries*. International Monetary Fund.

Kose, M. A., Sugawara, N., & Terrones, M. E. (2020). *Global recessions, centre for applied macroeconomic analysis, Crawford school of public policy, Australian National University*. (Working Paper 10/2020).

McKibbin, W., & Fernando, R. (2020). The global macroeconomic impacts of COVID-19: Seven scenarios. https://www.brookings.edu/research/the-global-macroeconomic-impacts-of-covid-19-seven-scenarios/

Mehrotra, S., & Parida, J. K. (2019). *India's employment crisis: Rising education levels and falling non-agricultural job growth, CSE*. (Working paper, 2019–04). Centre for Sustainable Employment, Azim Premji University.

MoSPI, India. https://www.mospi.gov.in/dataviz-quarterly-gdp-growth-rates

MoSPI; https://cpi.mospi.gov.in/Inflation_CurrentSeries_2012.aspx

Nataraj, G. (2017). *Impact of demonetization*. (Theme paper). Indian Institute of Public Administration, New Delhi.

Press Note on Periodic Labour Force Survey (Plfs), Annual Report (July 2023–June 2024).

OECD Interim Economic Assessment (2020): Corona Virus: The World Economy at Risk, 2nd March.

Rao, K., Mukherjee, S., Kumar, S., Sengupta, D. P., Tandon, S., & Nayudu, H. (2016). *Demonetization: Impact on the economy, national institute of public finance and policy* (Working Paper No. 182).

Rasel, M., Hossian, M. S., Sultana, A., & Kabir, M. H. (2019). Demonetization in India: An evaluation. *Asian Journal of Economics, Business and Accounting, 12*(2), 1–12, Article no. AJEBA.50607; ISSN: 2456-639X.

Reserve Bank of India. (2017, March 10). Macroeconomic impact of demonetisation - A preliminary assessment.

Sengupta, J. (2013, April-June, Summer). India and the Eurozone crisis. *World Affairs, The Journal of Internal Issues, 17*(2), 34–43. https://www.jstor.org/stable/48531683

Shirley, M. A. J (2017). Impact of demonetization in India special issue published in *International Journal of Trend in Research and Development (IJTRD)*.

Surico, P., & Galeotti, A. (2020). The economics of pandemic: The case of COVID-19. London Business School.

Trade and Development Report Update, UNCTAD, 4th March, 2020.

Vyas, M. (2017). *Using fast frequency household survey data to estimate the impact of demonetization on employment* (CMIE Working Paper).

Generating Employment in India: A Suggestion

Ambar Ghosh and Dipti Ghosh

Abstract Unemployment is a burning issue in India. In the post-reform period, employment had been more or less stagnant in the organized sector even though average annual growth rates of both GDP and value added of the organized sector at constant prices were quite high. Using a macro model that hopefully captures the salient features of the Indian economy, this paper suggests a way out. It derives the result that the larger the stock of infrastructure capital in the unorganized sector, the larger will be the levels of output and employment in both the sectors. It also shows that, if the government invests in infrastructure in the unorganized sector and finances it by taxing capitalists' income, employment will go up significantly. The policy will also heap considerable benefits on the poor. However, if the government finances its investment expenditure by imposing indirect taxes, employment and output levels are likely to contract in both the sectors.

Keywords Organized sector · Unorganized sector · Employment · Investment · Income tax · Indirect tax

JEL Classification E12 J21 O31

1 Introduction

Even though the average annual rate of growth of the real value added of the organized sector was quite high in India in the post-reform period, it experienced almost complete jobless growth (see Table 1). We find from Table 2 that GDP had grown at a high rate of around 6 percent per annum during 1994–1995–2014–2015. However, Table 3 reveals that the share of the organized sector in GDP increased from 36.8

Portions of this chapter draw from the author's publication Ghosh and Ghosh (2019a).

A. Ghosh (✉) · D. Ghosh
Economics, Jadavpur University, Kolkata, India
e-mail: ambarghosh@gmail.com

B. Chatterjee and A. K. Karmakar (eds.), *Analytical Issues in Growth & Structural Change, Macroeconomy, Security, and Sustainability of India's Economic Development*, India Studies in Business and Economics, https://doi.org/10.1007/978-981-95-5242-9_6

percent in 1993–1994 to 43.3% in 2003–2004 and further to 45.1% in 2010–2011. There are no reasons to believe that the trend has been reversed since 2010–2011. Thus, the real value added of the organized sector had grown at a higher rate than GDP. We also find from Table 4 that only 6% of the work force was employed in the organized sector in 2004–2005. Table 5 shows that the work force and the labour force had grown at an average annual rate of around 2%. Thus, the share of work force employed in the organized sector has dwindled continuously, whereas the share of the organized sector in GDP has steadily increased. Given the steady high growth rate of output of the organized sector and the complete stagnation in its level of employment, the unit labour requirement has gone down steadily and rapidly. Obviously, this has been brought about by labour saving technological and managerial changes taking place in the organized sector. The jobless growth in the organized sector has shifted the focus to the unorganized sector for job creation. ILO(2009) has made an attempt at suggesting a strategy for generating employment in India. It has recommended massive investments in sectors, which are naturally employment intensive. However, it has not derived its strategy from a macro-theoretic model. Hence, it has left the issue of the problem of financing of the required massive investments unexplored. Nor has it examined the issue of the possible conflict between the goal of employment generation and that of providing the masses with the basic necessities of life in adequate quantities at affordable prices. We have shown that, if the government invests in infrastructure in the unorganized sector and finances it by taxing capitalists' income, it will raise employment significantly and heap considerable benefits on the poor. This paper complements Ghosh and Ghosh (2019a, 2019b), which shows how labour saving technological and managerial changes in the organized sector produces strong recessionary forces on both the sectors of the economy.

Table 1 Employment in the organized sector (in million)

Year	Growth rate of GDP at constant (2004–2005) prices	Number of Workers employed
1994–1995	6.4	27.53
2000–2001	5.3	27.79
2001–2002	5.5	27.20
2003–2004	8.1	26.45
2004–2005	7.0	26.46
2005–2006	9.5	26.96
2006–2007	9.6	27.24
2007–2008	9.6	27.55
2008–2009	6.7	28.18
2009–2010	8.4	29.00
2010–2011	8.4	29
2011–2012	5.3	29.65

Source RBI

Table 2 Growth rate of GDP, Net FDI, foreign portfolio investment, government consumption and Gross Fiscal deficit (GFD)

Year	Growth rate of GDP at factor cost (at constant prices base 2004–2005)	Net FDI (US$ million)	Net portfolio investment (US$ million)	Total (US$ million)	Government consumption (in Rsbn)	GFD[a] (% of GDP)	Rate of GDCF[b]	Rate of NDCF
2000–2001	5.3	3270	2590	5860	3247.27	5.65	24.6	16.7
2001–2002	5.5	4734	1952	6686	3323.69	6.19	24.6	16.5
2002–2003	5.0	3157	944	4101	3317.53	5.91	25.4	17.3
2003–2004	8.1	2388	11,377	13,765	3409.62	5.48	27.3	19.5
2004–2005	7.0	3712	9291	13,003	3545.18	3.88	32.8	25.5
2005–2006	9.5	3033	12,492	15,525	3860.07	3.96	34.9	27.8
2006–2007	9.6	7693	6947	14,640	4005.79	3.38	36.2	29.2
2007–2008	9.6	15,891	27,434	43,325	4389.19	2.54	39.0	32.2
2008–2009	6.7	22,343	−14,032	8311	4845.59	5.99	35.6	27.9
2009–2010	8.4	17,965	32,396	50,361	5517.02	6.48	38.4	30.9
2010–2011	8.4	11,305	30,292	41,597	5843.52	5.87	39.8	32.5
2011–2012	6.5	22,006	17,171	39,177	6345.59	5.89	38.8	31.1
2012–2013	4.5	19,819	26,891	46,710	6620.33	5.06	38.9	30.9
2013–2014	4.7	21,564	4822	26,386	6873.89	4.85		

Source RBI
[a]Gross fiscal deficit, [b]Gross domestic capital formation

Table 3 Contributions of the organized sector and the unorganized sector to the value added of major sectors of production and NDP

Industry	1993–1994		2003–2004		2010–2011	
	Organized	Unorganized	Organized	Unorganized	Organized	Unorganized
Agriculture, forestry and fishing	3.5	96.5	4.1	95.9	5.8	94.2
Mining, manufacturing	64.2	35.8	60.5	39.5	64.5	35.5
Electricity, construction and services	47.1	58.9	53.1	46.9	42.2	51.8
NDP	36.8	63.2	43.3	56.7	45.1	54.9

Source CSO (2005): National Accounts Statistics 2005, Government of India and National Accounts Statistics 2012, Government of India

Table 4 Sectoral shares in work force (2004–2005)

	Organised Sector	Unorganized sector
Percentage of workforce employed 2004–2005	6	94

Source NSSO 61st round

Table 5 Labour force, work force and unemployment (in million)

	1993–1994	1999–2000	2004–2005	1999–2000 to 2004–2005 point to point annualised growth rate
Labour force	387.94	406.05	469.06	2.93
Work force	374.45	397.00	457.82	2.89
Number of unemployed	7.49	9.05	17.24	

Source NSSO and Report of the Task Force on Employment Opportunities (planning Commission)

2 The Model

Let the economy be broadly divided into two main sectors: the unorganized or the traditional sector and the organized or the modern sector. In India, the organized sector is defined as the one that consists of all **non-agricultural enterprises** employing more than ten employees or more without power and five employees or more with power. Thus, we define the organized sector as the one that consists of all large non-agricultural enterprises. The major feature of the organized sector is that it is an oligopoly. Producers in this sector set the prices and adjust their output to demand that comes forth at the prices set. The output in this sector is, thus, demand constrained. The unorganized sector, therefore, consist of all other non-agricultural enterprises (which are small) and agriculture. The latter is by far the dominant segment in the unorganized sector. The distinguishing feature of this sector is that the producers in this sector are credit constrained. They produce as much output as they can using the amounts of inputs they can purchase with the financial resources they have at their disposal and the markets clear through the adjustment in prices. We shall specify the features of the organized and the unorganized sector in detail below:

The Organized Sector

The output of this sector is denoted by Y. It is produced with capital and labour. The stock of capital is given, as the model is a short-run one. Production of the organized or the modern sector is highly import intensive and the production function is fixed coefficient.

In line with the tradition set by the structuralist writers such as Kalecki (1954), Rakshit (1982), Taylor (1983), Bose (1989) et al., we assume that the output of the modern or the organized sector is demand determined. Producers set the prices of their products and adjust their outputs to demand that comes forth at the prices set. The price of the output of the organized sector is denoted by P and it is fixed and assumed to be equal to unity for simplicity. The major components of aggregate demand for Y are consumption, investment, net export, and the demand arising from the unorganized or the traditional sector for Y, as it uses the goods produced in the organized sector as intermediate inputs in its production. It uses the output of the organized sector also for purposes of investment.

The consumption demand for the output of the organized/modern sector comes from both the workers and the capitalists of the organized sector, although quite a large part of the wage income is spent on the mass consumption goods produced by the unorganized sector. The average and marginal propensities to consume the output of the domestic organized sector and its foreign substitutes of workers and capitalists are assumed to be different and they are denoted by C_{wy} and C_c respectively.

Investment demand of the organized sector for Y, as standard, is assumed to be a decreasing function of the interest rate. In case of India, an important determinant of the cost of investment is the exchange rate (e) as a large part of investment demand of the organized sector represents demand for imported capital goods. So, an increase in e raises the cost of investment and, hence, given expectations, reduces investment demand for Y. Organized sector's production is highly import intensive. An increase in e, therefore, generates a strong cost-push. The corporate sector in India is heavily indebted to foreigners. An increase in e raises debt service charges on external loans in domestic currency substantially. All these adverse supply shocks demoralize the investors and dampen investment demand. Data on exchange rates, growth rates and capital formation given in Tables 2 and 6 show that in all the years of recession (2011–2012–2013–2014) exchange rate increased substantially indicating a strong inverse relationship between the exchange rate, rate of capital formation and growth rate in India. For all these reasons, we think that investment is highly sensitive to exchange rate in India. Hence, we have incorporated e as a determinant of investment and made it a decreasing function of e.

Table 6 Exchange rate of the Indian rupee vis-a-vis the US dollar (monthly average)

Year/ month	US$ average	Year/ month	US$ average	Year/ month	US$ average	Year/ month	US$ average
2008		Oct	46.7211	Jul	44.4174	Apr	54.4971
Jan	39.3737	Nov	46.5673	Aug	45.2788	May	55.1156
Feb	39.7326	Dec	46.6288	Sep	47.6320	Jun	58.5059
Mar	40.3561	2010		Oct	49.2579	Jul	60.0412
Apr	40.0224	Jan	45.9598	Nov	50.8564	Aug	64.5517
May	42.1250	Feb	46.3279	Dec	52.6769	Sep	64.3885
June	42.8202	Mar	45.4965	2012		Oct	61.7563
Jul	42.8380	Apr	44.4995	Jan	51.3992	Nov	62.7221
Aug	42.9374	May	45.8115	Feb	49.1671	Dec	61.7793
Sep	45.5635	June	46.5670	Mar	50.3213	2014	
Oct	48.6555	Jul	46.8373	Apr	51.8029	Jan	62.1708
Nov	48.9994	Aug	46.5679	May	54.4735	Feb	62.3136
Dec	48.6345	Sep	46.0616	June	56.0302	Mar	61.0021
2009		Oct	46.7211	Jul	55.4948	Apr	60.3813
Jan	48.8338	Nov	46.5673	Aug	48.3350	May	59.3255
Feb	49.2611	Dec	46.6288	Sep	54.3353	June	59.7143
Mar	51.2287	2011		Oct	52.8917	Jul	60.0263
Apr	50.0619	Jan	45.3934	Nov	54.6845	Aug	60.9923
May	48.5330	Feb	45.4358	Dec	54.6439		
June	47.7714	Mar	44.9914	2013			
Jul	48.4783	Apr	44.3700	Jan	54.3084		
Aug	48.3350	May	44.9045	Feb	53.7265		
Sep	48.4389	June	44.8536	Mar	54.5754		

Source RBI

Besides the organized sector's investment demand for the organized sector's output, the unorganized sector also requires the organized sector's output for investment purposes. We have made the unorganized sector's investment demand a decreasing function of interest rate and an increasing function of the aggregate infrastructure capital of the unorganized sector, denoted $\overline{K}$, for reasons we shall explain shortly.

Investment demand is, thus, inversely related to both r and e and is an increasing function of $\overline{K}$. In India, RBI seeks to keep r at a target level through its Liquidity Adjustment Facility and open market operations. We, therefore, regard it as a policy variable of the RBI and denote its exogenously given value by $\overline{r}$.

As standard, the net export of Y (denoted NX) depends positively on the real exchange rate $p \equiv \frac{P^{*}e}{P}$, (where P^{*} denotes the price of foreign goods), and foreign GDP (Y^{*}). It is also likely to depend negatively upon C, I and G, as they represent demand for both domestic and foreign goods. Thus, G, C and I enter as arguments in the net export function. Organized sector's workers' consumption demand for organized sector's output and its foreign substitutes is likely to be much less import intensive than capitalists' consumption demand. Hence, for simplicity and without any loss of generality, we only keep capitalists' consumption demand as an argument in the net export function. Similarly, unorganized sector's investment demand for Y, which we denote by I^A, is unlikely to be much import intensive. Following an increase in $\overline{K}$, which consists in rural electrification, setting up of flood control and irrigation facilities, investments in land reclamation and R&D that generates better seeds, production techniques, implements etc., producers in the unorganized sector will be induced to make complementary investments in facilities and implements such as new electric connection, pump sets, tube wells, better implements etc., as the increase in infrastructure capital relaxes crucial constraints operating on production. Import intensity of these investments is negligible and may, therefore, be ignored. For this reason, we have not incorporated I^A in the net export function. The organized sector also supplies the unorganized sector with intermediate inputs such as fertilizer, pesticide etc. Even though India has to meet a part of its fertilizer requirement with import, import intensity of the intermediate input demand of the unorganized sector is much less than those of I, G and capitalists' consumption. Hence, we have not explicitly considered intermediate input demand of the unorganized sector as a determinant of net export. This we have done for simplicity and without any loss of generality. Accordingly, Y is given by

$$
\begin{aligned}
Y = {} & C_{W_y}\cdot\left[w\frac{l_y}{L_0}Y(1-t_w)\right] + C_C\cdot\left[\left(Y - w\frac{l_y}{L_0}Y\right)(1-t)\right] \\
& + I\left(\underset{-}{\overline{r}}, \underset{-}{e}\right) + I^A\left(\underset{-}{\overline{r}}, \underset{+}{\overline{K}}\right) + G \\
& + \mathrm{NX}\left(\underset{+}{\frac{P^*e}{P}}, \underset{-}{C_C(1-t).\left(1 - w\frac{l_y}{L_0}\right)Y}, \underset{-}{I(\overline{r}, e)}, \underset{-}{G}, \underset{+}{\overset{*}{Y}}\right) + mA \qquad (1)
\end{aligned}
$$

In (1), w is the money wage rate of the organized sector workers which, as is standard in the Keynesian tradition or Keynes-Kalecki tradition, is assumed to be fixed in the short run. l_y is the unit labour requirement (measured in terms of labour hours) to produce a unit of Y and L_0 is the amount of labour time given by each worker in the given period. Hence, the number of workers needed to produce Y is given by $\frac{l_yY}{L_0}$. Total wage payment to labour is $w.\frac{l_yY}{L_0}$, which is also the real wage income of the organized sector workers, because the price of the organized sector output denoted by P is assumed to be equal to unity. In the structuralist tradition developed on the lines set by Keynes and Kalecki, the organized sector is assumed to be an oligopoly in consonance with reality. In such a scenario, prices display marked rigidity on account of oligopolistic interdependence among producers captured in a certain way in the kinked demand curve oligopoly model. In the Keynes-Kalecki (structuralist) tradition, producers set the prices on the basis of cost. We have, however, made prices rigid and independent of cost for analytical simplicity. Had we made P an increasing function of the cost of production, our results would have been stronger.

Workers pay taxes at the rate t_w on their income. $c_{W_Y}.\left[w\frac{l_y}{L_0}(1-t_w)\right]$ is the total consumption demand of the workers for the output of the organized sector and its foreign substitutes. (Since most of the workers are poor, we assume for simplicity and without any loss of generality that it represents demand for the output of only the domestic organized sector). After wage payments, the residue accrues to the producers as profit, as we have disregarded other factor payments for simplicity, i.e., we have assumed outstanding debt of the capitalists to the workers to be zero for simplicity. This does not matter, as the outstanding debt of the capitalists to the workers is fixed in the short period under consideration. So, the income of the producers is $\left[Y - w\frac{l_y Y}{L_0}\right]$ and if they pay tax at the rate t on their income, their disposable income is $\left[Y - w\frac{l_y Y}{L_0}\right](1-t)$. Therefore, their total consumption demand for Y is $C_c\left[Y - w\frac{l_y Y}{L_0}\right](1-t)$. We assume that quite a large part of it represents demand for foreign goods. Hence, we have made net export a decreasing function of capitalists' consumption demand. Signs of other partial derivatives of the NX function are quite self-evident.

Aggregate investment demand is decomposed into two components: $I(\overline{r}, e)$ and $I^A(\overline{r}, \overline{K})$, which give investment demands of the organized and the unorganized sectors respectively.

m denotes the fixed intermediate input requirement per unit of unorganized sector output. Therefore, total intermediate input requirement of Y of the unorganized sector is given by mA, where A is the total output of the unorganized sector.

The Unorganized Sector

The output of the unorganized sector is denoted by A. In what follows we shall seek to identify the factors that determine supply of and demand for A.

Supply of *A*

The unorganized sector is comprised of small rural and urban enterprises but the most dominant segment of this sector is agriculture. This sector absorbs most of the unskilled workers of the country. Its production function is fixed coefficient and the output of this sector is denoted by A which is produced with land, labour, capital and intermediate inputs bought from the organized sector. The stocks of land and capital used in the unorganized sector are given. In contrast with the tradition set by structuralist writers such as Rakshit (1982), Taylor (1983) et al., we have assumed the production function to be fixed coefficient even in agriculture. Those who are familiar with farming know that production techniques in agriculture recommend application of seed, fertilizer, pesticides etc. on a given piece of land in fixed optimum doses. Accordingly, the amount of labour needed to farm a piece of land in the optimum manner becomes fixed. The point is, deviation from the optimum recommended farming practices entails losses irrespective of prices. Applying labour in excess of the optimum to a given piece of land would yield insignificant result. This assumption helps us capture the fact that how much of the fixed amount of land and capital the producers in the unorganized sector can utilize depends crucially on the resources they have in their command to purchase intermediate inputs from the organized sector and labour.

Land usage can be increased with investments in agriculture which include investments in irrigation, electrification, flood control facilities, improvement in rural connectivity, land reclamation, agricultural research etc. This kind of investment is land augmenting as it enhances the usage of the same plot of land in a year and enables usage of more land for purposes of production. The infrastructure capital in the unorganized sector is denoted by K. The amount of land available to the unorganized sector is an increasing function of K. As K is given in the short run, we denote it by $\overline{K}$. As an increase in $\overline{K}$ makes possible greater number of cropping on the same plot of land or cultivation of new land leading to larger levels of production and income, it induces (and also makes it possible by relaxing the credit and thereby the resource constraint for) the unorganized sector's producers to undertake larger amount of complementary investment.

As most of the producers of the unorganized sector are financially weak and, therefore, subject to severe credit constraint, their purchasing power depends crucially on the relative price of their output in terms of the goods produced in the organized sector given by $\frac{P_A}{P}$, where P_A denotes price of the output of the unorganized sector. A ceteris paribus increase in $\frac{P_A}{P}$ enables the producers of the unorganized sector to purchase more intermediate inputs from the organized sector and labour and, thereby, allow them to bring more land under production in agriculture and, in general, to produce more. (This is possible in case of agriculture because of multiple cropping within a given period). Therefore, the supply of output of the unorganized sector is an increasing function of $\left(\frac{P_A}{P}\right)$.

Most of the production in the unorganized sector is carried out with the help of family labour and the unorganized sector workers also supplement their income by working outside their family firms in relatively larger firms that use both family labour and hired labour. There also exists large scale surplus labour in the unorganized sector. Hence, given everything else, if the government provides employment at the wage prevailing in the unorganized sector through employment guarantee schemes, it will augment unorganized sector's producers' income enabling them to buy more intermediate inputs from the organized sector and, thereby, bring more land under cultivation in agriculture and, in general, produce more. Let l_g be the total amount of employment generated in the unorganized sector through various government employment guarantee schemes. Hence, the supply function of the unorganized sector may be written as

$$A^S = A\left(\underset{+}{\frac{P_A}{P}}, \underset{+}{\overline{K}}, \underset{+}{l_g}\right) \tag{2}$$

A part of this supply of A is used for self consumption by the producers of A. Family enterprises keep the part of the produce that they consider absolutely necessary for survival for self consumption. However, for simplicity and without any loss of generality, we do not explicitly consider that part and assume the whole of the supply of A to be the marketable surplus of the unorganized sector.

Demand for *A*

The unorganized sector supplies principally the mass consumption goods, which belong to the category of necessities. So demand for A of a small number of rich organized sector producers and large landlords is likely to be fixed and, therefore, is ignored here for simplicity. The demand for A mainly comes from the organized sector workers and unorganized sector workers who do not have any family enterprises. For simplicity we assume that the latter spend all their income on A, while the former spend a fraction C_{wA} of their income on A.

Most of the output of A is produced in small firms using family labour and only a small fraction of output originates in the large firms. Let β be the fraction of total labour supplied by hired (landless or material means less) workers. Let l_A be the unit labour requirement for producing A. Therefore, the total labour required to produce A is $(l_A A)$. Now, since l_g denotes employment in the employment guarantee program in a given period, total employment in the unorganized sector is $(l_A A + l_g)$ and the total wage income is $w_A \cdot (l_A A + l_g)$ where w_A denotes the money wage rate in the A-sector. So, hired unorganized sector's workers' demand for A is $\frac{\beta w_A (l_A A + l_g)}{P_A}$. We assume w_A to be fixed. This assumption is standard in the Keynesian tradition. This also conforms to reality in the short run. On the other hand, total wage income of organized sector workers is $w\frac{l_y Y}{L_0}$ and their consumption demand for A is $C_{wA} \cdot w(1 - t_w)\frac{l_y Y}{L_0}$. So, the total demand for A is

$$A^D = \frac{C_{wA} \cdot w(1 - t_w)\frac{l_y}{L_0}Y}{P_A} + \frac{\beta w_A (l_A A) + \beta w_A l_g}{P_A} \tag{3}$$

The producers of the unorganized sector produce as much as they can with the resources they have at their disposal for purchasing intermediate inputs and labour and sell off their output at whatever prices they can do it. Producers do not have any control over either the aggregate output or the price. The price of A is, therefore, market clearing. The unorganized sector, accordingly, is in equilibrium when supply of A and demand for A become equal, i.e., when the following equation is satisfied:

$$\left(1 - \frac{\beta w_A l_A}{P_A}\right) A\left(\underset{+}{\frac{P_A}{P}}, \underset{+}{\overline{K}}, \underset{+}{l_g}\right) = \frac{C_{wA} \cdot w(1 - t_w)\frac{l_y}{L_0}Y}{P_A} + \frac{\beta w_A l_g}{P_A} \tag{4}$$

The LHS of (4) gives the net supply of A, which is defined as the supply of A net of the internal demand for A that production of A directly generates. Note that, for (4) to be satisfied for positive values of Y and l_g, $\frac{\beta w_A l_A}{P_A}$ has to be less than unity. We, therefore, assume this to be the case. If this were not the case, no producers would have produced A.

Following the structuralist tradition, we assume here that P_A clears the A-market. We have also ignored foreign trade in the output of the unorganized sector for simplicity.

The Foreign Exchange Market

The BOP consists of trade surplus and net inflow of foreign capital. The latter is assumed to be exogenously given for simplicity. The equilibrium in the foreign currency market is given by the following equation:

$$\mathrm{NX}\left(\underset{+}{\frac{P^*e}{P}},\ \underset{-}{C_c(1-t)\cdot\left(1-w\frac{l_y}{L_0}\right)Y},\ I(\underset{-}{\overline{r}}, e),\ \underset{-}{G},\ \underset{+}{\overset{*}{Y}}\right)+\overline{F}=0 \tag{5}$$

where NX, as we have already mentioned, stands for net export and $\overline{F}$ denotes the exogenously given net inflow of foreign capital.

The specification of our model is now complete. It consists of four Eqs. (1–5) in four endogenous variables Y, A, P_A and e. We solve them as follows:

Solving (5) for e, given the policy parameters and the exogenous variables, we get

$$e=e\left(\underset{+}{C_c(1-t)\cdot\left(1-w\frac{l_y}{L_0}\right)Y},\ \underset{-}{\overline{r}},\ \underset{+}{G},\ \underset{-}{Y^*},\ \underset{-}{\overline{F}}\right) \tag{6}$$

Signs of partial derivatives of (6) are quite self-evident from (5).

Substituting (2), (5) and (6) into (1), we get

$$\begin{aligned} Y={}& C_{Wy}\cdot\left[\left\{w\frac{l_y}{L_0}Y\right\}(1-t_w)\right]+C_C.\left[\left(Y-w\frac{l_y}{L_0}Y\right)(1-t)\right] \\ &+I\left(\overline{r}, e\left(\underset{+}{C_C(1-t).\left(1-w\frac{l_y}{L_0}\right)Y},\ \underset{-}{\overline{r}},\ \underset{+}{G},\ \underset{-}{Y^*},\ \underset{-}{\overline{F}}\right)\right) \\ &+I^A\left(\overline{r},\overline{K}\right)+G-\overline{F}+mA\left(\frac{P_A}{P}, l_g, \overline{K}\right) \end{aligned} \tag{7}$$

We can solve (4) and (7) for the equilibrium values of Y and P_A. The solution is shown in Fig. 1, where AA and YY represent (4) and (7) respectively. The solution corresponds to the point of intersection of these two schedules. In section A.1 in the appendix, we have derived the slopes of the YY and AA schedules and derived the stability condition. We have shown there that both YY and AA are upward sloping and the equilibrium is stable if YY is steeper than the AA schedule.

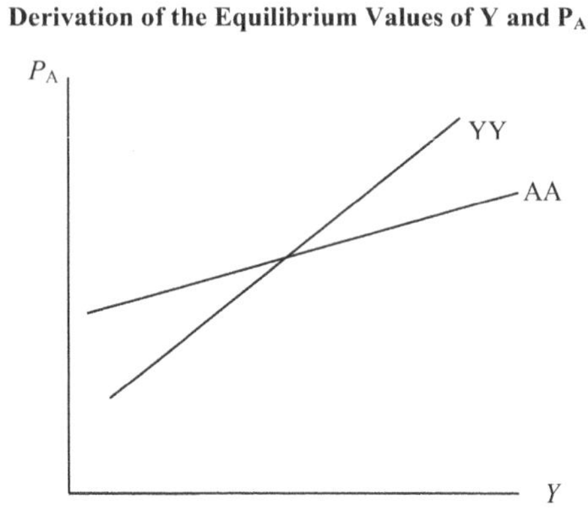

Fig. 1 Derivation of the equilibrium values of Y and P_A

For algebraic simplicity, we shall rewrite (4) and (7) as follows: The aggregate planned demand for Y as given by the R.H.S. of Eq. (7) in the text is denoted by $\overline{E}$. $\overline{E}$ is a function of P_A and Y, given the exogenous variables such as $\frac{wl_y}{L_0}$, $\overline{K}$, t, l_g and G, among others. Thus, we can rewrite Eq. (7) as

$$Y = \overline{E}\left(Y, \underset{+}{P_A}\right) \tag{8}$$

Equation (8) can be rewritten as

$$E = \overline{E}(Y, P_A) - Y = 0 \tag{9}$$

E denotes excess demand for Y.
We rewrite (9) as

$$E\left(Y, \underset{+}{P_A}\right) = 0;\ E\left(Y, \underset{+}{P_A}\right) \equiv \overline{E}\left(Y, \underset{+}{P_A}\right) - Y \tag{10}$$

Similarly, we can write (4) as

$$D \equiv A^D - A^S = D\left(\underset{-}{P_A}, \underset{+}{Y}\right) = 0 \tag{11}$$

We shall now examine how an exogenous increase in the stock of infrastructural capital in the unorganized sector affects the endogenous variables of the model.

3 The Effect of an Increase in $\overline{K}$

The organized sector employed only 6% of the workforce in 2004–2005 in India and it grew since then without generating any employment. The labour force, however, grew at the rate of almost 3% during 1999–2000–2004–2005 (see Tables 1, 4, and 5). There is no reason to suppose that these trends have changed much since then. Therefore, one can safely presume that almost all the workforce is employed in the unorganized sector. Since there is likely to be large scale surplus labour in the unorganized sector given the dominance of family enterprises and self-employed people, growth in the unorganized sector may be the most important way of generating gainful employment. We, therefore, examine here how an increase the stock of infrastructure capital in the unorganized sector is likely to affect the economy. We shall carry out this comparative static exercise using Fig. 2, where initial equilibrium (Y, P_A) corresponds to the point of intersection of YY and AA schedules representing (7) and (4) respectively. Following an increase in $\overline{K}$, as follows from (4), there emerges excess supply of A at any given (Y, P_A) on the initial AA schedule (since $\frac{\beta w_A l_A}{P_A}$ is less than unity). To restore equilibrium in the A sector at any given Y, P_A has to be lowered. Note that P_A need not be lowered to the level that restores output of the unorganized sector to its initial level, since a ceteris paribus fall in P_A also raises demand for A (see (4)). Thus, AA shifts downward. The new AA schedule is labeled AA_1 in Fig. 2. Let us now focus on YY. Corresponding to any given (Y, P_A) on the initial YY, there now emerges an excess demand for Y. This happens for two reasons. First, the increase in the supply of A raises the intermediate input demand for Y from the A-sector. Second, there takes place an increase in investment demand of the A sector (see (7)). The increase in investment demand is given by $I^A_{\overline{K}} d\overline{K}$.

Thus, at any given (Y, P_A) on the initial YY, there emerges an excess demand of $\left(mA_{\overline{K}} + I^A_{\overline{K}}\right)d\overline{K}$. Hence, to restore equilibrium in the Y-sector, at any given Y, P_A has to be lowered. If P_A is lowered to the level that restores supply of A to its initial level, excess demand for Y is not removed on account of the larger investment demand of the A sector (see (7)). Thus, to restore equilibrium in the Y-sector, P_A has to be lowered even below that level. Therefore, downward shift in the YY schedule will

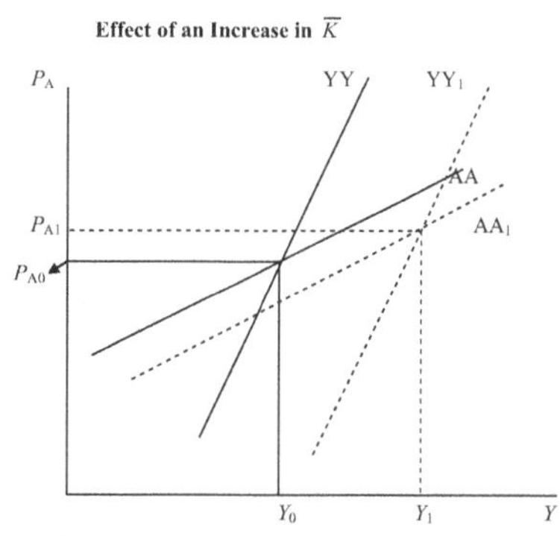

Fig. 2 Effect of an increase in $\overline{K}$

be larger than that of the AA schedule. The new YY schedule is labeled YY_1. Y will, therefore, be larger in the new equilibrium. Direction of change in P_A is, however, ambiguous. If P_A is higher or the same as before, A must be larger (see (2)). If P_A is less, A has to be greater to satisfy (4), since Y is larger. Hence, A must be larger in the new equilibrium. Accordingly, growth rates of both Y and A will go up. Employment in both the sectors will increase too.

The adjustment process may now be explained as follows. An increase in $\overline{K}$ consists in, for example, electrification of new areas, expansion of irrigation, flood control facilities, larger investment in R&D that yields better seeds, farming practices, better implements etc. Therefore, an increase in $\overline{K}$ induces the unorganized sector's producers to undertake complementary private investment, for example, in new electric connections, implements etc. Import intensities of these investments in India are practically nil. The increase in infrastructure capital enables the farmers and other producers, who are not resource constrained, to bring more land under production and, thereby, produce more A and demand more intermediate inputs from the organized sector. Thus, at the initial equilibrium Y, P_A and e, there emerges excess supply of A and excess demand for Y. P_A will fall to restore equilibrium in the A-sector. As P_A falls, supply of A falls, while demand for A rises (see (4). Hence, equilibrium in the A-sector will be restored at a higher level of A. Thus, even at this lower P_A, there will still exist excess demand for Y at the initial equilibrium Y. Hence, Y will expand raising demand for A. Thus, Y and P_A will go on rising until the new equilibrium is reached.

The above discussion yields the following proposition:

Proposition 1 *An increase in $\overline{K}$in the unorganized sector will bring about an increase in the growth rates of outputs of both the sectors and increase employment levels in both the sectors.*

We have proved this proposition mathematically in section A.2 in the appendix.

Since more than 95% of the work force is engaged in the unorganized sector, as follows from our above discussion, raising $\overline{K}$ is the most important way of generating employment.

4 Effect of an Increase in G to Raise $\overline{K}$ Financed by Taxation of Capitalists' Income

We shall examine here how an increase in G, which consists in investing in $\overline{K}$, financed by taxing the capitalists is likely to affect the economy. We shall study the effect of this using Fig. 2, where the initial equilibrium values of Y and P_A denoted by Y_0 and P_{A0} respectively correspond to the point of intersection of YY and AA schedules. Here, government expenditure rises by dG financed by taxing capitalists' income. Hence, $dG = d\left[t \cdot \left(1 - \frac{wl_y}{L_0}\right)Y\right]$ (see (7)). Let us now examine how YY and AA are affected by these changes. Focus on YY first. Corresponding to any (Y, P_A) on YY, as follows from (7), aggregate demand for Y changes by

$$Z = [(1 - C_c) \cdot \mathrm{d}G + I_e e_G \mathrm{d}G] \tag{12}$$

Let us now derive the value of $de = e_G dG$ from (5). Taking total differential of (5) treating Y and all exogenous variables other than G as fixed, setting $\mathrm{d}G = d\left[t.\left(1 - \frac{wl_y}{L_0}\right)Y\right]$, and, then, solving for de, we get

$$\mathrm{d}e = e_G \mathrm{d}G = \frac{-(-\mathrm{NX}_{CC} C_c - (-\mathrm{NX}_G))\mathrm{d}G}{\mathrm{NX}_p \frac{\partial p}{\partial e} + (-\mathrm{NX}_I)(-I_e)} \tag{13}$$

In the expression on the RHS of the above equation, $\mathrm{NX}_{\mathrm{CC}}$ denotes the partial derivative of NX with respect to capitalists' consumption. From the above it follows that $\mathrm{d}e < 0$, if $-\mathrm{NX}_{\mathrm{CC}} C_c > -\mathrm{NX}_G$. This means that e will fall if import intensity of capitalists' consumption is larger than that of government expenditure on $\overline{K}$, a condition which is quite likely to be satisfied. The reasons may be explained as follows. As we have already explained earlier, capitalists constitute a miniscule section of Indians, but they have in their command most of India's GDP. Hence, their consumption consists of the finest consumption items available globally from items of food and clothing to luxury cars, yachts, jets and islands. Since, India does not have any independent knowledge or technological base, almost all these consumption items are secured from abroad. Therefore, $-\mathrm{NX}_{\mathrm{CC}}$ is likely to be quite large. Government's investment in flood control, irrigation, electrification, road building, R&D etc., are carried out with domestic materials in the main. Only the high-tech capital goods and components are imported. Moreover, government can design its investments in such a way that their import intensity is minimized. Hence, $(-\mathrm{NX}_G)$ is unlikely to be very large. Thus, the value of de given by (13) is likely to be negative. Hence, the increase in aggregate demand for Y given by, as follows from (12), $[(1 - C_c) \cdot \mathrm{d}G + I_e e_G \mathrm{d}G]$ that takes place at any given (Y, P_A) on the initial YY is likely to be positive.

Thus, corresponding to any given (Y, P_A) on the initial YY schedule, there emerges excess demand for Y, if import intensity of capitalists' consumption is higher than that of government's expenditure on $\overline{K}$. Under these conditions, corresponding to any P_A, the Y-sector will be in equilibrium at a larger Y. Accordingly, YY shifts to the right. The AA schedule, as follows from (4), remains unaffected. Both Y and P_{A} will, therefore, go up in the new equilibrium under the condition specified above. A will go up too with the increase in P_A.

We shall now prove this result mathematically. Taking total differential of (10) and (11) treating all exogenous variables other than G as fixed and setting $\mathrm{d}G = d\left[t\left(1 - w\frac{l_y}{L_0}\right)Y\right]$, we get

$$E_Y \mathrm{d}Y + E_{P_A} \mathrm{d}P_A = -\varepsilon_5 \equiv -E_{\overline{G}} \mathrm{d}\overline{G} \tag{14}$$

$$D_Y \mathrm{d}Y + D_{P_A} \mathrm{d}P_A \equiv -\varepsilon_6 = -D_{\overline{G}} \mathrm{d}\overline{G} \tag{15}$$

$$\varepsilon_5 = (1 - C_c)\mathrm{d}\overline{G} + I_e e_G \mathrm{d}\overline{G} > 0 \; if \; -(\mathrm{NX_{cc}})C_c > -(\mathrm{NX}_G) \tag{16}$$

$$\varepsilon_6 = 0 \text{ (see (11) and (4))} \tag{17}$$

Solving (38) and (39), we get

$$\mathrm{d}Y = \frac{\begin{vmatrix} \underset{-}{-\varepsilon_5} & \underset{+}{E_{P_A}} \\ 0 & \underset{-}{D_{P_A}} \end{vmatrix}}{\Delta} > 0 \text{ (since } \Delta > 0) \tag{18}$$

$$\mathrm{d}P_A = \frac{\begin{vmatrix} \underset{-}{E_Y} & \underset{-}{-\varepsilon_5} \\ \underset{+}{D_Y} & 0 \end{vmatrix}}{\Delta} > 0 \tag{19}$$

$$\mathrm{d}A = A_{P_A}\mathrm{d}P_A > 0 \text{ (see (2))} \tag{20}$$

The adjustment mechanism may be briefly stated as follows. Following an increase in G by $\mathrm{d}G$ financed by taxation of capitalists' income, aggregate demand for Y at the initial equilibrium $(Y,\ P_A,\ e)$ will go up by $(1 - C_c)\mathrm{d}G$. However, the increase in G will be partly spent on imported goods lowering NX by $NX_G\mathrm{d}G$. On the other hand, the decline in capitalists' consumption will also reduce their demand for imported consumption goods raising net export by $-\mathrm{NX}_{cc}C_c \cdot \mathrm{d}G$. We have already argued that in Indian conditions, net export in the net is likely to rise lowering e. The fall in e will raise investment demand. Thus, at the initial equilibrium (Y, P_A), there emerges an excess demand for Y inducing the producers of Y to raise Y. The increase in Y will create an excess demand for A leading to a rise in both P_A and A. This is how Y, P_A and A will go on rising until the new equilibrium is reached.

This yields the following proposition:

Proposition 2 *If the government raises G and finances it by taxing capitalists' income, growth rates of both the sectors will go up if import intensity of capitalists' consumption(*$-NX_{cc}C_c$*) is larger than that of the government expenditure on* $\overline{K}$*, a condition which is highly likely to be satisfied in India. Employment in both the sectors will increase too.*

5 Effect of an Increase in G to Raise $\overline{K}$ Financed by Indirect Taxation of Sales of Y

Here, we consider the case where the increase in G to raise $\overline{K}$ is financed by indirect taxation. Usually, the government does not raise income tax rates to finance its additional expenditures for reasons that we shall explain later. Its favourite source of finance is indirect taxes and recently Government of India has undertaken an ambitious programme of reform of indirect taxation, which it refers to as Goods and Services Tax (GST). Under GST, efforts have been made to increase the coverage of indirect taxation over goods and services produced and producers and sellers of goods and services to the maximum possible extent. The objective is to raise as much revenue as possible from indirect taxation even though it is highly regressive and unjust. We assume that sales of Y are taxed at the rate τ so that from every unit of Y sold, capitalists pay to the government $P\tau$ as tax, where P is the price of Y set by the producers. Thus, buyers of Y face the price $P(1+\tau)$ and the government receives $P\tau Y$ as indirect tax revenue. Denoting the real value of government's indirect tax revenue by T, we have

$$T = \frac{P\tau Y}{P(1+\tau)} = \frac{\tau}{(1+\tau)}Y \equiv vY \quad v \equiv \frac{\tau}{(1+\tau)} \tag{21}$$

Workers' and capitalists' real incomes in this case are given by $\frac{wl_y}{L_0 P}(1-v)Y$ and $\frac{PY}{P(1+\tau)} - \frac{wl_y}{L_0 P}(1-v)Y = \left(1 - \frac{wl_y}{L_0 P}\right)(1-v)Y$. Incorporating these in (7) and setting $P = 1$ and $\mathrm{d}t = \mathrm{d}t_w = 0$ for simplicity, we rewrite it as follows:

$$\begin{aligned} Y = {} & C_{Wy} \cdot \left[\left\{w\frac{l_y}{L_0}Y\right\}(1-v)\right] + C_c \cdot \left[\left(Y - w\frac{l_y}{L_0}Y\right)(1-v)\right] \\ & + I(\overline{r}, e) + I^A\left(\overline{r}, \overline{K}\right) + G - \overline{F} \\ & + mA\left(\frac{P_A}{P}(1-v), l_g, \overline{K}\right) \equiv C \cdot (1-v)Y + I(\overline{r}, e) \\ & + I^A\left(\overline{r}, \overline{K}\right) + G - \overline{F} + mA\left(\frac{P_A}{P}(1-v), l_g, \overline{K}\right) \end{aligned} \tag{22}$$

where $C \equiv C_{Wy}.w\frac{l_y}{L_0} + C_c \cdot \left(1 - w\frac{l_y}{L_0}\right)$

Incorporating the indirect tax, we rewrite (4) and (5) as (23) and (24) respectively

$$\left(1 - \frac{\beta w_A l_A}{P_A}\right)A\left(\underset{+}{\frac{P_A}{P}(1-v)}, \underset{+}{\overline{K}}, \underset{+}{l_g}\right) = \frac{C_{wA}.w\frac{l_y}{L_0}Y}{P_A} + \frac{\beta w_A l_g}{P_A};$$

$$p_{A'} \equiv \frac{P_A}{P}(1-v), p_A \equiv \frac{P_A}{P} \tag{23}$$

And

$$\mathrm{NX}\left(\underset{+}{\frac{P^{*}e}{P}(1-v)}, \underset{-}{C_c(1-v)\cdot\left(1-w\frac{l_y}{L_0}\right)Y}, \underset{-}{I(\overline{r}, e, \overline{K})}, \underset{-}{G}, \underset{+}{\overset{*}{Y}}\right)+\overline{F}=0 \tag{24}$$

In the present case, the government raises G to raise $\overline{K}$ and finances it with indirect tax revenue. Therefore, in this case, we set

$$\mathrm{d}G = d(vY) \tag{25}$$

From (25), we get

$$\mathrm{d}v = \frac{\mathrm{d}G}{Y} - \frac{v}{Y}\mathrm{d}Y \tag{26}$$

To derive the impact of this policy on Y, we take total differential of (22) treating all exogenous variables other than $\mathrm{d}G$ as fixed, set $\mathrm{d}G = d(vY)$, use (26) and, then, solve for $\mathrm{d}Y$. This gives

$$\begin{aligned}\mathrm{d}Y &= C\cdot\mathrm{d}Y - C\cdot\mathrm{d}(vY) + I_e\mathrm{d}e + \mathrm{d}G + m\mathrm{d}A\\ &= C\cdot\mathrm{d}Y + (1-C)\cdot\mathrm{d}G + I_e\mathrm{d} + mvA\end{aligned} \tag{27}$$

To derive the value of de, we take total differential of (24) treat all exogenous variables other than G and v as fixed, use (25) and (26) and, then solve for de. This gives

$$\mathrm{d}e = \frac{B_g\mathrm{d}G + B_y\mathrm{d}Y}{B_e} \equiv b_g\mathrm{d}G + b_y\mathrm{d}Y \tag{28}$$

where

$$B_g \equiv \left[\left(\mathrm{NX}_{p/p}\frac{1}{Y} + (-\mathrm{NX}_G)\right) - \left((-\mathrm{NX}_{\mathrm{CC}})C_c\left(1 - w\frac{l_y}{L_0}\right)\right)\right] > 0 \tag{28i}$$

B_g gives the increase in BOP deficit due to a ceteris paribus unit increase in G. A part of it represents an increase in demand for imported goods. It also raises indirect tax rate pushing up domestic price level. As close substitutes of Indian goods are available almost in all countries, there is likely to take place substantial fall in net export and, therefore, large increase in BOP deficit. These two effects are captured by the first term of the expression on the RHS of (28i). A part of the unit increase in indirect tax revenue comes from the capitalists, whose consumption demand for imported goods falls lowering BOP deficit. The second term captures this. However, in the net, BOP deficit is likely to rise in Indian conditions and it is sensible to assume B_g to be positive.

$$B_y \equiv \left[(1-v)(-\mathrm{NX}_{\mathrm{CC}})C_c\left(1-w\frac{l_y}{L_0}\right)-\mathrm{NX}_{p'}p\frac{v}{Y}\right]<0 \tag{28ii}$$

B_y measures the increase in BOP deficit due to a ceteris paribus unit increase in Y. A part of it accrues to capitalists whose consumption demand for imports rises as a result. This is captured by the first term of the expression on the RHS of (28ii). The unit increase in Y also enables the government to reduce indirect tax rate, which lowers domestic price giving a boost to net export. This is given by the second term. The second term is likely to dominate for reasons we have already explained. Hence, B_y is likely to be negative.

$$B_e \equiv \mathrm{NX}_{p'}\frac{\partial(p(1-v))}{\partial e}+(-\mathrm{NX}_I)(-I_e)>0 \tag{28iii}$$

B_e measures the absolute value of the fall in BOP deficit that a ceteris paribus unit increase in e brings about. First, it raises real exchange rate and, thereby, raises net export. This is given by the first term on the RHS of (28iii). However, this term is likely to be small in India, since an increase in exchange rate also raises price level in India. Hence, its effect on real exchange rate is likely to be small. We have, however, not captured this in our model for simplicity. An increase in exchange rate also reduces investment in India and, thereby, lowers investment demand for imported goods. This is given by the second term. Thus, B_e is positive. Therefore,

$$b_g \equiv \frac{B_g}{B_e}>0 \text{ and } b_y \equiv \frac{B_y}{B_e}<0 \tag{28iv}$$

We shall now derive the value of dA. For that, we first take total differential of (23) treating all exogenous variables other than v as fixed, use (26) and, then, solve for dP_A. This yields

$$\mathrm{d}P_A=\frac{\overline{D}_g}{S_{P_A}}\mathrm{d}G+\frac{\overline{D}_y}{S_{P_A}}\mathrm{d}Y \tag{29}$$

where

$$S_{P_A}=\left(1-\frac{\beta w_A l_A}{P_A}\right)A_{P_A'}(1-v)\frac{1}{P}+\frac{C_{wA}w\frac{l_y}{L_0}Y+\beta w_A l_g+\beta w_A l_A A}{P_A^2}>0 \tag{29i}$$

S_{P_A} measures the absolute value of the fall in excess demand for A that a ceteris paribus unit increase in P_A brings about. The first term of the expression on the RHS of (29i) gives the increase in the supply of A that a unit increase in P_A leads to. The second term gives the absolute value of the fall in demand for A that a unit increase in P_A causes.

$$\overline{D}_g = \left(1 - \frac{\beta w_A l_A}{P_A}\right) A_{p_A'} p_A \frac{1}{Y} > 0 \qquad (29\text{ii})$$

$\overline{D}_g$ measures the increase in excess demand for A that a ceteris paribus unit increase in G brings about. A unit increase in G financed by additional indirect tax revenue, raises indirect tax rate pushing up the price of Y. This lowers net supply of A given by the expression on the RHS of (29ii) and, hence, excess demand for A goes up by the same amount.

$$\overline{D}_Y = C_{wA} \frac{w \frac{l_y}{L_0}}{P_A} - \left(1 - \frac{\beta w_A l_A}{P_A}\right) A_{p_A'} p_A \frac{v}{Y} > 0 \qquad (29\text{iii})$$

$\overline{D}_Y$ measures the increase in excess demand for A that a ceteris paribus unit increase in Y brings about. The first term of the expression on the RHS of (29iii) gives the increase in demand for A that it causes. The unit increase in Y also lowers indirect tax rate and thereby gives a boost to net supply of A given by the second term. We consider it sensible to assume the first term to dominate. Hence, we assume $\overline{D}_Y$ to be positive.

Now, using (23), we get

$$\mathrm{d}A = A_{p_A'} \mathrm{d}(p_A(1-v)) = A_{p_A'}((1-v)\mathrm{d}P_A - P_A \mathrm{d}v) \quad \because P = 1 \qquad (30)$$

Substituting (26) and (29) into (30) and rearranging terms, we write (30) as

$$\begin{aligned} \mathrm{d}A = {} & A_{P_{A'}} \left((1-v) \frac{\overline{D}_g}{S_{P_A}} - P_A \frac{1}{Y} \right) \mathrm{d}G \\ & + A_{P_{A'}} \left((1-v) \frac{\overline{D}_Y}{S_{P_A}} + P_A \frac{v}{Y} \right) \mathrm{d}Y \equiv A_g \mathrm{d}G + A_Y \mathrm{d}Y \quad A_g < 0, A_Y > 0 \qquad (31) \end{aligned}$$

Let us first focus on the first term on the RHS of (31). We shall argue that it is negative. Following an increase in G by dG, with Y remaining unchanged, v rises by $\frac{\mathrm{d}G}{Y}$ lowering $P_{A'}$ by $P_A \frac{\mathrm{d}G}{Y}$ at the initial equilibrium P_A. This creates an excess demand for A of $\overline{D}_g \mathrm{d}G$ at the initial equilibrium P_A. Hence, P_A rises by $\frac{\overline{D}_g}{S_{P_A}} \mathrm{d}G$ to remove the excess demand. The increase in P_A removes the excess demand for A not only by raising supply of A but also by lowering demand for A. Hence in the new equilibrium, A is less. Therefore, the first term in (31) is negative, i.e., $A_g < 0$. From (29i) and (29ii), we find that $(1-v)\frac{\overline{D}_g}{S_{P_A}} < (1-v)\frac{\left(1 - \frac{\beta W_A l_A}{P_A}\right) A_{P_{A'}} \frac{P_A}{Y}}{\left(1 - \frac{\beta W_A l_A}{P_A}\right)(1-v) A_{P_{A'}} \frac{1}{P}} = \frac{P_A}{Y}$.

Let us now focus on the second term. Following an increase in Y by $\mathrm{d}Y$, v falls by $\frac{v}{Y}\mathrm{d}Y$ raising p_A' by $P_A \frac{v}{Y} \mathrm{d}Y$ at the initial equilibrium P_A. This raises supply of A at the initial equilibrium P_A. The increase in Y also raises demand for A. Thus, there emerges an excess demand for A of $\overline{D}_Y dY$ at the initial equilibrium P_A. Accordingly,

P_A rises by $\frac{\overline{D}_Y dY}{S_{P_A}}$. As P_A and, therefore, $p_{A'}$ rises, supply of A increases further. Hence, $A_Y > 0$. One can also check from (29i) and (29iii) that $\overline{D}_Y$ and S_{P_A} are positive. Hence $A_Y > 0$.

Substituting (28) and (31) into (27) and, then, solving for dY, we get

$$\mathrm{d}Y = -\frac{\left[(-I_e)b_g + m\left(-A_g\right) - (1 - C)\right]\mathrm{d}G}{1 - [C + I_e b_Y + mA_Y]} < 0 \tag{32}$$

Let us now explain the expression on the RHS of (32). The numerator measures the excess supply of Y that is created at the initial equilibrium Y following the increase in G by dG financed by additional indirect tax revenue, when e and P_A adjust to keep the BOP and the market for A in equilibrium. Even though G increases by dG, the additional indirect tax revenue of dG comes from the workers and capitalists reducing their consumption demand by $C \cdot \mathrm{d}G$. Thus, in the net, demand for Y goes up by $(1 - C)\mathrm{d}G$. The hike in the indirect tax rate that has to be made to raise indirect tax revenue by dG at the initial equilibrium Y raises domestic price of Y substantially reducing net export and this is likely to be much larger than the decline in capitalists' consumption demand for imported goods. Moreover, a part of the additional government expenditure may be on imported goods. Therefore, e rises by $b_g\mathrm{d}G$ lowering investment demand by $(-I_e)b_g\mathrm{d}G$. The hike in the indirect tax rate and the consequent increase in the price of Y lowers A by $\left(-A_g\right)$ reducing demand for $Y$by $m\left(-A_g\right)$. Thus, in the net, aggregate demand for Y at the initial equilibrium Y falls by $\left[(-I_e)b_g + m\left(-A_g\right) - (1 - C)\right]\mathrm{d}G$, which, is highly likely to be positive in India. Let us explain. First, note that C, which denotes the marginal propensity to consume out of Y is likely to be quite high. We have already explained why $(-I_e)$ and b_g are likely to be quite large in India. Production of A is also highly Y-intensive. Hence, both m and $\left(-A_g\right)$ are likely to be quite large. For these reasons, $\left[(-I_e)b_g + m\left(-A_g\right) - (1 - C)\right]\mathrm{d}G$ is highly likely to be positive. There, thus, emerges an excess supply at the initial equilibrium Y and Y has to fall to remove this excess supply.

The denominator measures the decline in the excess supply of Y per unit fall in Y, when e and P_A adjust along with the decline in Y to keep the foreign currency market and A-market in equilibrium. The denominator is positive for reasons of stability (see (50, 52) and the discussion below it in the appendix). Per unit decrease in Y, excess supply falls by unity. However, the unit decline in Y also lowers demand in various ways. First, it directly reduces consumption demand of the workers and capitalists by C. The unit decrease in Y forces the government to raise the indirect tax rate, which, in turn, raises the price of Y. It, as we have already explained, is likely to create a BOP deficit even though the fall in consumption expenditure partly represents reduced consumption expenditure on imported goods also. Thus, e will rise by b_Y lowering $Ib_y\, I_e b_Y$. Again, the unit decrease in Y lowers demand for A at the initial equilibrium P_A and the rise in the price of Y reduces supply of A at the initial equilibrium P_A. For both these reasons, P_A will adjust to equilibrate the A market lowering A and demand for Y by A_Y and mA_Y respectively. Therefore, in the net, per unit decline in Y excess supply of Y falls by the denominator.

Substituting (32) into (31), we get

$$dA = A_g dG + A_Y \left\{ -\frac{\left[(-I_e)b_g + m(-A_g) - (1 - C)\right]dG}{1 - [C + I_e b_Y + mA_Y]} \right\} < 0 \qquad (33)$$

Thus, both Y and A are quite likely to decline if the government raises G and finances it by raising indirect tax collection.

The adjustment process may be explained as follows. Government raises G and finances it by raising indirect tax collection. As a result, demand for Y, given everything else, rises by $(1 - C)dG$. This will have its repercussions in the foreign currency market. A part of the additional government spending may be made on imported goods, while capitalists' demand for imported goods will fall. However, the major impact will come from the hike in the indirect tax rate and the increase in the price of Y that it brings about. As close substitutes of Indian products are available everywhere, this price rise will substantially reduce net export and in the net produce a large BOP deficit sending the exchange rate soaring. It will equilibrate the foreign currency market, as we have already explained mainly by reducing investment demand, which is highly import intensive. The rise in the price of Y will also reduce supply of A and create an excess demand in the A-market at the initial equilibrium P_A. P_A will rise to equilibrate the A-market. However, a rise in P_A not only raises supply of A but also lowers demand for A. Hence, in the new equilibrium A will be less. This will also lower demand for Y coming from the A sector. Thus, in the net, demand for Y is likely to fall creating an excess supply of Y at the initial equilibrium Y. Y will therefore fall to equilibrate the Y-sector. However, the fall in Y will reduce government's indirect tax collection inducing it to hike indirect tax rate further. This will again, through the process described above, will lower I and A and bring about a further contraction in Y. This process of contraction in Y and A will continue until the new equilibrium is reached. Our above discussion yields the following proposition:

Proposition 3*If the government raises G and finances it with indirect tax revenue, it is highly likely to reduce output and employment levels in both the organized and the unorganized sectors.*

6 Conclusion

There has taken place almost complete jobless growth in the organized sector in India in the post-reform period, even though its real value added has grown phenomenally. Given the Government of India's policy of non-interference with the technology choice of the entrepreneurs of the organized sector, one has to turn to the unorganized sector for employment generation. This paper shows that, an exogenous increase in infrastructure capital in the unorganized sector will raise output and employment

Table 7 Share of wage in the net value added of the organized manufacturing sector

Year	Wage/NVA	E/NVA
1990–1991	25.60837619	39.962135
1991–1992	24.77360615	38.24844028
1992–1993	23.62322467	38.68204933
1993–1994	19.89892122	32.3853645
1994–1995	20.29125577	32.5677205
1995–1996	20.06521796	32.36510722
1996–1997	16.87517837	29.48901451
1997–1998	17.89320363	31.46523061
1998–1999	17.06744177	30.67889995
1999–2000	16.97329792	30.8718755
2000–2001	19.26644502	35.3141847
2001–2002	19.01443998	35.38379755
2002–2003	17.22701817	32.00533666
2003–2004	15.01709971	28.74386123
2004–2005	12.94119363	24.78039248
2005–2006	12.07694285	23.73090671
2006–2007	11.19244953	22.42742604
2007–2008	10.59613904	21.89461019
2008–2009	11.32545249	24.52627358
2009–2010	11.64315067	24.82748124
2010–2011	12.1556146	26.01504869
2011–2012 (R)	13.08202487	28.13385202
2012–2013	13.01676982	27.94267692

Source Annual survey of industries, ministry of statistics and programme implementation
Where W = Wages to workers
E = Total emoluments, and NVA = Net value

levels in both the sectors. We have shown in this paper that, if the government invests in infrastructure in the unorganized sector and finances it by taxing the capitalists' income, employment will go up and there will take place expansion in both the sectors. However, if the government, as it normally does, finances the increase in its investment in the unorganized sector by raising indirect tax rates, it is highly likely to lower employment and output levels in both the sectors (Tables 7 and 8).

Table 8 Current account deficit in India

Year	Current a/c deficit as percentage of GDP
1990–1991	−1.9998
1991–1992	−0.62084
1992–1993	−1.37644
1993–1994	−0.40951
1994–1995	−0.76373
1995–1996	−1.45941
1996–1997	−1.54423
1997–1998	−1.66313
1998–1999	−2.31185
1999–2000	−2.99618
2000–2001	−1.36458
2001–2002	−1.66333
2002–2003	−1.79484
2003–2004	−2.50363
2004–2005	−4.23108
2005–2006	−6.01654
2006–2007	−6.79758
2007–2008	−7.77917
2008–2009	−10.0627
2009–2010	−8.48273
2010–2011	−7.45697
2011–2012	−10.4807
2012–2013	−11.245
2013–2014	−7.82023
2014–2015	−7.32151
2015–2016	−6.21191
2016–2017	−5.21381

Source RBI, Directorate General of Commercial Intelligence and Statistics

Appendix

Stability of Equilibrium

The aggregate planned demand for Y as given by the R.H.S. of Eq. (7) in the text is denoted by $\overline{E}$. $\overline{E}$ is a function of P_A and Y, given the exogenous variables such as $\frac{wl_y}{L_0}$, $\overline{K}$, t, l_g and G, among others. Thus, we can rewrite Eq. (7) as.

$$Y = \overline{E}\Big(Y, \underset{+}{P_A}\Big) \tag{34}$$

Equation (34) can be rewritten as.

$$E = \overline{E}(Y, P_A) - Y = 0 \tag{35}$$

E denotes excess demand for Y.

We rewrite (35) as

$$E\Big(Y, \underset{+}{P_A}\Big) = 0E\Big(Y, \underset{+}{P_A}\Big) \equiv \overline{E}\Big(Y, \underset{+}{P_A}\Big) - Y \tag{36}$$

Let us now explain the signs of the partial derivatives of $E(\bullet)$.

From (7), we get

$$\begin{aligned} E_Y = {} & C_{wy} \cdot (1 - t_w)\frac{wl_y}{L_0} + C_c \cdot (1 - t)\left(1 - \frac{wl_y}{L_0}\right) \\ & - (-I_e)e_Y - 1 < 0 \;\; 0 < \frac{wl_y}{L_0} < 1, \;\; e_Y > 0 \end{aligned} \tag{37i}$$

Let us explain the sign of E_Y. Note that $\frac{wl_y}{L_0}$ is the share of wage income in Y. Hence, it is positive but less than 1. Let us now derive the value of e_Y. Taking total differential of (5) in the text treating all exogenous variables as fixed and solving for $\frac{de}{dY}$, we get

$$\frac{de}{dY}(\equiv e_Y) = \frac{(-\mathrm{NX}_{cc})C_c(1 - t)\left(1 - w\frac{l_y}{L_0}\right)}{\mathrm{NX}_p \frac{\partial\left(\frac{P^* e}{P}\right)}{\partial e} + (-\mathrm{NX}_I)(-I_e)} > 0 \tag{37ii}$$

Let us explain the expression on the RHS of (37ii). NX_{cc} measures the change in net export per unit increase in capitalists' consumption. It is negative as a part (if not the whole) of the unit increase in capitalists' consumption represents additional demand for imported goods. Thus, the numerator gives the fall in net export that a unit increase in Y leads to as it raises capitalists' income. BOP, therefore, goes into deficit. To remove it, e has to rise so that net export is restored to its initial equilibrium value. The denominator gives the increase in net export due to a ceteris paribus unit increase in e. A unit increase in e raises net export in two ways. First, it raises net export by raising the real exchange rate given by the first term in the denominator. However, this term is likely to be small in India. Since production in India is highly import intensive, an increase in e raises P substantially. Hence, the effect of an increase in e on the real exchange rate is likely to be insignificant. (For simplicity, we have not made P an increasing function of e in our model). However, as we have already argued, in India investment is likely to be highly sensitive to exchange rate and an increase in e raises net export mainly by lowering I quite a large part of which represents demand for imported goods. This explains the sign of e_Y. It is, therefore, clear that E_Y is negative.

$$E_{P_A} = mA_{p_A} > 0 p_A \equiv \frac{P_A}{P} \quad (P \text{ is fixed and equal to unity by assumption}) \tag{37iii}$$

Similarly, we can write (4) in the text as

$$D \equiv A^D - A^S = D\Big(\underset{-}{P_A}, \underset{+}{Y}\Big) = 0 \tag{38}$$

Let us explain the signs of the partial derivatives of (38). From (4), we get

$$D_Y = C_{wA} \cdot (1 - t_w)\frac{wl_y}{L_0}\frac{1}{P_A} > 0 \tag{38i}$$

and

$$\begin{aligned} D_{P_A} = &-\left(C_{wA} \cdot (1 - t_w)\frac{wl_y}{L_0}Y + \beta w_A l_g\right)\left(\frac{1}{P_A^2}\right) \\ &-\left[\left(1 - \frac{1}{P_A}\beta w_A l_A\right)A_{p_A} + A\beta w_A(l_A)\frac{1}{P_A^2}\right] < 0 \end{aligned} \tag{38ii}$$

The first term on the RHS gives the fall in demand for A per unit rise in P_A, while the second term gives the rise in the supply of A. Both lead to a fall in the excess demand for A.

The solution of (4) and (7) or that of (37) and (38) is shown diagrammatically in the text in Fig. 1, where YY and AA schedules represent (37) (or (7)) and (38) (or (4)) respectively. The equilibrium values of Y and P_A correspond to the point of intersection of the two schedules. Their slopes in the (Y, P_A) plane are given by

$$\left(\frac{\mathrm{d}P_A}{\mathrm{d}Y}\right)_{YY} = \frac{E_{P_A}}{-E_Y} > 0 \tag{38iii}$$

And

$$\left(\frac{\mathrm{d}P_A}{\mathrm{d}Y}\right)_{AA} = \frac{-D_{P_A}}{D_Y} > 0 \tag{38iv}$$

The adjustment mechanisms of Y and P_A may be written as follows:

$$\frac{\mathrm{d}Y}{\mathrm{d}t} = \alpha \cdot E(Y, P_A) \quad \alpha > 0 \tag{39}$$

$$\frac{dP_A}{dt} = \beta \cdot D(Y, P_A) \quad \beta > 0 \tag{40}$$

Linearising $E(\bullet)$ and $D(\bullet)$ using Taylor's series in the neighborhood of the equilibrium values of Y and P_A denoted by Y_0 and P_{A0} respectively, we rewrite Eqs. (39) and (40) as follows:

$$\frac{dY}{dt} = \alpha \cdot E_Y \cdot (Y - Y_0) + \alpha . E_{P_A} . (P_A - P_{A0}) \tag{41}$$

$$\frac{dP_A}{dt} = \beta \cdot D_Y \cdot (Y - Y_0) + \beta \cdot D_{P_A} \cdot (P_A - P_{A0}) \tag{42}$$

We can write (41) and (42) as

$$\begin{bmatrix} \frac{d(Y-Y_0)}{dt} \\ \frac{d(P_A-P_{A0})}{dt} \end{bmatrix} = \begin{bmatrix} \alpha \\ \beta \end{bmatrix} \begin{bmatrix} \underset{-}{E_Y} & \underset{+}{E_{P_A}} \\ \underset{+}{D_Y} & \underset{-}{D_{P_A}} \end{bmatrix} \begin{bmatrix} (Y - Y_0) \\ P_A - P_{A0} \end{bmatrix} \tag{43}$$

From (43) it follows that the equilibrium is stable if

$$E_Y + D_{P_A} < 0 \tag{44}$$

And

$$\begin{vmatrix} \underset{-}{E_Y} & \underset{+}{E_{P_A}} \\ \underset{+}{D_Y} & \underset{-}{D_{P_A}} \end{vmatrix} (\equiv \Delta) > 0 \tag{45}$$

From (37i) and (38ii) it follows that (44) is satisfied.
(45) is satisfied if

$$\frac{-E_Y}{E_{P_A}} > \frac{D_Y}{-D_{P_A}} \tag{46}$$

The LHS and RHS of (46) represent the slopes of YY and AA respectively (see (38iii) and (38iv). Thus, for the equilibrium to be stable, the slope of YY has to be greater than that of AA.

We also give another interpretation of (46). (46) implies

$$E_Y + E_{P_A} \frac{D_Y}{-D_{P_A}} < 0 \tag{47}$$

The first term of the expression on the LHS of (47) gives the fall in excess demand for Y per unit increase in Y, when e adjusts to keep BOP in equilibrium and P_A remains unchanged. Let us now explain the second term. When Y increases, demand for A

rises at the initial equilibrium P_A. s a result will rise and equilibrate the A-market. Per unit increase in Y, P_A will go up by $\frac{D_Y}{-D_{P_A}} > 0$ raising supply of A and, thereby, demand for Y by $E_{P_A}\frac{D_Y}{-D_{P_A}} > 0$. Thus, the expression on the LHS of (47) gives the change in the excess demand for Y per unit increase in Y when e and P_A adjust to keep the BOP and the A-market in equilibrium. Therefore, (47) implies that, when Y increases and e and P_A adjust along with the increase in Y to keep the BOP and the A-market in equilibrium, excess demand for Y should fall. Alternatively, when Y declines and e and P_A adjust along with the decrease in Y to keep the BOP and the A-market in equilibrium, excess supply of Y should fall.

Effect of an Increase in $\overline{K}$

We shall derive mathematically the effect of an increase in $\overline{K}$. Taking total differential of (37) (or (7) in the text) and (A,4)(or (4) in the text) treating all exogenous variables other than $\overline{K}$ as fixed, we get

$$E_Y \mathrm{d}Y + E_{P_A}\mathrm{d}P_A = -\varepsilon_3 \equiv -E_{\overline{K}}\mathrm{d}\overline{K} \tag{48}$$

$$D_Y dY + D_{P_A}\mathrm{d}P_A \equiv -\varepsilon_4 = -D_{\overline{K}}\mathrm{d}\overline{K} \tag{49}$$

where

$$\varepsilon_3 \equiv E_{\overline{K}}\mathrm{d}\overline{K} = \left\{I^A_{\overline{K}} + mA_{\overline{K}}\right\}\mathrm{d}\overline{K} > 0 \text{ (from (7) in the text)} \tag{50}$$

Let us now focus on ε_4.

$$\varepsilon_4 = \frac{\beta w_A l_A}{P_A}A_{\overline{K}}\mathrm{d}\overline{K} - A_{\overline{K}}\mathrm{d}\overline{K} < 0 \left(\text{since}\frac{\beta w_A l_A}{P_A} < 1, \text{ see (4) in the text}\right) \tag{51}$$

From (48) and (49), we get

$$\mathrm{d}Y = \frac{\begin{vmatrix} \underset{-}{-\varepsilon_3} & \underset{+}{E_{P_A}} \\ \underset{+}{-\varepsilon_4} & \underset{-}{D_{P_A}} \end{vmatrix}}{\Delta} \tag{52}$$

From (52) it follows that, since $\Delta > 0$(see (45)

$$\mathrm{d}Y > 0\, if\ \frac{\varepsilon_3}{E_{P_A}} \text{ (absolute value of the vertical shift of YY)} > \frac{-\varepsilon_4}{-D_{P_A}}$$
$$\text{(absolute value of the vertical shift of AA)} \tag{53}$$

We shall now show that (53) is satisfied.

Substituting the values of $\varepsilon_3, \varepsilon_4, D_{P_A}$ and E_{P_A} given by (50), (51), (38ii) and (38iii) respectively into (53) and multiplying both sides by A_{P_A}, we have

$$\begin{aligned}
\frac{\varepsilon_3}{E_{P_A}}A_{P_A} &= \frac{\{I_{\bar{K}} + mA_{\bar{K}}\}\mathrm{d}\bar{K}}{mA_{P_A}}A_{P_A} \\
&= \left(\frac{I_{\bar{K}}}{m} + A_{\bar{K}}\right)\mathrm{d}\bar{K} > \frac{\left(1 - \frac{\beta w_A l_A}{P_A}\right)A_{\bar{K}}\mathrm{d}\bar{K}}{\left(1 - \frac{\beta w_A l_A}{P_A}\right)A_{P_A}}A_{P_A} \\
&= A_{\bar{K}}\mathrm{d}\bar{K} > \frac{-\varepsilon_4}{-D_{P_A}}A_{P_A} \\
&= \frac{\left(1 - \frac{\beta w_A l_A}{P_A}\right)A_{\bar{K}}\mathrm{d}\bar{K}}{\begin{pmatrix} C_{wA}\cdot(1-t_w)\frac{wl_y}{L_0}Y \\ +\beta w_A l_g + A\beta w_A(l_A) \end{pmatrix}\left(\frac{1}{P_A^2}\right) + \left[\left(1 - \frac{1}{P_A}\beta w_A l_A\right)A_{P_A}\right]}A_{P_A}
\end{aligned} \tag{54}$$

From (54) it is clear that (53) is satisfied.

From (48) and (49), one can easily deduce that the sign of $\mathrm{d}P_A$ is ambiguous. However, one can easily prove that whatever be the direction of change in P_A, A will be larger in the new equilibrium. If P_A is higher, as follows from (2) in the text, A must be larger. If P_A is the same or lower, as follows from (4) in the text, A must be larger to satisfy (4), since Y is larger.

References

Bose, A. (1989). Short-period equilibrium in a less developed economy. In M. Rakshit (Ed.), *Studies in the macroeconomics of developing countries,* Oxford University Press.

ILO. (2009). *Towards an employment strategy for India.* Geneva.

Kalecki, M. (1954). *Theory of economic dynamics: An essay on cyclical and long-run changes in capitalist economy.* George Allen and Unwin, Third Impression.

Rakshit, M. (1982). *Labour surplus economy: A neo-Keynesian approach.* Macmillan India Ltd.

Taylor, L. (1983). *Structuralist macroeconomics.* Basic Books.

Ghosh, D., & Ghosh, A. N. (2019a). High growth rate and stagnant unemployment in India: A macro-theoretic study. *Trade and Development Review, 12*(1–2), 23–63.

Ghosh, C., & Ghosh, A. N. (2019b).*Keynesian macroeconomics beyond the IS-LM model.* Springer.

Dynamic Connectedness of Indian Business Cycle with G-7 Economies

Zeeshan Nezami Ansari and Rajendra Narayan Paramanik

Abstract This study aims at exploring the business cycle connectedness among G7 countries and India using monthly industrial production data from April 1994 to December 2018. The variance decompostion method of generalized VAR model has been employed to estimate volatility spillover among all countries. Empirical findings suggest that US is net transmitter of volatility whereas Germany is the main recepient of spillover shocks. India is found to be weakly synchronized with G7 natios as far as industrial output based business cycle is concerned.

Keywords International business cycle · Dynamic volatility connectedness · VAR model

1 Introduction

The genesis of liteature on business cycle (BC) can be traced back to seminal work of Burns and Mitchell (1946). They defined BC as subsequent upward and downward movements of agggregate output and synchronization of BC is co-movement of cyclical outputs of two or more countries. The term international Busniess cycle (IBC) is recently gained attention of reseacrhers. IBC mainly focuses on those economies which have similar economic background like Euro-Area, European Union and OECD countries etc. The opening up of global economy and formulation of these groups started after break down of Breeton Woods Aggrements (1973) and rapid growth of globalization. The research on IBC received theoreatical contribution from Backus et al. (1992); Ahmed et al. (1993) and Baxter and Crucini (1994) whereas

Z. N. Ansari (✉)
Department of Economics, GITAM (Deemed to be) University Bengaluru, Bengaluru, Karnataka, India
e-mail: zeeshan_1921hs19@iitp.ac.in; znezami@gitam.edu

R. N. Paramanik
IIT Patna, Patna, Bihar, India
e-mail: rajendra@iitp.ac.in

B. Chatterjee and A. K. Karmakar (eds.), *Analytical Issues in Growth & Structural Change, Macroeconomy, Security, and Sustainability of India's Economic Development*, India Studies in Business and Economics, https://doi.org/10.1007/978-981-95-5242-9_7

modern empirical method dynamic volatility spillover of IBC was developed and discuss by Diebold and Rudebusch (1994).

Following this lineage of works, this paper analyzes the Indian business cycle sychronization with Global Business Cycle. It takes G7 countries as a representative of international economic order because it accountsfor 33% of global output and all countries' trade share as pecentage of GDP is more than 60%, except Japan and US in 2013 (O'Donnell, 2015). Recently developed method of dynamic volatility spillover (Diebold & Yilmaz, 2012) is employed gauge business cycle co-movement. The objective of this paper is to assess how Indian business cycle is connected to global business cycle and the effect of 2008 financial crisis on their dynamism. Futhermore, this method has some advantages over others. First it reqiures large number of data sets and second the it shows how the each micro unit connected to each others and reach to macro level.

The remainder of the chapter is orgaized as follows. In Sect. 2, review of existing literature in the context of IBC is briefed. Section 3 discusses the methodology which consists of time series filter and dynamic volatility connectedness. Section 4 contains description of data as well as interpreation of empirical results. Final Sect. 5 has concluding remarks.

2 Liteature Review

The IBC literature gained momentum after seminal work by Backus et al. (1992) where they found that there is discrepancy between model and data. When the transport cost of trade was introduced then the varibility of output reduces and cross correlation of output increases among US, Canada and six European Countries. IBC research was further extended by Baxter and Crucini (1994). They observed that closed economies has higher output correlation than open economies and domestic productivity shocks decreases for those economies which incorporate free asset's trade. Kose et al. (2003) found that output cross correlation decreases after globalization (1990s) and output fluctuation was more in developed economy than developing one.

However, the liteature on volatility connectedness in the context of IBC is very limited. With regard to G7 countries, some authors (Antonakakis & Badinger, 2016; Diebold & Yilmaz, 2013) found total connectedness of BC is increasing over time and reached their peak during fiancial crisis of 2008. Trade leads to less sycronization of BC and in case of directional volatility, US is the major transmitter and Germany is recepient of shocks. Futhermore, Antonakakis and Badinger (2016) stated growth and volatility of GDP have direct relation with themselves but bear an inverse relation with cross variables. In another work on G7 BC, in relation to stock market, Liow (2016) concluded that cyclical correlation (cohesion) between BC and stock market is positive in long run and negative in short run. Abosedra et al.(2019) investigate nexus among on G7 countries' growth and found that total connectedness is about 50%. Further European countries' own variance have larger than non-European countries which shows Eureopean countries have interdependence among themselves. Antonakakis et al. (2016) analyzed BC dyanmics for EU 15 and EU 28 countries and show that total connectedness is high duing 2008 recession. In their study, US is found to be dominated in spillover index whereas Spain is the largest transmitter of shocks.

There are some studies conducted on G7 countries BC by using dynamic factor loading model. Using this method, Del Negro and Otrok (2008) found that cross correlation among G7 countries decreased over time and more integrated economies did not grow strong co-movement with rest of the economies. Ahmed et al. (1993) found that the flexible exchange rate system (after 1973) becomes more volatile and makes world output shocks respond to the domestic output fluctuation more aggressively. Crucini et al. (2011) estimated weak correlation between G7's BC with variables like trade and oil proce whereas monetary policy is pro-cyclical and fiscal policy is counter cyclical to output. Furthermore, they claimed that growing importance of emerging economies like China and India leads to decline in G7's share in global output and India and China will be important factors in the determining IBC dynamics in future. In the context of of emerging nations very few studies are found. Fidrmuc et al. (2014) found China's BC is less synchronized with G7 BC and trade leads BC synchronization only in short term. Regarding India, only one research work is conducted by Fidrmuc and Korhonen (2010). They found India has negative cyclical correlation with OECD countries. Further, China and India have similar results in terms of comovement with OECD countries during 2008 financial crisis. Our study extends the existing work by incorporating the data till 2018 and we took monthly IIP data for analyzing the spillover/connectedness of BC volatility among G7 countries vis-à-vis India.

3 Econometric Methodology

The methodology consists of extraction of cyclical components of Index of Industrial Production (IIP) by HP filter (Hodrick & Prescott, 1997) and estimation of Volatility Connectedness Index by variance decomposition technique of Diebold and Yilmaz (2009, 2012).

Hodrick and Prescott (1997) said seasonally adjusted actual time series contains growth and cyclical components simultaneously. The growth component changes "smoothly" over time and cyclical one has average value of zero over time spread.

$a_t = g_t + c_{t,}$ where t = 1,2,3,……,T

$$c_t = a_t - g_t$$

$$\mathrm{Min}_{t=-1}^{g_t^T}\left[\sum_{t=1}^{t} c_t^2 + \Lambda \sum_{t=1}^{T}\left\{\left(g_t - g_{t-1}\right) - \left(g_{t-1} - g_{t-2}\right)\right\}^2\right]$$

Here Λ is smoothing parameter which penalizes the change in growth component. The smoothing parameter is suggested by authors to be 6.25 for annual data, 1600 quarterly data and 129,600 for monthly data.

Further, volatility connectedness is calculated by variance decomposition of generalized Vector Autoregressive (VAR) model (Pesaran & Shin, 1998). Generalized VAR helps in the estimation of directional volatility connectedness. That is a p-step ahead time horizon forecast for error variance of one market due to shocks in another market.

In particular Vector Autoregession (VAR) model will be

$$Y_t = \boldsymbol{\Phi}(L)Y_{t-p} + u_t \tag{1}$$

where as Y_t is N × 1 matrix, $\boldsymbol{\Phi}$ NPXNP coefficient matrix, u_t is N × 1 matrix, t = time period, N = numbers of variables and P = order of lags.

$\boldsymbol{\Phi}(L) = \phi^p L^p$ –where as L is lag operator till order p

$$Y_t - \boldsymbol{\Phi}(L)Y_{t-p} = u_t \tag{2}$$

$$Y_t\left(1 - \phi^p L^p\right) = u_t \tag{3}$$

$\phi^p L^p$-is invertible, that is determinant $|\,(1 - \phi^p L^p)\,| \neq 0$. So, Eq. (3) can be written as Moving Average Representation

$$Y_t = \boldsymbol{\Theta}(L)u_t \tag{4}$$

where as$\boldsymbol{\Theta}(L) = (1 - \theta^p L^p)$

$$\Theta(\mathrm{L}) = (1 - \phi^{\mathrm{p}}\mathrm{L}^{\mathrm{p}})^{-1}$$

The shocks u_t should be orthogonal that is errors are not contemporaneously correlated.

So p-step ahead error can be written as

$$u_{t+1,p} = Y_{t+1} - Y_{t+1,p} = \boldsymbol{\Theta}\left(L_p\right)\, u_t \tag{7}$$

Variance-covariance matrix of error is

$$E\left(u_{t+1,p}u_{t+1,p}\right) = \boldsymbol{\Theta}\left(L_p\right)u_t\boldsymbol{\Theta}\left(L_p\right)u_t \tag{8}$$

For generalized VAR model, there is no need of Cholesky Factorization which is inverse of lower triangular covariance matrix of error. The variables are not orthogonalized here. So moving average coefficient $\boldsymbol{\Theta}$ can be used for the estimation of variance decomposition. Variance decompositions are invariant to order of the variables. Each variable's variance decomposition the sum of the rows (total variance of equation) is not equal to 1. There is n number of equation, so, total variance of system is equal to N.

$\omega_{ij}(P)$ is P step ahead forecast variance decomposition in variable j due to shocks arise in the ith variable.

$$\omega^{e}_{P,ij} = \frac{\sigma_{jj}^{-1} \sum_{p=1}^{P} \left(u_i \boldsymbol{\Theta \Omega}\, u_j\right)^2}{\sum_{j=1}^{N} \sum_{p=1}^{P} \left(u_i \boldsymbol{\Theta \Omega \Theta} u_i\right)} \tag{9}$$

σ_{jj} is standard deviation of error of jth equation, Ω is variance matrix of error and $u_i$is selection vector where ith elements is one otherwise zero.

Cross variance is one variable's volatility attributed by another variables' shocks that is $i \neq j$ and total variance is one variable's volatility attributed by own variable's shocks as well as other variables' shocks, that is $i = j$and $i \neq j$. There is n number of variables.

ω^{e}_{ij} = variable variance/equation variance.

$\sum_{j=1}^{N} \varpi^{e}_{ij}$ = variables total variance/equation total variance = 1.

ω^{s}_{ij} = equation variance/system variance.

$\sum_{j=1}^{N} \omega^{s}_{ij}$ = equations total variance/system total variance = N.

$\sum_{j=1}^{N} \omega^{e}_{ij} / \sum_{j=1}^{N} \omega^{s}_{ij}$ = 1/N.

But equation's cross variance decomposition $i \neq j$ is represented as total volatility spillover at time t = 0 and represented as-.

$$V^{s}_{ij} = \sum_{\substack{i,j=1 \\ i \neq j}}^{N} \omega^{e}_{ij} / \sum_{i,j=1}^{N} \omega^{s}_{ij} = \frac{\text{Equations' cross variance decomposition}}{\text{System's total variance decomposition.}}$$

P step ahead total volatility connectedness can be shown as-

$$V^{s}_{ij}(\mathrm{P}) = \frac{\sum_{p=1}^{P} \sum_{\substack{i,j=1 \\ i \neq j}}^{N} \omega^{s}_{p,ij}}{\sum_{p=1}^{P} \sum_{i,j=1}^{N} \omega^{s}_{p,ij}} .100 \tag{10}$$

The advantage of generalized VAR model is that it helps in estimating total directional volatility spillover connectedness from one market to another market or all other markets as well as from all others markets to one single market.

Total directional volatility spillover/connectedness to i "form" all others express algebraically

$$V^{s}_{i\leftarrow *}(\mathrm{P}) = \frac{\sum_{p=1}^{P} \sum_{\substack{j=1 \\ i\neq j}}^{N} \omega^{s}_{p,ij}}{\sum_{p=1}^{P} \sum_{j=1}^{N} \omega^{s}_{p,ij}} 100 \tag{11}$$

On the other hand total directional volatility spillover/connectedness from i "to" all others

$$V^{s}_{i\rightarrow *}(\mathrm{P}) = \frac{\sum_{p=1}^{P} \sum_{\substack{i=1 \\ j\neq i}}^{N} \omega^{s}_{p,ji}}{\sum_{p=1}^{P} \sum_{j=1}^{N} \omega^{2}_{p,ij}} .100 \tag{12}$$

So net directional volatility connectedness of ith market is volatility's difference between i-th "to" all others and i-th "from" others can be represented as

$$NV^{s}_{i}(\mathrm{P}) = V^{s}_{i\rightarrow *}(\mathrm{P}) - V^{s}_{i\leftarrow *}(\mathrm{P}) \tag{13}$$

In the same way net pairwise volatility connectedness is difference between volatility running one to another and one from another, so net pairwise volatility spillover will be

$$NV^{e}_{ij}(\mathrm{P}) = \frac{\omega^{e}_{ij}(\mathrm{P}) - \omega^{e}_{ji}(\mathrm{P})}{N} .100 \tag{14}$$

The application of this method is to know each disaggregate unit's effect on other disaggregate unit as well as aggregate level of market, sector and economy (Diebold & Yilmaz, 2013). It also can be applied to assess portfolio's volatility distribution, risk sharing and risk mitigating among different markets (Abosedra et al., 2019). We have employed this method for volatiliaty spillover analysis of BC among major developed nations and India.

4 Data Description and Empricial Result

The Index of Industrial Production's (IIP) data of G7 countries (Canada, France, Italy, Germany, Japan, United Kingdom, United States of America) and India are taken from April 1994 to December 2018 OECD.stat database. Index of Industrial Production is most suitable proxy for monthly output for any country. Data series are seasonally adjusted by X-11 ARIMA techniques and trend and cyclical components are extracted by using Hodrick& Prescott filter with smoothing parameter of 129,600. Subsequently, generalized VAR model is applied with lag length 2 which is decided by optimal value of Akaike information criterion. Since the time peroid of our analysis ranges from April-1994 to December 2018, the sample size is 297. We have used rolling window length of 120 months for variance decompostion. Hence, available observation reduces to 177 and following Antonakakis and Badinger (2016) we used 12 months prediction horizon (Table 1).

It is evident from the Table 1 that cyclical components of all IIP series have zero mean. Japan, Germany and Italy have large variance as compared to other countries. All IIP cycle are negatively skewed except India. Kurtosis of France, Germany, Italy and Japan are leptokurtic and others are platykurtic. Jarque–Bera test shows that all cyclical series are non-normal. Augmented Dickey Fuller (ADF) test confirms all cyclical series are stationary (Fig. 1).

All the cyclical components show there is dip during 2008 financial crisis as their values vary between -5 to -25, as marked by red circle. From the graph it is evident that India is least affected among all nations and UK has lowest dip but it persists for few months. Japan, Germany and Italy have the deepest dip as well as large variance.

Volatility connectedness (shown in Table 2) resembles Loentief's Input-Output table. The Loentief's table states the markets in the row supply (transmit) their output to all other markets in the different columns within same row. On the other hand, the markets in the column demand (recipient) output from all other markets in the different rows within same column. But the connectedness table is just reverse of Lonetief's Input-Output table. It implies that all rows are "TO" economies and all the columns are "FROM" economies, meaning that the row countriesare recipient of shocks "FROM" other economies in the different columns within same row and column market is transmitter of shocks "TO" economies in the different rows within same column. Dynamic connectedness table can be divided in four qudrants where each qudrant seprated from others by broader line in Table 2. The second quadrant from Eq. (13) is pairwise directional connectedness one country receives and transmits to another country. The first quadrant from Eq. (11) is aggregation of all shocks received by row country from others countries excluding own country's shocks. In the third quadrant "contribution to others" from Eq. (12) is summation of all the shocks transmitted by column named country to other countries excluding own country's shock. The summation of all countries "contribution to others" is always equal to summation of all countries "contribution from others". The net spillover from Eq. (13) of each country is difference between "contribution to others" and "contribution from others". The negative integer of net spillover shows that country is net recipients of shocks and positive integer of net spillover shows that country is net transmitter of shocks. The total connectedness from Eq. (10) is either sum of all the shocks "contribution from others" or sum of all the shocks "contribution to others" divided by "contribution including own" economy.

In Fig. 2, total connectedness is shown with 1 year prediction horizon and it is found to be high, ranging between 50–60%. After 5 years, the total connectedness increases above 70% and remains high over the extended time period due to 2008 financial crisis.

The directional connectedness, as one country receives from others countries and one country transmits to others countries and net volatility connectedness is chronicled in Fig. 3. It represent that one country transmits volatility to others countries and the value varies between 5–35%. Figure 4 represents show one country receives

Table 1 Summary statistics

	Canada	France	Germany	Italy	Japan	UK	US	India
Mean	0	0	0	0	0	0	0	0
Variance	6.293	7043	12.771	16.767	23.678	2.742	6.975	3.306
Skewness	−1.026***	−0.765***	−0.818***	−0.40***	−1.462***	−0.561***	−0.548***	0.376***
Kurtosis	2.29***	3.389***	3.661***	3.495***	6.118***	1.762***	1.542***	0.575*
JB	117.035***	171.087***	198.987***	159.05***	569.047***	54.001***	44.291***	11.084***
ADF	−3.186**	−4.843***	−3.245**	−3.45***	−3.449***	−4.713***	−1.733**	−7.108***
Q(20)	1043.99***	947.967***	1125.045	1082.491***	871.256***	883.029***	1470.00***	561.403***
Q2(20)	657.848***	459.498***	531175***	467091***	275.747***	476.242***	681.798***	140.897***

Authors' Calculation. *Note* JB is Jarque–Bera Test, ADF is unit root test, Q (20) is Correlogram statistic at lag 20, Q2 (20) is Correlogram squared statistic at lag 20. *, ** and *** indicates the significance of statistic at 10%, 5% and 1% level respectively

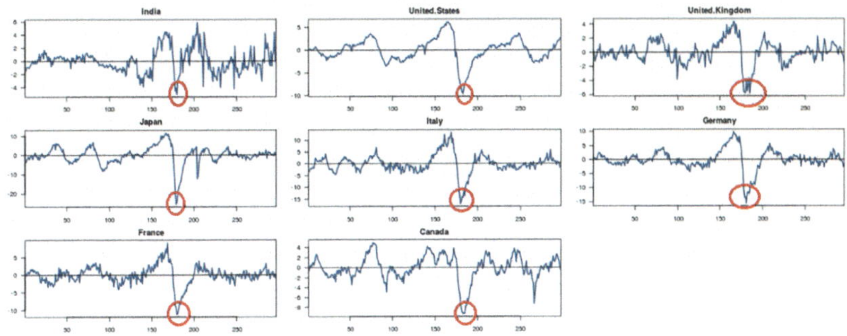

Fig. 1 Business cycles. Authors' calculation

volatility from all other countries and the value varies between 4–12%. It shows that US is the largest transmitter of volatility to other countries. Its volatility increases to 30% after 2008 financial crisis and then reduces to 10%. Canada's and Germany's volatility reduce after 2008 crisis (50 points). Pre-crisis volatility varies between 10–15% of these countries. India is least affected by 2008 global crisis and its dynamic volatility transmission to others countries is around 5%. As far as volatility received by different countries from all other countries is concerned, Fig. 4 showsGermany and India receive maximum volatility from all other countries and US is lowest receiver of volatility. The net volatility connectedness graph, as shown in Fig. 5 depicts India and France bear negative value throughout. Canada, Germany and Japan are volatility recipients after crisis because of negative value. Italy and UK, these two countries are found to be volatility transmitter to other countries post crisis period because of positive value and US is net volatility transmitter to all countries over complete time span.

It is evident from Table 2 that first diagonal represents own variance decomposition of each country. Countries in each column are transmitting shocks to rows' countries. India's shock to Canada mounts to 1.113 and that to France is around 2.494. India receives shocks from Canada which assumes value of 3.551 whereas from France it is 4.56. US is the highest transmitter of shocks to all others countries except for India. Germany is largest receiver of shocks form France, Italy, UK and US. The US receives minimal shocks from other countries and India is the least important transmitter of shocks. India receives highest shocks only from Italy and UK, valuing around 11.897% and 13.606% respectively. The values of cross country connectedness are not above 25%, so G7 nations are not pairwise synchronized. Five nations register negative net spillover/connectedness and these are Canada (−19.111%), France (−21.425), Germany (−47.572), Japan (−10.163) and India (−34.422). Italy; UK and US are transmitters of shocks to other countries because of positive net spillover value. US is 100%transmitter of shocks and Germany is 50% recipients of shocks. The total connectedness is 64.893 (65%) which is shown in fourth quadrant of the table.

Our findings are in consonance with other studies (Antonakakis & Badinger, 2016) as they too found US as largest transmitter and Germany is largest recipient of

Table 2 Dynamic Spillover Table

From To	Canada	France	Germany	Italy	Japan	UK	US	India	FROM others
Canada	37.758	5.923	4.757	8.341	10.158	7.991	23.959	1.113	62.242
France	7.392	25.453	7.973	15.915	6.897	13.829	20,048	2.494	74.547
Germany	7.118	10.875	16.279	18.077	8.12	13.846	23.129	2.556	83.721
Italy	5.434	9.598	6.000	31.156	10.487	14.511	20.271	2.544	68.844
Japan	6.139	8.882	6.701	13.175	30.268	8.882	23.925	2028	69.732
UK	6.375	7.168	3.54	15.394	9.327	33.141	21.646	3.409	66.859
US	7.122	6.114	4.802	7.968	8.433	5.617	57.655	2.291	42.345
India	3.551	4.562	2.377	11.879	6.147	13.606	8.734	49.144	50.856
Contribution TO others	43.131	53.122	36.149	90.748	59.569	78.281	141.712	16.435	519.147
Contribution including own	80.889	78.575	52.428	121.904	89.837	111.423	199.367	65.578	TCI
Net spillovers	−19.111	−21.42	−47.572	21.904	−10.16	11.423	99.367	−34.42	64.893

Authors' calculation

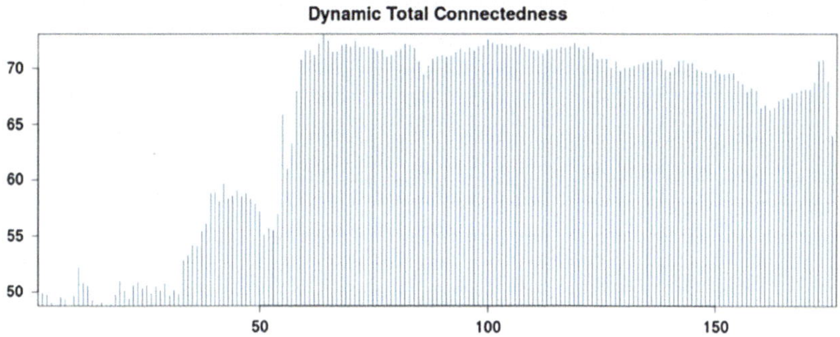

Fig. 2 Dynamic total connectedness. Authors' calculation

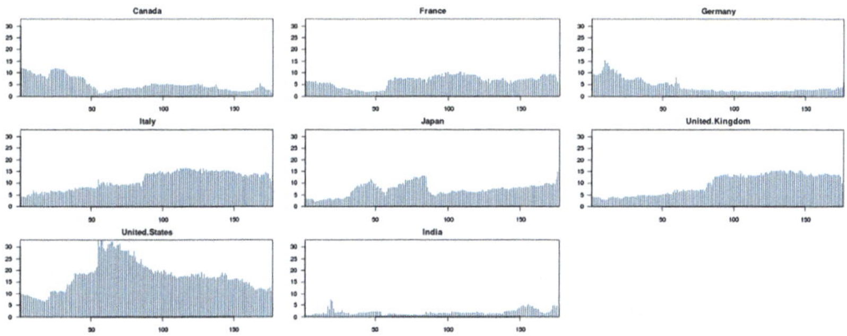

Fig. 3 Dynamic Connectedness of All Transmitting Economies. Authors' Calculation

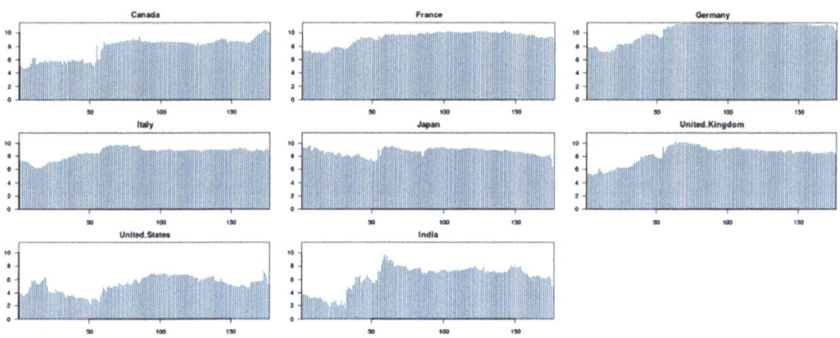

Fig. 4 Dynamic connectedness of all Recipient economies. Authors' calculation

shocks of BC. India is found to be poor transmitter as well as recipients of BC shocks. Further study highlights that India is asynchronous to developed world's business cycle dynamic too.

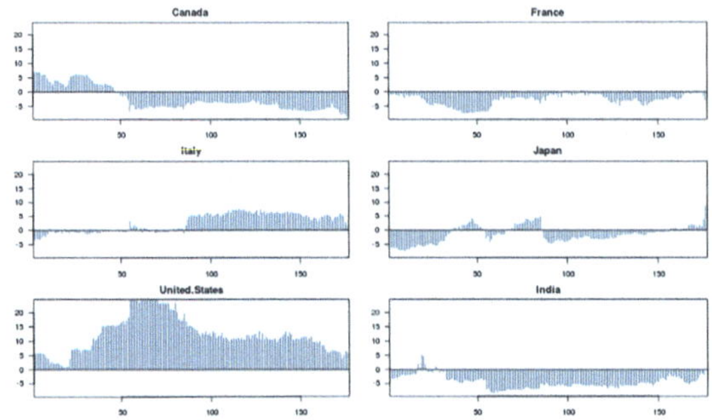

Fig. 5 Dynamic net connectedness. Authors' calculation

5 Conclusion

The study explores synchronicity and volatility spillover of Indian BC with G7 countries. Cyclical components of industrial outputs, as extracted by HP filter are used as BC component of output, varying from April 1994 to December 2018. Variance decomposition method of generalized VAR model reveals that Indian business cycle is asynchronous with G7 countries and there is strong spillover of BC volatility among G7 nations during post financial crisis period. Among G7 nations, US isfound to be net transmitter of volatility shock whereas Germany is net recipient. Future scope of the study lies in using different economic and financial factors like oil price, foreign investment and trade etc. to scrutinize the dynamics of global business cycle.

References

Abosedra, S., Arayssi, M., Sita, B. B., & Mutshinda, C. (2019). Exploring GDP growth volatility spillovers across countries. *Economic Modelling.*

Ahmed, S., Ickes, B. W., Wang, P., & Yoo, B. S. (1993). International business cycles. *The American Economic Review*, 335–359.

Antonakakis, N., & Badinger, H. (2016). Economic growth, volatility, and cross-country spillovers: New evidence for the G7 countries. *Economic Modelling, 52*, 352–365.

Antonakakis, N., Chatziantoniou, I., & Filis, G. (2016). Business Cycle Spillovers in the European Union: What is the Message Transmitted to the Core? *The Manchester School, 84*(4), 437–481.

Backus, D. K., Kehoe, P. J., & Kydland, F. E. (1992). International real business cycles. *Journal of Political Economy, 100*(4), 745–775.

Baxter, M., & Crucini, M. J. (1994). *Business cycles and the asset structure of foreign trade* (No. w4975). National Bureau of Economic Research.

Burns, A. F., & Mitchell, W. C. (1946). *Measuring Business Cycles*. National Bureau of Economic Research, Inc.

Crucini, M. J., Kose, M. A., & Otrok, C. (2011). What are the driving forces of international business cycles? *Review of Economic Dynamics, 14*(1), 156–175.

Del Negro, M., & Otrok, C. (2008). Dynamic factor models with time-varying parameters: Measuring changes in international business cycles. *FRB of New York Staff Report*, (326).

Diebold, F. X., & Rudebusch, G. D. (1994).*Measuring business cycles: A modern perspective* (No. w 4643). National Bureau of Economic Research.
Diebold, F. X., & Yilmaz, K. (2009). Measuring financial asset return and volatility spillovers, with application to global equity markets. *The Economic Journal, 119*(534), 158–171.
Diebold, F. X., & Yilmaz, K. (2012). Better to give than to receive: Predictive directional measurement of volatility spillovers. *International Journal of Forecasting, 28*(1), 57–66.
Diebold, F. X., & Yilmaz, K. (2013). *Measuring the Dynamics of Global Business Cycle Connectedness* (No. 13–070). Penn Institute for Economic Research, Department of Economics, University of Pennsylvania.
Fidrmuc, J., & Korhonen, I. (2010). The impact of the global financial crisis on business cycles in Asian emerging economies. *Journal of Asian Economics, 21*(3), 293–303.
Fidrmuc, J., Korhonen, I., & Poměnková, J. (2014). Wavelet spectrum analysis of business cycles of China and G7 countries. *Applied Economics Letters, 21*(18), 1309–1313.
Hodrick, R. J., & Prescott, E. C. (1997). Postwar US business cycles: An empirical investigation. *Journal of Money, Credit, and Banking*, 1–16.
Kose, M. A., Prasad, E. S., & Terrones, M. E. (2003). How does globalization affect the synchronization of business cycles? *American Economic Review, 93*(2), 57–62.
Liow, K. H. (2016). Linkages between cross-country business cycles, cross-country stock market cycles and cross-country real estate market cycles. *Journal of European Real Estate Research., 9*(2), 123–146.
O'Donnell, D. (2015). *G7 in figures: Summit of the G7 States in Elmau 2015*. Fed. Statistical Office of Germany.
Pesaran, H. H., & Shin, Y. (1998). Generalized impulse response analysis in linear multivariate models. *Economics Letters, 58*(1), 17–29.

Financial Deepening—Growth Nexus in South Africa and India: An Evidence from Cointegration and Causality

Mahendra Pal

Abstract The chapter examines the long-run and causal relationship between financial deepening and economic growth in South Africa and India with the help of new time series methodology for the period of 52 years (1971–2023). We attempt to discuss the theory of financial repression and liberalization and its application in South Africa and India; both countries are highly developing, emerging, and leading economies of BRICS. The financial sector reforms adopted by the South African economy in 1985 and Indian economy since 1991 onwards appear to be based on the theoretical backdrop of McKinnon-Shaw (1973) theory of financial liberalization. Further, the chapter analyzes the trends of GDP growth rate and financial deepening in South Africa and India. The study infers that financial deepening is not co-integrated with economic growth in South Africa and shows no long-run relationship, but in India both the variables are co-integrated and find long-run relationship and significant at 5% level. Granger causality results also show the difference in the direction of causality. In South Africa causality runs from growth to finance, which supports the hypothesis of Demand-Led Growth, while in India causality runs from finance to growth, which supports the hypothesis of Supply Led Growth. Further, our results are supported by the VECM, IRF and VDC. The paper finds that the liberalized financial system has not been able to increase effective growth rates in South Africa, while it has a proven record in India. Hence, we suggest further improvement in money and capital markets in South Africa through appropriate regulatory and macroeconomic policies. Indian programs of successful financial deepening and growth nexus should be the guide for the improvement in the financial system of South Africa and other SSA countries. India, with its sound financial system, is an ideal case study for

This chapter is an updated version of the paper presented at 50th Annual Conference of The Indian Econometric Society (TIES) at IGDR, Bombay 2013. I am thankful to Prof. K. L. Krishna, V. N. Pandit (Late), K. V. Bhanumurthy, Rama Chandran, and Narain Sinha for helpful comments, and Professor Rajiv Singh and Mr. Kanwal Kant D.U. for providing overall technical shape and assistance.

M. Pal (✉)
Department of Commerce, Delhi School of Economics, University of Delhi, New Delhi, India
e-mail: mahendra_dsc@yahoo.com

B. Chatterjee and A. K. Karmakar (eds.), *Analytical Issues in Growth & Structural Change, Macroeconomy, Security, and Sustainability of India's Economic Development*, India Studies in Business and Economics, https://doi.org/10.1007/978-981-95-5242-9_8

South Africa. Our findings regarding South Africa are consistent with the results of Odhiambo (2010).

Keywords Financial deepening · Growth · Co-integration · Causality · VECM · IRF · VDC

JEL Classification G_{21} · E_{44} · C_2

1 Introduction

During the last three decades the application of financial liberalization policy has become an important tool in the hands of policy makers in the developed and developing nations. The increasing financial deepening resulting from the policy of financial liberalization has become the policy advice to the emerging nations by the IMF/World Bank. The background of financial liberalization policy can be derived from the theory of financial repression developed by McKinnon-Shaw (1973). Classical theory considered the financial sector as playing only a minor role in the process of economic growth. The strategic role of financial development in promoting economic growth has been developed by Schumpeter (1911, 1934). The traditional monetary approach developed by Keynes (1936) often prescribes low interest rate policies in order to raise investment and thereby aggregate demand. In the McKinnon-Shaw model (1973), the traditional monetary policy is identified as one of financial repression that leads to disintermediation, decline in saving and economic growth. According to McKinnon-Shaw (1973) thesis, below-market interest rates discourage financial saving and at the same time, permit investments to take place where marginal returns to invested capital are poor, leading to overall low efficiency of investment.

Over the recent past, financial sector reforms, especially in Sub-Saharan Africa (SSA), have become a challenging task for policy makers, academicians, and practitioners. The focus has been on deregulation of the financial sector such as liberalization of interest rates, strengthening of the banking sector system, and introduction of new money market instruments in money and stock markets. At present, African countries are being integrated with the world economic system. The economic growth rate of the African economies has not increased up to the expectations with the financial sector reforms undertaken so far. The economic growth rate has not been impressive. The GDP growth rates for many of the SSA countries are far below 5 percent. In short, limited progress has been made by the financial sector in Africa toward improving financial saving mobilization, financial and bank intermediation processes. As reviewed from the literature, many of the economic problems associated with the difficulties in the financial sector have their origins in the past poor performance of the SSA's economies as a whole and moreover the financial sector in particular.[1]

South Africa continues to face a number of economic problems such as a high unemployment rate, high poverty level, and massive wealth and income disparities and improvement of millions. For example, as per Gini Index, which measures wealth inequality, South Africa tops the list of top 10 countries of wealth inequality in 2023. The Government of South Africa has tried various measures since 1994 to address these challenges; there still remains a big job to do for the Government of South Africa. Further South Africa has been trying to maintain her position as African economic power house, but on the other hand improvement of millions, has become a challenge.[2]

The Government of South Africa set up a National Planning Commission in 2007 to address the problems such as economic growth, poverty reduction and job creation in the country. Now South Africa is considered one of the best financial systems among the SSA countries. South Africa adopted a financial liberalization process in the 1980s. Following the De-Kock's recommendations (1978, 1985) ceiling on interest rates, reserve and liquidity ratios and credits was removed. Due to the process of financial liberalization, the real rate of interest turned positive in the 1980s liberalization process. Now South Africa is ranked as one of the best financial systems among the SSA countries. For a detailed discussion on this topic, see Odhiambo (2005, 2010).

Indian financial system has been changing from financial repression to liberalization, globalization, and privatization. Indian economy was financially repressed till the mid-1980s. S. Chakravarty Committee (1985) recommended first time the controlled deregulation for Indian economy. Further, in Indian economy, money and capital markets were completely deregulated under the SAP[3] which was introduced in the year of 1991. Bank Rate, CRR and SLR were brought down from their peak level to a reasonable low level. New money market instruments such as Ways and Means Advances (WMAs), autonomy to RBI, TR Bills of 91 days, T.R Bills of 182 days, T.R. Bills of 364 days, Dated Government securities, C.Ds, C.Ps were also introduced. Number of financial innovations, which can be used to control liquidity and money supply in Indian economy such as LAF, Repo and Reverse Repo Rate, MSS, and MSF, have also been introduced.

The study tries to compare the progress of financial system of South Africa with that of India. In both the countries the level of financial deepening has increased in the parallel form (i.e., more than 75%). South Africa adopted her financial sector reforms in 1985, while India adopted her financial sector reform process after New Economic Policy of 1991, in a massive scale with a theoretical background of McKinnon-Shaw Model, see Pal (1997, 2014a).

The basic objective of this chapter is to investigate empirically the two hypotheses such as Supply Leading Condition and Demand Following Condition developed by Patrick (1966). The basic research questions are: Is there any long-run relationship between financial deepening and the annual growth rate of GDP in South Africa and India? Second research question is to detect the direction of Grainger's causality between the two variables. The rest of the paper is organized as: Sect. 2 deals with the review of literature; Sect. 3 discusses the methodology; Sect. 4 deals with model specification; Sect. 5 deals with time series properties of the data; Sect. 6 deals with the empirical analysis and Sect. 7 concludes the chapter.

2 Literature Review (Theory and Empirics)

2.1 Theory of Financial Liberalization

The background of financial liberalization policy can be derived from the theory of financial repression developed by McKinnon-Shaw. Classical economic theory rejected the role of finance in the process of economic growth. Schumpeter (1911, 1934) identified the role of finance in promoting economic growth. The traditional monetary approach often prescribes low interest rate policies in order to raise investment and thereby aggregate demand. In the McKinnon-Shaw model (1973), the traditional monetary policy is identified as one of "financial repression" that leads to disintermediation, decline in investment, and worsening of market segmentation, a special feature in the developing economies, like India. Hence, McKinnon puts forward a hypothesis related to the basic complementarity between money and physical capital, as against the traditional theory which is based on a substitution relationship. There are four instruments of financial repression through which the government of any developing country tries to squeeze the banking sector in a particular country. These are high cash reserve ratio (CRR), high statutory liquidity ratio (SLR), high priority sector lending, and overvalued exchange rates.

2.2 Empirical Studies (South Africa and India)

Spears (1992), in his study on the role of financial intermediation in economic growth in SSA countries, tries to determine whether the development of the financial sector has been accompanied by economic growth in a sample of countries of SSA. Seck and Nil (1993), in their study of 9 emerging countries of Africa, explored that the real deposit rates in the commercial banks had a positive effect on financial savings, which is measured by the growth of M^3/GDP ratio, gross investment to GDP, and on the growth rate of output. Mwenda (1993) evaluates the impact of financial repression on the quantity and quality of investment in the commercial agriculture sector. Huw and Mahmood (1997), in their study, say that Asian countries have generally been more successful than African countries in liberalizing their financial system. Asia's experience with liberalization offers some useful lessons for Africa. Oyejide and Raheem (1999), in their study, reveal that political instability resulting from frequent changes of government may increase initiatives with high short returns rather than effective strategy that promote meaningful long-term development.

Ozturk (2007) investigated the long-run relationship between financial development and economic growth in South Africa for the period 1970–2003. With the help of VAR methodology, the author provides evidence of the existence of a long-run relationship between financial development and economic growth. Further, the study talks about a two-way Granger causal relationship between financial development and economic growth in South Africa. Odhiambo (2010) examines the deregulation of interest rate structure and its impact on the banking sector development and its relationship with economic growth in South Africa. With the help of VECM technique, he finds positive impact of interest rate deregulation on financial development in South Africa. Further, he also investigates that growth of financial intermediation, which is mainly caused by interest rate deregulation, does not Granger cause increase in investment and economic growth.

Akinlo and Egbetunde (2010) study the long-run and causal relationship between financial development and economic growth with the help of VECM for 10 countries in SSA. They conclude that financial development maintains a long-run relationship with economic growth in a sample of 10 countries of SSA. Mwenda and Mutoti (2011) talk about the impact of market-based financial sector reforms on the competitive efficiency of commercial banks and economic growth in Zambia.

Pal (2012) examines the financial sector reforms in Zambia for the period from 1986 to 2012. He provides the theoretical backdrop of financial repression and applies this theory in the Zambian financial system. His findings reveal the facts that Zambia adopted the policy of financial liberalization but the dose of financial liberalization has not been able to achieve a positive real rate of interest on the deposits of commercial banks and also has not been able to increase the level of financial deepening (M3/GDP) ratio. However, GDP growth rate has increased without the increase in financial deepening. Hence, in case of Zambia McKinnon-Shaw (1973) development paradigm does not seem to be applied during the study period.

Banerjee and Ghosh (1998) examine the impact of economic operations undertaken by industrial financial institutions in India. In their econometric study, they examine the "Supply Leading and Demand Following Condition". They use time series methodology for the period from 1961 to 1998 and conclude the existence of strong "Supply Leading Hypothesis" in case of Indian economy. Bell and Rousseau (2001) examine the role of financial intermediaries in influencing India's economic development. With the help of Vector Autoregressive (VAR) and Vector Error Correction Model (VECM), they evaluate the causal link and long-run relationship between financial intermediation and number of economic aggregates. They find the financial sector as an instrument in promoting economic growth and investment. In addition, they also reveal the fact that the role of financial sector in promoting industrial sector has gone beyond the passive support of Fiscal Policy in India.

Bhattacharya and Sivasubramanian (2003) investigate the causal direction between economic growth rate and the level of financial deepening in India for the period of twenty-eight years that is from 1971 to 1999. In their research, they apply modern time series technique that is unit root testing and Johansen's co-integration. Their results support "Finance -Led Growth" hypothesis in India.

Pradhan (2011) examine the long-run relationship between financial development and growth rate in India in a trivariate framework by incorporating stock market development. He finds that stock market development has substantial impact on finance-growth nexus, while financial development and economic growth are bidirectional, economic growth and stock market development are unidirectional. He concludes that stock market development is an integral part of economic growth, which is, in turn, associated with financial development in the Indian economy. Ray

(2013) traces the nexus and direction between economic growth and financial development in India using Granger Causality test for the period, 1990–91 to 2010–11. His results confirm the causal direction from finance to growth and thus supports the Supply Leading Condition of Patrick (1966). Pal (2013) traces finance-growth nexus in India with the help of co-integration technique and VECM developed by Johansen and Juselius (1990) for the period of 39 years that is from 1971 to 2010. His results confirm one co-integrating vector which tells about long-run equilibrium relationship. Further, Pairwise Granger causality shows unidirectional that is from finance to income. VECM model support the hypothesis of Finance- led growth in India.

Sabyasachi and Mandal (2014) re-examine the finance-growth relationship in India with the help of vector error correction model (VECM) for the period of post-reform period. They confirm in their study that financial deepening has a strong effect on the process of economic growth in India. Pal (2014a) examines theoretically and empirically the McKinnon-Shaw model in India. The paper reveals the facts that a basic complementarity exists between money and physical capital. With the help of two-stage least square and with time series data for the period of 39 years (1971–2010), he tests a simultaneous equation model for 'Money Demand Function' and 'Saving Function'. The study reveals positive and significant results for India. Sahoo (2014) examines the role of financial development in accelerating economic growth in India. To study this topic, he analyzes bank-based versus market-based financial systems. His findings also support the bank-based system in India and in this way he also joins the School of Supply Led growth hypothesis in India.

3 Methodology

3.1 Test of Integration

In the traditional statistical analysis, when an economic time series exhibits a significant trend, first differencing of the time series is required to obtain stationarity before estimation of any economic model. A time series is stationary if its mean, variance, and covariance are finite, and if they are independent of time. If, on the other hand, the variance increases over time, then the series becomes explosive. Any such series renders results of hypothesis testing unreliable. Hence, this type of time series, therefore, should not be used for the purpose of hypothesis testing. For a detailed analysis on this topic, see Stock and Watson (1996).

In the first step, the stationary of variables included in our analysis has been tested by a Unit Root Test. In this context, the ADF test and Phillips-Perron (PP) testing procedures have been applied. The ADF is based on the following three equations (i.e., first without any constant and trend; second with constant but no trend, while third with constant and trend). We do not produce the traditional three equations of unit root testing because these are available in Gujarati (2020) and Maddala (1992).

After confirming the order of integration of four variables of two countries, we directly deal with the co-integration test. Results of the order of integration can be obtained from the author on request.

3.2 *Test of Co-integration Test (Johansen and Juselius)*

After determining the order of integration of the four variables, we apply Johansen's co-integration test to ascertain whether or not the concerned variables share a common stochastic trend. We have applied the following unrestricted VAR model for estimation purposes.

$$Y_1 = A_0 + \sum_{j+1}^{p} AjY_{t-1} + \varepsilon i \tag{1}$$

where $Y_t = (Y, x, m)$ is a 3×1 vector of non-stationary 1 (1) variables, A_0 is a 3×1 vector of the constants, P is the number of lags, Aj is a 3×3 matrix of estimable parameters, and et is a 3×1 vector of the independent and identically distributed innovations. Johansen likelihood ratio (LR) tests are based on maximum eigenvalues and trace of the stochastic metrics. For detailed discussion, see Banerjee et al. (1993) and Johansen and Juselius (1990).

3.3 *Test of Pair Wise Granger Causality*

The Granger's pairwise test is based on the following two regressions:

$$\Delta Y_t = \alpha_0 + \sum\nolimits_{j=1}^{m} \alpha_j \Delta Y_{t-j} + \sum\nolimits_{j=1}^{m} \beta_j \Delta X_{t-1} + \epsilon_{1t} \tag{2}$$

$$\Delta X_t = \alpha_0 + \sum\nolimits_{j=1}^{m} \lambda_j \Delta X_{t-j} + \sum\nolimits_{j=1}^{m} \delta_j \Delta Y_{t-1} + \epsilon_{2t} \tag{3}$$

Equation (2) postulates that current ΔY is related to its past values as well as ΔX and Eq. (3) postulates a similar behavior for ΔX_t. It is assumed that the disturbances ϵ_{1t} and ϵ_{2t} are un-correlated and ΔX and ΔY are stationary process. For a detailed analysis on this topic, see Maddala (1992) and Gujarati (2020).

4 Model Specification

4.1 Model Specification, Data Source and Measurement of Variables

Following the methodology adopted by Patrick (1966), mainly two hypotheses have been tested empirically by the large number of studies undertaken on the issue of finance–growth nexus, namely the "Demand Following Condition" and "Supply Leading Condition". Equations 4 and 5 are related to two hypotheses as follows:

$$1.\quad \text{F.D.} = f(Y) \quad \text{Demand Following Condition} \tag{4}$$

$$2.\quad Y = f(\text{F.D.}) \quad \text{Supply Leading Condition} \tag{5}$$

Y = GDP Growth Rate
FD = Financial Development = M^3/GDP = Broad Money (C + DD + TD) / GDP)

M3 is a proxy for financial deepening (M3/GDP). Financial Development, Financial Intermediation Bank Intermediation, Financial Saving Financial Broadening (i.e., 7 terms are used interchangeably in the chapter). M3/GDP term is used by the RBI, while M2/GDP is defined and used by the IMF.

4.2 Data Source and Measurement of Variables

For estimation purposes we have used annual data sourced mainly from the World Development Indicators (WDI) published by the World Bank. The study covers a very long period of 52 years that is from 1971 to 2023. Most of the developing and financially repressed countries liberalized their economies during this period. S. Chakrvarty Committee (1985) introduced controlled economic liberalization in India, but New Economic Policy of 1991 introduced number of money, capital, trade and financial reforms, which ultimately increased the level of M3/GDP ratio and GDP growth rate in India. There are two methods of measurement of financial deepening—one is traditional and another is modern method.

Number of researchers notably Goldsmith (1969), Chakravorty Committee (1985), and Jadhav (1994) have recommended four traditional ratios to measure the level of financial development/financial deepening. These four ratios include Financial Ratio, Financial Interrelation Ratio, New Issue Ratio, and Intermediation Ratio. Due to problems of availability of systematic data series, empirical estimation becomes very difficult with these ratios. Hence, to avoid this problem, a number of empirical economists notably McKinnon (1973), Shaw (1973), Agarwal (1995), Pal

(1997, 2013), and Pradhan (2011) have used the ratios such as M1/GDP, M3/GDP, and TD/M3. M3/GDP ratio is the most popular indicator of financial development which promotes two things: accumulation of capital and promotion of investment in productive channel.

5 Trends of Financial Deepening & Growth Rate in South Africa & India

5.1 Time Series Properties of the Data (South Africa and India)

Table 1 demonstrates the upward trends of two concerned variables such as financial deepening (M3/GDP) ratio and the annual growth rate of GDP from 1971 to 2023 in both the countries—that is, South Africa and India. Further, both the Figs. 1 and 2 reveal the facts about the trend analysis of GDP growth rate and M3/GDP ratio of South Africa and India. When we talk about the M3/GDP ratio of India and South Africa, both are showing upward trends more or less in the same order, but when we talk about the annual growth of GDP, India's GDP growth rate remains higher than South Africa's GDP growth rate. Further, South Africa adopted her financial sector reforms in 1985, while India adopted her financial sector reforms process mainly after New Economic Policy of 1991 on a massive scale with a theoretical background of McKinnon-Shaw Model, see Pal (1997).

5.1.1 South Africa

Figures 3 and 4 demonstrate the plots of log GR and dlog GR, while Figures 5 and 6 demonstrate the plots of log M3 and dlog M3.

5.1.2 India

After showing and interpreting the empirical results on South Africa, now we intend to produce the empirical results about the Indian economy. Figures 7, 8, 9, and 10 demonstrate the plots of Log M3 and dlog M3 in India.

Table 1 Trends of financial deepening & growth rate in South Africa & India

South Africa			India	
Year	M3/GDP ratio (%)	GDP growth rate (%)	M3/GDP ratio (%)	GDP growth rate (%)
1971	57.66	4.28	23.37	1.64
1972	60.12	1.65	24.47	−0.55
1973	59.57	4.57	24.02	3.29
1974	56.49	6.11	22.84	1.18
1975	59.87	1.70	24.26	9.15
1976	57.70	2.25	28.03	1.66
1977	57.17	−0.09	29.48	7.25
1978	57.68	3.01	32.98	5.71
1979	56.45	3.79	35.39	−5.24
1980	52.08	6.62	34.47	6.74
1981	52.61	5.36	34.46	6.07
1982	52.59	−0.38	36.11	3.48
1983	52.34	−1.84	36.24	7.29
1984	53.52	5.10	38.16	3.82
1985	53.16	−1.21	39.53	5.25
1986	49.36	0.01	41.67	4.78
1987	50.48	2.10	42.63	3.96
1988	53.43	4.20	42.51	9.63
1989	53.67	2.39	42.82	5.95
1990	52.15	−0.32	42.18	5.53
1991	53.36	−1.02	43.42	1.06
1992	48.95	−2.13	44.15	5.48
1993	45.50	1.23	44.88	4.75
1994	47.61	3.20	46.02	6.66
1995	48.62	3.10	43.55	7.57
1996	49.36	4.30	44.69	7.55
1997	52.49	2.60	47.46	4.05
1998	55.07	0.50	48.91	6.18
1999	55.73	2.40	51.07	8.85
2000	52.71	4.20	54.65	3.84
2001	57.30	2.70	57.74	4.83
2002	58.25	3.70	62.62	3.81
2003	60.63	2.94	63.18	7.86
2004	61.59	4.55	64.64	7.92
2005	66.97	5.27	65.55	7.92
2006	73.18	5.60	68.06	8.07

(continued)

Table 1 (continued)

South Africa			India	
Year	M3/GDP ratio (%)	GDP growth rate (%)	M3/GDP ratio (%)	GDP growth rate (%)
2007	79.08	5.36	72.28	7.67
2008	80.80	3.19	77.37	3.09
2009	77.68	−1.54	79.08	7.86
2010	75.80	3.04	77.68	8.51
2011	74.63	3.28	78.84	5.24
2012	72.94	2.21	76.91	5.46
2013	71.01	2.48	78.18	6.39
2014	70.87	1.84	77.90	7.41
2015	73.46	1.19	78.01	7.99
2016	72.40	0.40	74.55	8.26
2017	72.18	1.41	74.15	6.81
2018	72.77	0.78	74.15	6.53
2019	74.12	0.15	76.05	4.04
2020	74.50	0.16	88.88	−7.97
2021	60.30	4.00	82.10	8.30
2022	65.41	2.10	83.00	7.10
2023	73.01	1.50	83.15	7.60

Source World Development Indicators (WDI), World Bank, Washington, DC

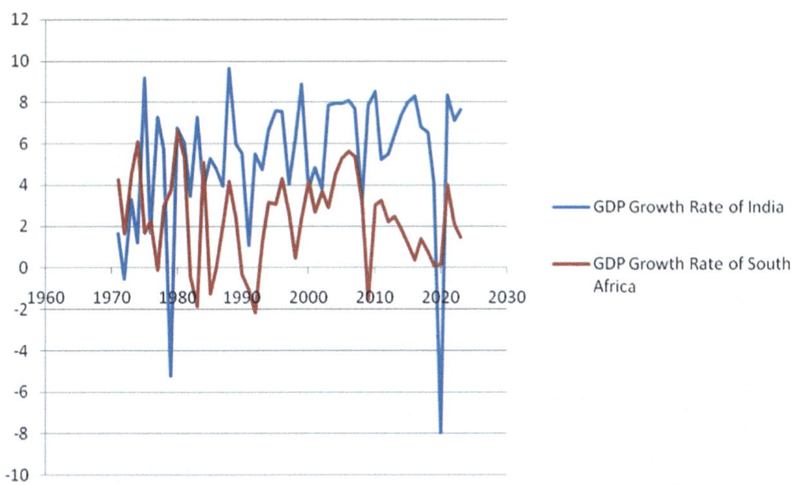

Fig. 1 Fluctuating trends of annual growth rates of GDP in India and South Africa

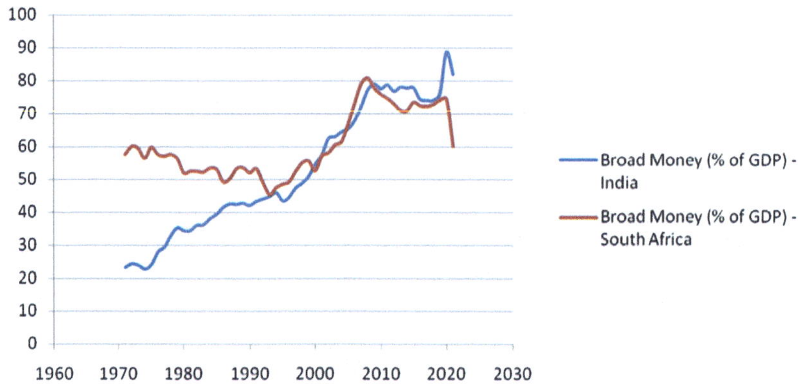

Fig. 2 Trends of financial deepening (M3/GDP) ratio in South Africa and India

Fig. 3 Plot of log GR

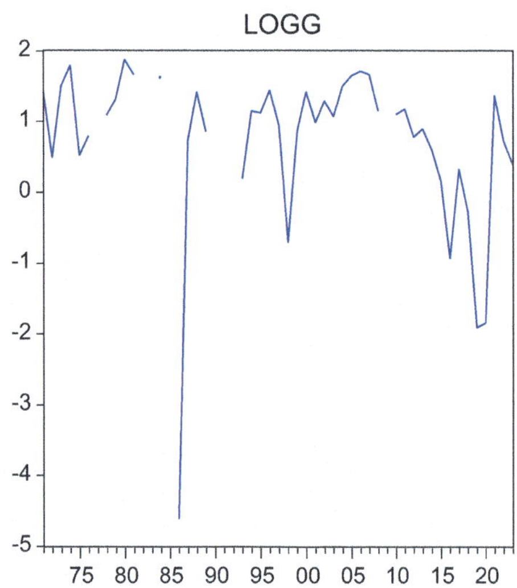

6 Empirical Results and Discussion

6.1 South Africa

In South Africa we tested the unit roots with the help of ADF and Phillips-Perron methodology but we do not find the stationarity at first-difference level. In this way the co-integration test does not apply in case of Trace Statistic, while Max-eigenvalue test indicates 1 co-integrating eqn(s) at the 0.05 level, hence there is no positive and long-run relationship between financial development (M^3) and GDP growth rate in South Africa. Table 2 and 3 demonstrate the results of co-integration.

Fig. 4 Plot of dlog GR

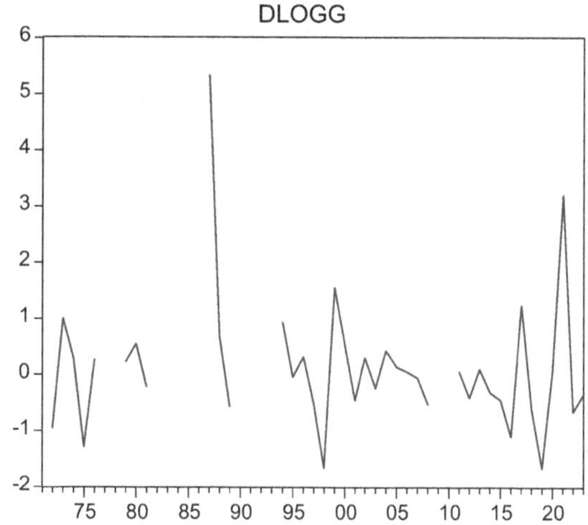

Fig. 5 Plot of log M3

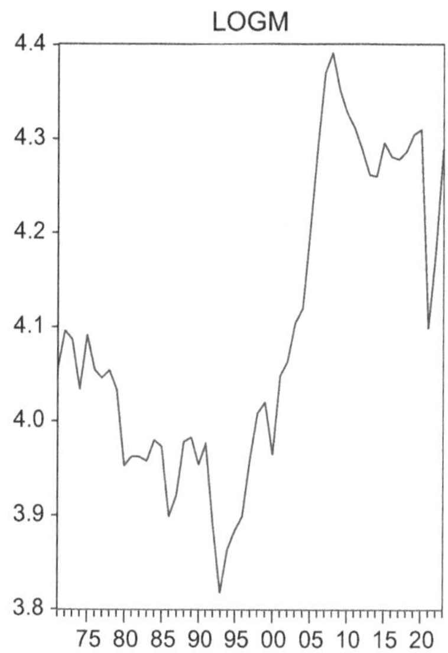

6.2 Granger Causality of South Africa

Table 4 demonstrates the Granger causality results in South Africa which are significant at the 5% level of significance. In South Africa, results reveal the facts that the annual growth of GDP causes financial development, financial deepening, financial depth, and financial intermediation; hence South Africa can be considered as a case of "Demand Following Hypothesis".

Fig. 6 Plot of dlog M3

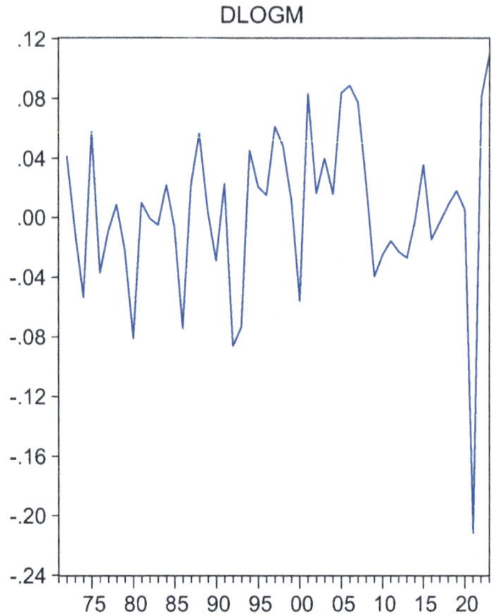

Fig. 7 Plot of log GR

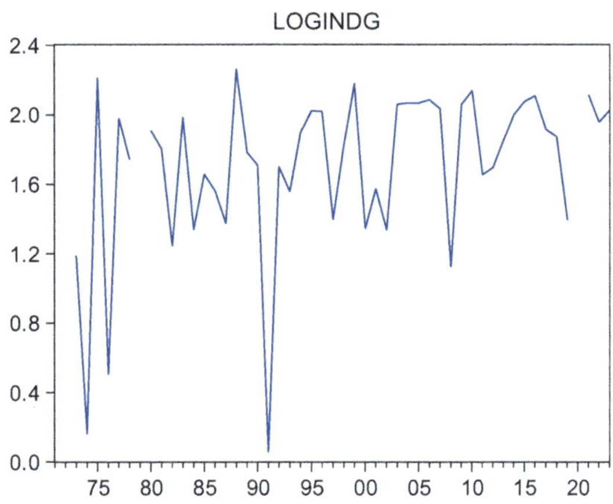

Table 5 demonstrates that in VECM in the lower panel. ECT term which is equal to −0.568002, shows that during one year period, the level of disequilibrium is corrected by more than 56%, which confirms a high speed of adjustment in South Africa. Further ECT term is also in minus which is correct as per Economic theory.

Theoretically, it is important to know the fact that the individual coefficient from VECM is very difficult to simplify and interpret the results. For this, it is important to analyze the dynamic properties of the model by examining the Impulse Response Function (IRF) and Variance Decomposition (VDC).

Figure 11 demonstrates the impulse response functions coming from standard deviation shocks to M3 with the response of GR traced out. Response from shocks

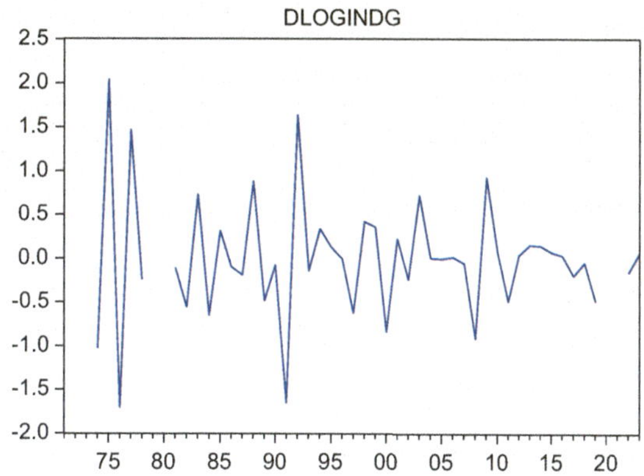

Fig. 8 Plot of dlog GR

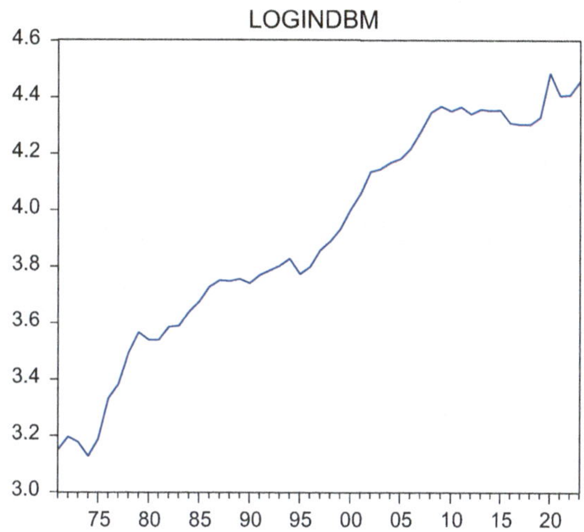

Fig. 9 Plot of log M3

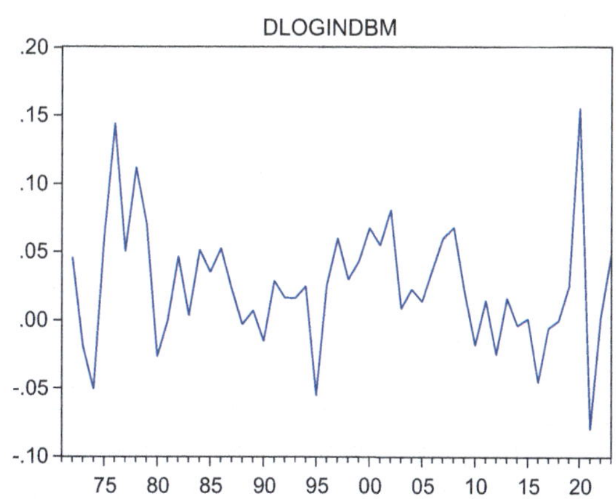

Fig. 10 Plot of dlog M3

Table 2 Results of Johansen co-integration test (trace statistic) for Finance and Growth

Included observations: 34 after adjustments
Trend assumption: linear deterministic trend (restricted)
Series: Log GR Log M3
Lags interval (in first differences): 1 to 1
Unrestricted co-integration rank test (Trace)

Hypothesized No. of CE(s)	Eigenvalue	Trace statistic	0.05 critical value	Prob.**
None*	0.448753	23.31025	25.87211	0.1008
At most 1	0.086090	3.060781	12.51798	0.8692

Trace test indicates no co-integration at the 0.05 level
*denotes rejection of the hypothesis at the 0.05 level
**MacKinnon-Haug-Michelis (1999) *p*-values

Table 3 Results of Johansen co-integration test (Max-Eigen value) for finance and growth

Hypothesized No. of CE(s)	Eigenvalue	Max-Eigen statistic	0.05 critical value	Prob.**
None*	0.448753	20.24947	19.38704	0.0374
At most 1	0.086090	3.060781	12.51798	0.8692

Max-eigenvalue test indicates 1 co-integrating eqn(s) at the 0.05 level
*denotes rejection of the hypothesis at the 0.05 level
**MacKinnon-Haug-Michelis (1999) *p*-values

Table 4 Results of Granger causality of South Africa

Pairwise Granger causality tests
Sample: 1971–2023
Lags: 2

Null hypothesis	Obs.	F-statistic	Probability
Log M3 does not Granger Cause Log GR	34	0.81184	0.4539
Log GR does not Granger Causes Log M3		3.67679*	0.0377
	GROWTH	⟶ FINANCE	

Significant at 5% level of significance

in the variable provides a path for GR. In the case of GR the path climbed up to 2 years, then declined up to 4 years, then turned negative after 4 years, and then became constant up to 10 years. Table 6 demonstrates the results from the Cholesky variance decomposition technique. A good proportion of the variance in GR shocks is attributable to shocks in M3 (Financial Deepening).

Table 5 Results of VECM for financial deepening and GDP growth rate

Error correction	D(LOGG)	D(LOGM)
CointEq1	−0.568002 (0.22141) [−2.56541]	0.042243 (0.01348) [3.13352]
D(LOGG(−1)	0.228053 (0.25760) [0.88531]	−0.022210 (0.01568) [−1.41605]
D(LOGG(−2)	−0.169520 (0.13511) [−1.25464]	0.011264 (0.00823) [1.36917]
D(LOGM(−1)	3.968535 (3.52435) [1.12603]	−0.235282 (0.21459) [−1.09642]
D(LOGM(−2)	1.284154 (3.14721) [0.40803]	−0.050600 (0.19163) [−0.26405]
C	−0.086616 (0.16914) [−0.51210]	0.018203 (0.01030) [1.76748]
R-squared	0.375491	0.434243
Adj. R-squared	0.239728	0.311253
Sum sq. resids	16.08863	0.059646
S. E. equation	0.836365	0.050925
F-statistic	2.765784	3.530704
Log likelihood	−32.60606	48.55672
Akaike AIC	2.662487	−2.934946
Schwartz SC	2.945376	−2.652057
Mean dependent	−0.06352	0.016952
S.D. dependent	0.959204	0.061362
Determinant resid covariance (dof adj.)		0.001543
Determinant resid covariance		0.000971
Log likelihood		18.29495
Akaike information criterion		−0.296204
Schwartz criterion		−0.363870

6.3 India

From Tables 7, 8, and 9, confirm the positive and long-run relationship between M3 and economic growth in India because in Table 7 the trace statistics is more than its critical value (i.e., 31.65951 more than 25.87211). Our results are also supported by the value of maximum eigenvalue in Table 8, which is also more than its critical value. Further, our normalized function value in Table 9 also supports the positive

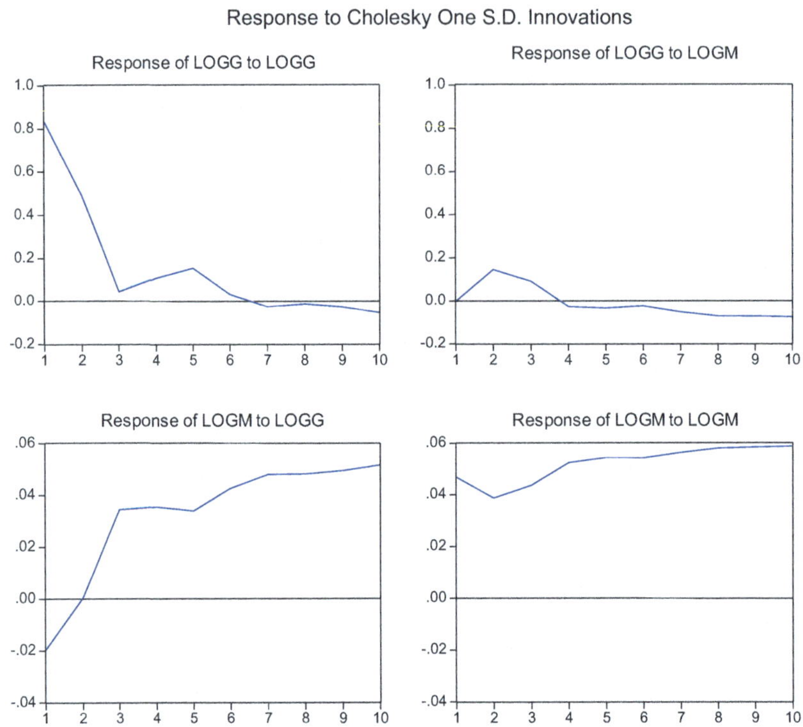

Fig. 11 Response to Cholesky One S.D. Innovations

results, which shows that one percent rise in M3 causes 0.22% rise in growth rate in India.

Table 10 demonstrates the Pairwise Granger causality results which confirm our hypothesis of strong causal direction from M3 to Growth in India at one lag and two lags also. It shows a unidirectional causal result that is from Financial Deepening (M3) to economic growth during the period of 52 years that is from 1971 to 2023. Financial Deepening causes the growth rate of income in Indian Economy.

Table 11 demonstrates that in VECM results. ECT term value is equal to − 0.4562297, which shows that during one-year period, the level of disequilibrium is corrected by more than 45%. ECT term is also in minus, which is very much correct as per Economic Theory. Our VECM reveals two important features: (a) GDP in India is Granger caused by FD, and the causality runs more from FD to GDP; (b) FD intends to increase the economic productivity in Indian economy.

Theoretically, it is important to know the fact that the individual coefficient from VECM is very difficult to simplify and interpret the result. For this, it is important to analyze the dynamic properties of the model by examining the Impulse Response Function (IRF) and Variance Decomposition (VDC). The impulse response functions coming from standard deviation shocks to M3 with the response of GDP are traced

Table 6 Variance decomposition of GR and M3

Period	S. E.	Log GR	Log M3
Variance decomposition of Log GR			
1	0.836365	100.0000	0.000000
2	0.980661	97.75948	2.240522
3	0.986045	96.90839	3.091613
4	0.992363	96.88259	3.117406
5	1.004865	96.85997	3.140029
6	1.005655	96.81565	3.184346
7	1.007198	96.58023	3.419773
8	1.009611	96.13218	3.867820
9	1.012292	95.68586	4.314145
10	1.016263	95.20931	4.790691
Variance decomposition of Log M3			
1	0.050925	14.92828	85.07172
2	0.064063	9.438610	90.56139
3	0.084948	21.94139	78.05861
4	0.106042	25.36341	74.63659
5	0.123977	26.10633	73.89367
6	0.141994	28.96513	71.03487
7	0.160223	31.75511	68.24489
8	0.177171	33.39280	66.60720
9	0.193066	34.70678	65.29322
10	0.208387	35.95386	64.04614

Table 7 Results of Johansen co-integration test (Trace statistic) for finance and growth

Included observations: 43 after adjustments
Trend assumption: linear deterministic trend (restricted)
Series: Log GR Log M3
Unrestricted co-integration rank test (Trace)

Hypothesized No. of CE(s)	Eigenvalue	Trace statistic	0.05 critical value	Prob.**
None*	0.445845	31.65951	25.87211	0.0085
At most 1	0.135805	6.276153	12.51798	0.4260

Trace test indicates 1 co-integrating eqn(s) at the 0.05 level
*denotes rejection of the hypothesis at the 0.05 level
**MacKinnon-Haug-Michelis (1999) *p*-values

Table 8 Co-integration for M3 and economic growth rate and financial deepening

Hypothesized No. of CE(s)	Eigenvalue	Max-Eigen statistic	0.05 critical value	Prob.**
None*	0.445845	25.38336	19.38704	0.0059
At most 1	0.135805	6.276153	12.51798	0.4260

Max-eigenvalue test indicates 1 co-integrating eqn(s) at the 0.05 level
*denotes rejection of the hypothesis at the 0.05 level
**MacKinnon-Haug-Michelis (1999) p-values

Table 9 Normalized co-integrating coefficients (standard error in parentheses)

Log GDP	Log M
1.000000	0.214023 (0.66978)

Table 10 Granger causality of India result

Pairwise Granger causality tests
Sample: 1971–2023
Lags: 2

Null hypothesis	Obs.	F-statistic	Probability
Log M3 does not Granger Cause Log GR	43	4.17490*	0.0230
Log GR does not Granger Causes Log M3		1.68557	0.1989
	FINANCE ⟶ GROWTH		

Significant at 5% level of significance

out in Fig. 12. Response from shocks in variable provides a path for GDP. The path increased up to 2 years, then starts declining till the year of 5 year and then becomes constant up to 10 years. Further, Table 12 demonstrates the results from Cholesky Variance Decomposition technique. A good proportion of the variance in GR shocks is attributable to M3. In this way Impulse response function (IRF) and variance decomposition (VDC) results confirm our empirical findings. It appears that Financial Deepening has made positive contribution in the Indian economy. Our empirical results reveal two important features: (a) GDP in India is Granger caused by Financial Deepening and the causality runs more from Financial Deepening to GDP (b) Financial Deepening intends to increase the economic productivity in Indian economy.

From the literature of financial liberalization and deepening, the theory of financial liberalization can succeed only if it is properly adopted in the order of sequencing of reform. There is support in the literature that financial liberalization should be

Table 11 VECM results for financial deepening and economic growth rate

Error correction	D(LOGINDG)	D(LOGINDBM)
CointEq1	−0.4562297 (0.28684) [−3.70346]	−0.055945 (0.02198) [−2.54548]
D(LOGINDG(−1)	−0.036397 (0.21711) [−0.16764]	0.020445 (0.01664) [1.22900]
D(LOGINDG(−2)	0.146203 (0.14836) [0.98546]	0.016260 (0.01137) [1.43042]
D(LOGINDBM(−1)	3.469484 (1.99703) [1.73732]	0.279376 (0.15302) [1.82580]
D(LOGINDBM(−2)	0.789752 (2.22638) [0.35472]	−0.043068 (0.17059) [−0.25247]
C	−0.098249 (0.08045) [−1.22130]	0.019210 (0.00616) [3.11660]
R-squared	0.662625	0.339524
Adj. R-squared	0.613011	0.242396
Sum sq. resids	5.785979	0.033969
S. E. equation	0.412524	0.031608
F-statistic	13.35562	3.495613
Log likelihood	−18.08870	84.66645
Akaike AIC	1.204435	−3.933322
Schwartz SC	1.457767	−3.679990
Mean dependent	−0.008058	0.025537
S.D. dependent	0.663132	0.036314
Determinant resid covariance (dof adj.)		0.000163
Determinant resid covariance		0.000118
Log likelihood		67.36066
Akaike information criterion		−2.668033
Schwartz criterion		−2.076925

combined with trade liberalization. Financial liberalization may be welfare-inducing for allowing banks to pay higher real deposit rates of interest, which enables them to expand their role in the economy as the efficient financial instruments. However, increased flow of finance needs to be conditioned by correct price signals; otherwise, investment may be taking place in the wrong sectors, i.e., not according to a country's comparative advantage and not where social rates of return are highest, and liberalization of foreign capital—that capital account convertibility should only follow

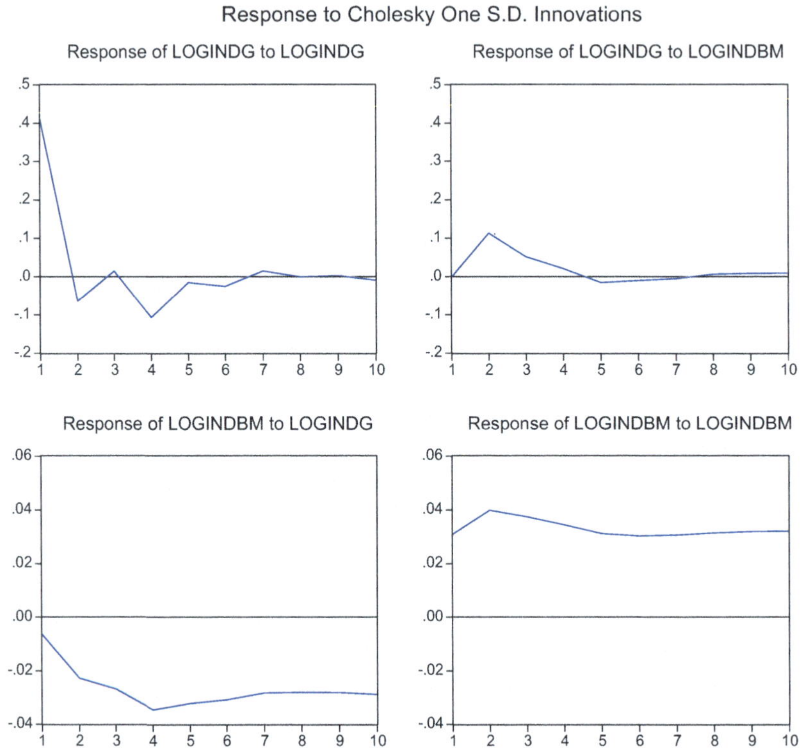

Fig. 12 Response to Cholesky One S.D. Innovations

domestic financial liberalization. Further, not only order but pace of liberalization in developing countries should be gradual. See McKinnon (1973) and Shaw (1973).

7 Conclusions

The chapter examines the long-run and causal relationship between financial deepening and economic growth in South Africa and India with the help of new time series methodology for the period of 52 years (1971–2023). We attempt to discuss the theory of financial repression and liberalization and its application in South Africa and India; both countries are highly developing, emerging, and leading economies of BRICS. The financial sector reforms adopted by the South African economy in 1985 and Indian economy since 1991 onwards appear to be based on the theoretical backdrop of McKinnon-Shaw (1973) theory of financial liberalization. Further the paper analyzes the trends of GDP growth rate and financial deepening in South Africa and India. The study finds that financial deepening is not co-integrated with economic growth in South Africa and shows no positive and long-run relationship, but in India

Table 12 Variance decomposition of GR and M3

Period	S. E.	Log GR	Log M3
Variance decomposition of Log GR			
1	0.412524	100.0000	0.000000
2	0.432625	93.07493	6.925067
3	0.436068	91.73005	8.269950
4	0.449259	91.97108	8.028924
5	0.449724	91.88323	8.116774
6	0.450484	91.86702	8.132979
7	0.450775	91.86861	8.131387
8	0.450835	91.84445	8.155545
9	0.450947	91.80394	8.196063
10	0.451132	91.76249	8.237508
Variance decomposition of Log M3			
1	0.031608	3.838962	96.16104
2	0.055770	17.70384	82.29616
3	0.072333	24.12595	75.87405
4	0.087212	32.11857	67.88143
5	0.098030	36.06020	63.93980
6	0.107123	38.36508	61.63492
7	0.114911	39.28507	60.71493
8	0.122390	39.81479	60.18521
9	0.129569	40.16990	59.83010
10	0.136547	40.56140	59.43860

both the variables are co-integrated and find long-run and positive relationship and significant at 5% level. Granger causality results also show the difference in the direction of causality. In South Africa causality runs from growth to finance, which supports the hypothesis of Demand-Led Growth, while in India causality runs from finance to growth, which supports the hypothesis of Supply Led Growth. Further our results are supported by the VECM, IRF, and VDC. The chapter finds that the liberalized financial system has not been able to increase effective growth rates in South Africa, while it has a proven record in India. Hence we suggest further improvement in money and capital markets in South Africa through appropriate macroeconomic policies. Indian programs of successful financial deepening and growth nexus should be the guide for the improvement in the financial system of South Africa and other SSA countries. One can understand that India, with its sound financial system serves as an ideal case study for South Africa. Our findings regarding South Arica are also consistent with the results of Odhiambo (2010).

Notes

1. For a detailed discussion on South African financial system, see Odhiambo (2005, 2010).
2. In mid-1996 Government of South Africa announced its long term strategy for 'Growth, Employment and Redistribution (GEAR) Programme but in 2001, due to world economic slowdown, GDP growth slowed down to 2.8%.
3. When a country is in economic crisis, then this particular country adopts SAP (Structural Adjustment Programme) of the IMF and the World Bank. SAP involves several steps to perform such as control on fiscal deficit, public sector reform (i.e.), charging correct prices of public utilities and reduction of unwanted subsidies, trade and exchange rate competitiveness, Central bank's autonomy and financial sector reforms which include mainly money and capital markets reforms. Now out of these comprehensive programmes, we chose to study 'Financial Sector Reform' Programmes theoretically and empirically in this paper. For a detailed discussion on this topic, see Pal (2016).

References

Abu, B. S., & Abu, Q. A. M. (2005). *Financial development and economic growth: Time series evidence from Egypt* (Discussion Paper No. 05-14n). Monaster Centre for Economic Research, Ben-Gurion University of Negev.

Abu, B. S., & Abu, Q. A. M. (2008). Financial development and economic growth: Empirical evidence from MENA countries. *Review of Development Economics, 12*(4), 803–817.

Agarwal, P. (1995). *Financial sector reforms in South Asia: Issues and evidence*. Paper presented at XIth World Congress of the International Economic Association, 18–22 December 1995, Tunis.

Agbetsiafa, D. (2003). The finance growth nexus: Evidence from Sub-Saharan Africa. *International Advances in Economic Research, 9*(2), 172.

Akinboade, O. A. (1998). Financial development and economic growth in Botswana: A test for causality. *Savings and Development, 22*(3), 331–348.

Akinlo, A., & Egbetunde, T. (2010). Financial development and economic growth: The experience of 10 Sub-Saharan African countries revisited. *The Review of Finance and Banking, 2*(1), 17–28.

Allen, D. S., & Ndikumana, L. (2000). Financial intermediation and economic growth in Southern Africa. *Journal of African Economies, 9*(2), 132–160.

Al-Yousif, Y. K. (2002). Financial development and economic growth: Another look at the evidence from developing countries. *Review of Financial Economics, 11*(2), 131–150.

Ang, J. B. (2008). A survey of recent developments in the literature of finance and growth. *Journal of Economic Surveys, 22*(3), 536–576.

Arestis, P., Demetriades, P., & Luintel, K. (2001). Financial development and economic growth: The role of stock markets. *Journals of Money, Credit and Banking, 33*(1), 16–41.

Atindehou, R. B., Gueyie, J. P., & Amenounve, E. K. (2005). Financial intermediation and economic growth: Evidence from Western Africa. *Applied Financial Economics, 15*(11), 777–790.

Banerjee, A., et al. (1993). *Cointegration, error correction, and econometric analysis of non-stationary data*. Oxford University Press.

Banerjee, S. S., & Ghosh, S. (1998). *Demand following and supply leading relationships: An empirical analysis for India* (MPRA Paper 22443). University Library of Munich.

Bhattacharya, P., & Sivasubramanian, M. N. (2003). Financial development and economic growth in India: 1970–1971 to 1998–1999. *Applied Financial Economics, 13*(12), 925–929.

Beck, T., & Honohan, P. (2007). *Making finance work for Africa*. The World Bank.

Bell, C., & Rousseau, P. L. (2001). Post-independence India: A case of finance-led industrialization. *Journal of Development Economics, 65*(1), 153–175.

Darrat, A. (1999). Are financial deepening and economic growth casually related? Another look at the evidence. *International Economic Journal, 13*(3), 19–35.
De Kock Commission. (1978). The *commission of inquiry into the monetary system and monetary policy in South Africa: Exchange rates in South Africa* (Interim Report, RPl 12/1978). Government Printer.
De Kock Commission. (1985). *The commission of inquiry into the monetary systems and monetary policy in South Africa* (Final Report, RP70/1984). Government Printer.
Demetriades, P. O., & Hussein, K. A. (1996). Does financial development cause economic growth? Time series evidence from 16 countries. *Journal of Development Economics, 51*(2), 387–411.
Demirguc-Kunt, A., &Levine, R. (2008). *Finance, financial sector policies, and long-run growth* (Policy Research Working Paper No. 4469).
Dickey, D., & Fuller, W. (1981). Likelihood ratio statistics for autoregressive time series with a unit root. *Econometrica, 49*(4), 1057–1072.
Egbetunde, T. (2009). *Financial intermediation and economic growth in sub-Saharan Africa (1980–2005)* (M.Sc thesis). Obafemi Awolowo University.
Engle, R. F., & Granger, C. W. J. (1987). Cointegration and error correction: Representation, estimation and testing. *Econometrica, 55*(2), 251–276.
Fowowe, B. (2011). Financial sector reforms and private investment in Sub-Saharan African countries. *Journal of Economic Development, 36*(3), 79–97.
Fry, M. (1988). *Money, interest and banking in economic development*. The John Hopkins University Press.
Ghali, K. H. (1999). Financial development and economic growth: The Tunisian experience. *Review of Development Economics, 3*(3), 310–322.
Ghirmay, T. (2004). Financial development and economic growth: In Sub-Saharan African Countries: Evidence from time series analysis. *African Development Review, 16*(3), 415–432.
Goldsmith, R. (1969). *Financial structure and development*. Yale University Press.
Greenwood, J., & Boyan, J. (1990). Financial development, growth, and the distribution of income. *Journal of Political Economy, 98*(5), 1076–1107.
Greenwood, J., & Bruce, S. (1997). Financial markets in development, and the development of financial markets. *Journal of Economic Dynamics and Control, 21*(1), 145–181.
Gujarati, D. N. (2020). *Basic econometrics* (6th ed.). Mc Graw Hill.
Habibullah, M. S., & Eng, Y. K. (2006). Does financial development cause economic growth? A panel data dynamic analysis for the Asian developing countries. *Journal of the Asian Pacific Economy, 11*(4), 377–393.
Huw, P., & Mahmood, P. (1997). *Financial indicators and financial change in africa and asia*. IMF Working. Paper No. 95/123.
Jadhav, N. (1994). *Monetary economics for India*. Macmillan.
Jayaratne, J., & Strahan, P. E. (1996). The finance-growth nexus: Evidence from bank-branch deregulation. *The Quarterly Journal of Economics, 111*(3), 639–670.
Johansen, S. (1988). Statistical analysis of cointegrating vectors. *Journal of Economic Dynamics and Control, 12*, 231–254.
Johansen, S., & Juselius, K. (1990). Maximum likelihood estimation and inference on cointegration with application to demand for money. *Oxford Bulletin of Economics and Statistics, 52*, 169–210.
Kasekende, L., Mlambo, K., Murinde, V., & Zhao, T. (2009). Restructuring for competitiveness: The financial services sector in Africa's four largest economies. In World Economic Forum (Ed.), *The Africa Competitiveness Report* (pp. 49–82). World Economic Forum.
Keynes, J. M. (1936). *The general theory of employment, Interest and money*. Palgrave Macmillan.
Khan, M., & Senhadji, A. S. (2003). Financial development and economic growth: A review and new evidence. *Journal of African Economies, 12*(2), 89–110.
King, R. G., & Levine, R. (1993a). Finance, entrepreneurship and growth: Theory and evidence. *Journal Monetary Economics, 32*(3), 513–542.
King, R. G., & Levine, R. (1993b). Financial and growth: Schumpeter might be right. *The Quarterly Journal of Monetary Economics, 108*(3), 717–737.

Kuznets, S. (1955). Economic growth and income inequality. *The American Economic Review, 45*(1), 1–28.
Lutz, B. (2008). Financial development and income in North Africa. *International Advance in Economic Research, 14*(4), 422–432.
Levine, R. (1997). Financial development and economic growth: Views and agenda. *Journal of Economic Literature, 35*(2), 688–726.
Lewis, W. A. (1995). *Theory of economic growth*. Allen and Unwin Ltd.
Luintel, K. B., & Khan, M. (1999). A quantitative reassessment of the finance-growth nexus: Evidence from a multivariate VAR. *Journal of Development Economics, 60*(2), 381–405.
Lutkepohl, H. (1982). Non-causality due to omitted variables. *Journal of Econometrics, 19*(2–3), 367–378.
Maddala, G. S. (1992). *Introduction to econometrics* (2nd ed.). Prentice Hall.
Odhiambo, N. M. (2004). Is financial development still a spur to economic growth? A causal evidence from South Africa. *Savings and Development, 28*(1), 47–62.
Odhiambo, N. M. (2005). Financial liberalization and financial deepening: Evidence from Three Sub-Saharan African (SSA) countries. In *African review of money, finance and banking* (pp. 5–23). Giordano Dell-Amore Foundation.
Odhiambo, N. M. (2007). Supply-leading versus demand-following hypothesis: Empirical Evidence from three SSA countries. *African Development Review, 19*(2), 257–280.
Odhiambo, N. M. (2008). Financial depth, savings and economic growth in Kenya: A dynamic causal linkage. *Economic Modeling, 25*(4), 704–713.
Odhiambo, N. M. (2010). Interest rate deregulation, bank development and economic growth in South Africa: An empirical investigation. *International Business & Economics Research Journal, 9*(11), 131–142.
Ozturk, I. (2007). Finance-growth nexus: Empirical evidence from South Africa. *Economic Studies Journal, 4*, 3–17.
McKinnon, R. I. (1973). *Money and capital in economic development*. The Brookings Institution Press.
Mwenda, A. (1993). *Credit rationing and investment behaviour under market imperfections: Evidence from commercial banking in Zambia* (PhD thesis. University of Gothenburg, Gothenburg.
Mwenda, A., & Mutoti, N. (2011). Financial sector reforms, bank performance and economic growth: Evidence from Zambia. *African Development Review, 23*(1), 60–74.
Pal, M. (1997). *Financial development in India: An empirical test of McKinnon-Shaw model*. A paper presented at Annual Conference Pennsylvania Economic Association, Annual Conference, Shippensburg, PA.
Pal, M. (2012). Financial sector reforms and economic growth in Zambia. *Indian Journal of African Studies, 18*(1 & 2), 151–162.
Pal, M. (2013). Finance-growth nexus in India: An evidence from co-integration and VECM. In *Econometrics applications in management*. Central University of Rajasthan. National Publishing House.
Pal, M. (2014a). Financial development in India—An empirical test of McKinnon-Shaw model. In A. N. Ghosh & A. K. Karmakar (Eds.), *Analytical issues in trade, development and finance: Essays in honor of Biswajit Chatterjee* (pp. 405–420). Springer.
Pal, M. (2014b). Financial policy of India—Theory & evidence from co-integration. *H. R. Journal of Management, 7*(1), 1–27.
Pal, M. (2016). The IMF conditionality theory and application in India. In D. Bhowmik (Ed.), *International monetary system: Past, present and future* (pp. 72–98). Regal Publication.
Pal, M. (2023). *Foreign capital and economic growth in India: Time series estimation*. Palgrave MacMillan (Springer Nature).
Pandit, V. N. (2001). *Structural modeling under challenge* (Working Paper No. 98). CDE, DSE.
Patrick, H. T. (1966). Financial development and economic growth in underdeveloped countries. *Economic Development and Cultural Change, 14*(2), 174–189.

Pill, H., & Pradhan, M. (1997). Financial liberalization in Africa & Asia. *Finance and Development, 34*(2), 7–10.
Pradhan, R. P. (2011). Financial development, growth and stock market development: The trilateral analysis in India. *Journal of Quantitative Economics, 9*, 134–145.
Raheem, M. I. (1993). Nigeria for Africa: A case for labour export. In T. A. Oyejide & M. I. Obadan (Eds.), *Applied economics and economic policy—In honour of Emmanuel C. Edozien*. Ibadan University Press.
Rajan, R. G., & Zingales, L. (1998). Financial dependence and growth. *American Economic Review, 88*(3), 559–586.
Ray, S. (2013). Does financial development promote economic growth in India? *International Journal of Economics Practices and Theories, 3*(3), 140–151.
RBI. (1985). *Committee to Review the Working of Monetary System* (Chairman S. Chakravarty), RBI Bulletin (1985).
Sabyasachi, K., & Mandal, K. (2014). Re-Examining the finance-growth relationship for a developing economy: A time series analysis of Post-Reform India. *The Journal of Developing Areas, 48*(1), 83–105.
Sahoo, S. (2014). Financial intermediation and growth: Bank-based versus market-based systems. *The Journal of Applied Economic Research, 8*(2), 93–114.
Schumpeter, J. A. (1911). *The theory of economic development*. Harvard University Press.
Schumpeter, J. A. (1934). *The theory of economic development an inquiry into profits, capital, credit, interest, and the business cycle*. Harvard University Press.
Seck, D., & El Nil, Y. H. (1993). Financial liberalization in Africa. *World Development, 21*(11), 1867–1881.
Shaw, E. S. (1973). *Financial Deepening in Economic Development*. Oxford University Press.
Spears, A. (1992). The role of financial intermediation in economic growth in Sub-Saharan Africa. *Canadian Journal of Development Studies, 13*(3), 361–379.
Stock, J. H., & Watson, M. W. (1996). Evidence on structural instability in macroeconomic time series relations. *Journal of Business and Economic Statistics, 14*(1), 11–30.
Waqabaca, C. (2004). *Financial development and economic growth in Fiji* (Working Paper 2004/03). Economics Department of Reserve Bank of Fiji.
Wolde-Rufael, Y. (2009). Re-examining the financial development and economic growth nexus in Kenya. *Economic Modeling, 26*(6), 1140–1146.
Wood, A. (1993). Financial development and economic growth in Barbados: Causal evidence. *Savings and Development, 17*(4), 379–390.
World Bank. (1989). *World development report 1989, financial systems and development*. Oxford University Press.
Xu, Z. (2000). Financial development, investment, and economic growth. *Economic Inquiry, 38*(2), 331–334.

Food and Nutrition Security in India

Temporal Trend of Food Security in India: Dimensions and Dilemmas

Supravat Bagli and Papita Dutta

Abstract Food security plays twin role in the process of development. First it contributes human development improving health indicators and second it accelerates growth improving productivity of labour. Food Security is a multidimensional concept. This chapter examines the six dimensions of food security; availability; accessibility; stability; utilization; agency; and sustainability in the context of Indian economy. Using secondary data the temporal trends of the indicators under the six dimensional framework have been analyzed. The analysis of per capita availability and accessibility of food grains shows that both are increasing. India is self-sufficient to produce its own food. Despite that, a persistent puzzle such that per capita consumption increases whereas per capita nutritional intake decreases had been identified in 2010s. After a persistent fall, per capita calorie and protein intake started rising since 2011–12. This study explores an inverse relation between women's participation in labour force and prevalence of undernutrition in recent time. The trend of sustainability indicators confirms sustainability of our agriculture not in an alarming situation. However, recent health and hunger indicators are disappointing. Some of them are deteriorating further in recent years. The analysis suggests for introducing universal PDS and extending procurement for some non-cereal products to improve the hunger situation. Opening of opportunity for employment for women, and investment in environmental friendly water management, and biotechnology for sustainability of agriculture may be effective for improving health and hunger statistics of India.

Keywords Food security · Hunger index · Indian Agriculture · Sustainability of food security · Public distribution system

S. Bagli (✉)
Presidency University, Kolkata, India
e-mail: supravat.bagli@gmail.com

P. Dutta
Gushkara Mahavidyalaya, Gushkara, India

B. Chatterjee and A. K. Karmakar (eds.), *Analytical Issues in Growth & Structural Change, Macroeconomy, Security, and Sustainability of India's Economic Development*, India Studies in Business and Economics, https://doi.org/10.1007/978-981-95-5242-9_9

1 Introduction

Access to food is the essential component of health status because without food we cannot survive. Life would be absolutely insecure if access to food is insecure. Food security increases the productivity of the labour force. Food security is not only essential for human development; it has an instrumental power in increasing productivity. Thus, food security system of a country plays twin role in the process of development. In this view, complete food security is crucial for inclusive sustainable development. However, even in this twenty-first century's world, a number of people die or tends to die only for the dearth of food. It is equally true for India (Narayan, 2021). Food security is, thus, our foremost priority for sustainable development. The second goal of the Sustainable Development Goals (SDGs) adopted by the United Nations (UN) in 2015 is to end all forms of hunger and malnutrition by 2030 ensuring access to sufficient and nutritious food in a sustainable manner. To achieve this goal UN has suggested the countries to eradicate all forms of malnutrition, stunting and wasting in children under 5 years of age, and address the nutritional needs of adolescent girls, pregnant and lactating women and older persons. The UN emphasizes agricultural productivity promoting sustainable agriculture with equal access to land, technology and markets.

Achievement of complete food security has been a major policy agendum of the Government of India since independence. During 1965s and 1960s we imported huge amount of food grains. During pre-green revolution time the assurance of sufficient food production and its price stability were the main challenges for development in India. Achievement of self-sufficiency in food grain production was in priority in the five years plans. Towards this goal the governments took several steps like extensive river valley irrigation, use of HYV technology, land reforms in favour of real farmers, and extension of service of financial institutions to the farmers etc. for improving the conditions of agriculture in India. All these initiative accelerated 'Green Revolution' at the end of 1960s. India has achieved self-sufficiency in food grains production in 1970s and has sustained it since then. But self-sufficiency in production did not ensure the access to sufficient amount of food grains at affordable prices for all. Public distribution system in India has been working since independence to ensure the access to basic food items at an affordable price for the poor households. Moreover, the national Food security Act, 2013, enacted to provide subsidized food grains to two third of Indians. This Act covers the PDS and other child nutritional development programs like midday meals scheme, Integrated Child Development Services Scheme and recognizes maternity entitlements. During the Covid 19 situation all these programs worked hard to ensure the food security for the people in India particularly for the marginalized sections.

Despite the presence of Right to Food Act, 2013 and widespread network of PDS in India only during the complete lockdown in March 2020 more than 200 people in India died as a result of starvation, financial distress and exhaustion (Aman et al., 2020). Narayan (2021) has reported that most of these households did not get free or subsidized food grains during that time, because they did not hold functional ration cards. Food and Agriculture Organization (FAO, 2022) reported that more than 17.6% of Indians are undernourished in 2020 which was 18.4% in 2001.The prevalence of undernourishment in India has increased 15% during 2019–20. No doubt, the situation has deteriorated during the Covid-19 situation in 2020–21. So, the problem of food security in India is a persistent problem. In 2010India had rank 67 out of 84 countries with hunger index value 0.24. Now in 2021 rank of India in accordance with its score in GHI 27.3 is 105 out of 127 countries (Concern Worldwide & Welthungerhilfe, 2021). According to International Food Policy Research Institute these statistics indicate the alarming hunger problem in India during the last decade. The GHI combined the indicators—share of undernourished people to the total population, prevalence of underweight children under age five years and infant mortality rate. Therefore, the public policies towards food and nutrition securities are not working in our expected direction. Food security in India is thus a persistent and challenging issue.

With this current scenario this chapter has tried to examine the temporal trend of the dimensions of food security and its dilemmas in India during the last two decades and try to focus the way forward. The remaining part of this chapter has five more sections. Section 2 has discussed the definitions and dimensions of food security. Section 3 deals with the analysis of the trend of the indicators of the dimensions of food security system focusing the dilemmas in the context of India. In Sect. 4 we have discussed the existing scenario and policies for food security in India. We shall propose some alternative policies for achieving complete food security in Sect. 5. Section 6 has concluded the chapter.

2 Definition and Dimensions of Food Security

In order to analyse the different dimensions of food security in India in recent times we should explain the definition and dimensions of food security. The concept of food security has evolved over time since 1970s. The first formal definition of food security appeared in World Food Conference; 1974 as: "[the] availability at all times of adequate world food supplies of basic foodstuffs, particularly so as to avoid acute food shortages in the event of widespread crop failure, natural or other disasters, to sustain a steady expansion of food consumption in countries with low levels of per capita intake and to offset fluctuations in production and prices" (United Nations, 1975).This definition basically emphasized on the production and supply side stability of the food items. And accordingly the nations started to take policy to produce more using new technology for achieving food security. Sen (1981) has shown that sufficient availability of food does not ensure the sufficient access to food. In his famous book *Poverty and Famines* he explained even where food was widely available in markets, famine situations arose because of the inaccessibility of food by a large section of people due to lack of purchasing power and entitlement to food. Against this backdrop Food and Agriculture Organisation (1982) defined food security as "ensuring that all people at all times have both physical and economic access to basic food they need". Further, in early 1980s short run instability in the supply of food created caused chronic food shortage and hunger in sub Saharan African countries (Clapp et al., 2022). Food and Agriculture Organisation (1982) has also upheld the importance of stability of food supply in short run. It formulated a conceptual framework for food security system mentioning three main dimensions of food security system. According to FAO (1982) three dimensions of food security are adequate food supply; maximum stability in the flow of supplies and affordable access to food who need it. In the same line World Bank (1986) defined food security "as access by all people at all times to enough food for an active, healthy life".

Further, in the 1990s, when nutritional aspects entered in to the literature of poverty the concept of food security has been widened. At the first conference on Nutrition 1992 (FAO 1992) the nutritional aspects of accessed food had been recognised as fourth pillar of food security system of a nation. Finally, adequacy of nutrition in food has been labelled as utilisation dimension of food security. With this end in view, FAO defined food security and modified several times. The latest definition of food security provided by FAO is as follows. Food Security exists when all people at all times, have physical, social and economic access to sufficient, safe and nutritious food to meet their dietary needs and food preference for an active and healthy life (FAO, 2001). At present, this is the globally accepted definition of food security. And global food security system formulated food security policies based on the four dimensions of food security system such that availability, accessibility, stability and utilisation of food. Majority of the studies in the literature of food security maintains a hierarchical order of these four dimensions such that availability of food necessary but not sufficient condition for access to food, access to food is necessary but not sufficient condition for proper utilisation; and stability in short run necessary for ensuring the affordable existence of other dimensions of food security. However, these dimensions are interconnected and complementary for smoothing the food security system of a nation.

However, progress towards achieving complete food security for all is not satisfactory. Food and Agriculture data, FAO (2022) tell us one third of world population faced food insecurity. From the same source we find that the condition of India is more serious relative to the world average. With this scenario Clapp et al. (2022) explained that we should expand the dimensions of food security system. They advocated to add two additional dimensions in the food security system for formulating policies towards complete food security. They have highlighted that the problem of hunger is chronic among the disadvantageous section of the society. To address this skewed distribution of the problem of food insecurity Clapp et al. (2022) argued to ensure the agency of the people with food system. In recent era there is a high interlinkage between food system and ecological system broadly environmental issues. The food security system for the people must be effective in a sustainable manner which is compatible with the concept of sustainable development. This fact justify the inclusion of sustainability of food security system as a new dimension of food security system and in the policy framework of food security. Clapp et al. (2022) has given a detailed account of the justification of these two new dimensions of food security system.

Therefore, food security system of a country is a multidimensional system. To address the problem of food insecurity countries frame their policies for food security based on the following its six dimensions.

(a) Availability of food
(b) Accessibility of food
(c) Stability in availability and accessibility of food
(d) Productive utilisation of food
(e) Agency of the people
(f) Sustainability of the availability, accessibility and utilisation of required food

Six dimensions of food security are definitely interconnected and complementary for an effective food security system. The concept of food security may be viewed as household level as well as at the economy level with the above dimensions. This study will try to give an account of the food security system and its outcomes in India in macroeconomic perspectives. In order to draw the glimpses of these dimensions of the food security system some selected indicators under each dimension have taken based on the report of FAO (2022) and on recent literature.

3 Trend of the Dimensions, Dilemmas and Development of the Food Security in India

In this section, we examine the trend of the indicators of the six dimensions of food security in the context of India for last two decades. We explore the dilemmas corresponding to each dimension. Finally, a detailed trend and comparison of the recent development of food security status of India which help to explore the policy options for achieving sustainable development goals in respect of food and hunger. This study explain the issues with the help of secondary data sources from different global agencies like FAOSTAT, World Bank, and national level source like RBI, Economic Survey, NSSO.

3.1 Availability of Adequate Food

Availability of food is the primary dimension of food security system. It includes the production, net import and procurement of food grains of a country. The production of sufficient food is necessary for achieving the complete of food security system. India has achieved self-sufficiency in production of food grains since 1970s. Although the productivity of food grains in India is relatively low compared to developed countries food shortage is not a serious problem in India. Figure 1 confirms that per capita food grains production and availability are increasing over time during the last two decades. Recently we observed a dilemma that per capita production is higher than the per capita availability. It was prominent during early 2010s where per capita availability was falling despite the increasing trend of per capita production. The figure displays that in 2003 and 2016 per capita production was less than the per capita availability. The PDS of our country successfully smoothed the gap between production and availability of food grains. Figure 2 shows that the share of procurement in net production and share of public distribution in net availability remains roughly unchanged during last two decades. In order to keep this stability in net availability, stocks with the Food Corporation of India is fluctuating. During late 2010s we see that stocks in government warehouses has increased significantly. With this situation we can recommend for increasing the per capita allotment of food for vulnerable section through PDS. However, in recent time diversification of diet among the current generation of forward and middle class Indians form nutri-cereals to high valued food items like milk, meat products, fruits and vegetables raises the demand for the high valued food items (Dev, 2018). To meet this rising demand for diversified food India should emphasise more to produce the non-cereal food items improving the agricultural production and productivity. It will definitely build the food security system resilient.

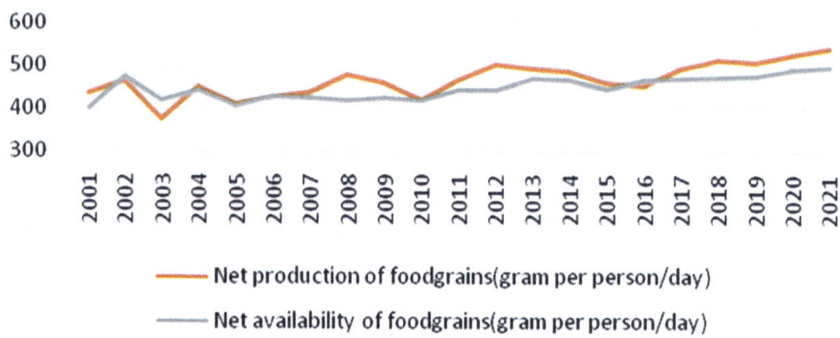

Fig. 1 Net production and net availability of food grains in India. *Source* compiled from data Economic Survey 2021–22 and World Bank

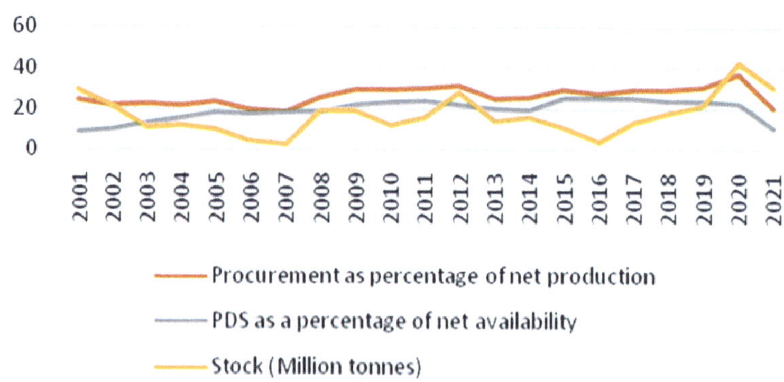

Fig. 2 Procurement, PDS and stocks in government granaries. *Source* compiled from data Economic Survey 2021–22

3.2 *Accessibility to Sufficient Food*

Sufficient amount of production of food grains/items does not ensure the access to sufficient food for all. Nobody would deny that in order to get access to sufficient food people need to have some purchasing power and accordingly require some entitlements. Or, there should have a strong public distribution system that ensures equitable access to food grains for maintaining healthy life. Therefore, accessibility of sufficient food is the most important dimension of food security system of a country. The trend of per capita GDP at constant price is a crude measure of the access to sufficient food. Figure 3 shows the trend of per capita GDP at constant price and per capita consumption expenditure for Indians during the last two decades. It indicates that both the indicators are increasing over time. There is a co-movement between the series. One can be satisfied with this picture for the trend of the access to food. A close look says that rate of change of income is higher than that of the per capita consumption. It means that the average propensity to consumption is falling. Average propensity to consumption was 0.64 in 2000 which is 0.58 in 2020. It happened due to concentration of income with the already rich people in the country. Therefore inequality in income and consumption is increasing over time which increases the inequality in access to food for the Indian. More specifically, vulnerability in access to food for the poor and marginal section of the society has been increasing during last two decades. Moreover, access to food depends on the price of the food items. Figure 4 shows the general inflation and inflation for food and beverage group based on consumer price index (CPI) with 2011–12 as base year. Price level plays dual role in the food security system in a country. One way it raises the income and thereby purchasing power of the farmers and indirectly income of the workers engaged in agriculture and allied activities, broadly rural people (Jacoby, 2013; Gulati et al., 2013). On the other way it reduces the purchasing power of the urban people who basically earn from off-farm employment. Therefore, inflation at low level is not bad. But when it fluctuates heavily it affects the access to food at least in short term. We see that during the period 2012–13 to 2018–19 price rise for food and beverage and general CPI has declined significantly. It definitely reduces the money income of the farmers particularly people of rural areas in India. The inflation for food and beverage was high or equal with general inflation up to 2016–17. However, during 2016–17 to 2018–19 the price rise for food and beverage was lower than the general price rise. So, the terms of trade was in favour of net food buyers. This situation adversely affect the access to food for the rural people who do not produce every components of food although it was the good period for the urban people who earn their livelihood from off-farm activities. However in recent years, price rise for food and beverage is increasing at a higher rate than that for general inflation. Thus the terms of trade are moving against industrial sector, thereby the off-farm sector of the economy particularly the low and fixed income group are facing hard times to get access to sufficient food when they need. Therefore, recent turning of the rise of food prices create difficulty in the smooth access to food for the people of India.

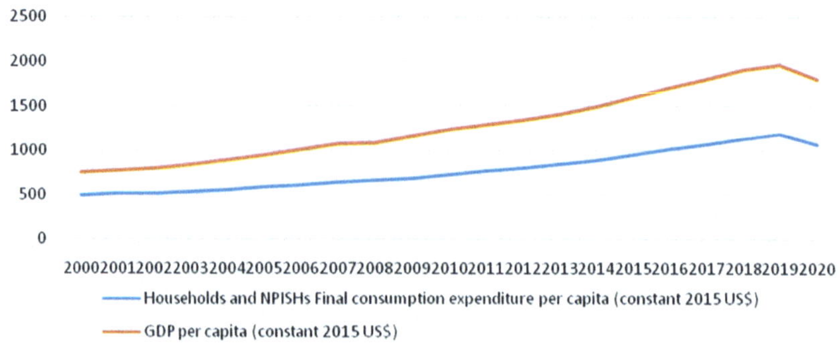

Fig. 3 Per capita consumption expenditure and per capita GDP during last two decades. *Source* compiled from data Economic Survey 2021–22 and World Bank

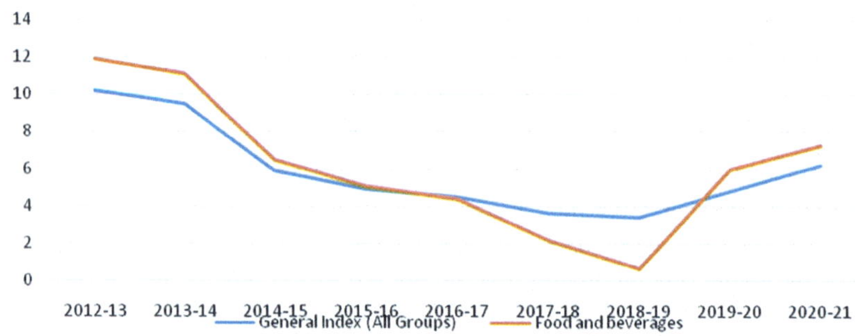

Fig. 4 Consumer Price Index (CPI) inflation. *Source* compiled from RBI, Annual Reports

The food security system in India thus may be strong in respect of availability but prominently weak in respect of the equitable access to food. In other words, the problem of food security system in India is not a problem of food shortage as shown in Fig. 1, rather a problem of existing distribution system or policy paralysis towards public distribution system. This problem is not new, long back it has been identified by Sen (1981). He analyzed how in accessibility of food by a large section of people with poor purchasing power and entitlement, not the shortage of food availability, caused, famine situations in 1970s. The access to sufficient food not only depends on availability of food on markets, but also on person's endowments of productive assets, employment status, and their rights within society. If the food entitlement failed—for example, recent pandemic resulted in job losses of many poor and non-poor workers, definitely hamper the access to food, in spite of the surplus production, stocks in government granaries and market availability. Therefore, the stability in supply of and in access to food is considered as third dimension of food security system of country.

3.3 *Stability in Food Security System*

The United Nations' Food and Agriculture Organization (FAO) has identified stability in food supply and in access along with the political stability as an important dimension of food security system of a country. Stability takes into account the vulnerability of the people to food insecurity due to temporary disruption inavailability, accessibility, or utilization of required food. Unexpected rainfall, political instability/terrorism, pandemic, epidemic, inflation, job losses may create instability in the food security system of a country. By stability in food security system we mean the short term volatility in production, variability in the indicators of access to food and in other economic and political factors. If there is high volatility in short term there is no certainty and smooth in access to food and its utilisation. This study measures the short term volatility or stability of the indicators of availability and accessibility and other factors computing the three years running coefficient of variation. Higher the value of the coefficient of variation lower the indication of stability.

Figure 5 shows that variability in food production is low in last decade comparted to that in the first decade of this millennium. Stability in production of food increases in recent years although the volume of production increases steadily. This type of trend in volatility in production may be justified with the statement; resilience to rainfall has been rising for Indian agriculture (Dev, 2018). Stability of food availability is however high during last five years (Fig. 6). It implies that our public distribution system successfully reduces the uncertainty in food availability in market for the last four five years. Therefore, the situation of the stability dimension of food availability is not so bad in India during the last two decades. Let us now see the variability in the indicators of the access to food. Figure 7 depicts the trend of variability of the indicators—per capita GDP and per capita consumption expenditure.

During 2002 to 2018 variability in per capita GDP was greater than the variability in per capita consumption expenditure. But in recent years the variability in per capita consumption is falling but it is greater than that in per capita GDP. It indicates that in spite of the stable income in average consumption fluctuate in short term. It may

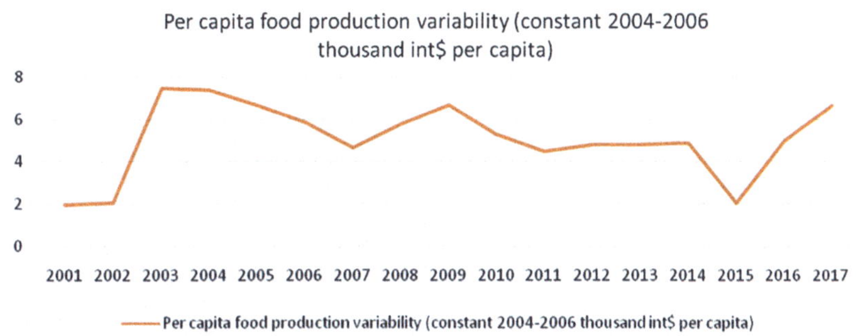

Fig. 5 Variability in per capita food production. 2022 *Source* Food and Agriculture Organization (FAO) Statistics (2022)

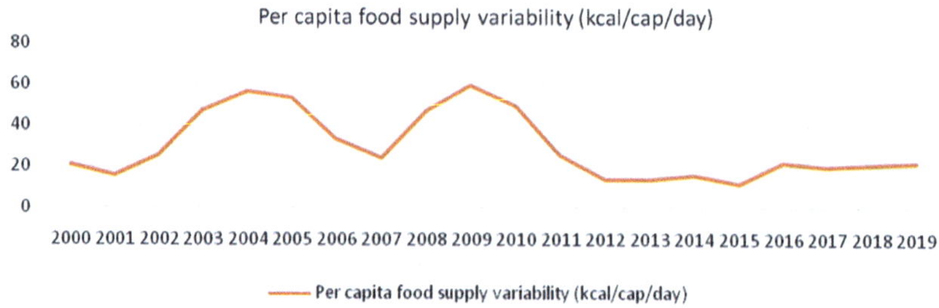

Fig. 6 Variability in per capita food Supply. 2022 *Source* Food and Agriculture Organization (FAO) Statistics (2022)

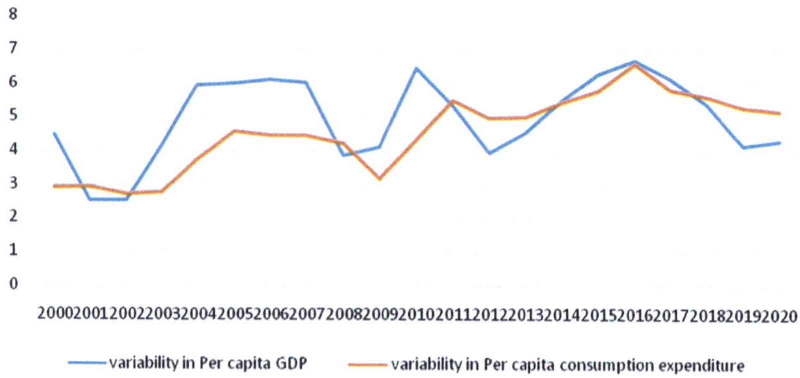

Fig. 7 Variability in per capita income and per capita consumption expenditure. *Source* compiled from data Economic Survey 2021–22 and World Bank

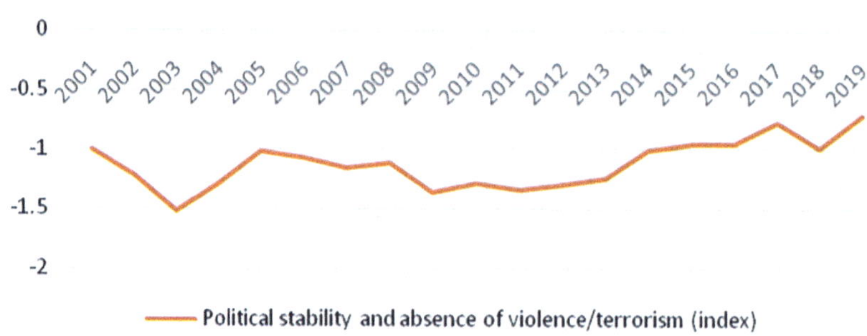

Fig. 8 Political stability and absence of violence/terrorism (index). 2022 *Source* Food and Agriculture Organization (FAO) Statistics ()

be due to factors other than income like job insecurity, price hike of the food and beverage relative to the general prices etc.

The United Nations' Food and Agriculture Organization (FAO) has considered political stability and absence of violence index as an indicator of stability in food security system. In accordance with FAO (2022) political stability and absence of violence index explores the perceptions of the chance that the government will be destabilized or overthrown by unconstitutional or violent means, including politically-motivated violence and terrorism. The value of the index ranges from −2 indicating strong political instability to 2 indicating strong political stability. In India the value of political stability did not fluctuate widely during the last two decades although it is negative throughout the period under consideration. In India political stability in average is consistently not good but recently it is slowly improving. Therefore, this indicator is not so important for explaining the food security system in India.

3.4 *Productive Utilisation of Accessed Food*

Access to sufficient food does not ensure the expected outcomes of the food security safety net. Success to food security system depends on proper utilization of food. Getting access to food many people may fail to utilise it for extracting sufficient energy and nutrition. Extraction of nutrition or utilisation of food is thus another dimension of food security system of a country identified by The United Nations' Food and Agriculture Organization (FAO). Extraction of nutrition from food closely connected with the absorption power which in turn positively correlated with health and hygiene standard of the households. Nutritional aspect of food security system encompasses the access to health care facility.

Table 1 presents the trend of nutritional data based on NSS data. Table 1 shows that recently per capita intake of calories has declined in rural and urban areas of India. However, protein intake have increased during 2009–10 to 2023–24. These, figures say that in respect of food utilisation in an average an Indian gets the minimum level of calorie and protein per day. This result is almost invariant across the rural and urban sector. But it is the average value. There is huge inequality in the consumption of food among different sections of our country. Thus if the average is equal to the minimum level, we can say a large section of population cannot consume minimum level of calories and protein. Moreover, NSSO data from different rounds shows per capita consumption of cereals and pulses has declined and consumption of high valued food has increases during 1983–84 to 2023–24. This is compatible with the Engle's law. However, the calorie and protein intake data generate a puzzle—calorie intake has fallen or remains almost unchanged despite the high prevalence of undernutrition in India.

Paucity of purchasing power, persistent high price of food and inadequate access to health care facility make the poor and vulnerable people suffering from malnutrition. This study, following FAO explores the temporal status of the Indian households in respect of the access to safe drinking water and sanitation to examine the proper utilisation of food security system.

Utilization ability of people increase if the access to basic amenities of health and hygiene, like use of safe drinking water, improved sanitation facility, increase.

Table 1 Per capita nutritional intake of Indian

	Calories (Kcal/day)		Protein (gm/day)	
year	Rural	Urban	Rural	Urban
2009–10	2147	2123	59.3	58.8
2011–12	2233	2206	60.7	60.3
2022–23	2233	2250	61.9	63.2
2023–24	2212	2240	61.8	63.4

Source NSS, 2023–24 and other past rounds on Consumer Expenditure Survey

Figure 9 displays the significant progress of the use of improved sanitation and access to safe drinking water for the households in India during last two decades. However, till now 9.5% of Indian households don't have access to safe drinking water, 29% of Indian households don't have access to improved sanitation in 2020. Here also we see the dilemma that despite the satisfactory level development in access to safe drinking water and sanitation, there is huge disparity in utilization of food i.e. nutritional intake. One point should be noted that more than 50% of the households use iodized salt with their food consumption. The situation is deteriorating recently (World Bank, 2022). An enormous scope have been there for further improvement of basic amenities of health and hygiene to accelerate the pace towards complete food security in India.

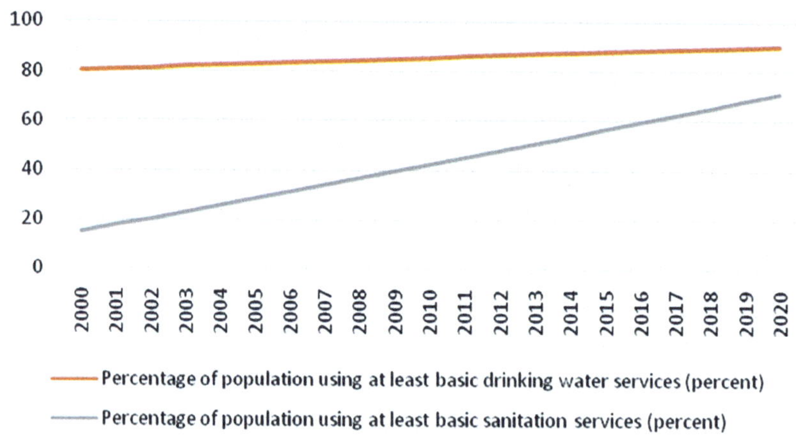

Fig. 9 Temporal status of the Indian Households in respect of the access to Safe Drinking Water and Sanitation. 2022 *Source* Food and Agriculture Organization (FAO) Statistics (2022)

3.5 Enhancement of Agency to the Food

In the literature of capability approach to development agency plays an important role for human development. The studies where food security is taken as an instrument of human development, agency plays vital to ensure food security at the household level and community level. Now a days, agency has been recognized as a non-material factors for reducing inequalities in socio economic aspects. It is an important for reducing inequities within food systems, including imbalances of power among actors within those systems (Clapp et al., 2022). According to Clapp et al. (2022) agency "refers to the capacity of individuals and groups to exercise a degree of control over their own circumstances and to provide meaningful input into governance processes". They have proposed to develop collective agency in the economy, particularly food policies for ensuring the equitable access to food systems at both individual and community levels. Indicators of agency varies depending on the nature of analysis. For example women's empowerment, decision making power, land ownership at the household level are the common indicators of agency at household level. At the national level, workforce participation, participation in governance, etc.

This study has considered only the female participation rate in labour force as an important indicator of agency of the consumer to food security system. Figure 10 displays that in recent times women's participation in labour force is falling. In 2014, 22% of the female aged 15 years above participated in labour force where as in 2020 it reduces to 18%. It may happen due to slowdown of Indian economy during late 2010s and broke out of Covid-19 pandemic in 2020. It is observed that there is an inverse relation between the prevalence of malnutrition and workforce participation rate of women. Therefore, the women's participation in labour force, an indicator of agency, is important factor to explain the recent scenario of food security in India.

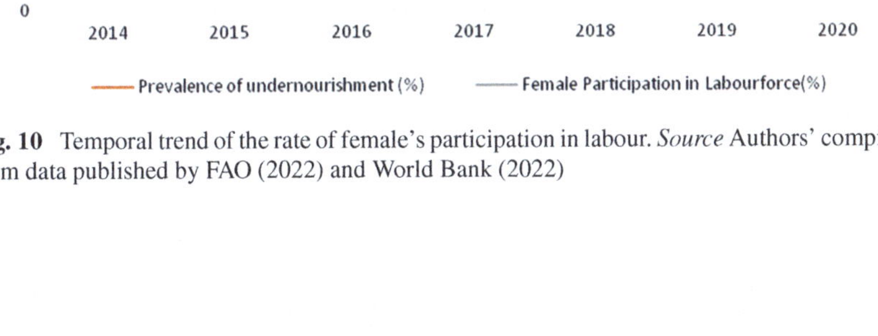

Fig. 10 Temporal trend of the rate of female's participation in labour. *Source* Authors' compilation from data published by FAO (2022) and World Bank (2022)

3.6 Sustainability of the Food Security

According to High Level Panel of Experts of the Committee on World Food Security considered the sustainability of food security as an important factors for achieving the sustainable development goals within 2030. Sustainability means that "food system practices that contribute to long-term regeneration of natural, social, and economic systems, ensuring the food needs of the present generations are met without compromising food needs of future generations" (HLPE, 2020). Sustainability is a long run concept. Stability of food security takes an account of short run volatility of food supply and demand due to supply demand shocks in short run, whereas sustainability of food security takes the account of ecosystem, livelihoods, climate change for long run food security system. Sustainable Development Goal-2 emphasized on sustainable agriculture for ending hunger. Therefore, sustainability should be an important dimension of food security system of a country. Although climate change and other issues of environment have some global perspectives, we take a crude indicators like use of chemical pesticides and chemical fertilizers for understanding the nature of food security in India in respect of sustainability. The data from FAOSTAT (2022) we find that in India share of agricultural land in total land falls slightly and share of cropland in agricultural land remains more or less unchanged. Figure 11 shows the trend of chemical pesticides used in agricultural during las two decades. Although in average the use of pesticides in India is significantly low compared to that in Japan, China even in America. The use of chemical pesticides in 2019 is not so high compared to that was in 2000. During the first decade the use of chemical pesticides reduced due to a prohibition or limit on using organochlorine pesticides, including HCH (BHC), DDT-aldrin etc. (2021). In recent years the use of chemical pesticides is slowly increasing which is not good for human health and norms of sustainability.

Figure 12 shows the trend of chemical fertilizer use in Indian agriculture. First we see that the components of nitrogen, Phosphate and Potash in fertilizer use have an increasing trend. Second, the use of nitrogen is increasing faster rate than the increasing rate of the use of phosphate and potash. Third, the average ratio of the use of the three major component of fertilizer maintains ratio 7:3:1 NPK. So far, the use of chemical fertilizer in per hector agricultural land has increased to almost double

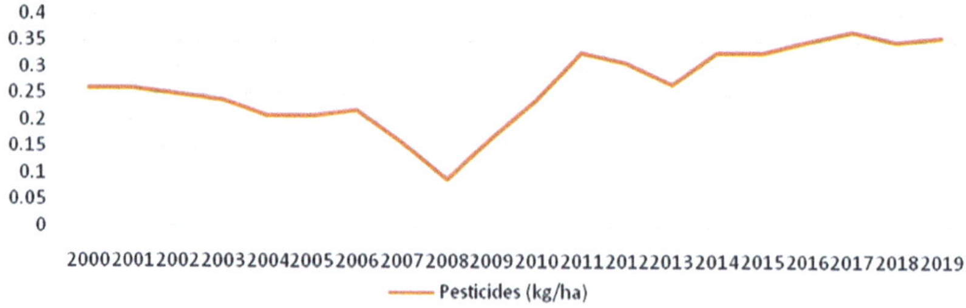

Fig. 11 Use of Chemical Pesticides in agriculture in India during 2000–2019. *Source* Authors' compilation from data published by FAO (2022)

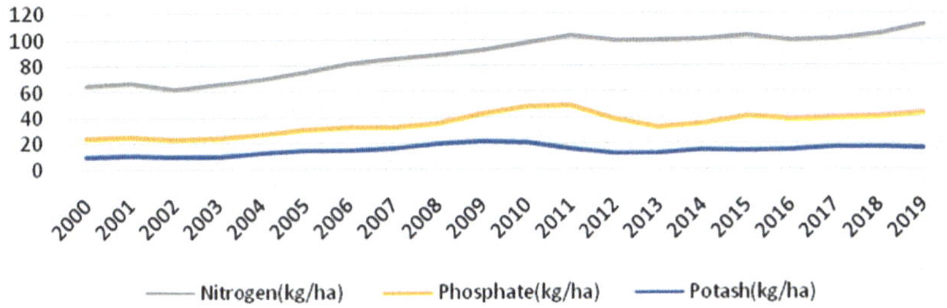

Fig. 12 Use of Chemical Fertilizer in agriculture in India during 2000–2019. *Source* Authors' compilation from data published by FAO (2022)

during last 20 years. So the indicators under sustainability are not in favour of the sustainability of the Indian agriculture.

The above analysis, therefore, claims that the problem of food security in India lies in the problem of accessibility to food, utilization of food, in agency power of people and in sustainability. India is in a good position in respect of average availability and stability in production. Against this backdrop, we should formulate food security policies putting more emphasis on the issues of accessibility to food and absorption of food and sustainability of food security for all.

4 Present Scenario of Hunger and Health: Are the Food Security Policies Working?

Despite the sufficient availability and stability of food production in India during last 50 years, India is home of the largest number of undernourished population (FAOSTAT, 2022). Undernourished person is not able to acquire enough food to meet the daily minimum dietary energy requirements, over a period of one year. FAO defines hunger as being synonymous with chronic undernourishment. Figure 13 shows that during the last two decades prevalence of under nourishment in India significantly higher than the world average. It is all time high compared to south Asian countries. The disappointing point is that during last two years the incidence of undernourishment in India and in the world is increasing. In India number of undernourished population increased 15% during 2019–20, where as in the World this change is 17% (Table 2). No doubt the situation is more disappointing during the pandemic times.

Further, Fig. 14 presents the scenario of child health and hunger index in India form the year 2000. All the indicators, except wasting, have slow downward sloping movement. Further the situation of wasting is more series among the households under marginalized castes and tribes. Therefore, the performance of the food security policies in our country is not satisfactory.

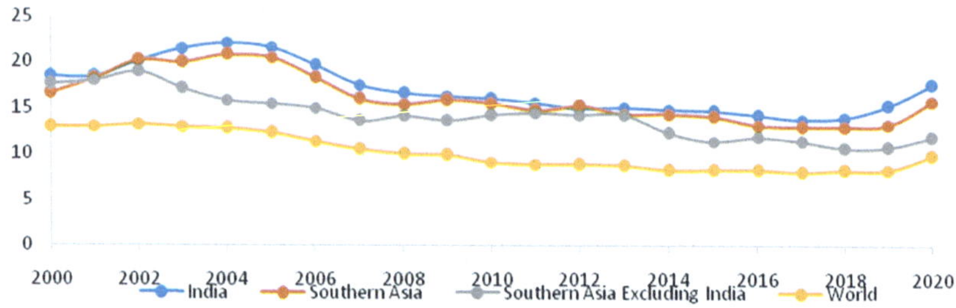

Fig. 13 Trend of the Prevalence of undernourishment (per cent of total Population). *Source* Authors' compilation from data published by FAO (2022)

Table 2 Number of undernourished population (per cent of total population)

Time period	India	Southern Asia	Southern Asia Excluding India	World
2019	208.6(15.3)	255.2(13.3)	58(10.7)	650.3(8.4)
2020	239.6(17.57)	305.7(15.8)	66.1(11.8)	768(9.9)
Change (%)	14.83	18.80	10.28	17.86

Source Authors' compilation from data published by FAO (2022)

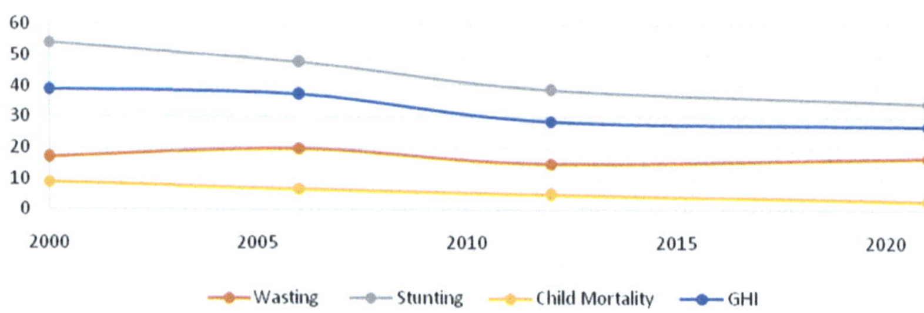

Fig. 14 Hunger and health statistics of India during last two decades. *Source* Authors' compilation from data published by NFHS, 2021, GHI

We have wide spread public distribution system and huge stock in our government granaries. In website we may find many programs for food security in India like the National Food Security Mission. We have Right to Food act 2013, which combines some programs like mid-day meal program. Basically all these national policies and programs for food security are connected with the PDS. It is really a good program for ensuring availability, accessibility, stability of food for all. Different programs introduce different types of ration cards and different eligibility criteria. This fact confused the beneficiaries and provider. Now a days, our PDS system is complex system to the poor and marginalized section for whom it is actually necessary. In 2013 the National Food Security Act ensured the supply of food grains for two third of our population through NFSA ration card. Now in 2022 our nation has added extra 20 crores but the ration card list remained unchanged. A large section of vulnerable population therefore remain outskirt of the PDS system. Further, as the current system is target based system it has some poor exclusion and rich inclusion like any other target based program. Therefore, despite the huge stock of food our PDS system fails to ensure food security of a large section of the people.

The government of India has also made some programs Rashtriya Krishi Vikas Yojana (RKVY), Pradhan Mantri Fasal Bima Yojana, the e-marketplace, as well as a massive irrigation and soil and water harvesting program for sustainability of Indian agriculture. However, we did not find any sound study indicating the successful story of these program regarding sustainability of food security In India.

5 Policy Prescriptions for Food Security in India

This study reveals that per capita net availability of food grains is increasing over time. But productivity of major crops in India are lower than that in many countries like China, Indonesia and others. It is a persistent problem of Indian agriculture. Moreover growth rate of the per capita availability and productivity of food grains have fallen during the reform periods (Bagli, 2014). Therefore, in order to improve the growth of food availability and productivity India need to improve the production condition of the food grains through investing more in technology, specifically biotechnologies, education particularly public investment in research and development, transport and storage facility, energy and better institutions. In this connection private investment and foreign investment may be allowed.

We have seen that situation of accessibility of food in India in recent years is deteriorating. In order to smooth the accessibility to basic food grains for the vulnerable the Government has a public distribution (PDS) system which has been modified time to time. No doubt that the PDS has no alternative to ensure the access to food for all in an equitable manner. At present, India introduced some supplementary programs such as targeted PDS including Antyodaya Anna Yojana (AAY), nutrition programs for children like mid-day meals, and ICDS to improve food and nutrition security of the children. These are under the Food Security Act 2013. However, many studies have criticized the present form and activities of the PDS in India in the ground of less inclusiveness, problem of elite capture, information asymmetries problem etc. (Dreze & Sen, 1989; Swaminathan, 2002; Bardhan & Mookherjee 2005; Narayan, 2021). Moreover it is very difficult to regularly update the eligible group. With this situation, we propose universal PDS to ensure the complete food security in India near future. After all the current stock and procurement can permit it. Moreover, at present government procures rice and wheat at MSP and extends subsidies for fertilizers, water, electricity, credit and seeds. These facilities usually go to the large farmers, few irrigated areas. This traditional policies accelerates inequality and adversely affect soil and water quality and product quality. These outcomes are against the sustainability of Indian agriculture. So, these limited scope of procurement and subsidies should be changed. It would more inclusive and diversified if the policy of procurement of MSP is applied for some non-cereal food. It will meet the diversified demand and utilization problem of food in present India. Hoarding of food grains sometimes causes food price inflation. Therefore, the access to food at an affordable price may be secured through PDS. The governments have to take some active policies like trade policy and procurement policy along with the PDS which control food price inflation.

We have explained that women's participation in labour force is closely connected with food security outcomes. For getting access to food people need to have purchasing power. Employment ensure this purchasing power. Adopting labour intensive technique in our manufacturing sector and/or through social protection programs we can increase employment. Apparel industry in our country has immense opportunity to create employment of our low skilled labour force particularly women. In rural India 75% of women engaged themselves in agriculture, but most of them don't have property right and access to other productive resources. Policies that ensure the property right of women in land and other productive assets are necessary to ensure food security in India. For this purpose government as well as NGOs may come forward to ensure livelihood security. In this connection micro finance groups is effective one. MGNREGS and group-centric micro enterprise are useful to increase access to food and nutrition. It ensures the life and livelihood security of the people.

Further, in order to enhance the agency of the people in food system we need some steps covering diet diversification, women's empowerment and development of awareness among the people regarding balanced diet, health and hygiene which will enhance the effective utilisation and sustainability food.

Indian agricultural use inputs like HYV seeds, fertilizers during last 60 years at a satisfactory level. Often production process use inputs at the lower ratio compared to the economically desirable point due inadequate capital formation, land and credit facility. Still now, a large number of Indian farmer don't have access to formal credit. The Governments have taken several initiatives like Krishan Credit Card, Crop insurance facility etc. financial inclusion in agricultural sector. India established river based irrigation system 60 years back, at present its functioning are not at satisfactory level. Despite the huge investment in canal irrigation recently one paradox appears such that net irrigated area under canal is shrinking due to urbanization. However, the cultivation of 50% of agrarian land exclusively depends on nature. Water management projects and other integrated farming methods are therefore, essential for improving the sustainability of food security. The government of India has initiated Accelerated Irrigation benefits program in 1996–97. Very recently Krishi Sinchani Yojana has been introduced. Financial constraints of the Government is a problem towards complete irrigation. Thus, the governments and appropriate authority have to allow private or foreign investment for improving the infrastructure like financial institutions, irrigation, storage and marketing facilities in agriculture for improving the sustainability of agriculture.

6 Conclusions

The concept of food security is a dynamic in nature. This chapter has given an account of the six dimensions of food security in India for last two decades. The dimensions of food security are availability, accessibility, stability, utilization, agency and sustainability. Agency and sustainability are the newly recognized dimensions, they are not incudes in global food security policy formulation. Based on the secondary data the temporal trends of the indicators have been analyzed and proposed a set of policy for achieving complete food security in India. The analysis of per capita production and availability of food grains shows that both are increasing but recently the gap between these two is widening. In the early 2010's there was puzzle such that although the per capita production increased, per capita availability decreased. So far, India is self-sufficient to produce its own food. It has a wide network of PDS. Despite that there is a persistent puzzle such that per capita consumption increases whereas per capita nutritional intake decreases (Deaton & Dreze, 2009). Further, in recent time prices of food is increasing over general price level. The indicators of stability of food security are more or less unchanged during the last two decades. It is observed that after a persistent fall for last 30 years per capita calorie intake and protein intake started upward rising since 2011–12. The study explores an inverse relation between women's participation in labour force and prevalence of undernutrition in recent time. However the trend of sustainability indicators confirms that sustainability of our agriculture is not in an alarming situation, but trend of the use of chemical fertilizer and pesticide should be checked for sustainability of food security. Despite the absence of red signal from the dimensions of food security in India health and hunger indicators are not good in a position. Some of them are deteriorating further in recent years. So, India has to traverse a long way to reach the destination notified by the sustainable development goals. In order to accelerate the speed of traverse we should introduce universal PDS and extend procurement for some non-cereal product. In addition to universal PDS, India has to take some policies for enhancing agency of people creating opportunity for employment of women, and for investment in environmental friendly water management, and biotechnology for sustainability of agriculture.

References

Aman, S. K, Thejesh, G., & Krushana. (2020). *Non virus deaths*. http://thejeshgn.com/project/covid19-india/non-virus-deaths/

Bagli, S. (2014). A study of food security in India. In P. K. Chattopadhyay (Ed.), *Growth and diversification aspects of rural development* (pp. 73–88). New Delhi Publishers.

Bardhan, P., & Mookherjee, D. (2005). Decentralising antipoverty program delivery in developing countries. *Journal of Public Economics, 89*(4), 675–704.

Clapp, J., Moseley, W. G., Burlingame, B., & Termine, P. (2022). The case for a six-dimensional food security framework. *Food Policy, 106*, 1–10.

Concern Worldwide and Welthungerhilfe. (2021). *2021 Global hunger index: Global hunger and food systems in conflict settings, regional, and national trends chapter 01*. https://www.globalhungerindex.org/pdf/en/2021.pdf
Deaton, A., & Dreze, J. (2009). Food and nutrition in India: Facts and interpretations. *Economic & Political Weekly, XLIV*(7), 42–65.
Dev, S. M. (2018). Transformation of Indian Agriculture? Growth, inclusiveness and sustainability. In *Presidential address delivered at the 78th annual conference of the Indian Society of Agricultural Economics*. 1–3 November 2018.
Dreze, J., & Sen, A. (1989). Public action for social security: Foundation and strategy. In E. Ahmad, J. Dreze, J. Hills, & A. Sen (Eds.), *Social security in developing countries*. OUP.
Economic survey 2021–22. Government of India, Department of economic affairs, economic division, Ministry of finance. Oxford University Press.
FAO. (1982). *World food security: A reappraisal of the concepts and approaches*. Director General's Report. https://books.google.co.in/books?id=cSwKMwEACAAJ
FAO. (1992). *International Conference on Nutrition: Final report of the Conference*. https://apps.who.int/iris/handle/10665/61254
FAO. (2001). *The state of food insecurity in the world 2001*. http://www.fao.org/docrep/003/y1500e/y1500e00.htm
FAO. (2022). *Food and agriculture data*. https://www.fao.org/faostat/en/#country
Gulati, A., Jain, S., & Hoda, A. (2013). *Farm trade: Tapping the hidden potential*. Discussion Paper No. 3. Commission for Agricultural Costs and Prices (CACP), Ministry of Agriculture, Government of India, New Delhi.
High Level Panel of Experts (HLPE). (2020). *Food security and nutrition: Building a global narrative towards 2030*. http://www.fao.org/3/ca9731en/ca9731en.pdf
Jacoby, H. (2013). *Food prices, wages and welfare in rural India*. Policy Research Working Paper Bo. 6412. Development Research Group, World Bank, Washington, DC.
Narayan, S. (2021). Time for universal public distribution system: Food mountains and pandemic hunger in India. *Indian Journal of Human Development., 15*(3), 503–514.
Nayak, P., & Solanki, H. (2021). Pesticides and Indian agriculture—a review. *International Journal of Research—GRANTHAALAYAH, 9*(5), 250. https://doi.org/10.29121/granthaalayah.v9.i5.2021.3930
NSS. (2024). *Key indicators of household consumer expenditure in India*. Ministry of statistics and programme implementation.
Sen, A. (1981). *Poverty and famines: An essay on entitlement and deprivation*. Oxford University Press.
Swaminathan, M. (2002). Excluding the needy: The public provisioning of food in India. *Social Scientists, 30*(3/4), 34–58.
United Nations. (1975). Report of the world food conference, Rome, 5–16 November 1974. https://digitallibrary.un.org/record/701143?ln=en
World Bank. (1986). *Poverty and hunger: Issues and options for food security in developing countries*. A World Bank Policy Study.
World Bank. (2022). *World development indicators*. 2021 Data. https://www.worldbank.org
World Bank Group. (2014). The context and conundrums of contemporary Agriculturein. *Republic of India Accelerating Agricultural Productivity Growth*, Washington, Ch2. https://documents1.worldbank.org/curated/en

Food Security in India Under Free Market Conditions: A Macro-Theoretic Study

Ambar Nath Ghosh and Dipti Ghosh

Abstract This chapter addresses the issue of food security in India. This chapter shows that under conditions of free market in India, food output is likely to be substantially less than its potential level given the stocks of available land and agricultural infrastructure. Because of the preponderance of small and marginal farmers in Indian agriculture, Indian farmers' bargaining strength vis-à-vis agricultural traders is very low; they have to keep a large fraction of their output for self-consumption; they are unable to secure credit on an adequate scale and interest rates charged on these loans are also fairly high. All these factors, as we have shown in this paper, make food output in India substantially less than its potential level, gravely threatening India's food security. Inadequate agricultural infrastructure makes India's food sector subject to vagaries of nature. In such circumstances, as our paper shows, even a one-period incidence of natural adversity depresses food output below its normal level for several periods. During these periods of below-normal food output, food output of the poorest of the farmers may be less than the subsistence level, making them starve and commit suicide. We have also shown that the policy of one-time loan waiver improves food output and farmers' economic condition only temporarily. However, in times of one-period incidence of natural adversity, the policy of one-time loan waiver can provide some relief to the farmers.

Earlier versions of the paper were presented in the following conferences

---

2nd South Asia Conference on Multidisciplinary Research 2019 (SAMR'19),Colombo, Sri Lanka organized by The International Research & Development Institution (TIRDI) on 8th November, 2019.

Third International Conference on Issues in Economic Theory and Policy organized by Economics Department, Presidency University, on 27th December 2019

A. N. Ghosh (✉) · D. Ghosh
Department of Economics, Jadavpur University, Kolkata, India
e-mail: ambarghosh@gmail.com

B. Chatterjee and A. K. Karmakar (eds.), *Analytical Issues in Growth & Structural Change, Macroeconomy, Security, and Sustainability of India's Economic Development*, India Studies in Business and Economics,
https://doi.org/10.1007/978-981-95-5242-9_10

Keywords Food security · Small and marginal farmers · Natural adversity · Loan waiver

JEL Code Q18 · Q12 · Q15 · H29

1 Introduction

Food security is an important aspect of economic development in all the countries of the world. The ranking of India in Global Hunger Index (2019) is 102 among 117 countries. This strongly underscores the extremely poor performance of the Indian economy relative to the other economies of the world in combating hunger. The data on per capita net availability of food grains in India also give evidential support to this. Table 1 in Chapter 3 shows that per capita net availability of food grains (per annum) in India has declined from 186.2 kg per year to 177.9 kg per year from 1991 to 2016. It reveals a food crisis in the Indian economy. The National Crime Records Bureau (NCRB) report for 2016 (NCRB, 2016) and the Government of India (2016) report underscore the country's grim agrarian crisis by revealing a high number of suicides of Indian farmers. Adoption of the New Economic Policy (NEP) in 1991 and constant monitoring by WTO since then has eroded the autonomy of the government in pursuing development policies regarding agriculture starting from input subsidy to the procurement programme. This paper seeks to show how free play of market forces endangers food security of most of the Indians.

Table 1 Per capita net availability of food grains (per annum) in India

Year	Per capita food grain (kg per year)
1991	186.2
2001	151.9
2011	170.9
2012	169.3
2013	179.5
2014	178.6
2015	169.8
2016	177.9
2017	178.4
2018	180.1
2019	180.5

Source Ministry of Agriculture & Farmers Welfare, Government of India

1.1 Literature Review

The existing literature points to four important features of Indian agriculture: (i) preponderance of small and marginal farmers who own and cultivate 85% of total agricultural land holdings and account for 40% of aggregate marketable surplus (NABARD, 2021), (ii) low prices received by farmers (Ahangar et al., 2013; Abishek, 2016; Mitra et al., 2017), (iii) inadequate supply of formal credit (Mohan, 2006; Golait, 2007; Government of India, 2014), (iv) decline in public investment in agriculture in the post-reform period (Mishra, 2006; Godara et al., 2014). Along with this, some studies have raised the issue of indebtedness of the farmers and farmers' suicide (Mishra, 2006; Jeromi, 2007; Sadanandan, 2014) in the context of Indian agriculture. There is, however, no theoretical study that incorporates all these major features of Indian agriculture and examines how India is likely to perform in the sphere of food security under free market conditions. The objective of the present chapter is precisely this.

2 The Basic Model

We have developed here a macro model which focuses principally on the food-producing sector of the economy. Here we abstract from foreign trade in food for simplicity. We shall explore the implications of foreign trade in food in our future research. We have incorporated in this model all the relevant salient features of the Indian agriculture delineated above.

2.1 Food Sector

The output of this sector is denoted by X. Production of food requires land, labour and industrial intermediate inputs. The farmers have a given amount of land and it is assumed for simplicity that sharecropping is the mode of cultivation for large landowners. Other farmers cultivate their own land with family labour. Sharecroppers also carry out cultivation using family labour. For simplicity, hired labour is ignored. The producers require "$1/a$" amount of industrial intermediate inputs to produce 1 unit of X. The production function is of fixed-coefficient type. The assumption of fixed-coefficient production function is a simple way of capturing the fact that how much food the farmers can produce depends crucially on how much industrial intermediate inputs they are able to buy. Given the preponderance of small and marginal farmers in the food sector, it may be quite realistic to assume that production of X is constrained by the availability of credit from the financial sector as the producers of this sector have very limited resources of their own to buy the essential inputs of production.

Farmers and sharecroppers cultivate land with family labour and keep α fraction of the total output for self-consumption. It is assumed that they consume only X. As their real income increases, their consumption also increases. So their consumption is an increasing function of X which in the simplest form is given by αX here. Hence, the marketable surplus of X becomes $(1-\alpha)X$. In keeping with reality (see Mitra et al., 2017), we assume that the farmers do not sell their produce directly to the consumers. Instead, they sell their produce to middlemen who are in all likelihood the representatives of the corporate sector. They are enormously mighty financially. The farmers most of whom are small and marginal have a perishable crop to sell after harvest and they have no storage facility of their own. All these factors make the bargaining strength of the middlemen infinitely large relative to the farmers. Accordingly, the middlemen offer the farmers the minimum possible price, denoted by $\overline{P}_X$, at which the farmers are willing to sell their marketable surplus. The determination of $\overline{P}_X$ can be shown with the help of the following equation:

$$\overline{P}_X = \frac{1}{a} P_Y \theta \ ; \ \theta > 1 \tag{1}$$

Let us explain (1). First, consider the non-food-producing sector, which constitutes the rest of the economy. We will refer to it as the industrial sector. We denote by Y the output of industrial goods produced by the industrial sector and P_Y denotes the price of Y. $1/a$ units of Y is required as intermediate inputs to produce 1 unit of X. So, the average variable cost of production of X is $\frac{1}{a}P_Y$. Since farmers on the average do not have any bargaining strength vis-à-vis the middlemen, the middlemen, a la Kalecki (1954) set $\overline{P}_X$ by applying the minimum possible mark-up to this average variable cost of production. This mark-up, denoted by θ, is taken to be exogenously given, and $\theta > 1$. θ is set at such a level that the farmers get the minimum profit they need to undertake production for the market. If farmers do not get a minimum profit from the marketable surplus of food, they will produce only for self-consumption using traditional technology and inputs that they can produce themselves. This explains (1).

Given the preponderance of small and marginal farmers in India and given their woefully limited purchasing power, to capture, hopefully, a crucial aspect of Indian reality, we assume that food output is constrained by the amount of industrial intermediate inputs the farmers can purchase. The amount of own fund the farmers have in their possession is denoted by S. Using S, they can produce $a\frac{S}{P_Y}$ amount of X and the revenue of the farmers from S, denoted by R_S, is given by

$$R_S = \overline{P}_X . a \frac{S}{P_Y}(1-\alpha) = \frac{1}{a} P_Y \theta . a \frac{S}{P_Y}(1-\alpha) = \theta(1-\alpha)S \tag{2}$$

In addition to their own fund, the farmers also borrow from both formal and informal credit markets. Given the lending norms of the lenders and the amount of collateral the farmers can offer, they get at the beginning of every period a fixed amount of loan from the lenders, which we denote by L_x. They use L_x to buy industrial intermediate inputs to produce X. They use a part of the sales proceeds from the sale of the output they produce with loan to pay off their outstanding debt along with interest at the end of every given period. They can use the rest either to augment their own consumption or to save in order to increase their own fund of the next period or for both. For simplicity, we assume that they use the rest of the sales proceeds to save to augment their own fund in the next period. We denote the amount of net revenue the farmers get from the sale of X produced with loan after paying back the loan along with interest by R_L. It is given by

$$R_L = \overline{P}_X a\frac{L_X}{P_Y} - (1 + r_0)L_X = \theta\frac{1}{a}P_Y a\frac{L_X}{P_Y} - (1 + r_0)L_X = [\theta - (1 + r_0)]L_X \quad (3)$$

In (3), r_0 denotes the interest rate on the outstanding loans of the farmers. We shall explain it shortly. We assume that $[\theta - (1 + r_0)] > 0$ because otherwise the farmers will not borrow. The sum of R_S and R_L constitutes farmers' own fund in the next period. Therefore, denoting farmers' own funds in periods $t-1$ and t by S_{t-1} and S_t, respectively, we get

$$S_t = \theta(1 - \alpha)S_{t-1} + [\theta - (1 + r_0)]L_x \quad (4)$$

The RBI regulates interest rates in the formal credit markets. Moneylenders in the informal credit market fix their interest rates by applying fixed mark-ups to the formal lending rates. These mark-ups cover their transactions cost, profit margin and risk premia. The smaller a farmer, the higher the interest rate he faces. We denote the average interest rate faced by farmers to be r_0.. We take it to be given. We can solve (4) for the steady state value of S. We assume $\theta(1 - \alpha)$ to be less than unity for the sake of existence of a meaningful steady state and for its stability.

The output of food in period t is given by

$$X_t = a\frac{S_t}{P_Y} + a\frac{L_X}{P_Y} \quad (5)$$

Substituting the steady state value of S in (5), we can derive the steady state value of X.

Following Kalecki (1954), we assume that the industrial sector is an oligopoly and producers fix P_Y by applying a fixed mark-up to the average variable cost of production. The only variable input that is used in production is labour. Labour requirement per unit of Y and the money wage rate in industry, as standard, are assumed to be fixed. Hence, P_Y is fixed in (5).

Derivation of the steady state value of S:

The steady state value of S, denoted by $\overline{S}$, as follows from Eq. (4), is given by

$$\overline{S} = \frac{[\theta - (1 + r_0)]L_X}{1 - \theta(1 - \alpha)} \quad (6)$$

Let us explain the RHS of (6). At $S_{t-1} = 0$, excess of S_t over S_{t-1} is given by $[\theta-(1 + r_0)]L_X$—see (4). Per unit increase in S_{t-1}, S_t goes up by $(1-\alpha)\theta$, vide (4), reducing (S_t-S_{t-1}) by $[1-(1-\alpha)\theta]$. Therefore, to reduce (S_t-S_{t-1}) by $[\theta-(1 + r_0)]L_X$, S_{t-1} has to rise from zero by $\frac{[\theta-(1+r_0)]L_X}{1-\theta(1-\alpha)}$. This explains Eq. (6).

Substituting (6) into (5), we get the steady state value of X, denoted by $\overline{X}$. It is given by

$$\overline{X} = \frac{a}{P_Y}\left[\frac{[\theta-(1+r_0)]L_X}{1-\theta(1-\alpha)} + L_x\right] \tag{7}$$

The derivation of the steady state values of S and X are illustrated graphically in Fig. 1. The right-side panel of Fig. 1 shows the steady state value of S whereas the left-side panel shows that of X. In the right-side panel the SS curve represents equation (4) in the (S_{t-1}, S_t) plane. The steady state value of S, denoted by $\overline{S}$ is given by the point of intersection of SS and the 45^0 line. If the resources of the farmers are lower than $\overline{S}$, say S_0, in a given period, then it will increase in the next period to S_1. S will go on.

Increasing from S_1 to S_2 and so on, until it reaches $\overline{S}$. In the left-side panel the XX curve represents (5). It shows the values that X assume corresponding to different values of S. The steady state value of X corresponds to the steady state value of S on XX.

We shall now identify the major determinants of X and, thereby, seek to explain why India's food security is extremely fragile in free market conditions.

Determination of the Steady State Values of S and X

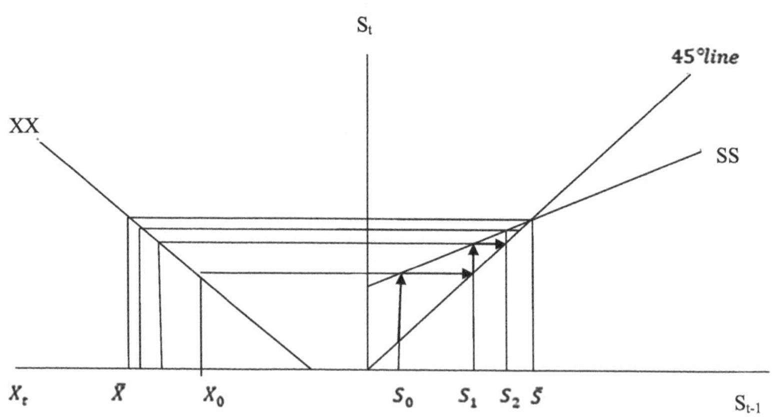

Fig. 1 Determination of the steady state values of S and X

3 The Effect of a Fall in L_X

In the pre-reform period, financial institutions were non-profit making social organizations, which were an integral part of planning. Interest rates were administered by the planners at low levels and the financial institutions disbursed credit to different sectors including the food sector at these administered interest rates on such a scale that the planned production and investment targets in all the different sectors of production were fulfilled. In the post-reform period, under the New Economic Policy, financial institutions have become commercial profit-seeking organizations. Hence, they have become extremely averse to lending to small and marginal farmers who have very little collateral to offer. Financial institutions consider it extremely risky to lend to such producers and, therefore, charge very high interest rates on such loans. Small and marginal farmers, therefore, have to borrow from the indigenous money lenders (NSSO 70th round), who give them very small amount of loans at very high interest rates. We, therefore, examine here how a decline in L_X for exogenous reasons affects X. We shall do this with the help of Fig. 2, where the initial steady state S corresponds to the point of intersection of the 45^0 line and the SS schedule representing (4) corresponding to the initial L_X. The initial steady state X corresponds to the initial steady state S on the XX schedule representing (5) corresponding to the initial value of L_X. A ceteris paribus fall in $L_X$by dL_X, as follows from Eq. (4), will shift the SS curve downward by $[\theta - (1 + r_0)]$. Let us explain. A fall in $L_X$by dL_X in period $t-1$ will reduce farmers' own fund in period t by the amount $[\theta-(1 + r_0)]dL_X$, given the value of S_{t-1}. Hence, at any given S_{t-1}, S_t will be less by this amount and SS curve will shift down in the first quadrant of Fig. 2. As a result, the steady state value of S will fall from $\overline{S}$ to $S\prime$ $S\prime$. The contraction in the steady state value of S will be larger than the fall in L_X. One unit fall in $L_X$in period $t-1$ will reduce S_t by $[\theta-(1 + r_0)]$—see (4).Therefore, vide (2) and (4), the revenue of the farmers in period $t + 1$ and S_{t+1} will shrink by $[\theta-(1 + r_0)](1-\alpha)\theta$. In the similar manner, S_{t+2} will fall by $[\theta-(1 + r_0)][(1-\alpha)\theta]^2$. The process of contraction in S will continue until the fall in S that takes place in each period eventually falls to zero. Thus, the total change in S due to a unit reduction in $L_X$or the fall in the steady state value of S will be

$$\begin{aligned} d\overline{S} &= -[\theta - (1 + r_0)]dL_X - [\theta - (1 + r_0)](1 - \alpha)\theta dL_X \\ &- [\theta - (1 + r_0)][(1 - \alpha)\theta]^2 dL_X - \ldots\ldots\ldots\ldots \\ &= -\frac{[\theta - (1 + r_0)]}{1 - (1 - \alpha)\theta} dL_X \end{aligned} \tag{8}$$

One can easily check that the value of $d\overline{S}$ yielded by (6) following a ceteris paribus unit fall in L_X tallies with (8).

Let us now examine how X will behave following a ceteris paribus decline in L_X bydL_X. From (5) it follows that following a change in L_X by $dL_X < 0$, the value of X_t corresponding to any given S_t will fall by $[(adL_X)/P_Y]$. XX schedule in the left panel

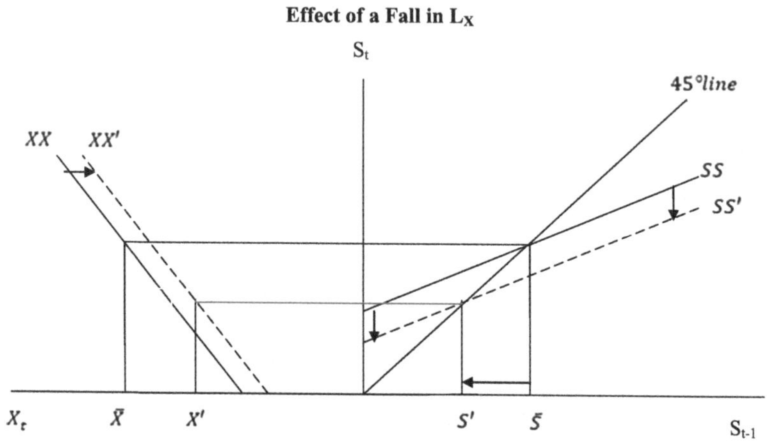

Fig. 2 Effect of a fall in L_X

of Fig. 2 will, therefore, shift to the left. The new XX schedule is labelled XX′. The new steady state X corresponds to the new steady state S on XX′. The new steady state X is labelled X′. From (5) it follows that the fall in the steady state value of X is given by

$$d\overline{X} = \frac{a}{P_Y}\left[d\overline{S} + dL_X\right] = \frac{a}{P_Y}\left[\frac{\theta - (1 + r_0)}{1 - \theta.(1 - \alpha)} + 1\right]dL_X \tag{9}$$

Let us now examine how X falls over time. In period 0, L_X falls by dL_X lowering X by $(a/P_Y)dL_X$. This will reduce farmers' revenue from the sale of X in period 0 and their own fund in period 1, S_1, by θdL_X and $[\theta - (1 + r_0)]dL_X$,, respectively—see (2), (3) and (4). Therefore, X in period 1 will fall by $(a/P_Y)[\theta - (1 + r_0)]dL_X$. Hence, farmers' revenue from the sale of X in period 1 and, thereby, their own fund in period 2 will fall by $[\theta(1 - \alpha)][\theta - (1 + r_0)]dL_X$. Hence, X in period 2 will fall by $(a/P_Y)[\theta(1 - \alpha)][\theta - (1 + r_0)]dL_X$. This will reduce farmers' revenue from the sale of X and, thereby, their own fund in period 3 by $[\theta(1 - \alpha)]^2[\theta - (1 + r_0)]dL_X$. Therefore, X in period 3 will go down by $(a/P_Y)[\theta(1 - \alpha)]^2[\theta - (1 + r_0)]dL_X$. The process of contraction will go on until the fall in S that takes place in each successive period eventually falls to zero. Thus, the total fall in X is given by

$$dX = \frac{a}{P_Y}dL_X + \frac{a}{P_Y}[\theta - (1 + r_0)]dL_X + \frac{a}{P_Y}[\theta(1 - \alpha)][\theta - (1 + r_0)]dL_X + \frac{a}{P_Y}[\theta(1 - \alpha)]^2[\theta - (1 + r_0)]dL_X + \ldots\ldots\ldots = \frac{a}{P_Y}\left[1 + \frac{[\theta - (1 + r_0)]}{1 - \theta(1 - \alpha)}\right]dL_X \tag{10}$$

It is clear that (10) tallies with (9). The above analysis yields the following proposition:

Proposition 1: A given fall in L_X brings about a large and cumulative fall in X.

One can easily deduce that the effect of an increase in r_0 is similar.

Following the adoption of the New Economic Policy (NEP), the policy of directed credit has been shelved and financial institutions have become profit-driven. Under such circumstances, they are likely to supply most of their loans to large corporations whom they regard as quality borrowers and unlikely to provide much loan to small and marginal farmers who produce the bulk of the aggregate food output in India. Financial institutions are likely to consider it extremely risky to lend to small and marginal farmers as they have little to offer by way of collateral and there is a great deal of uncertainty associated with both food output and food prices. Hence, under the new economic policy, provision of credit to the food sector is likely to be woefully inadequate leading to large-scale underutilization of land and infrastructure available to the food sector. In times of recession and perceptible increase in the incidence of bank frauds, as is the case at the present in India, financial institutions will tighten credit standards and their perception as regards the riskiness of lending to the small and marginal farmers will worsen, and credit supply to the food sector as a result will fall substantially, weakening India's food security to a considerable extent. In the Nehru-Mahalanobis era, financial institutions functioned under the administered interest rate and directed credit programme. Under this programme, the financial institutions had to lend to the food sector as much credit as was necessary to achieve the food production targets specified in the plans at interest rates fixed for the food sector by the planners. These interest rates were fixed at low levels so that the farmers could afford to take as much loan as was necessary to lfulfill the plan targets. Clearly, liberalization of the financial sector under the NEP, as our above analysis suggests, has gravely threatened India's food security by lowering supply of credit and raising cost of credit substantially to the farmers.

4 The Effect of an Increase in P_Y

During the Nehru-Mahalanobis era, prices of almost all the essential non-agricultural goods were administered by the government. Under the New Economic Policy, however, the government is allowing the prices to be set by market forces. Since then, prices of all essential industrial intermediate inputs have been rising continuously. The government is also regularly raising the prices of the essential industrial intermediate inputs still under its control. Of late, hiking indirect tax rates on essential industrial intermediate inputs such as diesel has become a favourite source of raising revenue of the government. We, therefore, consider it important to examine the effect of an increase in P_Y on the steady state values of S and X. We can explain this graphically with help of Fig. 3, where the initial steady state S denoted by $\overline{S}$ corresponds to the point of intersection of SS representing (4) and the 45^0 line. The steady state value of X corresponds to $\overline{S}$ on XX representing (5) in the second quadrant. The SS curve and the steady state value of S following a ceteris paribus increase in Pyremain unaltered (see Eq. (4)). But it alters the XX schedule in two ways. First it reduces the horizon intercept of the XX schedule. The horizontal intercept of this schedule shows the amount of X that is produced with the help of loan when $S_t = 0$. An increase in P_Y lowers the purchasing power of the given amount of loan taken by the farmers in order to buy indispensable inputs from the industrial sector. Hence the amount of X produced contracts. Second it makes XX schedule steeper. For both these reasons, a smaller amount of X gets produced at any S_t because of the higher input costs. So, XX schedule rotates as well as shifts to the left. The steady state value of X falls to X''. As we derive from (5), the fall in the steady state value of X is given by

$$d\overline{X} = -a\frac{[\overline{S} + L_X]}{P_Y^2}dP_Y \tag{11}$$

From (11) we get the following proposition:

Proposition 2: A rise in P_Y brings about a large fall in X.

The industrial sector, as we have already specified, is an oligopoly and P_Y is set by applying a fixed mark-up to the average variable cost of production. Government's policies play a crucial role in the determination of P_Y in India. Government imposes indirect taxes on the production and sales of industrial products. It also administers the prices of many essential intermediate inputs such as oil, railway fares, power tariffs, coal prices etc. If the government raises indirect tax rates and the administered prices noted above, P_Y will rise, threatening India's fragile food security. Moreover, under the New Economic Policy, with all the safeguards protecting the small and medium industrial enterprises from competition from the large corporations gone,

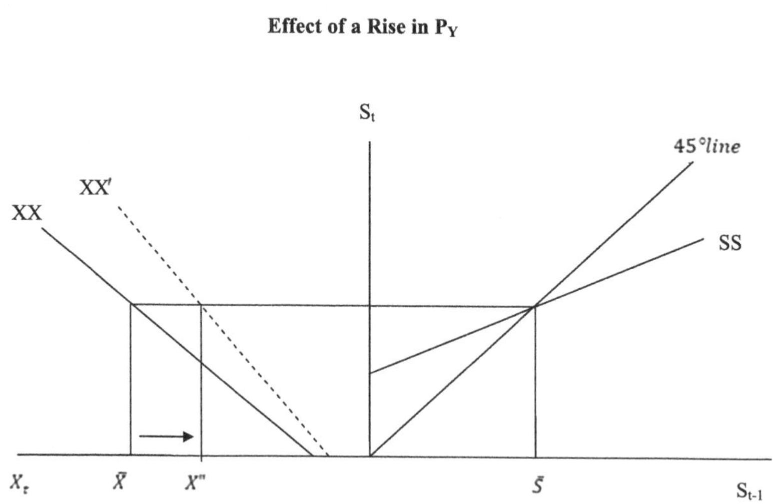

Fig. 3 Effect of a rise in P_Y

the corporate sector is growing in India at a much faster rate than the rest of the industrial sector. The consequent increase in the degree of concentration is also putting substantial upward pressure on industrial prices, threatening gravely India's food security.

5 Loan Waiver

We have delineated above the kind of terrible exploitation and deprivation farmers are subject to in India. They often take to the streets to draw the attention of the government and the people to their plight. They demand government intervention to ensure that they get just prices for their produce, cushion against uncertainties, adequate infrastructure and adequate loans on reasonable terms. Political parties in India often recommend loan waiver to give relief to the farmers. We examine here what kind of impact a one-time loan waiver is likely to produce on the farmers' economic condition and India's food security.

Suppose in a given period, period 0, $L_X(1+r_0)$ is waived. This waiver is applicable to period 0 only. We shall examine its impact using Fig. 4, where SS represents Eq. (4). With $L_X(1+r_0)=0$, SS, as follows from (4), shifts upward by $L_X(1+r_0)$. The new SS is labelled SS′. The equation of the SS′ schedule, as follows from (4), is given by

$$S_t = \theta(1-\alpha)S_{t-1} + \theta L_x \tag{4a}$$

Using (4a), we can derive the value of S_1. It is given by (assuming that $S_0 = \overline{S}$)

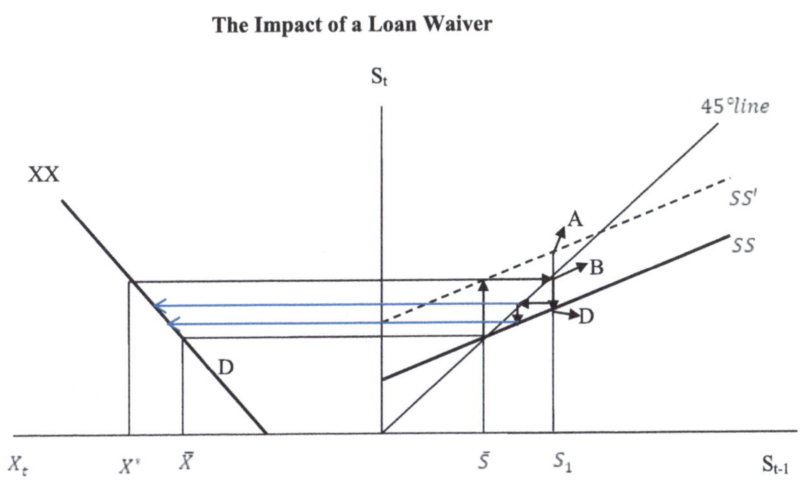

Fig. 4 The impact of a loan waiver

$$S_1 = \theta(1-\alpha)S_0 + \theta L_x = \theta(1-\alpha)\overline{S} + \theta L_x \tag{4b}$$

In period 1, however SS',, moves back to SS, since the loan waiver here, as is usually the case, a one-time programme. The XX schedule, however, as follows from (5), remains unaffected. Suppose in period 0, the economy was in the steady state with $S_0 = \overline{S}$. In period 0, there is loan waiver and the farmers' saving of $L_X(1 + r_0)$ on account of the loan waiver will be added to their own fund in period 1. In period 1, therefore, S will increase from $\overline{S}$ by $L_X(1 + r_0)$ and X by $L_X(1 + r_0).(a/P_Y)$ from $\overline{X}$ to X^* in Fig. 4—see (5). However, from period 2 onward S and along with it X will go on falling until they become equal to $\overline{S}$ and $\overline{X}$ again. The time paths of S and X are shown in Fig. 4 with arrows. Thus, a one-time loan waiver will raise X only temporarily.

Let us now compute the time paths of S and X using (4), (4a) and (5). The loan waiver takes place in period 0. As a result, farmers' own fund in period 1, as follows from (4), rises by $dS_1 = L_X(1 + r_0)$. They will use it to buy industrial intermediate inputs to produce more X in period 1. The additional X they will produce in period 1 is $dX_1 = a.\frac{L_X(1+r_0)}{P_Y}$. They will use α fraction of it for self-consumption and sell off the rest for augmenting their own fund in the next period. The additional sales revenue in period 1 will, therefore, be $\theta(1-\alpha)L_X(1 + r_0)$. If the loan waiver were permanent, i.e., if $L_X(1 + r_0)$ were zero in every period, S_2 in period 2 would have gone up by the whole of the additional sales revenue in period 1. Let us explain this point a little more. If the loan waiver were permanent, i.e., if the loan waiver had taken place in every period, the value of S_t in every period from period 1 onward would have been given by (4a) and S would have increased from period 1 onward along SS$'$ representing (4a) in Fig. 4. Hence, if there had taken place loan waiver in period 1, S in period 2 would have increase by AB as shown in Fig. 4 and $AB = \theta(1-\alpha)L_X(1 + r_0)$. It is clear from (4a) that if S_1 rises by $L_X(1 + r_0)$, S_2 will go up by $\theta(1-\alpha)L_X(1 + r_0)$. However, in period 1, there is no loan waiver and the farmers have to pay debt service charges of $L_X(1 + r_0)$, which is given by the length AD in Fig. 2, for the L_X amount of loan taken at the beginning of period 1. Therefore, total change in S in period 2 is given by $dS_2 = \theta(1-\alpha)L_x(1 + r_0) - L_x(1 + r_0) = -[1 - \theta(1-\alpha)]L_x(1 + r_0)$, which equals, in terms of Fig. 4, AB−AD = −BD. In period 2, therefore, X and, thereby, sales revenue decline by $dX_2 = a\frac{dS_2}{P_Y} = -\frac{a}{P_Y}[1 - \theta(1-\alpha)]L_X(1 + r_0)$ and $-\theta(1-\alpha)[1 - \theta(1-\alpha)]L_X(1 + r_0)$, respectively. Farmers' own fund in period 3 will, therefore, fall by $dS_3 = -\theta(1-\alpha)[1 - \theta(1-\alpha)]L_X(1 + r_0)$ lowering X and sales revenue in period 3 by $dX_3 = (dS_3/P_Y)$ and $-\ [\theta(1-\alpha)]^2[1 - \theta(1-\alpha)]L_X(1 + r_0)$, respectively. This process of contraction will continue until the fall in S that takes place in each successive period eventually falls to zero. When that happens, the economy achieves a new steady state (or the initial steady state?). Thus, the total changes in S and X are given by the following:

$$\begin{aligned} dS &= L_X(1 + r_0) - [1 - \theta(1-\alpha)]L_X(1 + r_0) - \theta(1-\alpha)[1 - \theta(1-\alpha)] \\ &\quad L_X(1 + r_0) - [\theta(1-\alpha)]^2[1 - \theta(1-\alpha)]L_X(1 + r_0) - \ldots\ldots\ldots\ldots\ldots = 0 \end{aligned} \tag{12}$$

$$dX = \frac{a}{P_Y} L_X(1+r_0) - \frac{a}{P_Y}[1-\theta(1-\alpha)]L_X(1+r_0)$$
$$- \frac{a}{P_Y}\theta(1-\alpha)[1-\theta(1-\alpha)]L_X(1+r_0) -$$
$$\frac{a}{P_Y}[\theta(1-\alpha)]^2[1-\theta(1-\alpha)]L_X(1+r_0) - \ldots\ldots\ldots\ldots\ldots = 0 \quad (13)$$

From the above analysis we get the following proposition:

Proposition 3: The policy of one-time loan waiver increases food output and farmers' economic condition for some periods of time following the implementation of the policy, but not permanently.

Even though the one-time policy of loan waiver does not improve farmers' economic condition and food output permanently, it may be of great help to the farmers in times of stress caused by adverse natural factors. We shall show this in the next section.

6 Adverse Natural Shock

Food production largely depends on the state of nature in India where there is a huge deficiency in infrastructural facilities to combat natural adversities. The scenario has become all the more depressing on account of the drastic decline in public investment in infrastructure in the post-reform period (Mishra, 2006; Godara, 2014). An adverse natural shock drastically reduces food output corresponding to any given stocks of land, infrastructure and the amount of intermediate inputs used. Outputs of many of the small and marginal farmers become so low that they have to use a larger fraction of the outputs for self-consumption for survival. We incorporate the following modifications to capture the impact of natural adversities. We assume that the average productivity of the industrial inputs instead of being a is aN, where N represents the state of nature. It is unity when the state of nature is normal and the worse the state of nature, the smaller is the value it assumes. Similarly, the fraction of food output kept for self-consumption is now (α/N) instead of being α.. It is now reasonable to rewrite (1) as

$$\overline{P}_X = \frac{1}{aN} P_Y \theta \quad (14)$$

Let us explain (14) in detail. N is less than unity when nature is worse than normal. N is greater than unity when nature is better than normal. In (14), we adhere to the principle that the traders apply a fixed mark-up to the average variable cost of production to determine the price they offer to the farmers. They take into account the value of N, while computing the average variable cost of production. Thus, in times of adverse natural shock that depresses output below its normal level, traders' offer price becomes higher than its normal level and conversely. To induce farmers to undertake production for the market, they should be assured of some minimum profit. To ensure that, the traders have to take into account the value of N for computing the average variable cost of production and they have to fix θ in such a manner that this condition is fulfilled.

Incorporating all the changes noted above in (4) and (5), we get

$$S_t = (1 - \frac{\alpha}{N})\theta.S_{t-1} + [\theta - (1 + r_0)]L_X \tag{15}$$

Note that the revenue from the sale of marketable surplus of food produced with farmers' own fund is $\overline{P}_X\left(1 - \frac{\alpha}{N}\right)\frac{S_{t-1}}{P_Y}aN = \theta\left(1 - \frac{\alpha}{N}\right)S_{t-1}$. Again, net revenue from the sale of food produced with loan is given by $\overline{P}_X\frac{L_X}{P_Y}aN - (1 + r_0)L_X = [\theta - (1 + r_0)]L_X$. This explains (15). The food output as follows from Eq. (5) now becomes

$$X_t = aN\frac{S_t}{P_Y} + aN\frac{L_X}{P_Y} \tag{16}$$

7 The Impact of a Fall in N

Let us examine the impact of a one-period fall in N from one on the production of food and farmers' economic condition. We shall do this first with the help of Fig. 5, where the SS schedule in the first quadrant represents (15), for $N = 1$. The XX schedule in the second quadrant represents (16), with $N = 1$. Let us now examine how these schedules will shift following a decline in N by $dN < 0$. Let us focus on the SS schedule first. Deterioration in the state of nature in period 0, captured by a fall in N by dN from one, will keep the vertical intercept of SS unchanged, but reduce its slope by $\frac{\alpha\theta}{N^2}dN$. Hence, SS will rotate downward. The new SS schedule is labelled SS$'$. Focus now on XX. Both its horizontal intercept and slope become smaller. It, therefore, shifts to the left and become steeper. The new XX is labelled XX$'$. If the shock lasts only for one period, in the next period, both SS and XX will move back to their old positions. We shall now describe how S and X will behave over time following a one-period adverse natural shock. Suppose initially the economy was in steady state with $S = \overline{S}$ and $X = \overline{X}$, respectively. Also suppose that the one-time adverse natural shock occurs in period 0 lowering X in period zero to X$'$—see Fig. 5. As a result, S in period 1 will fall to S$'$—See Fig. 5. From the next period, period 2, however, S and X will start rising back towards their initial steady state values as shown by the arrows in Fig. 5. Let us now compute the changes in S and X over time using (15) and (16).

Let us suppose that the economy was in steady state with $X = \overline{X}$ and $S = \overline{S}$ and the adverse natural shock occurred in period 0. X in period 0, therefore, as follows from (16), fell from its steady state value $\overline{X}$ by (denoting the value of dN in period 0 by dN_0)

The Impact of a One-Period Adverse Natural Shock

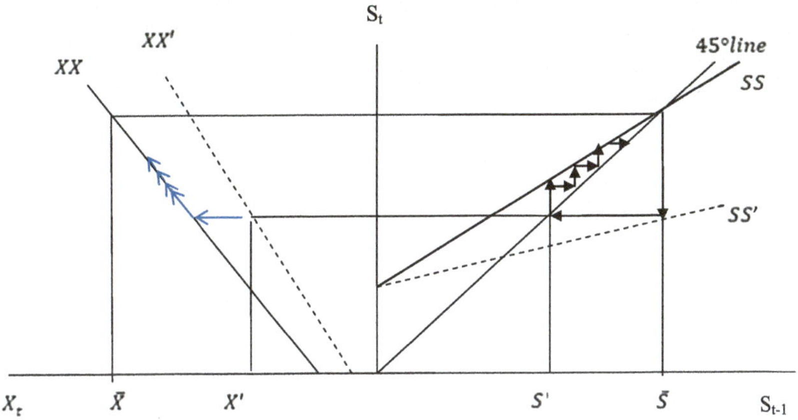

Fig. 5 The impact of a one-period adverse natural shock

$$dX_0 = a\left[\frac{\overline{S} + L_X}{P_Y}\right] dN_0 \tag{17}$$

from $\overline{X}$ to X' as shown in Fig. 5. This reduces farmers' revenue from the sale of X in period 0 lowering farmers' own fund in period 1. As we derive from (15), the fall in S in period 1 is given by

$$dS_1 = \alpha\theta\overline{S}\frac{1}{N^2}dN_0 < 0 \because dN_0 < 0 \text{ and } S_0 = \overline{S} \tag{18}$$

Note that, the larger the absolute value of dN_0, i.e., the greater the intensity of the adverse natural shock, the more is the fall in S_I. In period 1, N again rises by $-dN_0$ to 1. This means that the value of dN in period 1 is $-dN_0$. As a result, X in period 1 changes by, as follows from (16) (and also using (17))

$$\begin{aligned} dX_1 &= \left[\frac{aN}{P_Y}\right].dS_1 + \left[\frac{S_1}{P_Y}a + \frac{L_X}{P_Y}a\right](-dN_0) \\ &= \left[\frac{aN}{P_Y}\right].dS_1 + \left[\frac{\overline{S}}{P_Y}a + \frac{L_X}{P_Y}a\right](-dN_0) \\ &= \left[\frac{aN}{P_Y}\right].dS_1 + [-dX_0] \end{aligned} \tag{19}$$

(Note that the initial value of $S_1 = \overline{S}$. It dropped from $\overline{S}$ by dS_1 in period 1 because of the adverse natural shock in period 0.)

From (19), it is clear that if dS_1 were 0, X_1 would have been equal to $\overline{X}$. However, the larger is $|dS_1|$, the smaller is dX_1 relative to $(-dX_0)$. From the above discussion it follows that the larger the $-dN_0$, i.e., the greater the intensity of the natural shock, the lower is X_1 relative to $\overline{X}$.

Let us now focus on period 2. From (15) it follows that (setting $N = 1$)

$$S_2 = \theta(1-\alpha)S_1 + L_X.[\theta - (1 + r_0)] \tag{20}$$

Note that

$$S_1 = \overline{S} - (-dS_1) \tag{21}$$

Substituting (21) into (20) and rearranging terms, we get

$$\begin{aligned} S_2 &= \theta(1-\alpha)\overline{S} + L_X.[\theta - (1 + r_0)] - \theta(1-\alpha)(-dS_1) \\ &= \overline{S} - \theta(1-\alpha)(-dS_1) \end{aligned} \tag{22}$$

It is clear from (21) and (22) that S_2 is larger than S_1, since $\theta.(1-\alpha) < 1$.. Again, (setting N = 1)

$$\begin{aligned} X_2 &= \frac{a}{P_Y}[S_2 + L_X] = \frac{a}{P_Y}\left[\overline{S} - \theta(1-\alpha)(-dS_1) + L_X\right] \\ &> \frac{a}{P_Y}\left[\overline{S} - (-dS_1) + L_X\right] = X_1 \end{aligned} \tag{23}$$

Let us now focus on period 3. From (15), (20) and (22), we get (setting $N = 1$)

$$\begin{aligned} S_3 &= \theta(1-\alpha)S_2 + L_X.[\theta - (1 + r_0)] \\ &= \theta(1-\alpha)\overline{S} + L_X.[\theta - (1 + r_0)] - [\theta(1-\alpha)]^2(-dS_1) \\ &= \overline{S} - [\theta(1-\alpha)]^2(-dS_1) > S_2 \end{aligned} \tag{24}$$

Therefore, as follows from (16) (setting $N = 1$)

$$\begin{aligned} &X_3 = \frac{a}{P_Y}[S_3 + L_X] = \frac{a}{P_Y}\left[\overline{S} - [\theta(1-\alpha)]^2(-dS_1) + L_X\right] > \\ &\frac{a}{P_Y}\left[\overline{S} - \theta(1-\alpha)(-dS_1) + L_X\right] = X_2 \end{aligned} \tag{25}$$

This is how slowly over time S and X will move up to their initial respective steady state values. The above analysis yields the following proposition:

Proposition 4: A one-period adverse natural shock will reduce food output in the period in which the shock occurs. The food output will not go back to its initial steady statelevel right in the next period. It will take many periods of time before it gets close to its initial steady statevalue. The greater the intensity of

the adverse natural shock, the longer it will take for the food output to reach its initial steady statevalue.

The above proposition points to one reason why farmers commit suicide in India. Following a significant adverse natural shock, many farmers' food output falls well below the subsistence level, leaving them hungry. Since it will take long for food output to move back to its initial level, many farmers, being unable to bear the pain of hunger, may commit suicide. The larger the preponderance of small and marginal farmers, the greater is likely to be the incidence of farmer suicide following a significant adverse natural shock.

It is also clear from the analysis of this section and that of the previous one that the deleterious impact of an adverse natural shock may be mitigated through a policy of loan waiver. One can easily work out that through a policy of loan waiver along with a suitable amount of transfers to farmers for the purpose of enabling them to increase purchases of industrial intermediate inputs, it may be possible to restore food output to its initial steady state level in the period just next to the one in which the adverse natural shock occurs.

8 The Impact of a Decrease in $\overline{P}_X$

Given the preponderance of small and marginal farmers in Indian agriculture, the bargaining strength of the farmers is very low relative to that of the agricultural traders. The less the relative bargaining strength of the farmers, the smaller is the value of θ and, therefore, the lower is $\overline{P}_X$—see (1). We shall here examine the impact of a decline in θ using Fig. 6, where the initial steady state S, labelled $\overline{S}$, corresponds to the point of intersection of the SS schedule representing (4) and the 45^0 line. The initial steady state X corresponds to $\overline{S}$ on the XX schedule representing (5) in the second quadrant. Following a fall in θ by $d\theta < 0$, both the vertical intercept and the slope of the SS schedule become smaller, It, therefore, shifts downward and becomes flatter. The XX schedule, however, remains unaffected. Hence, steady state values of both S and X go down making India's food security more fragile.

The fall in the steady state value of S, as we derive from (6), is given by

$$d\overline{S} = \frac{L_X d\theta}{1-\theta(1-\alpha)} + \frac{[\theta-(1+r_0)]L_X}{[1-\theta(1-\alpha)]^2}(1-\alpha)d\theta < 0 \tag{26}$$

The fall in $\overline{S}$, as follows from (5), lowers the steady state value of X by

$$d\overline{X} = a.\left(\frac{d\overline{S}}{P_Y}\right) = \left(\frac{a}{P_Y}\right)\left\{\frac{L_X d\theta}{1-\theta(1-\alpha)} + \frac{[\theta-(1+r_0)]L_X}{[1-\theta(1-\alpha)]^2}(1-\alpha)d\theta\right\} < 0 \tag{27}$$

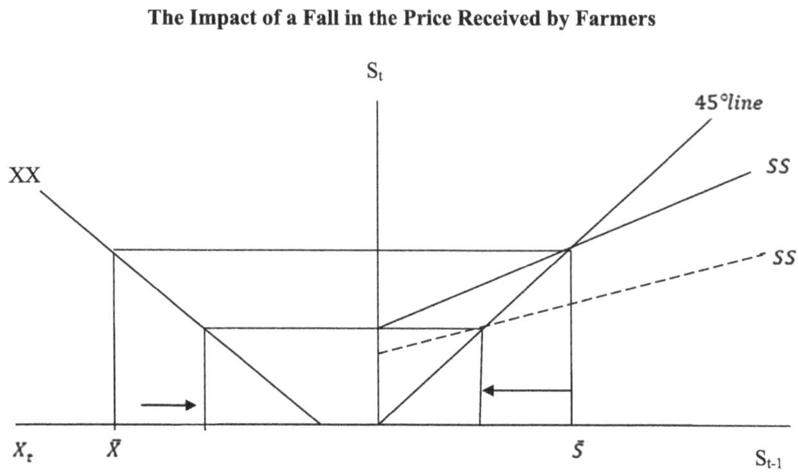

Fig. 6 The impact of a fall in the price received by farmers

Let us examine how S and X fall following a decline in θ using (4) and (5). Suppose the fall in θ takes place in period 0. From (4) it follows that

$$S_1 = [\theta(1-\alpha)]S_0 + [\theta - (1+r_0)]L_X \tag{28}$$

We assume that initially the economy was in steady state so that $S_0 = \overline{S}$ and S_1 would have been equal to $\overline{S}$ if θ had stayed unchanged. Following the decline in θ and the consequent fall in the sales revenue, S_1 falls, as follows from (28), by

$$dS_1 = [(1-\alpha)S_0 + L_X]d\theta = \left[(1-\alpha)\overline{S} + L_X\right]d\theta \tag{29}$$

Therefore, in period 1, X falls from its steady state value $\overline{X}$ by

$$dX_1 = \frac{a}{P_Y}dS_1 \tag{30}$$

This fall in X lowers farmers' own fund in period 2 further. From (4), we know that

$$S_2 = [\theta(1-\alpha)]S_1 + [\theta - (1+r_0)]L_X \tag{31}$$

One should note that θ in (31) is the new lower θ.. From (31), it follows that

$$dS_2 = [\theta(1-\alpha)]dS_1 \tag{32}$$

Hence, as follows from (5), X in period 2 falls by

$$dX_2 = \frac{a}{P_Y} dS_2 \tag{33}$$

Similarly, in period 3,

$$dS_3 = [\theta(1-\alpha)]dS_2 = [\theta(1-\alpha)]^2 dS_1 \tag{34}$$

And

$$dX_3 = \frac{a}{P_Y} dS_3 \tag{35}$$

Thus, through successive periods, there will take place a cumulative decline in S and X until the fall in X that takes place in each successive period eventually falls to zero. Thus, the total fall in S and X is given by (using (29) and (6))

$$\begin{aligned} dS &= dS_1 + [\theta(1-\alpha)]dS_1 + [\theta(1-\alpha)]^2 dS_1 \\ &+ \ldots\ldots\ldots\ldots\ldots = \frac{1}{1-[\theta(1-\alpha)]} dS_1 \\ &= \left[\frac{L_X}{1-[\theta(1-\alpha)]} + \frac{[\theta-(1+r_0)]L_X}{[1-\theta(1-\alpha)]^2} (1-\alpha) \right] d\theta \end{aligned} \tag{36}$$

and

$$\begin{aligned} dX &= \frac{a}{P_Y} dS_1 + \frac{a}{P_Y}[\theta(1-\alpha)]dS_1 + \frac{a}{P_Y}[\theta(1-\alpha)]^2 dS_1 + \ldots\ldots\ldots\ldots\ldots = \\ &\frac{a}{P_Y} \frac{1}{1-[\theta(1-\alpha)]} dS_1 = \frac{a}{P_Y} \left[\frac{L_X}{1-[\theta(1-\alpha)]} + \frac{[\theta-(1+r_0)]L_X}{[1-\theta(1-\alpha)]^2} (1-\alpha) \right] d\theta \end{aligned} \tag{37}$$

The above analysis yields the following proposition:

Proposition 5: A given fall in θ will lead to a cumulative fall in food output greatly jeopardizing India's food security.

From our above discussion, we find that under free market conditions, the greater the preponderance of the small and marginal farmers, the less is the bargaining strength of the farmers relative to the agricultural traders and, hence, the lower is the price the farmers' produce fetches. This lower price will bring about a large fall in food output, substantially undermining India's food security.

9 Conclusion

India has made a transition from a planned economy to a market economy. In consequence, the financial institutions, which were social organizations disbursing credit in accordance with the pattern specified in the plans, have turned into profit-seeking firms. Public investment that grew phenomenally in the plan era, creating agricultural infrastructure at a rapid pace, tapered off in the post-reform period, leaving agriculture vulnerable to the vagaries of nature. Small and marginal farmers, the producers of the major part of agricultural output in India, who enjoyed considerable protection in the plan era, have become subject to extremely exploitative and discriminatory market forces in the post-reform period. All these factors, the study in this chapter shows, have considerably weakened India's food security and have led to gross underutilization of land and infrastructure available for food production. The paper also shows that the policy of one-time loan waiver improves food security only temporarily. However, it may be of considerable use in mitigating the impact of a one-period adverse natural shock. Adverse natural shocks, as this chapter shows, may be one important reason why so many farmers in India commit suicide every year.

References

Ahangar, G. B., Ganie, A. H., & Padder, M. J. (2013). A study on institutional credit to agriculture sector in India. *International Journal of Current Research and Academic Review, 1*(4), 72–80.

Golait, R. (2007). Current issues in agriculture credit in India: An assessment. *RBI Occasional Papers, 28*, 79–100.

Godara, R. L. (2014). Agriculture credit in India: An analytical study. *International Journal of Latest Trends in Engineering and Technology, 3*(4).

Government of India. (2014). NSSO 70th round (Dec 2013). Income, expenditure, productive assets and indebtedness of agricultural households in India. Government of India, Report No. 576(70/33/3).

Government of India. (2016). *State/UT-wise suicides by farmers and agricultural labourers due to bankruptcy or indebtedness during 2014 and 2015*. Ministry of Agriculture and Farmers Welfare.

Government of India. (2017). *Pocket book of AGRICULTURAL STATISTICS 2017*. Government of India, Ministry of Agriculture & Farmers Welfare.

Jeromi, P. D. (2007). Farmer's indebtedness and suicides: Impact of agricultural trade liberalisation in Kerala. *Economic and Political Weekly, 42*(31), 3241–3247.

Kalecki, M. (1954). *Theory of economic dynamics: An essay on cyclical and long-run changes in capitalist economy*. George Allen and Unwin, London, Third Impression.

Mitra, S., Mookherjee, D., Torero, M., &Visaria, S. (2017). *Asymmetric information and middleman margins: An experiment with Indian potato farmers*. Boston University. http://open.bu.edu

Mishra, S. (2006). Farmer's Suicides in Maharashtra. *Economic and Political Weekly, 41*(16), 1538–1545.

Mohan, R. (2006). Agricultural credit in India – Status, issues and future agenda. *Economic and Political Weekly, 41*, 1013–1021.

NABARD. (2021). *National Paper (NABARD) - PLP 2020–21*. https://www.nabard.org/auth/writereaddata/CareerNotices/2309195333Paper%20on%20Market%20Linkages%20on%20Agriculture%20Commodities.pdf

National Crime Records Bureau. (2016). *State/UT-wise total number of suicides by farmers and agricultural labourers from 2013 to 2015*. Accidental Deaths & Suicides in India' for relevant years.

Sadanandan, A. (2014). Political economy of suicide: Financial reforms, credit crunches and farmer suicides in India. *The Journal of Developing Areas, 48*(4), 287–307.

Sriram M. S. (2007). *Productivity of rural credit: A review of issues and some recent literature*. Indian Institute of Management Ahmedabad. Working Paper No. 2007-06-01.

Sketching the Trajectory of Food and Nutrition Security in India: A Contextual Analysis

Purba Chattopadhyay

Abstract Food, apart from being a basic necessity, signifies our culture, our emotion, history, socialization, economic conditions, geographical location, and stage of the developmental process. The world today has diverse cuisines and innumerable options of food constituted through a complex permutation and combination of spices, animal or plant origin ingredients tempered at various moderations of temperature and time. However, this same world houses millions of hungry people. In the context of the above, the present chapter looks into the concept of hunger in the Indian economy. It then analyses the concept of food security and its three dimensions and tries to trace the path of food security for India. Next, it looks into the concept of nutrition security and brings out the differences between food and nutrition security. Finally, it concludes that nutrition security is a much wider term than food security and to achieve nutrition security an integrated approach of multiple sectors is needed for it to succeed.

Keywords Food · Hunger · Food security · Nutrition · Nutrition security · India

JEL Classification H8 · I0 · I1 · I3

P. Chattopadhyay (✉)
Department of Home Science, University of Calcutta, Kolkata, India
e-mail: pchomesc@caluniv.ac.in

B. Chatterjee and A. K. Karmakar (eds.), *Analytical Issues in Growth & Structural Change, Macroeconomy, Security, and Sustainability of India's Economic Development*, India Studies in Business and Economics,
https://doi.org/10.1007/978-981-95-5242-9_11

1 Sketching the Trajectory of Food and Nutrition Security in India: A Contextual Analysis

"The universe is nothing except for life and everything that lives has to feed itself."
Jean-Antheleme Brillat-Savarin (1755–1826)[1]

The world around us is nothing but a collage of vibrant lives which thrives from time immemorial through evolution change and competition to survive. The common chain which binds all living things is the requirement of nutrition to sustain life. Food, a complex compound of protein, fats, vitamins, minerals, foliage, and water, is essential for the existence of any form of life on earth. Coming to the most dominant and intelligent of the life forms known to us, namely the human beings, we see that food forms essential pillars of human existence. Apart from a basic necessity, it signifies our culture, our emotion, history, socialization, economic conditions, geographical location, stage of the developmental process, and many more things. Going back in time, human existence can be traced back to some millions of years ago, from when we have traversed a long-long journey to reach the present world. This journey of humankind over the years has seen the evolution of the modern human and the process has also witnessed a significant change in the living and working conditions of the humans with ever-changing dynamics of socialization, cultural, political, and geographical divisions and manifestations of diverse subgroups embodying the uniqueness of their journey so far. Considering food, the composition of the food basket had undergone a sea change from the simple nomadic existence to the complex modern societies adding diversities to our food basket in every sense, be it variety, taste, flavours, shape, or size. The world today has diverse cuisines and innumerable options of food constituted through a complex permutation and combination of spices, animal or plant origin ingredients tempered at various moderations of temperature and time. However, this same world houses more than 800 million people[2] going hungry and more than 2 billion people suffering from malnutrition. These are the people who are unable to have even the basics that our ancestors some billions of years ago could provide for themselves, even though there are sufficient food, knowledge, and resources for all. As a species we have made significant progress and breakthrough making life easier and more comfortable, however, we still have not reached a position where none of our fellow beings starve to death. Data reveals some 8.8% of people worldwide are undernourished, meaning their calorie intake is less than their basic energy needs. There are 663 million undernourished individuals in the world. Twenty-two per cent of children under five are "stunted," or visibly shorter than average for their age, as a result of malnutrition or recurring illnesses. Extreme food insecurity affects about 697 million people worldwide, or

---

[1] Symons M. (2014) Brillat-Savarin and Food. In: Thompson P., Kaplan D. (eds) Encyclopaedia of Food and Agricultural Ethics. Springer, Dordrecht. https://doi.org/10.1007/978-94-007-6167-4_4-6.

[2] https://www.fao.org/state-of-food-security-nutrition.

9% of the total population. One in four people, or 1.9 billion people globally, suffer from moderate to severe food insecurity.

In the context of the above, the chapter aims to look into the concept of hunger and tries to understand food security. Therefore, the study will examine the development of food security for India and concentrate on the Indian context. The disparities in food and nutrition security and their significance in the Indian context will also be examined in this study. Lastly, the chapter will try to look into the trends and analyse the consequences of the same for the future.

1.1 Understanding the Concept of Hunger

To understand food and nutrition security one has to first contextualize the problem in a given socioeconomic historical and cultural setting. An understanding of the population's background and dynamics is very important before having any discussion on food security. With a growth rate of almost 1% (0.97), India's population increased from 1.21 billion in 2011 to 1.39 billion in 2021. Additionally, data from different NSSO rounds show that the percentage of the population living below the poverty line (BPL) increased at a rate of 2.12% between 1991 and 2001, then decreased to 1.76% year between 2001 and 2011. Despite the lack of official statistics, the United Nations projected that 364 million people in the nation were impoverished in 2019, making about 28% of the entire population and approximately 25% of the world's undernourished poor (absolute) population.

According to the 2019 NITI Aayog study, the poverty ratio in rural areas was 32.75%, while in urban areas it was 8.81%. This indicates that poverty is concentrated more in rural areas. Additionally, Adivasis and Dalits were particularly affected by the high rates of poverty and malnutrition. According to the Global Nutrition Report (2016), India is ranked 114th out of 132 nations in terms of stunting in children under five, 120th out of 130 countries in terms of under-five wasting, and 170th out of 185 countries in terms of anaemia prevalence. According to the NFHS-4 study, undernutrition and a lack of access to basic healthcare services are the biggest problems facing the SC and ST social groups. The fact that vulnerable groups in society receive the least amount of development and welfare initiatives is indicative of this.

The world bank data also shows a grim picture of the prevalence of mass poverty. The recent pandemic also hit the vulnerable groups the most, with severe crisis stories of people emerging who were incapable of ensuring their minimum basic requirements for sustenance. The concept of poverty here meant the absolute number of poor who were incapable of ensuring their minimum calorie requirement needed for sustaining life. The stark number of poor was the reason why India ranked 101 out of 116 countries in 2021 in the Global Hunger Index.[3] The score of India was 27.5, i.e., between 20.0 and 34.9 which placed it in the range where the hunger

[3] https://www.globalhungerindex.org India.

levels may be considered as serious. This dense concentration of poor in a country makes the issue of food security so relevant and important. Oxfam's good enough to eat Index places India among the 30 worst performing nations among a total of 125 countries. This throws light on not only the availability of food but also the quality of food intake by the people. The concept of hunger that emerges out of the above data is reflective of the extreme condition of these poor people and tells a story that contradicts the success story of India as a self-sufficient nation in food-grain productivity. To understand the dynamics of poverty and food insecurity, we have to look into the food productivity trends and the interplay of demand and supply side of food.

1.2 Food Security

The definition of food security is flexible and has transformed and expanded significantly since it was first coined in the early 1970s at the World Food Summit, 1974 where its focus was mainly on food supply ensuring the availability of food. However, in 1983, the FAO extended the concept to include accessibility, both physical and economic of the available food. The definition broadened further in 1986 when the World Bank in its report on Poverty and Hunger considered the dynamism of the concept of food security and defined food security as access of all people at all times to enough food for an active, healthy life. The meaning further underwent refinement in 1996 which stressed the aspect of human security of which food security was a part. The concept also took accessibility into account and can be broadly defined as existing when everyone, everywhere, has physical, social, and financial access to enough wholesome food that satisfies their dietary requirements and food choices for an active and healthy life. The application of this idea to the family level, with individuals living in households as the main focus of concern, is known as household food security. Therefore, one may begin with the food supply element. Food production and rural residents' socioeconomic standing in India are indicators of the expansion of agriculture and rural wealth. The nation has achieved remarkable strides in food and agricultural output over the last forty years. These changes have been triggered by the green revolution of the 1960s, which increased the productivity of food grains especially staples like wheat and rice; the White revolution or Operation Flood of the 1970s which catapulted India to one of the major milk-producing countries in the world; and the Blue Revolution in 1985 through its multidimensional activities resulting in a surge in fisheries and productivity from aquaculture and fisheries. These revolutions also brought about increased levels of inputs-use, mechanization, and policy support. The success of the revolution showcased the public and private investments in infrastructure, research, and extension. This was accompanied by adequate price support and incentives and other agricultural support policies which led to noteworthy growth in food production and hence amplified the availability of food grains per capita. Concerning Food security, this was a significant leap, particularly in the Indian context as the availability of food is the primary pillar of food security, and this series of revolutions helped in ensuring the availability of subsidized staple food to the people. The adoption of a new agricultural strategy resulted in a rise in food-grain productivity increased from 115.6 million tonnes in 1960–61 to 316.06 million tonnes in 2020–21. This leap was indeed commendable. Further, India registered record-breaking food-grain production in seven years in the past decade which remained undisturbed even during the incidence of droughts. However, all this success stories were marred by the farmer protests and several cases of farmer suicides. The NSSO data reveals that between the decades about 34 million farmers moved out of agriculture. This amounts to about a 2.04% annual rate of exit from farming. Structurally, the Indian agriculture system has about 78% of farmers who are smallholders having less than 2 ha of farm holding, owning about 33% of total cultivated land. These smallholders along with the landless agricultural workers constitute the most vulnerable rural population often constituting the bulk of hungry undernourished masses. This has a serious repercussion for the food security frontier of the country. Another important aspect of understanding the Indian agricultural system is that these marginal, smallholders or landless labourers cannot afford modern irrigation facilities and are left susceptible to climatic changes and the uncertainty of the monsoon. This increases their vulnerability. The WHO states that three pillars determine food security: food availability, food accessibility, and food use and misuse (Matthew J Burton et al., 2021). To this, the FAO adds a fourth pillar: the stability of the first three dimensions of food security over time. So, regarding the dimension availability, we can see that although productivity has significantly increased over time yet the plight of the average farmer who is responsible for the gross productivity and hence the availability of food grains for this huge populous country is not very comforting. Moreover, the basis of the prosperity of a profession lies in the attitude of the people involved in it. Here too, the trends are very gloomy which questions the sustainability of agriculture in the Indian scenario in long run. The success story of Indian agriculture has to assure good returns to the average small landowners to landless labourers or else soon it will have its aftermaths on the gross agricultural productivity. What makes things more challenging is the average annual growth of the population at the rate of 0.99% as of 2020 (WB report). Now let us come to food accessibility. It is a well-known fact that productivity and hence the availability of food does not ensure food accessibility. The available food may be inaccessible due to price and other barriers. According to the 2020 Global Food Security Index, India is ranked 71st out of 113 large nations. Since the Covid epidemic, there has been an approximate 9.7 crore increase in the number of people experiencing moderate to severe food poverty. Regretfully, this occurred at a time when the government go-downs held an unparalleled 100 million tonnes of food grains. This contrast again showcases that the availability of food does not necessarily ensure accessibility. These data not only reveal the inaccessibility of food for the people but also show the instability in the dimensions of availability and also accessibility. In conclusion, the FAO assessment estimates that almost 40% of India's food production is wasted annually as a result of disjointed food systems and ineffective supply chains (Matthew J Burton et al., 2021). Even before the meal is delivered to the customers, this loss takes place. It's interesting to note that India spends about Rs 1.5

lakh crore yearly on free and inexpensive food grains, but a 2016 study calculated that Rs 92,651 crore is wasted every year due to farm produce waste. According to the 2021 Food Waste Index Report, an amazing 50 kg of food is wasted annually per person in Indian households. In the course of the pandemic-induced lockdown, some 65 lakh tonnes of food grains continued to rot in go-downs across India for the first quarter of 2020. Coming to misuse, the Public Distribution System, which includes 60,000 ration stores, enables Ration cardholders designated BPL, entitled to 35 kg of grain. However, because food intended for the undernourished population has been exploited, this tool is rife with corruption. More than 60% of the food grains have been squandered, whether they were lost in transportation, sold on the illegal market, tainted by middlemen, or deteriorated in other ways. The inadequacy of the system is demonstrated by the fact that 21% of people remain undernourished in spite of the installation of five million ration stores and 750 billion rupees. The idea that malnutrition and food insecurity in India cannot be solely ascribed to a lack of food supply but rather to the fact that the food produced is not being used in a transparent and compliant manner has been reinforced by the repeated failures of initiatives like the Public Distribution System. Additional instances of carelessness and misconduct in the Public Distribution System include incorrect grain weighing, inconsistent distributions among households eligible for the programme, the substitution of inferior food and supplies for open market sales, issues obtaining ration cards for eligible families, and the creation of fake ration cards for fair price stores. Many people believe that hunger and malnutrition are issues that only affect underdeveloped and under-resourced areas. However, India's recent economic expansion shows that food security is not a problem that is solely related to a nation's economic resources; rather, these resources must be managed morally and appropriately for the country as a whole to benefit from prosperity. However, going back to the basic understanding of food, we can see that food security only addresses a part of the concept of food viz. that of dealing with hunger. Food, on the other hand, has a bigger meaning than hunger satiation; food is an essential connotation of vitamins, minerals, fats, proteins, and fibres, which not only provide us with energy to sustain life but also have a crucial role in ensuring good health and well-being. Food security addresses the issue of direct hunger and the availability of food notwithstanding the quality to address hunger. However, the very essence of food is to provide nutrition, and proper intake of nutrition not only requires stable availability and accessibility of food over time but also requires the quantity and quality of the food to be balanced in the components like micronutrients and macronutrients. For this, one has to understand nutrition security, which is a deeper concept than food security.

1.3 Nutrition Security

Before discussing nutrition security let us first look into some of the health indicators of the Indian population. In 2016, non-communicable diseases accounted for 61% of all fatalities. In 2019, undernutrition was the principal cause of morbidities for all ages, contributing to about seventeen per cent of all disability-adjusted life years (DALYs) and the principal cause of death for children under five in all Indian states, accounting for 68.2% of all under-5 deaths. In 2017, this rate was 6.8 times higher in Uttar Pradesh, Bihar, Assam, and Rajasthan than in any other state. In India, undernutrition related health indicators like the prevalence of low birth weight were 21.4% in 2017, stunting was at about 40%, wasting 16%, underweight 32.7%, anaemia in children 60%, and anaemia in reproductive age group women about 55%. In comparison to the 2022 targets, India would have an excess prevalence of low birthweight of 8.9%, stunting of 9.6%, underweight of 4.8%, anaemia in children of 11.7%, and anaemia in women of 13.8%. States differ significantly in terms of the pervasiveness of malnutrition pointers, their rates of growth, and the discrepancies between predicted incidence and goals. According to the initial indicators, a significant portion of the populations inadequate nutritional consumption is represented in the health parameters. Now coming back to food security, we have seen that it is defined as the obtainability and the access of food to all people; however, security concerning the nutrition stresses the intake of a wide assortments of foods with diverse nutrient composition that provides the essential building blocks for a healthy life. The average Indian diet is about 2280 cal. The average was fewer than 2400 cal, indicating hunger and poverty in nine large states. Of the adults in the NFHS-4 study, over half had a normal nutritional status, but about 90% of the children suffered from either over nutrition or moderate to severe undernutrition. Of the undernourished majority experienced varying degrees of Chronic Energy Deficiency.

Food is a healthy assortment of nutrients in form of proteins, fat, carbohydrates, vitamins, minerals which gives the body the requisite energy to carry out the day-to-day activities. These nutrients are present in most foods consumed daily in various proportions. Interestingly, the nutrient content of the food varies based on what food it is (meaning the category of food), how the food has been produced (type of farming organic, etc.), how fresh the food is, how the food is been cooked, processed or stored, how long it has been stored, what are the conditions in which the food is being prepared. The problem with nutritional intake is that it not only depends upon the amount and quality of the food being consumed but also depends upon the physiological endowment of an individual to assimilate and digest the food. The ability to digest the food again depends on the genetic makeup as well as external conditions like incidence of diseases, susceptibility to infections, etc., which leads to loss of nutrients. Further, the efficacy of food consumed to provide the nutrition depends on the cultural practices, social norms, family dynamics, perception, and educational levels of one who is cooking or is in charge of distribution of food. Considering the Indian household these multifarious conditions causes wide diversities in nutritional intake across the country. The NSSO data reveals that the food basket for an average Indian household has become more diversified. However, this broadening of the food basket entails the ready to use fast foods rather than variety of cereals or pulses. Significantly one of the most nutritious foods, the cereals and pulses known for its high protein content is witnessing a steady decline in per capita consumption. Further a direct association with income is being observed by the fact that higher the household income more the diversity in the food basket. The demand for fruits and vegetables both locally available and exotic variety are on rise. This surge in demand is making horticulture lucrative. With globalization of cuisines, changing tastes and preferences, prevalence of popular mass media, and rapid urbanization, there is a steady rising demand for this emerging food and hence has its positive consequence in form of crop diversification. The more the expenditure driven crop diversification the more is the bias towards production of non-cereal crops on one hand, and on the other hand demand of high value-added commodities like milk, fish, nuts, berries, eggs, etc. The emerging demand patterns for the fine cereals and high value commodities have a direct consequence on the incentive to produce and hence resource allocation. The nutritious coarse cereals and millets, the grains for the poor are witnessing a steady decline in productivity. The paradox is which the average nutrition consumption of the population is getting better off at disaggregated levels the bottom percentile of the populations, the poorest of the poor's consumption basket is further shrinking. The decline in the coarse cereal's productivity has had an adverse effect on the rural poor and the vulnerable sections of the society.

India as of today presents a unique case study of a dual society existing with one country. There is one half that is susceptible to the core, any external shocks like the droughts or pandemic, as observed recently expose the extreme susceptibility. These are the people whose felt need is for food security; however, what they deserve is nutrition security. Quite interestingly there is another half within the same who are eating good, rather at times eating energy-dense calorie intense food far exceeding the body's requirement. This is leading to rise in lifestyle diseases like cardiovascular diseases, diabetes, obesity, and related morbidities. For ensuring nutrition security one has to do away with malnutrition, be it undernutrition or be it overnutrition. Thus, nutrition security entails not only the availability of food but has to be a specific basket of food with an appropriate combination of macro and micronutrients, designed for individuals taking into account their work profile, age, sex, and other requirements. Along with such detailing, it also requires basic knowledge of the people who are consuming the food as well as ensuring safe and hygienic availability of the food.

Thus, while dealing with hunger, it is food that is of primary importance. When India became independent, it was a war-devastated country with a long history of colonization. Poverty, illiteracy, unemployment, and poor health were rampant, and quite naturally the concept of welfare cantered around the provision of food to the masses who were incapable of making the basic provision of food for them. The main issue was to provide food to deal with huger satiation in the macro sense of the term. However, as discussed above the main function of food is to provide nutrition and that is why not only is the quantity of the food intake but also it is the quality composition and the condition of the food available complemented with the knowledge of how to cook or eat the food in what quantities that is extremely, important. This concept of food is a micro concept which is also a multidimensional notion needing a holistic understanding of the cultural practices the educational and knowledge base of the individual the community engagement, and the circumstances of the people to make any successful intervention. In India, the approach to food has always been food-centric and less nutrition centric. However, recently the awareness is increasing, and disaggregated surveys on cereal consumption are done for the first time. Performance-wise a lot has been done; but looking at the millions of starving people, poor health indicators, incidences of mortality and morbidities, poor indicators of maternal and child health, it is obvious that proper nutrition security requires an integrated effort on part of the government, non-governmental agencies, civil society, and necessitates voluntary participation of masses. Then only the impact could be felt at the macro levels with improvement in the general health indicators.

2 Conclusions

In conclusion to the above discussion, nutrition security is a much wider term than food security. However, for both food or nutrition security availability of food or in the latter case a balanced food basket depends primarily on productivity. The discussion on productivity has shown that despite significant achievements much needed to be done for the vulnerable marginal and small farmers. Nutrition is still not given priority in planning and execution, even in the fields of agriculture and health. Furthermore, in objectives of the government of India sponsored programmes, nutrition enhancement is not a stated objective with quantifiable metrics for monitoring at the policy level. Poor targeting, accountability, and governance have resulted from a top-down strategy that did not involve the community in planning or execution or make them aware of the issue.

The external shock of the pandemic has a further profound impact on the delicate system already plagued with malnutrition. Further rise in price is making accessibility difficult for a large section of society. At 13%, the country's yearly wholesale inflation rate reached its highest level in a decade. Fuel and food prices were important considerations.

The food sector is interconnected and interdependent, though perilously. And that is why any policy decision is it the export or import of food grains, giving incentives to farmers announcing food programmes or other welfare programs should have a heavy basis in assuring nutrition security. The most important point here is if nutrition security may be ensured for the masses, then many indicators like health and education are bound to get better. The two ways the causal relationship has to be recognized between nutrition with all other social parameters of well-being.

References

Banik, N. (2018). *Benefit-cost analysis of farmer distress: Analysis of interventions addressing farmer distress in Rajasthan*. Woking Paper Copenhagen Consensus Centre.

Cotton, C. P., Hashem, F. M., Marsh, L. E., & Dadson, R. B. (2009). Broadening perspectives: Educating underrepresented youth about food agricultural sciences through experiential learning. *NACTA Journal, 53*(4), 23–29.

Crush, J. (2016). *No. 01: Hungry cities of the global South.* https://core.ac.uk/download/157834980.pdf
Economic Survey. (2017–2018). *Ministry of Finance, GOI.*
FAO. (2011). FAOSTAT. Food and Agriculture Organization of the United Nation.
F.A.O. (2014). Retrieved from http://faostat3.fao.org/download/FB/CL/E on January 5, 2019.
Gibson, R. B. (2006). Beyond the pillars: Sustainability assessment as a framework for effective integration of social, economic and ecological considerations in significant decision-making. *Journal of Environmental Assessment Policy and Management, 8*(03), 259–280.
Godoy, D., & Dewbre, J. (2010). *Economic importance of agriculture for poverty reduction.* OECD Food, Agriculture and Fisheries Working Papers, No. 23, OECD Publishing.
Haddad, L. J., Hawkes, C., Achadi, E., Ahuja, A., Ag Bendech, M., Bhatia, K., Bhutta, Z., et al. (2015). *Global nutrition report 2015: Actions and accountability to advance nutrition and sustainable development.* International Food Policy Research Institute.
Haddad, L., Hawkes, C., Udomkesmalee, E., Achadi, E., Bendech, M. A., Ahuja, A., Bhutta, Z., De-Regil, L., Fanzo, J., Fracassi, P., & Grummer-Strawn, L. M. (2016). Global nutrition report 2016: From promise to impact: Ending malnutrition by 2030. *International Food Policy Research Institute.*
Jayne, T. S., Mather, D., & Mghenyi, E. (2010). Principal challenges confronting smallholder agriculture in sub-Saharan Africa. *World Development, 38*(10), 1384–1398.
Labour Ministry Report. (2012, July 18). *Ministry of labour and employment.* Retrieved from https://labour.gov.in/annual-reports on November 10, 2018.
National Sample Survey Organization GoI. (2005). Retrieved from http://www.mospi.gov.in/national-sample-survey-office-nsso on December 9, 2018.
NCAER. (2017). *Kharif outlook report.* Report No. 2017-12-1.
NCAER Annual Reports. (2015, 2016, and 2017). Retrieved from Annual Reports http://www.ncaer.org/annual_reports.php as of December 2, 2018.
NSSO. (2014). *Household consumption of various goods and services in India 20ll-12, NSS 68th Round.* Ministry of Statistics and Programme Implementation, GOI.
Puri, V. K., & Misra, S. K. (2017). *Indian economy* (35th ed.). Himalaya Publishing House.
Sharma, A. (2007). The changing agricultural demography of India: Evidence from a Rural youth perception survey. *International Journal of Rural Management, 3*(1), 27–41.
Sharma, A., & Bhaduri, A. (2009). The "Tipping Point" in Indian Agriculture: Understanding the withdrawal of the Indian Rural youth. *Asian Journal of Agriculture and Development, 6*(1362-2016-107622), 83.
Sumberg, J., Anyidoho, N. A., Leavy, J., te Lintelo, D. J. H., & Wellard, K. (2012). Introduction: The young people and agriculture 'problem' in Africa. *IDS Bulletin, 43*(6), 1–8.
Swaminathan, M. S. (2011). *Production, income, and equity – key driver for sustainable development.* Future Agricultural Extension. Westville Publishing House, New Delhi.
Symons, M. (2014). Brillat-Savarin and food. In P. Thompson & D. Kaplan (Eds.), *Encyclopaedia of food and agricultural ethics.* Springer. https://doi.org/10.1007/978-94-007-6167-4_4-6
The Centre for Study of Developing Societies (CSDS). (2015). State of Indian farmers: A report. Retrieved from https://www.lokniti.org/pdf/Farmers_Report_Final.pdf on January 1, 2019.
The World Bank Annual Report. (2007). Retrieved from http://siteresources.worldbank.org/EXTANNREP2K7/Resources/English.pdf as of February 12, 2018.
White, B. (2012). Agriculture and the generation problem: Rural youth, employment and the future of farming. *IDS Bulletin, 43*(6), 9–19.

Child Undernutrition in India: Proximate Socio-demographic Determinants

Basudha Mukhopadhyay

Abstract The extent of child undernutrition in India is quite high, its prevalence and incidence require explanation. Searches for socio-demographic and economic factors that affect child undernutrition in our country have been made in the literature, but those are exercises based on averages. Using the unit-level information obtainable from NFHS 3, NFHS 4 and NFHS 5, this paper makes an attempt to identify the main social, demographic and economic factors operating in India across the major states, which tend to determine the extent and prevalence of child undernutrition in India and pose a major challenge towards achieving our commitment for sustainable development.

Keywords Stunting · Wasting · Underweight · Morbidity

JEL Classification Code: H51; I15: J13; O53

1 Introduction

Although there is no consensus among biologists and nutritionists about how undernutrition is to be defined and by what standard it needs to be measured, it is generally recognized that both undernutrition and over nutrition are serious problems of the human race. Undernutrition is a condition where the body does not have adequate amounts of one or more nutrients and usually reflects as outcomes of the various anthropometric indicators of human body. For analytical purposes, one may distinguish between input-based and output-based indicators and measurements to characterize the phenomenon of undernutrition. In input-based analysis, dietary intake is used for nutritional assessment, whereas in out-based analysis one considers

---

B. Mukhopadhyay (✉)
Department of Commerce, J D Birla Institute, Kolkata, West Bengal, India
e-mail: rc.basudha@gmail.com

B. Chatterjee and A. K. Karmakar (eds.), *Analytical Issues in Growth & Structural Change, Macroeconomy, Security, and Sustainability of India's Economic Development*, India Studies in Business and Economics,
https://doi.org/10.1007/978-981-95-5242-9_12

the disorderly consequences (referred as *failures*) on the human body as indicators of nutritional inadequacies or deprivations thereof. Since the early 1980s, the WHO, UNICEF and the World Bank have shifted to output-based analysis, based on comparing measurement of anthropometric indicators with a specified reference in order to assess the nutritional status of the population. The anthropometric approach hinges on the assumption that people's physical appearance reflects their nutrition status, and it is sufficient to work with such outcome indicators. The principal indicators used under this category are height-for-age, weight-for-height and weight-for-age, and for the undernourished, these are reflected in retardation of body size (stunting), low weight-for-height (wasting) and underweight for children under the age of 5 years.

2 Factors Influencing Undernutrition in India

Latest analysis and research on child undernutrition, emphasizes that rural India still houses a good number of children with stunting. Since this form of child undernutrition exhibits long-term undernutrition, hence it can be said that higher income alone cannot help in reducing its prevalence. Though income, no doubt, is one of the most important factors influencing child undernutrition, other demographic factors like household size, whether household head is male, mother's age at marriage, her education, age composition of children, etc. also contributes towards nutritional deprivation. Attention must also be given to enhancing women's autonomy through more remunerative employment opportunities for them to improve hygiene and sanitation facilities of the household (vide (https://www.tandfonline.com/doi/full/10.1080/02692170500031711)).

There have been numerous studies on each of the three indicators of undernutrition and their proximate determinants in India and the states, and most of such studies have relied on explicit econometric/statistical formulations like multiple regression analysis, logistic regression and even panel data analysis to drive home the strength of alternative social, demographic and economic factors influencing undernutrition among children and mothers in our countries.

India has a population of 1.3 billion and ranks high among the undernourished countries of the world. India now has landed up in a position where acute undernutrition among under 5 children and mothers poses a danger to our declared goal of Sustainable development (SDG) and cannot be ignored or set aside as an artefact. It is well established that undernutrition is responsible for the occurrence of large array of diseases and disabilities, leading to lower brain development among the children, which lower their potentials as individuals. The consequences of poor nutrition are affecting the country's socio-economic growth and productivity.

A longitudinal study conducted by Devi and Geervani (1994) in four villages of Medak district of Andhra Pradesh, and the study by Radhakrishna and Ravi (2004), showed a strong influence of socio-economic status and parental care on the control of infectious diseases and food intake. These two factors are considered as two major causes for undernutrition among children in developing countries. Vinod et al. (1999) used multivariate analysis of the effects of selected demographic and socio-demographic factors on child undernutrition and found that the strongest predictors of child nutrition in India are child's age, child's birth order, mother's education and household standard of living. According to the study by Irudaya and Navaneetham (1994), educated mothers use better antenatal and post-natal care, which results in better health of the mother and child. The studies by Mahapatra (2000) and George et al. (2000) also tend to support the importance of mothers' education in influencing the extent of undernutrition among children below 5 years. In a study by Rajaretnam and Hallad (2000), it was found that Indian children become less and less underweight but more and more stunted after reaching 2 years of age. It also found out that the sex of the child, birth weight, order of birth, mother's education, antenatal care and incidence of illness are important predictors of child undernutrition. In a study by Chakraborty (2011) on "Determinants of nutritional status in children under 5 years in India: a multilevel approach", and Chatterjee (1996), the factors associated with nutritional status of children aged <3 years were estimated by using data from NFHS 2. There are certain studies which say that disease and diet are one of the important determinants of child nutritional status. This is because a child with inadequate diet is more prone to poor nutritional status (Dreze & Sen, 1989). This further leads to the risk of disease and recurrent illness caused by disease can damage child nutritional status. Again, inadequate diet makes the child receptive to diseases and infection. Infection in turn leads to loss of appetite, impairs the absorption capacity of nutrients from food and thus impairs the possibility of growth of the child. Some study identified certain categories of care for mothers, namely, mother's physical health, reproductive health support, autonomy and respect in the family and educational opportunities. These factors are important for the promotion of health and well-being of both the mother and the child. The importance of supporting mothers to obtain extra high-quality foods, reduce their workload at home, ensuring that they attend antenatal care clinics and receive professional care during childbirth are taken up in a number of literature on child health. Again, poor maternal nutrition can lead to low birth weight of children in developing countries. Anaemic mothers are found to be less active care givers to children. This adversely affects the nutritional status of children.

The social and demographic determinants of child undernutrition are the factors that characterize the environment which influences the lifelong development and heath outcome of a child (Pal, 1999; Pathak & Singh, 2009). These determinants act at different levels of influence of child nutritional status and interact with one another. These arrays of determinants are not always of biological and genetic in nature. But they firmly establish their influence in the interaction between individuals and social and physical environment of the child. That is why government and policymakers are attempting to understand the social determinants of child undernutrition.

It has been recognized in the literature that education increases the ability of the mother to understand the importance of giving good care to the children (Shroff et al., 2009). However, there are studies which reveal that educated mothers are likely to be involved in various economic activities, for which they must stay away from home, and this reduces the time available for child care. Thus, literature discloses that maternal education has both positive and negative effects on child undernutrition. It is also known that breastfeeding practices along with complementary feeding norms also play a vital role in child survival, growth and development. Studies reveal that children residing in households with proper hygiene practices play a notable role in reducing the level of stunting. Again, children in households with poor hygiene practices are more susceptible to higher episodes of diarrhoea, which in turn raises the possibility of the risk of undernutrition and proneness to other diseases. Health practices at home, which include immunization of children, play a significant role towards child growth and development. There is enough evidence in literature that children who are fully immunized tend to have a better growth status than those who are not.

In India, it is observed that there is a decline in the prevalence of undernutrition from NFHS 3 to NFHS 4 and in some cases in NFHS 5. There are evidences in literature which shows the extent and type of undernutrition differ sharply due to variation of socio-demographic factors, levels of literacy, climate, religion and cultural beliefs. Studies by Rajaram et al. (2003), Rao et al. (2004) and Dasgupta et al. (1990) showed that mortality and morbidity rates differ among the socio-demographic groups across the world. There are also growing evidences which suggest that in India there exists gap in the prevalence of undernutrition among children between the rich and the poor. This paper is an attempt to study the interplay of socio-demographic variables and the status of child undernutrition in India using controls for various traditional and accepted predictors of undernutrition at individual, maternal, household and community characteristics. The conceptual framework of the study is based on the econometric methodology of different forms for analysing determinants of undernutrition.

3 Methodology

3.1 Data

The nationally representative unit-level dataset for healthcare estimation of the people of India is available through National Family Health Survey (NFHS). This study used the publicly available unit-level dataset from NFHS 3, 4 and 5. This data set is the authentic data that is available on important maternal and health care indicators including nutritional status for children under five years of age, following standard anthropometric components. These surveys follow stratified two-stage sampling techniques. The 2001 and 2011 census served as the sampling frame for the selection of PSUs. Details on the sampling procedure can be found at IIPS, 2007, 2014 and 2019–20. The three NFHS surveys have been conducted under the stewardship of the Ministry of Health and Family Welfare (MoHFW), Government of India (also see Mukhopadhyay, 2020).

3.2 Study Sample

Of the total 46,665 children from NFHS 3 and 2,19,796 children from NFHS 4, a subset of 36,066 children from NFHS 3 and a subset of 1,71,029 from NFHS 4, and a subset of 1,35,231 are considered for this paper from NFHS 5 respectively from 29 states in India. The data of NFHS 5 has been used to calculate the status of height-for-age only.

Ten thousand five hundred and nine-nine children (22.7%) from NFHS 3 and forty-eight thousand seven hundred and sixty-seven children (22%) from NFHS 4 and around 19% children from NFHS 5 were excluded who were missing either antropometric data or were not included among the 29 states considered for the study. Three indices of nutritional status were calculated for children: height-for-age, weight-for-height and weight-for-age. The first indicator, which is height-for-age look into linear growth retardation and is a signal for chronic undernutrition. The weight-for-height indicator juxtaposes body mass to body length and indicates acute undernutrition. The weight-for-age is a composite measure of both chronic and acute undernutrition. These three indices of nutritional status are expressed in z-scores within the range of −5 to +5 standard deviation from the WHO reference population (vide Mukhopadhyay, 2020, op cit.).

NFHS 3, NFHS 4 and NFHS 5 used the new International Reference Population released by the World Health organization in 2006. This new standard is constructed based on children from Ghana, Norway, The United States of America, India, Brazil and Oman who are raised in healthy situations following recommended feeding practices and whose mothers could avail proper nutrition and other childcare facilities.

These three indicators of child undernutrition are expressed as standard deviation units (z-scores) from the median of the International Reference Population (WHO, 2006). The computation of z-scores was done in order to get appropriate anthropometric indicator relative to the International Reference Population with respect to particular age. The z-score is calculated with the help of the following formula

$$z_i = (A_i - \mu)/\sigma$$

where z_i mentions the z-score for the specific indicator for the child. μ and σ are the median and standard deviation of the International Reference Population.

Children with the height-for-age z-score <−2 SD (Standard Deviation) from the median of the International Reference Population are regarded as short for their age (Stunted). Children whose weight-for-height z-score <−2SD from the median of the International Reference Population, a child is said to be thin for his/her height or wasted. Since weight-for-height (underweight) is composite indicator of chronic as well as acute undernutrition, it which takes into consideration both height-for-age as well as weight-for-height. Children with z-score <−2SD from the median of the reference population are classified as underweight.

3.3 Methods Used

The study objective that has been taken here is addressed through multilevel regression econometric technique. Here we initiated multilevel regression of height-for-age, weight-for-height and weight-for-age on certain covariates which are considered as proximal and intervening covariates. We employ multi- level linear regression model by allowing cluster level random effects. Certain amount of correlation of under-nutrition parameters between children is allowed in multilevel approach by taking consideration of community/household effect.

The NFHS data is stratified in nature which means that the children are nested into mothers, mothers are nested into households, household are nested into Primary Sampling Units (PSUs) and PSUs are nested into states. Taking all these factors into consideration, we used the multilevel regression model in order to evaluate the parameters for nutritional status among children. Previous studies have shown that there is a possibility of under-estimation of parameters if single level model is used for stratified field type of data, and also it has been found that siblings in a household usually show similar characteristics with their mother (https://equityhealthj.biomedical.com/articles/https://doi.org/10.1186/1475-9276-9-19). There is a possibility that children from a specific community may have in common certain community level factors, mainly the availability of health facilities in a particular community. That means that the undiscernible heterogeneity in the resulting variable is also correlated at the level of the cluster. Hence that may result to an estimation problem if we consider the OLS technique of estimation.

We test variance component or random intercept model following the trend and practice of contemporary literature. We introduced the model covariates in stages. The subsequent changes in the model fit were then observed through log-likelihood values. The analysis was carried out using STATA for hierarchical linear models using maximum likelihood for multilevel analysis. Though, similar work had been done in Kanjilal et al., (2010). Nutritional status of children in India: household socio-economic condition as the contextual determinant, International Journal for Equity in Health, 2010, but the uniqueness of this paper lies in working with huge datasets from NFHS 3, NFHS 4 and NFHS 5.

The usefulness of the variance component model is that it corrects the problem of correlated observations in the cluster, by introducing random effect at each cluster. That implies that subjects within the same cluster are allowed to have a shared random intercept. The two clusters which we have considered are community and household. This is because NFHS give details on children of one mother chosen from a particular household. Hence, we consider the following regression equation,

$$z_{ij} = \beta^{/} x_{ij} + \delta_i + \mu_{ij} \tag{1}$$

where z_{ij} is the height-for-age, weight-for-height and weight-for-age for the child(ren) from the jth household in the ith community. The vector of the regression coefficients is represented by β corresponding to the effects of fixed covariates $x_{ij.}$ x_{ij}

are the observed characteristics of the child, the household and the community. The random community effect 'i' denoted the deviation of community i's mean z-score from the grand mean. Likewise, 'j' is a random household effect that denotes the deviation ij household's mean z-score from the ith community mean. The error terms are $\boldsymbol{\delta}_{\mathbf{i}}$ and$\boldsymbol{\mu}_{\mathbf{ij}}$. It is assumed that the error terms are normally distributed with zero mean and variances $\sigma^2{}_c$ and $\sigma^2{}_h$ of community and household respectively. The values of $\sigma^2{}_c$ and $\sigma^2{}_h$ may probably be larger when the observations of the cluster show greater homogeneity and are not explained by the covariates taken under consideration.

We need to affirm the appropriateness of the multilevel model. This is possible, if we test the variances of the random section of the model chosen, and then see if the variances are different from zero for both the households and communities. The evaluation of the intra-class correlation (ICC) is thereafter conducted, and it showed the extent of correlation between child undernutrition with both household and communities. If the ICC so derived distinguishably differs from zero then it indicates that the random effect models is suitable and appropriate for this study. The proportion of variation is explained by the ICC coefficient. The formula to find the correlation between children's status of nutrition in the very same community as well as household is

$$\rho c = \sigma^2 c / \left(\sigma^2 c + \sigma^2 h\right) \rho c = \sigma^2 c / \left(\sigma^2 c + \sigma^2 h\right) \rho c = \sigma^2 c / \left(\sigma^2 c + \sigma^2 h\right) \quad (2)$$

The total variability in the individual height-for-age, weight-for-height and weight-for-age z-scores is then divided into two separate parts, namely, variance in children's nutritional status among households within communities and variances between communities. The objective of introducing covariates at each level in the variance component model is that, it helps to examine that the perceived distinction in anthropometric scores is traceable to variables at all the levels taken under consideration.

The analysis is presented in the following tables. Four models are used for the analysis in addition to the conventional OLS model which does not take into consideration the cluster random effects.

The OLS model we usually fit $Z_i = \beta_0 + \beta_1 x_i + e_i \text{where } e_i \sim N\left(0, \sigma^2\right) Z_i = \beta_0 + \beta_1 x_i + e_i \text{where } e_i \sim N\left(0, \sigma^2\right) Z_i = \beta_0 + \beta_1 x_i + e_i \text{where } e_i \sim N\left(0, \sigma^2\right)$ $Z_i = \beta_0 + \beta_1 x_i + e_i \text{where } e_i \sim N\left(0, \sigma^2\right) Z_i = \beta_0 + \beta_1 x_i + e_i \text{where } e_i \sim N\left(0, \sigma^2\right)$ $Z_i = \beta_0 + \beta_1 x_i + e_i \text{where } e_i \sim N\left(0, \sigma^2\right) Z_i = \beta_0 + \beta_1 x_i + e_i \text{where } e_i \sim N\left(0, \sigma^2\right)$

Here, Z_i is the z-score of the ith individual and X_i are the children, mother and household specific variables. But when the data is clustered, using this model causes problems. If we fit this model to the clustered data, we do not get correct answers. This model does not show how much variation is there at each level of cluster. By using this model, we cannot find out how much effect household has on the community after control of individual child, mother and household level variables.

3.4 Variables Used in the Regression Model

This paper uses height-for-age, weight-for-height and weight-for-age as the outcome variables, signifying the three undernutrition parameters. The height-for-age (stunting) is the indicator of chronic undernutrition due to long-term deprivation of food, while weight-for-height (wasting) is an indicator of acute undernutrition due to recent illness or food deprivation. Weight-for-age (underweight) is a composite of the previous two measures of nutritional status. These measures are expressed in the form of z-scores standard deviation (SD) from the median of the 2006 WHO International Reference Population. This continuous standard deviation of z-scores provides expected changes in the value of the regress and variable due to one unit change in the regressors no matter whether the child is stunted/wasted/underweight or not. This approach differs from the conventional approach of employing dichotomous variable on probability of a child being undernourished. (0 = otherwise, 1 = stunted/wasted/underweight). This study attempts to develop a deterministic model instead of modelling the probability of stunting/wasting/underweight. This paper attempts to find out the influencing role of household socio-demographic variables on child undernutrition status in twenty-nine states in India.

3.5 Explanatory Variables

The causes of stunting, wasting and underweight are multiple and often interdependent. It is observed from various literatures that there is a tendency of socio-demographic clustering of risk factors for poor health. Association is observed between rural living conditions and poor health and that is why rural health has become a new arena of research. On the other hand, urban environments may pose threat to health that is less salient in rural environments. Hence, rural and urban living environments have a tendency to place different kinds of demand on their inhabitants. It has been observed in various literatures that in developing countries including India, the rural children tend to be comparatively poorer than their urban counterpart and socio-economic status is strongly associated with health. Overall living standards and health standard are poorer in rural children than the urban children. Hence, rural–urban place of residence is considered as an explanatory variable in the study.

The other explanatory variables are chosen based on available literature on the subject. Here we consider certain individual characteristics of a child as the impending determinant of child undernutrition. We considered square of child's age, sex of the child, birth order, size of the child at birth, complete doses of immunization, child suffered from recent illness mainly from diarrhoea or acute respiratory disorder and recommended feeding practice denoted by exclusive breastfeeding for more than six months.

Apart from the child level covariates, we considered the mother-level controls. These includes education of mothers in terms of number of years of education, mother's body mass index (BMI base = 18.5), mother's status of anaemia, mother's availing Mother and Child Protection Card, place of birth of the child, mother's decision-making power in terms of autonomy for taking medical help.

The household level factors that are considered, except for rural–urban differences, controls are included for ethnicity of the household, i.e., whether they belong to scheduled casters and scheduled tribe households, either the household has the piped water facility, and whether the household owns a house of its own. The last two factors are used as an indicator of the nature of asset the household has. Since the community characteristic is regarded a distant covariate of child undernutrition in the model, hence the percapita NSDP and different states are considered in each of the models as controls or as fixed effects of the multilevel model.

4 Results

4.1 Role of Socio-demographic Conditions

Tables 1 and 7 show significant association between socio-economic status and child nutritional status. Here, the dependent variable is the continuous standard deviation of HAZ score. Given this form of dependent variable, a higher coefficient recommends better nutritional status of children among children living in the urban areas as compared to those living in rural areas.

From the OLS model, it is revealed that better nutritional outcome is observed from the children living in urban areas than rural areas. It can be seen that nearly 40% (0.25–(−0.13)) and 32% better nutritional status among children living in urban areas compared to those living in the rural areas in NFHS 4 and 3 respectively. All the variance component models also support these findings. As we introduce the covariates at each level, the results of variance component models depict the extent to which observed differences in HAZ scores are allocated to predictors operating at each level. Here, we observe that after the introduction of the child level covariates with state level fixed effect, the impact of rural–urban place of residence becomes a bit stronger which is echoed in both the NFHSs. The result is around 53% (0.40–(−0.13)) and 41% (0.296–(−0.111)) higher incidence of inferior nutritional status among children residing in rural areas than the ones coming from urban areas in the two NFHSs respectively. But it is interesting to observe that the gap between rural–urban places of residence gradually gets reduced when we introduced the mother-level covariates and other household-level covariates. Model 4 and 5 show similar estimates as that of OLS.

The results of the OLS model indicate that better nutritional outcomes in terms of higher height-for-age values are significantly associated with being male and among children of larger than average size at birth. It can also be witnessed that there is an

Table 1 Association (β_s) from ordinary least squares and multilevel linear regression models (main effects) between (height-for-age) and rural–urban place of residence, controlling for various other covariates; twenty-nine Major States, India, NFHS 4

Predictors	OLS	Model 1	Model 2	Model 3	Model 4
Exp(B)(SE)					
Urban residence	0.247*** (0.026)		0.391*** (0.040)	0.212*** (0.023)	0.212*** (0.023)
Rural residence	−0.131*** (0.020)	-	−0.139*** (0.020)	−0.136*** (0.020)	−0.135*** (0.021)
Controls					
Individual characteristics					
Child age (months)	−0.079 (0.002)	–	−0.074 (0.006)	−0.078 (0.002)	−0.089 (0.002)
Sex (base: male) female	−0.005*** (0.001)	–	−0.025*** (0.001)	−0.015*** (0.002)	−0.005*** (0.001)
Order of birth	−0.021 (0.008)	–	−0.019 (0.018)	−0.022 (0.008)	−0.021 (0.008)
Size at Birth	0.245* (0.022)	–	0.258* (0.023)	0.245* (0.022)	0.215* (0.021)
Suffered (*base: no illness*) recent illness	−0.022 (0.025)	–	−0.022 (0.025)	−0.022 (0.025)	−0.020 (0.022)
Duration of exclusive breastfeeding (*base: less than 6 months*)	−0.039* (0.016)	–	−0.035* (0.012)	−0.033* (0.015)	−0.031* (0.011)
Completed Immunization	0.001 (0.012)	–	0.001 (0.012)	0.001 (0.012)	0.001 (0.012)
Mothers' characteristics					
Years of education	0.035*** (0.005)	–		0.032*** (0.004)	0.034*** (0.007)
BMI of mother≥ 18.5 (*base= 18.5*)	0.022** (0.005)	–		0.019** (0.005)	0.020** (0.004)
Suffers from anaemia	0.152 (0.064)	–		0.147 (0.061)	0.149 (0.064)
Mother and Child Protection Card	0.025** (0.002)	–		0.022** (0.002)	0.023** (0.002)
Institutional delivery (*base = home delivery*)	0.084*** (0.021)	–		0.082*** (0.020)	0.081*** (0.023)
Decision-making power	−0.051 (0.032)	–		−0.051 (0.032)	−0.050 (0.038)
Household characteristics					
Ethnicity SC ST	−0.101*** (0.019)	-	−0.101*** (0.019)	–	−0.111*** (0.012)

(continued)

Table 1 (continued)

Predictors	OLS	Model 1	Model 2	Model 3	Model 4
Water source (piped water)	0.021** (0.001)	–	0.022** (0.001)	–	0.024** (0.001)
Owns a house	0.210 (0.021)	–	0.216 (0.022)	–	0.211 (0.021)
States					
Per capita NSDP	0.172*** (0.022)	–	0.315*** (0.029)	0.216*** (0.027)	0.191*** (0.027)
Haryana	−0.152* (0.085)	–	−0.147* (0.082)	−0.149* (0.085)	−0.150* (0.084)
Himachal Pradesh	0.163* (0.091)	–	0.161* (0.088)	0.162* (0.085)	0.163* (0.090)
Punjab	0.131 (0.077)	–	0.133 (0.073)	0.130 (0.072)	0.130 (0.077)
Rajasthan	−0.145*** (0.042)	–	−0.144*** (0.043)	−0.143*** (0.044)	−0.141*** (0.040)
Uttarakhand	−0.255* (0.102)	–	−0.245* (0.112)	−0.250* (0.102)	−0.250* (0.102)
Chhattisgarh	0.131* (0.071)	–	0.129* (0.068)	0.130* (0.069)	0.133* (0.070)
Madhya Pradesh	0.013* (0.060)	–	0.016 (0.061)	0.014 (0.056)	0.017* (0.059)
Uttar Pradesh	−0.165* (0.063)	–	−0.164* (0.063)	−0.163* (0.063)	−0.165* (0.063)
Bihar	−0.129* (0.065)	–	−0.129* (0.065)	−0.129* (0.065)	−0.129* (0.065)
Jharkhand	−0.255 (0.052)	–	−0.254 (0.052)	−0.255 (0.051)	−0.254 (0.051)
Odisha	0.213*** (0.085)	–	0.211*** (0.084)	0.210*** (0.084)	0.210*** (0.082)
West Bengal	0.163** (0.066)	–	0.161** (0.062)	0.162** (0.060)	0.162** (0.065)
Arunachal Pradesh	0.025 (0.056)	–	0.024 (0.053)	0.026 (0.056)	0.022 (0.056)
Assam	0.035* (0.065)	–	0.031* (0.063)	0.034 (0.063)	0.033 (0.064)
Manipur	0.288* (0.054)	–	0.284* (0.051)	0.285 (0.050)	0.287 (0.051)
Mizoram	0.301* (0.024)	–	0.302* (0.022)	0.302 (0.023)	0.303 (0.022)
Nagaland	0.024* (0.002)	–	0.023* (0.001)	0.022 (0.002)	0.020 (0.002)

(continued)

Table 1 (continued)

Predictors	OLS	Model 1	Model 2	Model 3	Model 4
Gujrat	−0.298*** (0.063)	–	−0.297*** (0.061)	−0.296*** (0.060)	−0.295*** (0.061)
Maharashtra	−0.102** (0.045)	–	−0.103** (0.045)	−0.103** (0.045)	−0.101** (0.045)
Andhra Pradesh	0.045* (0.066)	–	0.046* (0.065)	0.042* (0.064)	0.044 (0.063)
Tamil Nadu	0.327** (0.061)	–	0.326** (0.061)	0.322** (0.062)	0.325** (0.060)
Karnataka	−0.035 (0.066)	–	−0.034 (0.067)	−0.034 (0.065)	−0.033 (0.064)
Delhi	−0.023* (0.088)	–	−0.025* (0.088)	−0.022 (0.087)	−0.021 (0.085)
Meghalaya	0.075 (0.068)	–	0.076 (0.065)	0.073 (0.065)	0.073 (0.069)
Sikkim	0.021 (0.078)	–	0.022 (0.079)	0.025 (0.074)	0.025 (0.074)
Tripura	0.030 (0.082)	–	0.031 (0.83)	0.032 (0.084)	0.035 (0.080)
Goa	0.009 (0.074)	–	0.005 (0.073)	0.008 (0.072)	0.005 (0.071)
Jammu & Kashmir	−0.041 (0.081)	–	−0.041 (0.079)	−0.044 (0.081)	−0.045 (0.079)
Constant	−1.119*** (0.076)				
N	1,70,006	1,70,058	1,70,006	1,70,006	1,70,006
Log likelihood	R^2 0.177				
X^2 statistics	151.270		3926.7	4097.6	3922.9
P value	0.000		0.000	0.000	0.000

Significant at ***$p < 0.001$, **$p < 0.01$, *$p < 0.05$
Source Calculation from NFHS 4 unit data

apparent inverse association between duration of breastfeeding and height-for-age nutritional status. It is observed that those children whose duration of breastfeeding is more than a year, has increased incidence of stunting. In this respect, let us mention that the available literature mentions (Mazumdar, 2010) about the nonlinear effect of breastfeeding duration and nutritional status. Prolonged breastfeeding signals delayed onset of weaning, which in turn may lead to nutritional deprivations that may lead to chronic undernutrition.

It is found that mothers who have certain years of education, have normal BMI values, possess Mother and Child Protection Card and have given birth in an institution are found to be benefitting from better nutritional status in NFHS 4. Among the household-level characteristics, it seems that there is an inverse association between those belonging to SC and ST ethnic group and long-term undernutrition. A clear positive association is also observed between availability of piped water and height-for-age z-scores. This implies that those communities belonging to SC and ST and non-availability of piped water are more probable from suffering from long-term undernutrition.

From the state level characteristics, it is clear that that states with higher per capita NSDP have a significant position association with height-for-age *z*-scores. This finding is unique and is not observed by studies conducted earlier. The results of OLS are more or less consistent with the results of the others models where the covariates are introduced in phased manner.

By phased manner, we mean that in the rest of the models along with rural–urban differences, all the other covariates are introduced step-by step where the null model does not include any covariates. In Model 2, first the child-level covariates are introduced, and Model 3 and 4 includes mother-level covariates and all the covariates respectively.

The calculated intra-class correlation coefficient (ICC) values presented in Tables 2 and 8 differs from zero. The immediate implication is that child height-for-age z-scores are correlated with households and communities (PSUs). It can also be witnessed that intra-class correlation coefficient values for household level are much higher than the ICC values of PSUs. The lower panel of Tables 2 and 8 helps us to infer that the residual variance is distributed across the PSUs and households. The estimates from Model 1 (null model) indicate that the variation in height-for-age has a substantial group level component. Incidentally, the null model contains no observed covariates. If we combine the community (PSUs) and Household level estimates, the total variances are 0.505 and 0.575 of which 65% and 61% is attributed to household-level variation in anthropometric scores. We can also observe that the variance decomposition pattern in Model 2, Model 3 and Model 4, are consistent to the observations on null model variance decomposition. The pattern is similar across PSU and household levels. Further, it can also be discerned that the household heterogeneity is partially accounted by the covariates of the model. The values of $\sigma^2{}_c$ and $\sigma^2{}_h$ are significantly different, which indicates that the homogeneity of within cluster observations is not explained by the observed covariates used in the model. A look on the intra-household correlation shows that it is quite large in Model 4. It is also seen that this value is large in all the other models too. This result suggests that the height outcomes of two individual children who belong to the same family are more homogeneous. As can be seen in all the models that the overall higher values of $\sigma^2{}_h$, that is, the variance at the household level gives the indication that there is higher homogeneity at the household level. Similar results are for both NFHS 4 and 3. From these results it can also be inferred that the choice of one-level model with a similar set of data might not have yielded the desired result.

For analysing the status of children from NFHS 5 across all the states, it can be observed from Table 13 that similar significant association between socio-economic status and child nutritional status through HAZ score. From the OLS model, it is revealed that better nutritional outcome is observed from the children living in urban areas than rural areas. Here too, the variance component models also support the same

Table 2 Random coefficients, intra-class correlation and variance decomposition estimates (height-for-age) NFHS 4

Random coefficients, Intra-class correlation and Variance Decomposition estimates				
	Model 1	Model 2	Model 3	Model 4
Random effects				
σ^2_c Community-PSU	0.196	0.085	0.065	0.049
(S.E)	(0.022)	(0.017)	(0.010)	(0.009)
Proportions of overall (null model) explained by the covariates of the model (in %)		51.546	69.145	69.001
$\sigma^2{}_h$ (Household)	0.309	0.496	0.456	0.412
(S.E)	(0.021)	(0.035)	(0.034)	(0.031)
Proportions of overall (null model) explained by the covariates of the model (in %)		−31.112	−22.072	−27.551
Residual^2	1.755	1.502	1.509	1.510
(S.E)	(0.025)	(0.019)	(0.021)	(0.024)
Intra-class correlation				
ρ(PSU)	0.081*	0.039*	0.021*	0.024*
ρ(household)	0.215*	0.243*	0.244*	0.219*
Variance Decomposition (in %)				
PSU	35.2	14.7	9.9	10.3
Household	64.8	85.3	90.1	89.7

Significance level *$p < 0.05$
Source Calculation from NFHS 4 unit data

findings. It is also evident from the table that after the introduction of the child level covariates with state level fixed effect, the impact of rural–urban place of residence becomes a bit stronger.

The results of the models indicate that better nutritional outcomes in terms of higher height-for-age values are significantly associated with being male and among children of larger than average size at birth. Same as the results of the previous two rounds, the findings of NFHS 5 also depict the inverse association between duration of breastfeeding and height-for-age nutritional status.

Mothers, who have certain years of education, have normal BMI values, possess Mother and Child Protection Card and have given birth in at institutions so that their children are benefitting from better nutritional status.

From the state level characteristics, states with higher Per capita NSDP have a significant positive association with height-for-age *z*-scores.

Thus, it can be said that the survey to gauge the status and improvement of health of children, before and also after the pandemic, failed to reveal a notable impact on the nutritional status of children of our country.

Table 3 Association (β_s) from ordinary least squares and multilevel linear regression models (main effects) between (weight-for-age) and rural–urban place of residence, controlling for various other covariates; twenty-nine major states, India, NFHS 4

Predictors	OLS	Model 1	Model 2	Model 3	Model 4
Exp(B)(SE)					
Urban residence	0.391*** (0.019)		0.396*** (0.018)	0.309*** (0.018)	0.308*** (0.019)
Rural residence	−0.104*** (0.034)	–	−0.104*** (0.035)	−0.105*** (0.032)	−0.105*** (0.032)
Controls					
Individual characteristics					
Child age (months)	−0.027 (0.000)	–	−0.045 (0.004)	−0.034 (0.001)	0.059 (0.002)
Sex (base: male) female	−0.003*** (0.001)	–	−0.013*** (0.002)	−0.019*** (0.003)	−0.018*** (0.002)
Order of birth	−0.001 (0.008)	–	−0.002 (0.009)	−0.001 (0.008)	−0.002 (0.008)
Size at birth	0.245 (0.022)	–	0.258 (0.023)	0.245 (0.022)	0.225 (0.021)
Suffered (*base: no illness*) recent illness	−0.022** (0.005)	–	−0.020** (0.006)	−0.021** (0.005)	−0.020** (0.006)
Duration of breastfeeding (*base: less than 6 months*)	−0.014* (0.014)	–	−0.017* (0.013)	−0.018* (0.014)	−0.017* (0.012)
Completed Immunization	0.003* (0.010)	–	0.002* (0.011)	0.002* (0.010)	0.005* (0.011)
Mothers' characteristics					
Years of Education	0.012 (0.001)	–	–	0.013 (0.001)	0.011 (0.012)
BMI of mother	0.006** (0.003)	–	–	0.005** (0.002)	0.005** (0.001)
Suffers from anaemia	0.027 (0.010)	–	–	0.024 (0.008)	0.026 (0.008)
Mother and child protection card	0.002* (0.001)	–	–	0.005* (0.002)	0.006* (0.003)
Institutional delivery	0.045** (0.004)	–	–	0.044** (0.005)	0.041** (0.003)
Decision-making power	0.032** (0.005)	–	–	0.033** (0.002)	0.033** (0.007)
Household characteristics					
Ethnicity SC ST	−0.066** (0.013)	–	−0.065** (0.014)	–	−0.061*** (0.012)

(continued)

Table 3 (continued)

Predictors	OLS	Model 1	Model 2	Model 3	Model 4
Water source (piped water)	0.011** (0.002)	–	0.012** (0.002)	–	0.014** (0.001)
Owns a house	0.105** (0.051)	–	0.106** (0.052)	–	0.106** (0.051)
States (household size)					
Per capita NSDP	0.101*** (0.020)	–	0.107*** (0.021)	−0.109*** (0.022)	−0.111*** (0.021)
Haryana	0.092* (0.015)	–	0.097* (0.012)	−0.099 (0.015)	−0.093 (0.014)
Himachal Pradesh	0.045* (0.091)	–	0.041* (0.091)	0.042* (0.095)	0.043* (0.091)
Punjab	0.117** (0.077)	–	0.117* (0.073)	0.118* (0.072)	0.118* (0.072)
Rajasthan	0.201* (0.034)	–	0.202* (0.034)	0.203 (0.038)	0.203 (0.036)
Uttarakhand	−0.015* (0.092)	–	−0.015 (0.092)	−0.012 (0.093)	−0.013* (0.093)
Chhattisgarh	0.001* (0.025)	–	0.002 (0.026)	0.002 (0.026)	0.0033 (0.025)
Madhya Pradesh	−0.029* (0.019)	–	−0.026* (0.016)	−0.026* (0.017)	−0.029* (0.019)
Uttar Pradesh	−0.055** (0.031)	–	−0.054** (0.032)	−0.051** (0.032)	−0.051** (0.032)
Bihar	−0.056* (0.024)	–	−0.055* (0.023)	−0.0529* (0.026)	−0.053* (0.026)
Jharkhand	0.196* (0.083)	–	0.195 (0.083)	0.196 (0.072)	0.195 (0.077)
Odisha	0.175* (0.055)	–	0.178* (0.059)	0.178* (0.054)	0.178* (0.054)
West Bengal	0.099 (0.021)	–	0.095 (0.021)	0.096 (0.021)	0.097 (0.022)
Arunachal Pradesh	0.042 (0.023)	–	0.045 (0.025)	0.046 (0.025)	0.043 (0.026)
Assam	0.055* (0.024)	–	0.054 (0.027)	0.055 (0.027)	0.056 (0.026)
Manipur	0.162* (0.045)	–	0.165 (0.045)	0.166 (0.047)	0.166 (0.047)
Mizoram	0.258* (0.015)	–	0.254 (0.016)	0.254 (0.016)	0.255 (0.015)
Nagaland	0.009* (0.019)	–	0.011 (0.019)	0.013 (0.019)	0.009 (0.015)

(continued)

Table 3 (continued)

Predictors	OLS	Model 1	Model 2	Model 3	Model 4
Gujrat	−0.152* (0.021)	–	−0.157* (0.022)	−0.157* (0.021)	0.155** (0.020)
Maharashtra	−0.117* (0.025)	–	−0.119* (0.025)	−0.119* (0.025)	−0.119* (0.025)
Andhra Pradesh	0.022* (0.015)	–	0.023* (0.016)	0.22 (0.019)	0.022 (0.019)
Tamil Nadu	0.016* (0.062)	–	0.015 (0.061)	0.015 (0.062)	0.015 (0.063)
Karnataka	−0.022 (0.034)	–	−0.027 (0.035)	−0.027 (0.036)	−0.027 (0.036)
Delhi	−0.007 (0.037)	–	−0.009 (0.039)	−0.009 (0.031)	−0.009 (0.032)
Meghalaya	0.066* (0.051)	–	0.065 (0.052)	0.065 (0.052)	0.066 (0.051)
Sikkim	0.009* (0.021)	–	0.010 (0.025)	0.011 (0.025)	0.011 (0.021)
Tripura	0.026 (0.035)	–	0.027 (0.036)	0.028 (0.039)	0.028 (0.041)
Goa	0.011 (0.047)	–	0.012 (0.049)	0.012 (0.048)	0.015 (0.047)
Constant	−1.112*** (0.088)				
N	1,70,006	1,71,058	1,70,006	1,70,006	1,70,006
Log likelihood	R^2 0.152				
X^2 statistics	126.570		3058.6	3177.2	3099.9
P value	0.000		0.002	0.002	0.002

Significant at ***$p < 0.001$, **$p < 0.01$, *$p < 0.05$
Source Calculation from NFHS 4 unit data

Both Tables 3 and 9 shows significant association between socio-demographic status and child nutritional status. Here the dependent variable is the continuous standard deviation of weight-for-age z-score. It is evident from the tables that the nutritional status of children living in urban areas is much better than those living in the rural areas of India. From the OLS model, it can be seen that 50% better nutritional status (0.391−(−0.104)) is enjoyed by the children living in urban areas in NFHS 4 whereas it was 43% in NFHS 3 compared to those living in the rural areas. All the variance component models also support these findings.

Once we introduce covariates at each level, the results of various variance component models show the expense of the pronounced differences in weight-for-age z-scores are allocated to covariates operating at each level. The introduction of the child level covariates with state level fixed effect depicts a similar picture of the impact of rural–urban place of residence. It shows a similar 50% (0.396−(−0.104)) and 44%

Table 4 Random coefficients, intra-class correlation and variance decomposition estimates (weight-for-age) NFHS 4

Random coefficients, intra-class correlation and variance decomposition estimates				
	Model 1	Model 2	Model 3	Model 4
Random effects				
$\sigma^2{}_c$ community- PSU	0.127	0.061	0.052	0.033
(S.E)	(0.009)	(0.006)	(0.006)	(0.007)
Proportions of overall (null model) explained by the covariates of the model (in %)		46.323	52.296	53.118
$\sigma^2{}_h$ (Household)	0.401	0.475	0.488	0.449
(S.E)	(0.033)	(0.041)	(0.041)	(0.039)
Proportions of overall (null model) explained by the covariates of the model (in %)		−26.225	−20.745	−21.466
Residual^2	1.056	1.029	1.025	1.021
(S.E)	(0.025)	(0.019)	(0.021)	(0.024)
Intra-class correlation				
ρ(PSU)	0.065*	0.034*	0.019*	0.020*
ρ(household)	0.196*	0.167*	0.188*	0.184*
Variance decomposition (in %)				
PSU	29.5	11.9	8.3	11.8
Household	70.5	88.1	91.7	88.2

Significance level *$p < 0.05$
Source Calculation from NFHS 4 unit data

higher incidence of poor nutritional status among children residing in rural areas in NFHS 4 and NFHS 3 respectively. As in HAZ score results, it can be observed that the gap between rural–urban places of residence gradually gets less with the introduction of the mother-level covariates and other household-level covariates. Around 41% and 40%, respectively, better nutritional status for children residing in urban areas are observed in Model 4 and 5.

The results of the OLS model and the other models with separate covariates reveal that better nutritional outcomes in terms of higher weight-for-age values are significantly associated with being female, duration of breastfeeding and complete immunization. An inverse association is observed between duration of breastfeeding and weight-for-age nutritional status. It is observed that those children whose duration of breastfeeding is longer than 6 months has increased incidence of underweight. The results are similar to the observations we found from Table 1. This affirms that prolonged breast feeding does not increase the nutritional status of children. It can be also concluded that female children are more prone to adverse nutritional status than their male counterpart. This implies that girl children are still relatively neglected in our country. Again, complete immunization is also an essential component to

Table 5 Association (β_s) from ordinary least squares and multilevel linear regression models (main effects) between (weight-for-height) and rural–urban place of residence, controlling for various other covariates; twenty-nine major states, India, NFHS 4

Predictors	OLS	Model 1	Model 2	Model 3	Model 4
Exp(B)(SE)					
Urban Residence	0.269*** (0.023)		0.266*** (0.022)	0.269*** (0.021)	0.271*** (0.023)
Rural Residence	−0.095*** (0.031)	–	−0.099*** (0.032)	−0.099*** (0.030)	−0.095*** (0.031)
Controls					
Individual characteristics					
Child age (months)	−0.055*** (0.002)	–	−0.054*** (0.009)	−0.051*** (0.010)	0.053*** (0.012)
Sex male	−0.019** (0.025)	–	−0.021** (0.025)	−0.022** (0.022)	−0.021** (0.023)
Order of birth	−0.016 (0.007)	–	−0.025 (0.010)	−0.025 (0.011)	−0.025 (0.011)
Size at birth	0.312 (0.039)	–	0.325 (0.036)	0.311 (0.035)	0.322 (0.034)
Suffered (*base: no illness*) recent illness	−0.109* (0.053)	–	−0.105* (0.052)	−0.102* (0.052)	−0.111* (0.056)
Duration of breastfeeding	0.061* (0.028)	–	0.062* (0.028)	0.065* (0.029)	0.066* (0.031)
Completed immunization	0.015* (0.001)	–	0.016* (0.003)	0.017* (0.002)	0.019* (0.002)
Mothers' characteristics					
Years of education	0.029** (0.016)	–	–	0.027*** (0.014)	0.022*** (0.014)
BMI of mother	0.011** (0.006)	–	–	0.012** (0.007)	0.012** (0.008)
Suffers from anaemia	0.101** (0.051)	–	–	0.102** (0.051)	0.103** (0.052)
Mother and child protection card	0.066* (0.011)	–	–	0.065* (0.012)	0.066* (0.013)
Institutional delivery	0.051** (0.025)	–	–	0.054** (0.026)	0.059** (0.024)
Decision-making power	−0.016 (0.011)	–	–	−0.015 (0.010)	−0.015 (0.010)
Household characteristics					
Ethnicity SC ST	−0.057** (0.029)	–	−0.058** (0.023)	–	−0.060*** (0.023)
Water source (piped water)	0.055** (0.012)	–	0.052** (0.011)	–	0.054** (0.011)

(continued)

Table 5 (continued)

Predictors	OLS	Model 1	Model 2	Model 3	Model 4
Owns a house	−0.098 (0.021)	–	−0.096 (0.019)	–	−0.096 (0.018)
States (household size)					
NSDP	0.123*** (0.042)	–	0.122*** (0.043)	0.122*** (0.045)	0.123*** (0.044)
Haryana	−0.039* (0.021)	–	−0.036* (0.017)	−0.039* (0.016)	−0.036* (0.018)
Himachal Pradesh	0.088* (0.074)	–	0.082* (0.072)	0.083* (0.073)	0.086* (0.071)
Punjab	0.129** (0.076)	–	0.127** (0.069)	0.128 (0.065)	0.127 (0.066)
Rajasthan	−0.333** (0.021)	–	−0.332** (0.022)	−0.333** (0.026)	−0.335** (0.029)
Uttarakhand	0.068* (0.029)	–	0.066 (0.025)	0.065 (0.025)	0.065 (0.021)
Chhattisgarh	0.025* (0.016)	–	0.022 (0.016)	0.022 (0.015)	0.022 (0.015)
Madhya Pradesh	−0.054** (0.022)	–	−0.059* (0.022)	−0.058* (0.022)	−0.058* (0.022)
Uttar Pradesh	−0.062** (0.021)	–	−0.063** (0.021)	−0.061** (0.025)	−0.063** (0.022)
Bihar	−0.046* (0.031)	–	−0.047* (0.033)	−0.046* (0.032)	−0.045* (0.032)
Jharkhand	−0.177 (0.078)	–	−0.178 (0.076)	−0.178 (0.069)	−0.177 (0.069)
Odisha	−0.125 (0.074)	–	−0.124 (0.072)	−0.121 (0.071)	−0.121 (0.073)
West Bengal	−0.132 (0.025)	–	−0.136 (0.022)	−0.133 (0.026)	−0.135 (0.023)
Arunachal Pradesh	−0.109* (0.011)	–	−0.107* (0.012)	−0.104* (0.016)	−0.106* (0.018)
Assam	−0.041* (0.017)	–	−0.044* (0.016)	−0.045* (0.014)	−0.047* (0.015)
Manipur	0.119* (0.033)	–	0.120 (0.034)	0.126 (0.035)	0.127 (0.035)
Mizoram	0.102* (0.021)	–	0.109 (0.024)	0.111 (0.027)	0.112 (0.025)
Nagaland	0.185* (0.093)	–	0.184 (0.096)	0.181 (0.092)	0.187 (0.099)
Gujrat	0.144* (0.035)	–	0.148 (0.036)	0.147 (0.035)	0.147 (0.039)

(continued)

Table 5 (continued)

Predictors	OLS	Model 1	Model 2	Model 3	Model 4
Maharashtra	−0.095* (0.033)	–	−0.096* (0.034)	−0.099* (0.036)	−0.095* (0.035)
Andhra Pradesh	−0.116* (0.056)	–	−0.121* (0.057)	−0.121* (0.057)	−0.122* (0.051)
Tamil Nadu	0.091* (0.027)	–	0.096 (0.026)	0.092 (0.022)	0.096 (0.021)
Karnataka	−0.055* (0.022)	–	−0.061 (0.022)	−0.062 (0.019)	−0.063 (0.022)
Delhi	−0.097 (0.025)	–	−0.098 (0.025)	−0.095 (0.024)	−0.095 (0.029)
Meghalaya	0.061 (0.041)	–	0.059 (0.042)	0.053 (0.043)	0.053 (0.044)
Sikkim	0.121* (0.036)	–	0.122 (0.035)	0.121 (0.035)	0.121 (0.033)
Tripura	0.052 (0.033)	–	0.054 (0.030)	0.050 (0.034)	0.050 (0.031)
Goa	0.165 (0.021)	–	0.159 (0.021)	0.159 (0.019)	0.159 (0.022)
Constant	−1.127*** (0.088)				
N	1,70,006	1,71,058	1,70,006	1,70,006	1,70,006
Log likelihood	R^2 0.419	−40281.20	−39458.55	−38459.19	−38122.17
X^2 statistics	211.245		2985.6	2944.7	2901.1
P value	0.001		0.001	0.001	0.001

Significant at ***$p < 0.001$, **$p < 0.01$, *$p < 0.05$
Source Calculation from NFHS 4 unit data

better nutritional standard of the child population of our country. It is imperative that children obtaining all the required vaccines enjoy a better nutritional outcome than those deprived from complete immunization doses.

Among the mother-level variables, it can be observed that mother's education having normal BMI positively influence the nutritional score of children. Here too, the mother possessing with Mother and Child Protection Card in NFHS 4 can ensure their children with better nutritional outcome. It can also be seen that mother who has the power of taking her own decision in terms of autonomy in taking decision for medical help can give their children a healthier nutritional life.

A look into the household-level predictors, reveals that those households having access to piped water and owns their own house have a positive association with weight-for-age z-scores. Again, a negative association is observed with SC and ST ethnic group and the nutritional status. That means those households belonging to SC and ST ethnic groups contribute to worse nutritional status of children in India.

Table 6 Random coefficients, Intra-class correlation and variance decomposition estimates (weight-for-height) NFHS 4

Random coefficients, intra-class correlation and variance decomposition estimates				
	Model 1	Model 2	Model 3	Model 4
Random effects				
σ^2_c Community- PSU	0.145	0.089	0.060	0.041
(S.E)	(0.011)	(0.011)	(0.013)	(0.019)
Proportions of overall (null model) explained by the covariates of the model (in %)		39.385	56.211	58.598
σ^2_h (Household)	0.389	0.452	0.444	0.454
(S.E)	(0.047)	(0.050)	(0.051)	(0.056)
Proportions of overall (null model) explained by the covariates of the model (in %)		−26.225	−20.745	−21.466
Residual^2	1.139	1.144	1.141	1.145
(S.E)	(0.021)	(0.029)	(0.026)	(0.027)
Intra-class correlation				
ρ(PSU)	0.071*	0.042*	0.025*	0.029*
ρ(household)	0.206*	0.212*	0.213*	0.219*
Variance decomposition (in %)				
PSU	31.7	25.5	15.1	18.8
Household	68.3	74.5	84.9	81.2

Significance level *$p < 0.05$
Source Calculation from NFHS 4 unit data

From the state level characteristics, it can be observed that there is a positive association between per capita NSDP and weight-for-height z-scores. Again, this is a unique result, not observed by any other study before. That means states with higher per capita NSDP contribute to better nutritional status of children in our country.

The results of OLS are more or less consistent with the results of the other models where the covariates are introduced in phased manner. Here too, the calculated intra-class correlation coefficient values presented in Tables 4 and 10 differs from zero. The implication is similar to the earlier height-for-age z-scores. Indeed, the weight-for-height z-scores are correlated with households and communities (PSUs). The higher values of ICC for household level indicate that the z-scores are more correlated to predictors at the household level than the community (PSUs).

The lower panel of Tables 4 and 10 shows that the residual variance is distributed across the PSUs and households. From Table 4, we observe that in Model 1 (null model) indicates that the total variance is 0.528 of which 76% is attributed to household-level variation in anthropometric scores. In Model 2, the variance decomposition pattern that is observed is that the total variance is 0.536, of which 90% is variation in household level. In Model 3 and Model 4, the variation attributed to

Table 7 Association (β_s) from ordinary least squares and multilevel linear regression models (main effects) between (height-for-age) and rural–urban place of residence, controlling for various other covariates; twenty-nine major states, India, NFHS 3

Predictors	OLS	Model 1	Model 2	Model 3	Model 4
Exp(B)(SE)					
Urban residence	0.211*** (0.020)		0.296*** (0.021)	0.202*** (0.021)	0.199*** (0.020)
Rural residence	−0.109*** (0.017)	–	−0.111*** (0.016)	−0.112*** (0.015)	−0.113*** (0.016)
Controls					
Individual characteristics					
Child age (months)	−0.061 (0.018)	–	−0.053 (0.019)	−0.066 (0.018)	−0.065 (0.017)
Sex (base: male) female	0.016** (0.009)	–	0.022** (0.006)	0.018** (0.005)	0.019** (0.007)
Order of birth	−0.034 (0.011)	–	−0.035 (0.015)	−0.033 (0.018)	−0.031 (0.014)
Size at birth	0.189* (0.031)	-	0.193* (0.032)	0.191* (0.036)	0.188* (0.033)
Suffered (*base: no illness*) recent illness	−0.051* (0.019)	–	−0.053* (0.018)	−0.052* (0.016)	−0.051* (0.017)
Duration of breastfeeding (*base: less than 6 months*)	−0.075* (0.029)	–	−0.078* (0.021)	−0.077* (0.022)	−0.077* (0.026)
Completed immunization	0.095* (0.017)	–	0.092* (0.017)	0.093* (0.016)	0.094* (0.015)
Mothers' characteristics					
Years of education	0.055** (0.016)	–		0.054** (0.014)	0.058** (0.015)
BMI of mother≥ 18.5 (*base= 18.5*)	0.043* (0.011)	–		0.045* (0.012)	0.051* (0.014)
Suffers from anaemia	0.185* (0.051)	–		0.181* (0.052)	0.188* (0.056)
Institutional delivery (*base = home delivery*)	0.077*** (0.015)	–		0.078*** (0.014)	0.077*** (0.013)
Decision-making power	0.033* (0.019)	–		0.034* (0.018)	0.035* (0.017)
Household characteristics					
Ethnicity SC ST	−0.154*** (0.024)	–	−0.156*** (0.025)	–	−0.153*** (0.021)
Water source (piped water)	0.065** (0.011)	–	0.063** (0.012)	–	0.064** (0.013)
Owns a house	0.195* (0.034)	–	0.194* (0.039)	–	0.197* (0.038)
States					

(continued)

Table 7 (continued)

Predictors	OLS	Model 1	Model 2	Model 3	Model 4
Per capita NSDP	0.187** (0.099)	–	0.191** (0.095)	0.192** (0.099)	0.191** (0.096)
Haryana	0.108 (0.064)	–	0.109 (0.061)	0.111 (0.065)	0.111 (0.064)
Himachal Pradesh	0.188* (0.082)	–	0.181* (0.084)	0.181* (0.082)	0.181* (0.085)
Punjab	0.124 (0.061)	–	0.125 (0.064)	0.126 (0.065)	0.124 (0.069)
Rajasthan	−0.109** (0.031)	–	−0.108** (0.040)	−0.111** (0.040)	−0.111** (0.040)
Uttarakhand	−0.187* (0.092)	–	−0.187* (0.093)	−0.186* (0.097)	−0.185* (0.102)
Chhattisgarh	0.122 (0.064)	–	0.123* (0.061)	0.121* (0.062)	0.126* (0.063)
Madhya Pradesh	0.025 (0.005)	–	0.027 (0.004)	0.026 (0.005)	0.025 (0.006)
Uttar Pradesh	−0.101* (0.057)	–	−0.103* (0.051)	−0.104* (0.053)	−0.106* (0.054)
Bihar	−0.151* (0.039)	–	−0.156* (0.037)	−0.153* (0.035)	−0.152* (0.034)
Jharkhand	−0.184* (0.033)	–	−0.186* (0.034)	−0.192* (0.038)	−0.192* (0.033)
Odisha	0.144* (0.071)	–	0.146* (0.072)	0.147* (0.071)	0.148* (0.072)
West Bengal	0.141* (0.043)	–	0.145* (0.042)	0.145* (0.045)	0.146* (0.041)
Arunachal Pradesh	0.003 (0.012)	–	0.004 (0.017)	0.009 (0.017)	0.010 (0.017)
Assam	0.027 (0.016)	–	0.027 (0.017)	0.028 (0.016)	0.028 (0.016)
Manipur	0.321 (0.027)	–	0.326 (0.026)	0.325 (0.026)	0.325 (0.029)
Mizoram	0.253 (0.033)	–	0.256 (0.037)	0.255 (0.036)	0.254 (0.035)
Nagaland	0.041 (0.017)	–	0.044 (0.018)	0.043 (0.018)	0.044 (0.017)
Gujrat	−0.205*** (0.046)	–	−0.206*** (0.046)	−0.209*** (0.046)	−0.209*** (0.045)
Maharashtra	−0.153* (0.033)	–	−0.156* (0.035)	−0.157* (0.034)	−0.154* (0.033)

(continued)

Table 7 (continued)

Predictors	OLS	Model 1	Model 2	Model 3	Model 4
Andhra Pradesh	0.095 (0.056)	–	0.096 (0.055)	0.099 (0.054)	0.098 (0.052)
Tamil Nadu	0.112* (0.025)	–	0.118* (0.026)	0.119* (0.026)	0.119* (0.028)
Karnataka	−0.011 (0.008)	–	−0.012 (0.007)	−0.016 (0.005)	−0.017 (0.006)
Delhi	−0.084 (0.019)	–	−0.083 (0.017)	−0.081 (0.016)	−0.086 (0.017)
Meghalaya	0.045 (0.021)	–	0.047 (0.022)	0.048 (0.023)	0.049 (0.024)
Sikkim	0.134 (0.051)	–	0.136 (0.052)	0.137 (0.051)	0.133 (0.051)
Tripura	0.055 (0.041)	–	0.056 (0.044)	0.049 (0.045)	0.050 (0.046)
Goa	0.014 (0.035)	–	0.019 (0.033)	0.019 (0.032)	0.019 (0.033)
Jammu & Kashmir	−0.056 (0.055)	–	−0.057 (0.056)	−0.058 (0.057)	−0.059 (0.054)
Constant	−1.126*** (0.043)	−1.111*** (0.021)	−1.132*** (0.025)	−1.140*** (0.024)	−1.141*** (0.021)
N	35,112	36,000	35,229	35,229	35,227
Log likelihood	R^2 0.149	−33352.36	−39845.26	−38971.31	−39668
X^2 statistics	158.394		4388.49	4622.3	4411.5
P value	0.000		0.000	0.000	0.000

Significant at ***$p < 0.001$, **$p < 0.01$, *$p < 0.05$
Source Calculation from NFHS 3 unit data

household level are 90% and 93%, respectively, which only confirms that the results are consistent to the observations on null model variance decomposition. The pattern is similar across PSU and household levels. The values of $\sigma^2{}_c$ and $\sigma^2{}_h$ are significantly different which indicates that the homogeneity of within cluster observations is not explained by the observed covariates used in the model. A look on the intra-household correlation shows that it is quite large around 0.184 (Model 4). It is 0.196 in the null model. It is also seen that this value is large in all the other models too. This result suggests that the weight-for-age outcomes of two individual children who belong to the same family are more homogeneous. A higher value of $\sigma^2{}_h$ indicates that there is higher homogeneity at the household level. Similar results are observed from Table 10 for NFHS 3. The results proved that the choice of one-level model with a similar set of data might not have yielded the desired result.

The results of Tables 5 and 11 indicate significant association between household socio-demographic profile and nutritional status of children. Here the dependent variable is the continuous standard deviation of weight-for-height *z*-score. As explained

Table 8 Random coefficients, intra-class correlation and variance decomposition estimates (height-for-age) NFHS 3

Random coefficients, intra-class correlation and variance decomposition estimates				
	Model 1	Model 2	Model 3	Model 4
Random effects				
$\sigma^2{}_c$ Community- PSU	0.209	0.099	0.078	0.044
(S.E)	(0.026)	(0.021)	(0.015)	(0.011)
Proportions of overall (null model) explained by the covariates of the model (in %)		45.965	71.231	66.934
$\sigma^2{}_h$ (household)	0.366	0.412	0.455	0.465
(S.E)	(0.025)	(0.032)	(0.035)	(0.033)
Proportions of overall (null model) explained by the covariates of the model (in %)		−33.688	−25.636	−29.514
Residual^2	1.965	1.632	1.611	1.651
(S.E)	(0.029)	(0.025)	(0.023)	(0.028)
Intra-class correlation				
ρ(PSU)	0.085*	0.050*	0.036*	0.031*
ρ(household)	0.277*	0.254*	0.291*	0.243*
Variance decomposition (in %)				
PSU	34.9	11.6	8.2	12.2
Household	65.1	88.4	91.8	87.8

Significance level *$p < 0.05$
Source Calculation from NFHS 3 unit data

earlier, this continuous standard deviation of weight-for height z-score is effective of furnishing expected change in the value of the dependent variable due to one-unit changes in the regressors regardless of whether a child is wasted or not.

From the OLS model, it is revealed that better nutritional outcome is observed from the children living in urban areas than rural areas. It can be seen that nearly 36 per cent better nutritional status (0.269−(−0.095)) and 30% in NFHS 4 and NFHS 3 respectively among children living in urban areas compared to those living in the rural areas. In Model 2, it is 36% (0.266−(−0.099)) and 30%, respectively, in Model 3 it is 37% (0.269−(−0.099)) and in Model 4 it is 37% (0.271−(−0.095)) and 28%, respectively, in NFHS 4 and NFHS 3, respectively. Hence, all the variance component models also support these finding. As we introduce the covariates at each level, the results of variance component models depict the extent to which observed differences in weight-for-height z-scores are allocated to predictors operating at each level. It is observed that after the introduction of the child level covariates with state level fixed effect, the impact of rural–urban place of residence remains the same. Further, from the results of the OLS model, it can be inferred that better nutritional outcomes in terms of higher weight-for-height values are significantly associated

Table 9 Association (β_s) from ordinary least squares and multilevel linear regression models (main effects) between (weight-for-age) and rural–urban place of residence, controlling for various other covariates; twenty-nine major states, India, NFHS 3

Predictors	OLS	Model 1	Model 2	Model 3	Model 4
Exp(B)(SE)					
Urban residence	0.325*** (0.021)		0.341*** (0.022)	0.297*** (0.022)	0.298*** (0.023)
Rural residence	−0.101*** (0.027)	–	−0.102*** (0.028)	−0.102*** (0.029)	−0.102*** (0.027)
Controls					
Individual characteristics					
Child age (months)	−0.034*** (0.009)	–	−0.049*** (0.010)	−0.044*** (0.012)	0.048*** (0.010)
Sex (base: male) female	−0.011*** (0.009)	–	−0.019*** (0.007)	−0.023*** (0.005)	−0.020*** (0.009)
Order of birth	−0.035 (0.017)	–	−0.033 (0.015)	−0.038 (0.016)	−0.033 (0.017)
Size at birth	0.281 (0.040)	–	0.285 (0.039)	0.284 (0.038)	0.83 (0.040)
Suffered (*base: no illness*) recent illness	−0.065 (0.022)	-	−0.066 (0.020)	−0.064 (0.021)	−0.066 (0.023)
Duration of Breastfeeding (*base: less than 6 months*)	−0.046* (0.023)	–	−0.049* (0.027)	−0.045* (0.025)	−0.042* (0.025)
Completed Immunization	0.018* (0.008)	–	0.017* (0.009)	0.016* (0.009)	0.019* (0.008)
Mothers' characteristics					
Years of education	0.051** (0.018)	–	–	0.052** (0.017)	0.056** (0.018)
BMI of mother	0.022** (0.011)	–	–	0.023** (0.011)	0.024** (0.012)
Suffers from anaemia	0.041 (0.015)	–	–	0.043 (0.016)	0.041 (0.016)
Institutional delivery	0.039** (0.012)	–	–	0.038** (0.009)	0.039** (0.009)
Decision-making power	0.049** (0.014)	–	–	0.047** (0.013)	0.047** (0.014)
Household characteristics					
Ethnicity SC ST	−0.094** (0.050)	–	−0.093** (0.048)	–	−0.096*** (0.047)
Water source (piped water)	0.031** (0.011)	–	0.033** (0.012)	–	0.036** (0.011)
Owns a house	0.143** (0.035)	–	0.141** (0.036)	–	0.142** (0.037)
States (household size)					

(continued)

Table 9 (continued)

Predictors	OLS	Model 1	Model 2	Model 3	Model 4
NSDP	0.127*** (0.033)	–	0.126*** (0.032)	−0.125*** (0.035)	−0.125*** (0.035)
Haryana	0.086* (0.021)	–	0.085 (0.022)	−0.089 (0.022)	−0.086 (0.022)
Himachal Pradesh	0.064* (0.030)	–	0.065* (0.031)	0.066* (0.031)	0.066* (0.031)
Punjab	0.158* (0.061)	–	0.155* (0.062)	0.154* (0.061)	0.154* (0.061)
Rajasthan	0.239 (0.051)	–	0.234 (0.053)	0.233 (0.054)	0.234 (0.052)
Uttarakhand	−0.022* (0.009)	–	−0.023* (0.010)	−0.023* (0.011)	−0.023* (0.009)
Chhattisgarh	0.053* (0.016)	–	0.053* (0.017)	0.053* (0.017)	0.052* (0.017)
Madhya Pradesh	−0.032* (0.021)	–	−0.033* (0.022)	−0.033* (0.022)	−0.032* (0.022)
Uttar Pradesh	−0.076** (0.025)	–	−0.078** (0.026)	−0.078** (0.026)	−0.078** (0.026)
Bihar	−0.019* (0.010)	–	−0.020* (0.010)	−0.020* (0.010)	−0.021* (0.010)
Jharkhand	0.055 (0.016)	–	0.056 (0.017)	0.057 (0.017)	0.057 (0.016)
Odisha	0.044* (0.031)	–	0.047* (0.032)	0.046* (0.032)	0.046* (0.032)
West Bengal	0.065 (0.029)	–	0.066 (0.030)	0.067 (0.032)	0.067 (0.033)
Arunachal Pradesh	−0.087* (0.036)	–	−0.089* (0.035)	−0.088* (0.036)	−0.088* (0.035)
Assam	0.043 (0.022)	–	0.045 (0.023)	0.043 (0.023)	0.044 (0.023)
Manipur	0.115 (0.035)	–	0.117 (0.034)	0.117 (0.037)	0.117 (0.036)
Mizoram	−0.199** (0.023)	–	−0.195** (0.024)	−0.193 (0.025)	−0.194 (0.025)
Nagaland	0.034* (0.021)	–	0.033* (0.022)	0.032* (0.021)	0.033* (0.021)
Gujrat	−0.106* (0.052)	–	−0.105* (0.051)	−0.105* (0.052)	0.106** (0.052)
Maharashtra	0.159 (0.079)	–	−0.156 (0.077)	−0.155 (0.077)	-0.155 (0.077)

(continued)

Table 9 (continued)

Predictors	OLS	Model 1	Model 2	Model 3	Model 4
Andhra Pradesh	0.051 (0.022)	–	0.055 (0.020)	0.055 (0.020)	0.056 (0.020)
Tamil Nadu	0.039 (0.050)	–	0.038 (0.051)	0.039 (0.051)	0.039 (0.050)
Karnataka	−0.062 (0.025)	–	−0.065 (0.026)	−0.064 (0.027)	−0.064 (0.027)
Delhi	−0.057 (0.035)	–	−0.058 (0.036)	−0.058 (0.035)	−0.059 (0.035)
Meghalaya	0.029 (0.011)	–	0.029 (0.013)	0.028 (0.013)	0.028 (0.013)
Sikkim	0.027 (0.015)	–	0.029 (0.014)	0.029 (0.015)	0.028 (0.015)
Tripura	0.070 (0.028)	–	0.069 (0.029)	0.070 (0.027)	0.070 (0.027)
Goa	0.033 (0.007)	–	0.034 (0.007)	0.035 (0.007)	0.034 (0.007)
Constant	−1.295*** (0.088)		–		
N	35,112	36,000	35,229	35,229	35,227
Log likelihood	R^2 0.166	−36101.20	−39709.23	−38845.64	−39233
X^2 statistics	155.251		4309.23	4597.8	4463.61
P value	0.001		0.001	0.001	0.001

Significant at ***$p < 0.001$, **$p < 0.01$, *$p < 0.05$
Source Calculation by author from NFHS 3 unit data

with being male and among those children who suffered from major illness like diarrhoea or acute respiratory diseases. Here, we find that unlike the previous two cases of child stunting and child underweight in NFHS 4, the weight-for-height z-scores are positively associated with the duration of breastfeeding of the children. It can be observed that those children whose duration of breastfeeding is longer than 6 months, has decreased incidence of wasting. Prolonged breastfeeding is therefore not a cause of acute undernutrition.

From all the models in Tables 5 and 12, it can be observed that mothers who have certain years of education, possess Mother and Child Protection Card and had given birth in at institutions can keep their children secured with comfortable nutritional status. Among the household-level characteristics, it can be observed that there is an inverse association between those belonging to SC and ST ethnic group and acute undernutrition. A clear positive association is also observed between availability of piped water and weight-for-height z-scores. This implies that those communities belonging to SC and ST and non-availability of piped water are more probable from suffering from wasting.

Table 10 Random coefficients, intra-class correlation and variance decomposition estimates (weight-for-age), NFHS 3

Random coefficients, intra-class correlation and variance decomposition estimates				
	Model 1	Model 2	Model 3	Model 4
Random effects				
$\sigma^2{}_c$ Community- PSU	0.111	0.064	0.048	0.029
(S.E)	(0.016)	(0.009)	(0.010)	(0.008)
Proportions of overall (null model) explained by the covariates of the model (in %)		29.121	41.222	45.459
$\sigma^2{}_h$ (Household)	0.435	0.401	0.426	0.389
(S.E)	(0.025)	(0.029)	(0.033)	(0.032)
Proportions of overall (null model) explained by the covariates of the model (in %)		−25.313	−26.361	−21.342
Residual^2	1.128	1.419	1.411	1.599
(S.E)	(0.021)	(0.018)	(0.022)	(0.023)
Intra-class correlation				
ρ(PSU)	0.059*	0.038*	0.022*	0.021*
ρ(household)	0.184*	0.168*	0.176*	0.159*
Variance decomposition (in %)				
PSU	32.7	20.4	10.6	8.5
Household	67.3	79.6	89.4	91.5

Significance level $*p < 0.05$
Source Calculation from NFHS 3 unit data

From the state level characteristics, again it is confirmed that that states with higher Per capita NSDP have a significant position association with weight-for-height z-scores. The results of OLS are more or less consistent with the results of the other models where the covariates are introduced in phased manner.

The calculated intra-class correlation coefficient values presented in Tables 6 and 12 are different from zero, implying that weight-for-height *z*-scores are correlated with households and communities (PSUs). Here too the values of household-level ICC are higher. This indicates that the *z*-scores are more correlated to the covariates at the household level than the community (PSUs). The lower panel of Table 6 shows that the residual variance is distributed across the PSUs and households. A look at Model 1 (null model), indicates that the total variance is 0.534 of which 68 Per cent is attributed to household-level variation in anthropometric scores. In Model 2, the total variance is 0.541 of which 75% is variation in household level, whereas in Model 3 and Model 4, the variation attributed to household level are 85% and 81% respectively. The results are thus consistent to the observations on null model variance decomposition.

Table 11 Association (β_s) from ordinary least squares and multilevel linear regression models (main effects) between (weight-for-height) and rural–urban place of residence, controlling for various other covariates; twenty-nine major states, India, NFHS 3

Predictors	OLS	Model 1	Model 2	Model 3	Model 4
Exp(B)(SE)					
Urban residence	0.275*** (0.019)		0.277*** (0.020)	0.279*** (0.019)	0.268*** (0.018)
Rural residence	−0.021*** (0.008)	–	−0.020*** (0.009)	−0.019*** (0.010)	−0.016*** (0.010)
Controls					
Individual characteristics					
Child age (months)	−0.049 (0.011)	–	−0.054 (0.010)	−0.051 (0.011)	0.053 (0.011)
Sex (base: male) female	−0.025* (0.015)	–	−0.021* (0.016)	−0.022* (0.017)	−0.021* (0.016)
Order of birth	−0.033 (0.012)	–	−0.037 (0.011)	−0.036 (0.012)	−0.036 (0.012)
Size at birth	0.253 (0.029)	–	0.255 (0.028)	0.256 (0.028)	0.254 (0.027)
Suffered (*base: no illness*) recent illness	−0.174* (0.050)	–	−0.173* (0.049)	−0.171* (0.048)	−0.172* (0.047)
Duration of breastfeeding (*base: less than 6 months*)	−0.043* (0.015)	–	−0.045* (0.019)	−0.047* (0.017)	−0.047* (0.015)
Completed immunization	0.025* (0.007)	–	0.024* (0.009)	0.027* (0.010)	0.028* (0.010)
Mothers' characteristics					
Years of education	0.036** (0.011)	–	–	0.035*** (0.012)	0.033*** (0.011)
BMI of mother	0.055 (0.023)	–	–	0.051** (0.025)	0.054** (0.022)
Suffers from anaemia	−0.152** (0.029)	–	–	−0.153** (0.028)	−0.157** (0.027)
Institutional delivery	0.083** (0.019)	–	–	0.081** (0.017)	0.084** (0.020)
Decision-making power	−0.047 (0.030)	–	–	−0.046 (0.031)	−0.043 (0.031)
Household characteristics					
Ethnicity SC ST	−0.097** (0.014)	–	−0.099** (0.016)	–	−0.098*** (0.015)
Water source (piped water)	0.035** (0.008)	–	0.036** (0.007)	–	0.034** (0.008)
Owns a house	−0.117 (0.015)	–	−0.118 (0.013)	–	−0.116 (0.013)
States (household size)					

(continued)

Table 11 (continued)

Predictors	OLS	Model 1	Model 2	Model 3	Model 4
NSDP	0.141*** (0.055)	–	0.143*** (0.056)	0.143*** (0.054)	0.143*** (0.053)
Haryana	−0.021* (0.006)	–	−0.023* (0.009)	−0.025* (0.010)	−0.027* (0.011)
Himachal Pradesh	0.065 (0.047)	–	0.066 (0.048)	0.066 (0.045)	0.067 (0.047)
Punjab	0.201 (0.013)	–	0.203 (0.017)	0.203 (0.019)	0.203 (0.015)
Rajasthan	−0.254** (0.039)	–	−0.256** (0.042)	−0.254** (0.043)	−0.256** (0.041)
Uttarakhand	0.053 (0.018)	–	0.054 (0.021)	0.057 (0.020)	0.058 (0.019)
Chhattisgarh	0.153 (0.020)	–	0.159 (0.023)	0.157 (0.024)	0.158 (0.021)
Madhya Pradesh	−0.041** (0.011)	–	−0.042* (0.016)	−0.045* (0.015)	−0.046* (0.014)
Uttar Pradesh	−0.011** (0.006)	–	−0.012** (0.004)	−0.012** (0.003)	−0.011** (0.005)
Bihar	−0.089* (0.051)	–	−0.085* (0.054)	−0.087* (0.049)	−0.084* (0.050)
Jharkhand	−0.201* (0.072)	–	−0.202* (0.074)	−0.203* (0.077)	−0.203* (0.075)
Odisha	0.099* (0.025)	–	0.096* (0.027)	0.092* (0.024)	0.098* (0.024)
West Bengal	−0.189* (0.060)	–	−0.185* (0.059)	−0.187* (0.055)	−0.184* (0.056)
Arunachal Pradesh	−0.156* (0.020)	–	−0.154* (0.026)	−0.155* (0.023)	−0.156 (0.020)
Assam	−0.166* (0.087)	–	−0.162* (0.084)	−0.160* (0.085)	−0.161* (0.086)
Manipur	0.217 (0.051)	–	0.214 (0.052)	0.210 (0.053)	0.219 (0.054)
Mizoram	0.069 (0.019)	–	0.074 (0.020)	0.078 (0.021)	0.075 (0.022)
Nagaland	0.208 (0.088)	–	0.209 (0.085)	0.211 (0.084)	0.209 (0.086)
Gujrat	−0.127* (0.033)	–	−0.136* (0.032)	−0.132* (0.034)	0.139* (0.030)
Maharashtra	−0.052* (0.009)	–	−0.058* (0.006)	−0.062* (0.013)	−0.063* (0.014)

(continued)

Table 11 (continued)

Predictors	OLS	Model 1	Model 2	Model 3	Model 4
Andhra Pradesh	−0.029* (0.011)	–	−0.030* (0.012)	−0.046* (0.022)	−0.041* (0.019)
Tamil Nadu	0.076 (0.031)	–	0.081 (0.035)	0.073 (0.041)	0.075 (0.039)
Karnataka	−0.025 (0.009)	–	−0.029 (0.016)	−0.45 (0.011)	−0.041 (0.008)
Delhi	−0.052 (0.021)	–	−0.057 (0.019)	−0.049 (0.030)	−0.044 (0.031)
Meghalaya	0.012 (0.032)	–	0.023 (0.031)	0.026 (0.025)	0.017 (0.021)
Sikkim	0.056 (0.025)	–	0.057 (0.022)	0.057 (0.024)	0.061 (0.031)
Tripura	0.035 (0.021)	–	0.036 (0.020)	0.037 (0.021)	0.041 (0.025)
Goa	0.161 (0.011)	–	0.145 (0.019)	0.146 (0.019)	0.110 (0.024)
Constant	−1.184*** (0.059)				
N	35,112	36,000	35,229	35,229	35,227
Log likelihood	R^2 0.422	−40399.74	−39407.09	−30259.52	−31233.10
X^2 statistics	199.301		2845.05	2981.1	2814.3
P value	0.002		0.002	0.000	0.002

Significant at ***$p < 0.001$, **$p < 0.01$, *$p < 0.05$
Source Calculation from NFHS 3 unit data

5 Discussion

The NFHS provides data that reflects the fact that there is widespread undernutrition among the children in our country. In this paper, we find that child undernutrition in India is widely varied across the rural–urban areas of the states in India. From the variance component models, we find that there is clustering of observations at the community and at the household level. That means in the 29 states of India, children in the households who shared similar communities showcase similar nutritional status. The result is true for all the measures of undernutrition namely, stunting, wasting and underweight. Intra-household correlation is more prominent as compared to intra-community correlation. Hence, it can be understood that children from a cluster or community do not share stronger correlation in terms to their nutritional status. Nevertheless, the observations at the household level are not independent which proves the fact that children belonging to a particular household share common characteristics in the process of their growth. This is a distinctive observation not carried by most of the studies conducted earlier. It is also seen that children from the

Table 12 Random coefficients, intra-class correlation and variance decomposition estimates (weight-for-height) NFHS 3

Random coefficients, Intra-class correlation and Variance Decomposition estimates				
	Model 1	Model 2	Model 3	Model 4
Random effects				
σ^2_c Community- PSU	0.121	0.054	0.041	0.037
(S.E)	(0.014)	(0.012)	(0.010)	(0.018)
Proportions of overall (null model) explained by the covariates of the model (in %)		42.727	42.365	49.163
σ^2_h (Household)	0.431	0.496	0.412	0.453
(S.E)	(0.032)	(0.037)	(0.035)	(0.042)
Proportions of overall (null model) explained by the covariates of the model (in %)		−21.549	−19.711	−18.208
Residual^2	1.026	1.101	1.129	1.133
(S.E)	(0.019)	(0.022)	(0.031)	(0.030)
Intra-class correlation				
ρ(PSU)	0.055*	0.051*	0.031*	0.033*
ρ(household)	0.192*	0.207*	0.241*	0.239*
Variance decomposition (in %)				
PSU	28.8	25.9	11.4	15.1
Household	71.2	74.1	88.6	84.9

Significance level *$p < 0.05$
Source Calculation from NFHS 3 unit data

households in the rural areas of all the states in our country have higher prevalence of worst nutritional status. Such association is consistent across the different variance component models applied in this study. This reaffirms the fact that better nutritional status is enjoyed by the children living in urban parts of the country having favourable socio-demographic background. This is true in all the models where there are controls at the individual, maternal and community characteristics. This also emphasizes that the differences in the availability of resources to the families in urban and rural parts of the country act as an important determinant to child undernutrition. Hence, we can infer that the prevailing socio-demographic status is an important determinant of the level of nutritional achievement among children of our country. If we look forward to the betterment of such socio-demographic condition, then it is expected to improve nutritional growth of the children through better nutritional intake and reduced morbidity.

The uniqueness of this paper is the consideration of huge set of individual level data set for both NFHS 3 and NFHS 4and also from NFHS 5. This paper observed certain distinctive results not observed by most of the studies in literature. Here, we have seen that percapita NSDP significantly influences all the conventional undernutrition

Table 13 Association (β_s) from ordinary least squares and multilevel linear regression models (main effects) between (height-for-age) and rural–urban place of residence, controlling for various other covariates; twenty-nine major states, India, NFHS 5

Predictors	OLS	Model 1	Model 2	Model 3	Model 4
Predictors					
Exp(B)(SE)					
Urban residence	0.211^{***} (0.018)		0.401^{***} (0.046)	0.229^{***} (0.039)	0.216^{***} (0.018)
Rural residence	-0.173^{**} (0.022)		-0.187^{***} (0.039)	-0.190^{***} (0.036)	-0.177^{**} (0.022)
Controls					
Individual characteristics					
Child age (months)	−0.064 (0.010)		−0.087 (0.013)	−0.093 (0.019)	
Sex (base: male) female	-0.002^{***} (0.001)		-0.029^{**} (0.006)	-0.022^{**} (0.008)	
Order of birth	−0.027 (0.004)		−0.030 (0.015)	−0.051 (0.064)	
Size at birth	0.251^{*} (0.021)		0.299^{*} (0.050)	0.501^{*} (0.059)	
Suffered (*base: no illness*) recent illness	−0.026 (0.031)		−0.045 (0.036)	−0.039 (0.044)	
Duration of breastfeeding (*base: less than 6 months*)	-0.041^{*} (0.014)		-0.049^{*} (0.016)	−0.061 (0.029)	
Completed immunization	0.002 (0.15)		0.006 (0.019)	0.006 (0.019)	
Mothers' characteristics					
Years of education	0.041^{*} (0.004)			0.046^{**} (0.012)	
BMI of mother ≥ 18.5 (*base= 18.5*)	0.031^{*} (0.002)			0.026 (0.010)	0.038 (0.014)
Suffers from anaemia	0.143 (0.059)			0.194 (0.014)	0.152 (0.009)
Mother and child protection card	0.029^{*} (0.005)			0.052^{**} (0.012)	0.019^{**} (0.022)
Institutional delivery (*base = home delivery)*	0.075^{**} (0.035)			0.041^{***} (0.044)	0.033^{***} (0.018)
Household characteristics					
Ethnicity SC ST	0.099^{**} (0.025)		0.036^{***} (0.026)		-0.150^{***} (0.036)

(continued)

Table 13 (continued)

Predictors	OLS	Model 1	Model 2	Model 3	Model 4
Water source (piped water)	0.022*** (0.005)		0.029*** (0.018)		0.060** (0.022)
Owns a house	0.300 (0.025)		0.243 (0.051)		0.209 (0.031)
States					
Per capita NSDP	0.186** (0.031)		0.353*** (0.095)	0.303** (0.045)	0.022*** (0.074)
Haryana	−0.162 (0.054)		−0.166* (0.077)	−0.201* (0.081)	−0.201* (0.055)
Himachal Pradesh	0.126* (0.064)		0.201* (0.097)	0.199 (0.081)	0.130* (0.083)
Punjab	0.134 (0.094)		0.159 (0.099)	0.190 (0.099)	0.112 (0.051)
Rajasthan	0.190** (0.055)		0.196*** (0.074)	0.196*** (0.083)	0.144*** (0.046)
Uttarakhand	−0.031* (0.121)		−0.333*** (0.212)	−0.322* (0.153)	−0.277* (0.119)
Chhattisgarh	0.039** (0.069)		0.139* (0.073)	0.169 (0.081)	0.180* (0.079)
Madhya Pradesh	0.101 (0.081)		0.023 (0.066)	0.019 (0.074)	0.088* (0.009)
Uttar Pradesh	−0.116 (0.071)		−0.188 (0.059)	−0.199 (0.019)	−0.171 (0.013)
Bihar	−0108* (0.087)		−0.136* (0.084)	−0.077* (0.039)	−0.109* (0.057)
Jharkhand	−0.301 (0.088)		−0.333 (0.088)	−0.208 (0.055)	−0.259 (0.098)
Odisha	0.199*** (0.076)		0.041*** (0.099)	0.280*** (0.044)	0.090*** (0.092)
West Bengal	0.153 (0.075)		0.233 (0.091)	0.197 (0.056)	0.199 (0.069)
Arunachal Pradesh	0.039 (0.084)		0.022 (0.041)	0.029 (0.060)	0.022 (0.056)
Assam	0.070 (0.061)		0.099* (0.022)	0.049 (0.083)	0.033 (0.064)
Manipur	0.294 (0.058)		0.219 (0.099)	0.295 (0.058)	0.287 (0.051)
Mizoram	0.258 (0.051)		0.345 (0.055)	0.220 (0.026)	0.303 (0.022)
Nagaland	0.035 (0.008)		0.090 (0.009)	0.049 (0.012)	0.020 (0.002)

(continued)

Table 13 (continued)

Predictors	OLS	Model 1	Model 2	Model 3	Model 4
Gujrat	0.199** (0.056)		0.301*** (0.091)	0.284*** (0.055)	0.295*** (0.061)
Maharashtra	−0.109 (0.089)		−0.199 (0.036)	−0.144 (0.059)	−0.101 (0.045)
Andhra Pradesh	0.081 (0.072)		0.081 (0.054)	0.066 (0.058)	0.044 (0.063)
Tamil Nadu	0.301 (0.056)		0.419 (0.095)	0.402 (0.033)	0.325 (0.059)
Karnataka	−0.051 (0.074)		−0.061 (0.088)	−0.043 (0.001)	0.044 (0.018)
Delhi	−0.061 (0.071)		−0.055 (0.097)	−0.055 (0.055)	−0.050 (0.055)
Meghalaya	0.062 (0.071)		0.085 (0.083)	0.061 (0.019)	0.090 (0.041)
Sikkim	0.035 (0.062)		0.086 (0.88)	0.066 (0.039)	0.084 (0.011)
Tripura	0.056* (0.051)		0.066 (0.052)	0.088 (0.044)	0.059 (0.062)
Goa	0.021 (0.076)		0.015 (0.091)	0.018 (0.021)	0.049 (0.022)
Jammu & Kashmir	−0.058 (0.095)		−0.084 (0.064)	−0.049 (0.050)	−0.059 (0.041)
Constant	−1.123** (0.071)				
N	1,34,200	1,34,566	1,34209	1,34,191	1,34,899
Log likelihood	$R^2$0.183		−44005011		
X^2 statistics	143.105		2994.5	2922.0	2922.1
P value	0.001		0.003	0.001	0.001

Significant at ***$p < 0.001$, **$p < 0.01$, *$p < 0.05$
Source Calculation from NFHS 5 unit data

parameters for NFHS 3 and for NFHS 4and from NFHS 5 which is used to understand the status of stunting of children of our country. Also, the result that intra-household correlation is more prominent to intra-community correlation, is also quite discrete from studies conducted on earlier.

References

Chakraborty, R. et al. (2011). Use of mid-upper arm circumference in determining undernutrition and illness in rural adult Oraon men of Gumla District, Jharkhand, India, National Library of Medicine 11(3).

Chatterjee, B. (1996), Economics of health, nutrition and development- theory and evidence. In A. Banerjee & B. Chatterjee (Eds.), Economic theory, trade and quantitative economics-essay in honour of Professor P.N. Roy, University of Calcutta, 1996.

Dasgupta, P., & Ray, D. (1990). Adapting to undernourishment: The biological evidence and its implications. In J. Dreze & A. Sen (Eds.), *Political economy of hunger* (Vol. I, pp. 191–246). Clarendon Press.

Devi, P. Y., & Geervani, P. (1994). Determinants of nutrition status of pre-school children in Andhra Pradesh. journals.sagepub.com.

Dreze, J., & Sen, A. K. (1989). *Hunger and public action*. Clarendon Press, Oxford.

George, K. A., et al. (2000). Anaemia and nutritional status of pre-school children in Kerala. *The Indian Journal of Pediatrics, 67*, 575–578.

Handbook of Statistics on the Indian Economy 2004-05: RBI Bulletin Mumbai, Reserve Bank of India 2005.

International Institute for Population Sciences (IIPS) & ORC MACRO: National Family Health Survey (NFHS-3), 2005-06.

International Institute for Population Sciences (IIPS) & ORC MACRO: National Family Health Survey (NFHS-4), 2015-16.

International Institute for Population Sciences (IIPS) & ORC MACRO: National Family Health Survey (NFHS-5), 2019-21.

Irudaya, R., & Navaneetham, K. (1994). Maternal and child Immunization on infant survival. *Janasamkhya, 12*(1–2), 159–82.

Kanjilal et al. (2010). Nutritional status of children in India: household socio-economic condition as the contextual determinant. *International Journal for Equity in Health.*

Mahapatra, A., et al. (2000). Nutritional status of preschool children in the drought affected Kalahandi district of Orissa. *India Journal of Medical Research, 111*, 90–94.

Mazumdar, S. (2010). Determinants of inequality in child malnutrition in India: The poverty-undernutrition linkage. *Asian Population Studies.*

Mukhopadhyay, B. (2020). Minimum acceptable diet and child undernutrition in India. *ARTHA BEEKSHAN, 29*(2 & 3), 3–37.

Pal, S. (1999). An analysis of childhood malnutrition in rural India: Role of gender, income and other household characteristics. *World Development, 27*(7), 1151–1171.

Pathak, P. K., & Singh, A. (2009). Geographical variation in poverty and child malnutrition in India. In K. K. Singh, R. C. Yadava, & A. Pandey (Eds.), *Population, poverty and health: Analytical approaches Hindustan Publishing Corporation.*

Radhakrishna, R., & Ravi, C. (2004). Malnutrition in India. *Economic and Political Weekly, 39*, 671–676.

Rajaram, et al. (2003). Analysis of childhood malnutrition in Kerala and Goa. *Journal of Biological Science, 35*(3), 335–351.

Rajaretnam and Hallad Js. " Determinants of nutritional status of young children in India: an analysis of 1992-93 NFHS data, 2000, Medicine, Demography India

Rao, et al. (2004). Nutritional status of children in north-east India. *Asia-Pacific Population Journal/ United Nations, 19*(3), 39–56.

Shroff, M., Griffiths, P., Adair, L., Suchindran, C., & Bentley, M. (2009). Maternal autonomy is inversely related to child stunting in Andhra Pradesh, India. *Maternal and Child Nutrition, 5*, 64–74.

Vinod K. M. et al. (1999). An inventory model for deteriorating items with time dependent demand and holding cost under partial backlogging. *Yugoslav Journal of Operations Research, 24*(1), 87–98.

Wagstaff, A., & Watanabe, N. (2000). Socioeconomic inequalities in child malnutrition in developing world. Policy Research Working paper 2434 World Bank, Washington D.C.
World development report 1993: Investing in health. Washington, DC: The World bank 1993.
World Health Report 1999: Making a Difference. Geneva. WHO 1999.
World Health Report 2006: Working Together for Health. Geneva. WHO 2006.
https://equityhealthj.biomedical.com/articles/10.1186/1475-9276-9-19
https://www.tandfonline.com/doi/full/10.1080/02692170500031711

India and Sustainable Development Goals

Tourism Development and Environmental Pollution: A Dynamic Analysis

Manash Ranjan Gupta and Priya Brata Dutta

Abstract We develop a two sector dynamic model of a less developed economy with intertemporal utility maximizing behaviour of the household. The model consists of an imported traded good sector and a non-traded tourism service sector serving international tourists. Revenue earned from tourism finances imports. The model takes care of the negative effect of tourism development on environmental pollution. Environmental quality and capital stock accumulate over time. We analyse properties of the long-run equilibrium and show that the unique long-run equilibrium point satisfies saddle point stability.

Keywords Environmental pollution · Non-traded tourism service · Capital accumulation · Economic growth · Long-run equilibrium · Abatement expenditure · Intertemporal optimization

JEL Classification F18 · F64 · O44 · Q56 · Z32

1 Introduction

International tourism plays an important role in the economic development of many small less developed countries. It is an important source of foreign exchange earnings in those countries. For example, in 1995, income of HongKong from tourism was

Another paper related to the present one has already been published in the Journal of International Trade and Economic Development. See Gupta and Dutta (2017). However, the model developed in that paper is built on an exogenous savings framework; and does not solve any Ramsey Problem.

M. R. Gupta
Economic Research Unit, Indian Statistical Institute, Kolkata, India
e-mail: manrangup@gmail.com

P. B. Dutta (✉)
Economics and Politics Department, Visva-Bharati University, Shantiniketan, West Bengal, India
e-mail: priyabratadutta@gmail.com

B. Chatterjee and A. K. Karmakar (eds.), *Analytical Issues in Growth & Structural Change, Macroeconomy, Security, and Sustainability of India's Economic Development*, India Studies in Business and Economics,
https://doi.org/10.1007/978-981-95-5242-9_13

about one billion US dollars; and this was about 8% of its GDP. In Cyprus, tourism activities contributed to about 20% of its GDP in 2014. In 2012, Jamaica earned about 15 billion US dollars from tourism; and it was about 4.5% of her GDP. In Spain, tourism activities shared 10.9% of the Gross Domestic Product (GDP) and 11.9% of total employment in 2014. In Canary Islands, 31.4% of GDP and 35.9% of employment were obtained from the tourism sector in that year.

Quality of environment has an interesting relationship with tourism development; and there exist many empirical works focusing on this aspect. Davies and Cahill (2000) and Tisdell (2001) point out two conflicting features. Tourists prefer a region with an attractive environmental quality but environmental quality is worsened due to expansion of tourism. According to Crouch and Louvière (2001) and Brau and Cao (2005), the quality of the environment, both natural as well as man-made, is essential to attract tourists. A programme of tourism development leads to many constructional activities which generate negative environmental effects; and these activities are linked with development of transportation infrastructure like roads and railways and development of tourism facilities like resorts, hotels, restaurants, markets, parks etc. Tourism development causes deforestation; and this deforestation is responsible for landslides in mountains, floods in seashores and river banks and reduction of the natural growth rate of forest animals. Empirical evidence related to these problems can be found from the works of Sun and Walsh (1998), Gossling (2000, 2002), Jim (2000), Maddison (2001) etc.

There exists substantial discussion about how tourism expansion generates economic benefits in a backward economy. A few works discuss these effects without developing formal economic models.[1] Copeland (1991) first develops a static short-run competitive general equilibrium model of a small open economy and attempts to find out welfare effects of tourism expansion. However, Copeland (1991) does not consider the problem of environmental pollution. A few static general equilibrium models are also developed extending Copeland (1991) model and reanalysing its results.[2] A few dynamic models of tourism development also exist in the literature, and the small set consists of the works of Hazari and Sgro (1995), Schubert et al. (2011), Cerina (2007), Marsiglio (2015, 2016) etc. The effects on environmental quality of tourism development are analysed by the dynamic models of Cerina (2007) and Marsiglio (2015, 2016). These models incorporate intertemporal optimizing behaviour of households and show that long-run equilibrium is a saddle point. However, these models are one sector aggregative models of tourism development and do not consider the existence of a non-tourism sector. Hence, these models are not suitable to apply to those economies where the non-tourism sector also plays a significant role in economic development. These models are suitable to analyse economic growth of those small island countries and of small landlocked hill

[1] See, for example, Mathieson and Wall (1982), Pearce (1989), and Gray (1970, 1982) etc.

[2] Chao et al. (2004) introduces the effect of cash in advance constraint which creates a distortion; Chao et al. (2005) emphasizes on the role of imperfect competition and of social externalities created by tourism. Hazari and Sgro (2015) analyse various issues related to tourism development in different chapters of their book.

countries where tourism is the only source of income. Problems of resource allocation between the tourism sector and the non-tourism sector are always important in many less developed economies like India, Pakistan, Bangladesh etc. However, an aggregative one-sector model is not suitable to analyse these problems.

This chapter deals with an intertemporal analysis of the resource allocation problem between the tourism sector and the non-tourism sector. So a dynamic two sector model of a backward economy is developed with an imported traded good sector and with a non-traded tourism service sector. The model focuses on international tourism; and so an exogenous increase in the demand for tourism service coming from the international tourists is viewed as tourism development in the host country. Revenue is earned from the tourism sector, and this revenue finances import. Tourism development leads to environmental degradation. Environmental quality changes over time[3]; and so the negative environmental effects of tourism expansion are intertemporal in nature. Capital accumulation, which is the source of economic growth, also takes place over time. The representative household maximizes her lifetime utility defined as the discounted present value of utility over the infinite time horizon. These three features clearly justify why we should consider a dynamic intertemporal model in place of a static one period model.

This dynamic model is used to derive a few interesting results related to properties of the long-run equilibrium. The unique long-run equilibrium is either a saddle point or unstable in this model. Existing dynamic models of tourism development like Cerina (2007), Marsiglio (2015, 2016) etc. also show that the long-run equilibrium is either a saddle point or unstable.

The basic short-run equilibrium model is developed in Sect. 2. In Sect. 3, we introduce the dynamic analysis with intertemporal optimization behaviour of the representative household along with intertemporal accumulation of capital and degradation of environmental quality. Properties of long-run equilibrium are analysed in Sect. 3. Concluding remarks are made in Sect. 4.

2 The Short-Run Equilibrium Model[4]

2.1 Description

Our model is an otherwise identical two sector Heckscher-Ohlin-Samuelson (HOS) trade model as developed by Jones (1965) with the modification that the exportable sector is replaced by a non-traded tourism service sector.[5] We consider a small open two sector economy with two factors of production—capital and labour. Sector 1

[3] See, for example, Gupta and Barman (2009, 2010), Economides and Philippopoulos (2008), Greiner (2005) etc.

[4] This section is similar to a section of Gupta and Dutta (2017).

[5] An HOS model is available in any standard textbook on International Trade Theory and so need not be discussed in detail in this paper.

produces a traded good whose total demand is met by domestic production as well as by import. Sector 2 produces the non-traded tourism service. Expenditure on imports is financed by the revenue earned from tourism; and the price of the non-traded tourism service stands for the terms of trade. Both the factors are perfectly mobile between these two sectors; and so factor prices are equalized across the sectors. The price of the traded good is exogenously given; and hence seller's effective price of this good is changed following exogenous changes in the values of the policy parameter. The equilibrium price of the non-traded tourism service is determined by the supply–demand equality in the competitive domestic market. The tourism service is a normal good; and this implies that its level of demand varies negatively with its price, and positively with the income of the rest of world as well as with the environmental quality of the host country. The increase in income of the outside world raises international tourists flow to the host country; and this increase in tourist flow is defined as tourism development in this model. Residents of the host country consume only the traded good; and the tourism service is consumed only by international tourists. So the demand for tourism service remains independent of changes in national income of the host country. Improvement in the quality of environment also leads to an increase in the demand for tourism service because international tourists always prefer a better quality of environment. Production function of each of these two sectors obeys all standard neo-classical properties including constant returns to scale. Factor endowments and environmental quality of the host country are exogenously given in the short run. Factor prices in both the sectors are perfectly flexible and this flexibility ensures full utilization of these factor endowments. All markets are perfectly competitive; and the representative firm in each of these two sectors is a profit maximizer.

Following notations are used here.

K = Capital stock.
L = Labour endowment.
a_{ji} = Per unit requirement of the jth factor in ith sector for $j = \mathrm{L}, \mathrm{K}$ and $i = 1, 2$.
P = Relative price of the non-traded tourism service.
w = Wage rate.
r = Rental rate on capital.
X_i = Level of output of ith sector for $i = 1, 2$.
$\mathrm{Y_S}$ = National income of the host country.
$\mathrm{Y_N}$ = Income of the rest of the world.
E = Quality of environment.
θ_{ji} = Cost share of jth factor in ith sector for $j = \mathrm{L}, \mathrm{K}$ and $i = 1, 2$.
λ_{ji} = Proportion of jth factor employed in ith sector for $j = \mathrm{L}, \mathrm{K}$ and $i = 1, 2$.
S^h_{ji} = The elasticity of factor output coefficient of jth factor in hth sector with respect to price of ith factor for $i, j = \mathrm{L}, \mathrm{K}$ and $h = 1, 2$.

For example, $\mathrm{S}^1_{\mathrm{LK}} = \left(\frac{\mathrm{r}}{\mathrm{a_{L1}}}\right)\left(\frac{\partial \mathrm{a_{L1}}}{\partial \mathrm{r}}\right)$, $\mathrm{S}^1_{\mathrm{LL}} = \left(\frac{\mathrm{W}}{\mathrm{a_{L1}}}\right)\left(\frac{\partial \mathrm{a_{L1}}}{\partial \mathrm{W}}\right)$ etc. $\mathrm{S}^h_{ji} > 0$ for $j \neq i$; and $\mathrm{S}^h_{jj} < 0$.

Also, $\mathrm{S}^h_{ji} + \mathrm{S}^h_{jj} = 0$ for $j \neq i$.

$\hat{x} = \frac{dx}{x}$ = Relative change in x.
The model is described by following equations.

$$1 = a_{L1}w + a_{K1}r; \tag{1}$$

$$P = a_{L2}w + a_{K2}r; \tag{2}$$

$$a_{L1}X_1 + a_{L2}X_2 = L; \tag{3}$$

$$a_{K1}X_1 + a_{K2}X_2 = K; \tag{4}$$

$$D_2(P, Y_N, E) = X_2 \text{ with } \frac{\partial D_2}{\partial P}\left\langle 0;\ \frac{\partial D_2}{\partial Y_N}\right\rangle 0 \text{ and } \frac{\partial D_2}{\partial E} > 0; \tag{5}$$

and

$$Y_S = X_1 + PX_2 = wL + rK. \tag{6}$$

We normalize the price of the traded good to unity. Equations (1) and (2) stand for competitive equilibrium conditions in sectors 1 and 2. The right hand side in each of these two equations represents the marginal cost of production. Marginal cost and the average cost are equal because production function satisfies constant returns to scale. Price is equal to marginal cost when a competitive firm maximizes profit; and all firms are identical in each of these two sectors. Factor-output coefficients, a_{ji}, are also functions of factor price ratios, $\left(\frac{w}{r}\right)$, because the Iso-product curve for each of these two production sectors is smooth convex and the representative competitive firm maximizes profit. Equations (3) and (4) represent equilibrium conditions in the labour market and in the capital market respectively. $(a_{L1}X_1 + a_{L2}X_2)$ stands for demand for labour and $(a_{K1}X_1 + a_{K2}X_2)$ represents demand for capital. Supply demand equality in each of these two input markets is automatically attained by the flexibility of factor prices, w and r. Both the sectors pay same prices to each of these two factors because both the factors are perfectly mobile between these two sectors. Equation (5) represents the demand supply equality for non-traded tourism service. Left hand side of this equation stands for the demand function for tourism service; and the demand for tourism service varies inversely with its price, directly with income of the rest of the world and also positively with product quality represented by the quality of environment. This Eq. (5) solves for the equilibrium value of the relative price of the non-traded tourism service. Equation (6) shows total factor income of the host country; and it is equal to national income in the absence of indirect taxes and subsidies.

2.2 Working of the Short-Run Equilibrium Model

w, r, P, X_1, X_2 and Y_S are six unknowns in this model. We have six independent equations with six unknowns. L, K, Y_N and E are four parameters.

Equations (1) and (2) simultaneously determine w and r in terms of P. So each a_{ji} is also determined. Equations (3) and (4) solve for X_1 and X_2 as functions of P. Equation (6) is used to find the value of Y_S in terms of P. Finally, Eq. (5) solves for the equilibrium value of P.

Using Eqs. (1) and (2), we obtain

$$\hat{r} = \frac{\theta_{L1}\hat{P}}{|\theta|}; \tag{7}$$

and

$$\hat{w} = -\frac{\theta_{K1}\hat{P}}{|\theta|}. \tag{8}$$

Here, $|\theta| = (\theta_{L1}\theta_{K2} - \theta_{L2}\theta_{K1})$ represents the capital intensity ranking between the two sectors; and sector 2 representing tourism sector is assumed to be more labour intensive, i.e., $|\theta| < 0$. Hazari and Sgro (2015) assume that tourism sector is more labour intensive than the non-tourism sector. This makes sense when share of industry in the non-tourism sector is high and/or when agriculture is highly mechanized.

Using Eqs. (3), (4), (7) and (8), we obtain

$$\hat{X}_1 = \frac{\lambda_{K2}\hat{L} - \lambda_{L2}\hat{K}}{|\lambda|} + \widehat{CP}; \tag{9}$$

and

$$\hat{X}_2 = \frac{\lambda_{L1}\hat{K} - \lambda_{K1}\hat{L}}{|\lambda|} + \widehat{FP}. \tag{10}$$

Here,

$$|\lambda| = (\lambda_{L1}\lambda_{K2} - \lambda_{L2}\lambda_{K1}) < 0$$

because sector 1 is capital intensive. Here

$$C = \frac{\lambda_{K2}A - \lambda_{L2}B}{|\lambda|} < 0;$$

and

$$F = \frac{\lambda_{L1}B - \lambda_{K1}A}{|\lambda|} > 0.$$

This is so because
$|\theta| < 0;\ S^h_{ij} > 0$ and $S^h_{jj} < 0$. Hence

$$A = \frac{1}{|\theta|}\left[\left(\lambda_{L1}S^1_{LL} + \lambda_{L2}S^2_{LL}\right)\theta_{K1} - \left(\lambda_{L1}S^1_{LK} + \lambda_{L2}S^2_{LK}\right)\theta_{L1}\right] > 0;$$

and

$$B = \frac{1}{|\theta|}\left[\left(\lambda_{K1}S^1_{KL} + \lambda_{L2}S^2_{KL}\right)\theta_{K1} - \left(\lambda_{K1}S^1_{KK} + \lambda_{K2}S^2_{KK}\right)\theta_{L1}\right] < 0;$$

From Eqs. (6), (7) and (8), we have

$$\hat{Y}_S = \frac{wr}{PY_S|\theta|}(a_{L1}K - a_{K1}L)\hat{P} + \frac{WL}{Y}\hat{L} + \frac{rK}{Y}\hat{K}. \tag{11}$$

Finally, using Eqs. (5) and (10), we obtain

$$\hat{P} = \frac{1}{D}\left[\frac{\lambda_{L1}}{|\lambda|}\hat{K} - \frac{\lambda_{K1}}{|\lambda|}\hat{L} - e_{MN}\hat{Y}_N - e_E\hat{E}\right]; \tag{12}$$

where

$$D = [e_P - F] < 0. \tag{13}$$

Here $e_p < 0$ and $e_{MN} > 0$ stand for the price elasticity of demand and income elasticity of demand for tourism service respectively; and $e_E > 0$ represents the elasticity of demand for tourism service with respect to environmental quality.

Using Eq. (12), Eqs. (7), (8), (9), (10) and (11) can be modified as follows.

$$\hat{r} = \frac{\theta_{L1}}{|\theta|}\frac{1}{D}\left[\frac{\lambda_{L1}}{|\lambda|}\hat{K} - \frac{\lambda_{K1}}{|\lambda|}\hat{L} - e_{MN}\hat{Y}_N - e_E\hat{E}\right]; \tag{7A}$$

$$\hat{w} = -\frac{\theta_{K1}}{|\theta|}\frac{1}{D}\left[\frac{\lambda_{L1}}{|\lambda|}\hat{K} - \frac{\lambda_{K1}}{|\lambda|}\hat{L} - e_{MN}\hat{Y}_N - e_E\hat{E}\right]; \tag{8A}$$

$$\hat{X}_1 = \frac{1}{|\lambda|}\left[\lambda_{K2} - \lambda_{K1}\frac{C}{D}\right]\hat{L} - \frac{1}{|\lambda|}\left[\lambda_{L2} - \lambda_{L1}\frac{C}{D}\right]\hat{K} - \frac{C}{D}\left[e_{MN}\hat{Y}_N + e_E\hat{E}\right]; \tag{9A}$$

$$\hat{X}_2 = -\frac{\lambda_{K1}}{|\lambda|}\left[1 + \frac{F}{D}\right]\hat{L} + \frac{\lambda_{L1}}{|\lambda|}\left[1 + \frac{F}{D}\right]\hat{K} - \frac{F}{D}\left[e_{MN}\hat{Y}_N + e_E\hat{E}\right]; \tag{10A}$$

and

$$\begin{aligned}\hat{Y}_S = {} & \frac{w}{Y_S}\left[-\frac{1}{D}\frac{r}{|\theta|}(a_{L1}K - a_{K1}L)\frac{\lambda_{K1}}{|\lambda|} + L\right]\hat{L} \\ & + \frac{r}{Y_S}\left[\frac{1}{D}\frac{w}{|\theta|}(a_{L1}K - a_{K1}L)\frac{\lambda_{L1}}{|\lambda|} + K\right]\hat{K} \\ & - \frac{wr}{Y|\theta|}(a_{L1}K - a_{K1}L)\frac{1}{D}\left[e_{MN}\hat{Y}_N + e_E\hat{E}\right]. \end{aligned} \tag{11A}$$

Here, $\left[1 + \frac{F}{D}\right] > 0$, $|\lambda| < 0$ and $(a_{L1}K - a_{K1}L) < 0$.

Hence, using Eqs. (7A), (8A), (9A), (10A) and (11A), we can establish the following proposition.

Proposition 1 *In the short-run equilibrium, (i) Price of the non-traded tourism service varies directly with Southern capital endowment, tourism development and Southern environmental quality but ambiguously with Southern labour endowment; (ii) Wage rate varies directly with capital endowment, tourism development and Southern environmental quality but ambiguously with labour endowment; (iii) rental rate on capital varies inversely with capital endowment, tourism development and Southern environmental quality but ambiguously with labour endowment; (iv) Level of output of the traded good varies inversely with tourism development and Southern environmental quality but ambiguously with capital stock and labour endowment; (iv) Level of output of the non-traded tourism service varies directly with labour endowment, tourism development and Southern environmental quality but inversely with capital stock; and finally, (v) National income of the host country varies directly with capital endowment, tourism development and Southern environmental quality but ambiguously with labour endowment.*

We now turn to explain the intuition behind this proposition, and this can be explained conveniently in terms of Rybczynski (1955) effect and Stolper-Samuelson (1941) effect.

Due to Rybczynski effect, an exogenous increase in capital (labour) endowment lowers (raises), the supply of non-traded tourism service because the tourism sector is more labour intensive than the traded good sector. Demand for non-traded tourism service remains unaffected. So the increase in capital (labour) endowment leads to an increase (decrease) in the price of the non-traded tourism service. On the other hand, tourism development, which takes place in the form of an exogenous increase in income of the outside world and/or an improvement in the environmental quality of the host country, raises the demand for tourism service but keeps its supply unchanged. So the relative price of the tourism service goes up in these two cases.

Due to Stolper-Sameulson effect, wage rate (rental rate on capital) varies directly (inversely) with the price of the labour intensive non-traded tourism service. So wage rate (rental rate on capital) varies positively (negatively) with capital endowment, tourism development and environmental quality. However, an increase in labour endowment lowers (raises) the wage rate (rental rate on capital).

Changes in factor endowments have two different types of effects on the output composition of these two sectors. Direct effect is similar to the Rybczynski effect;

and the indirect effect comes from the consequent change in the price of the tourism service. Due to Rybczynski effect, an increase in capital (labour) endowment raises (lowers) the production of traded good and lowers (raises) the supply of tourism service at the given price because the tourism service sector is more labour intensive. However, the indirect effect works in the opposite direction for the traded good when factor endowments are expanded; and thus the net effect on the level of output of the traded good is ambiguous. In the case of non-traded tourism service, the indirect effect also works in the opposite direction. However, its magnitude is weaker than that of the direct effect; and so the sign of the net effect on the output of tourism sector is dominated by the direct effect. Tourism development or improvement in environmental quality raises the demand for tourism service; and so its relative price goes up. This in turn, generates an adverse (favourable) effect on the output of the traded good (tourism service).

Due to an increase in any factor endowment, national income is also increased due to the direct effect. However, the increase in capital endowment raises the price of the tourism service. So the net effect of an expansion of capital endowment on Southern national income is always positive. On the contrary, a rise in labour endowment leads to a fall in the price of the tourism service; and so the final effect on national income is ambiguous. Finally, tourism development or improvement in environmental quality raises the demand for tourism service; and consequently raises its price which, in turn, leads to an increase in national income.

3 The Dynamic Analysis[6]

Capital stock and environmental quality change over time; and, in order to analyse properties of this intertemporal behaviour, we move to a dynamic analysis. The representative household in the host country supplies labour and capital; and maximizes her lifetime utility subject to the budget constraint. The lifetime utility is defined as the infinite integral of the discounted present value of instantaneous utility; and discounting is made at a constant rate, ρ.

The instantaneous utility function of the representative household is given by

$$u(c) = \frac{C^{1-\sigma}}{1-\sigma} \text{ with } \sigma > 0. \tag{14}$$

The instantaneous utility appears to be a positive and concave function of her level of consumption, C of the traded good. Tourism service is consumed only by international tourists.[7] Domestic consumers consume only traded good which is a Solow

[6] Optimal control theory of this chapter is done according to Gupta and Dutta (2021).

[7] In many less developed countries, there exists a very high degree of economic inequality; and rich domestic consumers also consume tourism service there. We ignore this realistic feature for the sake of simplicity.

(1956) type of aggregate commodity satisfying the dual role of being consumed as well as of being invested. Its demand is met by domestic production and import; and the import is financed by income earned from tourism.[8] σ represents the constant elasticity of marginal utility with respect to consumption.[9]

We rule out the possibility of depreciation of capital stock for the sake of technical simplicity. So the aggregate budget constraint of the household who allocates his income between consumption of traded goods and savings (investment) is given by

$$\dot{K} = Y_S - C. \tag{15}$$

Here Y_S is total income of this household; and it is given by Eq. (6). Number of households in the host country is normalized to unity; and so, in the absence of taxes and subsidies, Y_S represents the national income.

Using Eqs. (6) and (15) we have

$$\dot{K} = WL + rK - C. \tag{16}$$

The representative household maximizes the discounted present value of utility over the infinite time horizon given by

$$\int_0^\infty u(C)e^{-\rho t}dt$$

with respect to C subject to Eqs. (14) and (16). The growth rate of consumption derived from this maximization exercise is given by[10]

$$\frac{\dot{C}}{C} = \frac{1}{\sigma}(r - \rho). \tag{17}$$

Environmental quality is degraded due to the expansion of the tourism sector because tourism development, on the one hand, leads to deforestation and destruction of hills and seashores due to construction of roads and hotels and, on the other hand, generates pollution due to use of various non-eco-friendly consumer goods. However, there is a positive rate of its automatic natural improvement. The intertemporal rate of change in the environmental quality is given by

$$\dot{E} = \eta E - \frac{\psi(X_2)}{(1 + v)}. \tag{18}$$

There are two sources of improvement in the quality of environment- natural improvement and abatement activity. Here, η stands for the constant natural rate of

---

[8] Tourism sector only generates factor income in the hands of domestic consumers; and this is allocated between consumption of traded good and investment.

[9] Consumption, c, is not a composite good even though it is a two sector model.

[10] Derivation of Eq. (17) is shown in the Appendix (A).

improvement of environmental quality; and v represents the rate of pollution abatement expenditure which is assumed to be financed exogenously by the government. If it is financed by taxation, then abatement expenditure is to be subtracted from income to obtain the rate of capital accumulation.[11] $\psi(X_2)$ represents the rate of degradation of environmental quality caused by the expansion of tourism sector. Expansion of tourism activity takes place with the arrival of tourists. Cerina (2007) assumes that pollution flow varies positively with the size of the tourist arrival and inversely with the rate of abatement expenditure. Here $\frac{\psi(X_2)}{(1+v)}$ represents the effective pollution flow and $\psi'(X_2)$. $\eta(1 + v)$ represents the aggregate rate of improvement in environmental quality.

3.1 Long-Run Equilibrium

In the long-run equilibrium, $\dot{C} = \dot{K} = \dot{E} = 0$; and hence, from Eqs. (6), (15), (17) and (18), we find that,

$$r = \rho; \tag{19}$$

$$wL + rK = C; \tag{20}$$

and

$$(1 + v)\eta E = \psi(X_2). \tag{21}$$

From the comparative static results presented in the short-run equilibrium model, we find that r and X_2 are functions of K and E. Hence Eqs. (19) and (21) solve for long-run equilibrium values of K and E in terms of parameters, ρ, η and u. Then Eq. (20) solves for the long-run equilibrium value of C. Since Eqs. (19) and (21) are independent of C, the comparative steady state effects on K and E can be analysed using only these two equations provided that the long-run equilibrium point is stable. The stability analysis of this long-run equilibrium point is done in the next subsection; and it is found that either this long-run equilibrium satisfies saddle point stability with a unique transitional path or there exists infinite number of transitional paths around the long-run equilibrium point leading to indeterminacy. The condition required for indeterminacy is given by

$$\left(\psi'(X_2)\frac{X_2}{\psi}\right)\left(\frac{\partial X_2}{\partial P}\frac{P}{X_2}\right)\left(\frac{\partial P}{\partial E}\frac{E}{P}\right) > 1. \tag{A}$$

[11] This is more realistic but would complicate the technical analysis. Ideally the abatement decision of the government should be endogenized; and we shall take care of this problem in our future research.

If condition (A) is not satisfied then the equilibrium satisfies saddle point stability. Left hand side of this inequality (A) is the product of three elasticities- the elasticity of degradation of environmental quality with respect to the level of output of tourism service, the own price elasticity of supply of tourism service and the elasticity of its equilibrium price with respect to environmental quality. So the problem of indeterminacy arises when the demand for tourism service is highly elastic to environmental quality and when the negative environmental degradation effect of tourism development is very strong. Existing dynamic models on tourism development like Cerina (2007), Marsiglio (2015, 2016) study environmental implications of tourism development but do not point out the possibility of indeterminacy of transitional growth path. Next subsection deals with technical analysis related to transitional dynamics.

3.2 Stability of Long-Run Equilibrium[12]

The transitional dynamic properties of the long-run equilibrium depend on the sign of latent roots of the Jacobian matrix corresponding to dynamic Eqs. (16) (17) and (18). It is given by

$$J = \begin{bmatrix} \frac{\partial \frac{\dot{C}}{C}}{\partial c} & \frac{\partial \frac{\dot{C}}{C}}{\partial K} & \frac{\partial \frac{\dot{C}}{C}}{\partial E} \\ \frac{\partial \frac{\dot{K}}{K}}{\partial C} & \frac{\partial \frac{\dot{K}}{K}}{\partial K} & \frac{\partial \frac{\dot{K}}{K}}{\partial E} \\ \frac{\partial \frac{\dot{E}}{E}}{\partial C} & \frac{\partial \frac{\dot{E}}{E}}{\partial K} & \frac{\partial \frac{\dot{E}}{E}}{\partial E} \end{bmatrix}.$$

Using Eqs. (7A), (10A), (16)–(18), we have

$$\frac{\partial \frac{\dot{C}}{C}}{\partial c} = 0;$$

$$\frac{\partial \frac{\dot{C}}{C}}{\partial K} = \frac{1}{\sigma}\frac{r}{K}\frac{\theta_{L1}}{|\theta|}\frac{1}{D}\frac{\lambda_{L1}}{|\lambda|} < 0;$$

$$\frac{\partial \frac{\dot{C}}{C}}{\partial E} = -\frac{1}{\sigma}\frac{r}{K}\frac{\theta_{L1}}{|\theta|}\frac{1}{D}e_E < 0$$

$$\frac{\partial \frac{\dot{K}}{K}}{\partial C} = -\frac{1}{K} < 0;$$

$$\frac{\partial \frac{\dot{K}}{K}}{\partial K} = \frac{C}{K^2} - \frac{wL}{K^2} + \frac{\lambda_{L1} wr}{|\lambda||\theta| DK^2 P}(a_{L1}K - a_{K1}L);$$

[12] See Benhabib and Perili (1994) for such an analysis in the model of endogenous growth of Lucas (1988).

$$\frac{\partial \frac{\dot{K}}{K}}{\partial E} = -\frac{e_E wr}{KE|\theta|DP}(a_{L1}K - a_{K1}L) > 0;$$

$$\frac{\partial \frac{\dot{E}}{E}}{\partial C} = 0;$$

$$\frac{\partial \frac{\dot{E}}{E}}{\partial K} = -\frac{1}{E}\frac{1}{(1+v)}\psi\prime(X_2)\frac{X_2}{K}\frac{\lambda_{L1}}{|\lambda|}\left(1+\frac{F}{D}\right) > 0;$$

and

$$\begin{aligned}\frac{\partial \frac{\dot{E}}{E}}{\partial E} &= \frac{\psi}{E^2}\frac{1}{(1+v)}\left\{1+\psi'(X_2)\frac{X_2}{\psi}\frac{F}{D}e_E\right\}\\ &= \frac{\psi}{E^2}\frac{1}{(1+v)}\left\{1-\left(\psi'(X_2)\frac{X_2}{\psi}\right)\left(\frac{\partial X_2}{\partial P}\frac{P}{X_2}\right)\left(\frac{\partial P}{\partial E}\frac{E}{P}\right)\right\}.\end{aligned}$$

The determinant corresponding to this Jacobian matrix is given by

$$\mathrm{Det}(J) = \frac{r}{\sigma K^2E^2}\frac{\theta_{L1}}{|\theta|}\frac{1}{D}\frac{\lambda_{L1}}{|\lambda|}\frac{\psi}{(1+v)}\left\{1-\left(\psi'(X_2)\frac{X_2}{\psi}\right)\left(\frac{\partial X_2}{\partial P}\frac{P}{X_2}\right)\left(\frac{\partial P}{\partial E}\frac{E}{P}\right)\right\};$$

and, trace of the Jacobian matrix is given by

$$\begin{aligned}\mathrm{Tr}(J) = &\frac{C}{K^2} - \frac{wL}{K^2} + \frac{\lambda_{L1}wr}{|\lambda||\theta|DK^2P}(a_{L1}K - a_{K1}L)\\ &+ \frac{\psi}{E^2}\frac{1}{(1+v)}\left\{1-\left(\psi'(X_2)\frac{X_2}{\psi}\right)\left(\frac{\partial X_2}{\partial P}\frac{P}{X_2}\right)\left(\frac{\partial P}{\partial E}\frac{E}{P}\right)\right\}\end{aligned}$$

Sign of Det(J) depends on condition (A); and the sign of the last element of Tr(J) is also conditional on condition (A). In order to determine the sign of the latent roots of the J matrix we apply the Routh-Hurwitz Theorem. The characteristic equation obtained from J matrix is given by

$$-q^3 + \mathrm{Tr}(J)q^2 - M(J)q + \mathrm{Det}(J) = 0, \tag{22}$$

where q is the latent root.

Here,

$$\begin{aligned}M(J) = &\begin{bmatrix}\frac{\partial \frac{\dot{C}}{C}}{\partial C} & \frac{\partial \frac{\dot{C}}{C}}{\partial K}\\ \frac{\partial \frac{\dot{K}}{K}}{\partial C} & \frac{\partial \frac{\dot{K}}{K}}{\partial K}\end{bmatrix} + \begin{bmatrix}\frac{\partial \frac{\dot{K}}{K}}{\partial K} & \frac{\partial \frac{\dot{K}}{K}}{\partial E}\\ \frac{\partial \frac{\dot{E}}{E}}{\partial K} & \frac{\partial \frac{\dot{E}}{E}}{\partial E}\end{bmatrix} + \begin{bmatrix}\frac{\partial \frac{\dot{C}}{C}}{\partial C} & \frac{\partial \frac{\dot{C}}{C}}{\partial E}\\ \frac{\partial \frac{\dot{E}}{E}}{\partial C} & \frac{\partial \frac{\dot{E}}{E}}{\partial E}\end{bmatrix}\\ = &\frac{1}{\sigma}\frac{r}{K^2}\frac{\theta_{L1}}{|\theta|}\frac{1}{D}\frac{\lambda_{L1}}{|\lambda|} + \frac{\psi}{E^2}\frac{1}{(1+v)}\left\{\frac{C}{K^2} - \frac{wL}{K^2}\right.\end{aligned}$$

$$+\frac{\lambda_{L1} wr}{|\lambda||\theta|DK^2P}(a_{L1}K - a_{K1}L)\bigg\}\bigg\{1 - \left(\psi'(X_2)\frac{X_2}{\psi}\right)\left(\frac{\partial X_2}{\partial P}\frac{P}{X_2}\right)\left(\frac{\partial P}{\partial E}\frac{E}{P}\right)\bigg\}$$
$$-\frac{1}{E}\frac{1}{(1+v)}\psi'(X_2)\frac{X_2}{K}\frac{\lambda_{L1}}{|\lambda|}\left(1+\frac{F}{D}\right)\frac{e_E wr}{KE|\theta|DP}(a_{L1}K - a_{K1}L).$$

The number of positive roots in the characteristic Eq. (22) is equal to the number of variations of signs in the scheme

$$\left\{-1,\ Tr(J), -M(J) + \frac{Det(J)}{Tr(J)}, Det(J)\right\}. \tag{23}$$

The number of negative roots will determine the nature of transitional paths around the long-run equilibrium point. In this model we have two state variables, K and E, and only one control variable, C. The properties of transitional dynamics depends on the relationship between number of state variables and number of negative latent roots. The long-run equilibrium is saddle point stable (unstable) if the number of negative latent roots is equal to (less than) the number of state variables. However, it faces indeterminacy with infinite number of transitional path when number of negative latent roots is greater than the number of state variables. We now consider two cases.

Case (i): Condition (A) is satisfied So Det(J) is positive. If

$$\frac{C}{K^2} + \frac{\lambda_{L1} wr}{|\lambda||\theta|DK^2P}(a_{L1}K - a_{K1}L) < \frac{wL}{K^2}$$
$$-\frac{\psi}{E^2}\frac{1}{(1+v)}\left\{1 - \left(\psi'(X_2)\frac{X_2}{\psi}\right)\left(\frac{\partial X_2}{\partial P}\frac{P}{X_2}\right)\left(\frac{\partial P}{\partial E}\frac{E}{P}\right)\right\},$$

then Tr(J) is negative.

Then, whatever be the sign of $\left\{-M(J) + \frac{Det(J)}{Tr(J)}\right\}$, we have only one variation in sign in the scheme (23). So the characteristic Eq. (22) has only one positive root and two negative roots; and thus number of negative latent roots is exactly equal to the number of state variables. Hence the long-run equilibrium point satisfies saddle point stability with a unique transitional path.

If, on the other hand,

$$\frac{C}{K^2} + \frac{\lambda_{L1} wr}{|\lambda||\theta|DK^2P}(a_{L1}K - a_{K1}L) > \frac{wL}{K^2}$$
$$-\frac{\psi}{E^2}\frac{1}{(1+v)}\left\{1 - \left(\psi'(X_2)\frac{X_2}{\psi}\right)\left(\frac{\partial X_2}{\partial P}\frac{P}{X_2}\right)\left(\frac{\partial P}{\partial E}\frac{E}{P}\right)\right\}$$

then Tr(J) is positive. In that case,

M(J) is negative because

$$\left\{\frac{C}{K^2} - \frac{wL}{K^2} + \frac{\lambda_{L1}wr}{|\lambda||\theta|DK^2P}(a_{L1}K - a_{K1}L)\right\} > 0$$

and

$$\left\{1 - \left(\psi'(X_2)\frac{X_2}{\psi}\right)\left(\frac{\partial X_2}{\partial P}\frac{P}{X_2}\right)\left(\frac{\partial P}{\partial E}\frac{E}{P}\right)\right\} < 0.$$

So $\left\{-M(J) + \frac{Det(J)}{Tr(J)}\right\}$ is positive; and hence we have only one variation in sign in the scheme (23). So here also the characteristic Eq. (22) has only one positive root and two negative roots; and thus the number of negative latent roots is equal to the number of state variables. Hence the long-run equilibrium point once again satisfies saddle point stability in this case.

Case (ii): Condition (A) is not satisfied In this case, Det(J) is negative. If

$$\frac{C}{K^2} + \frac{\lambda_{L1}wr}{|\lambda||\theta|DK^2P}(a_{L1}K - a_{K1}L) + \frac{\psi}{E^2}\frac{1}{(1+v)}\left\{1 - \left(\psi'(X_2)\frac{X_2}{\psi}\right)\left(\frac{\partial X_2}{\partial P}\frac{P}{X_2}\right)\left(\frac{\partial P}{\partial E}\frac{E}{P}\right)\right\} < \frac{wL}{K^2},$$

then Tr(J) is negative.

Then M(J) is also negative because

$$\left\{\frac{C}{K^2} - \frac{wL}{K^2} + \frac{\lambda_{L1}wr}{|\lambda||\theta|DK^2P}(a_{L1}K - a_{K1}L)\right\} < 0$$

and

$$\left\{1 - \left(\psi'(X_2)\frac{X_2}{\psi}\right)\left(\frac{\partial X_2}{\partial P}\frac{P}{X_2}\right)\left(\frac{\partial P}{\partial E}\frac{E}{P}\right)\right\} > 0.$$

So, $\left\{-M(J) + \frac{Det(J)}{Tr(J)}\right\}$ is positive.

Hence we have two variations in sign in the scheme (23). So the characteristic Eq. (22) has two positive roots and only one negative root; and hence the number of negative latent roots is less than the number of state variables. So the long-run equilibrium is unstable in this case.

However, if

$$\frac{C}{K^2} + \frac{\lambda_{L1}wr}{|\lambda||\theta|DK^2P}(a_{L1}K - a_{K1}L) + \frac{\psi}{E^2}\frac{1}{(1+v)}\left\{1 - \left(\psi'(X_2)\frac{X_2}{\psi}\right)\left(\frac{\partial X_2}{\partial P}\frac{P}{X_2}\right)\left(\frac{\partial P}{\partial E}\frac{E}{P}\right)\right\} > \frac{wL}{K^2},$$

then Tr(J) is positive.

Then, whatever be the sign of $\left\{-\mathrm{M(J)} + \frac{\mathrm{Det(J)}}{\mathrm{Tr(J)}}\right\}$, we have two variations in sign in the scheme (23). So the characteristic Eq. (22) has two positive roots and only one negative root in this case too; and this implies that the number of negative latent roots falls short of the number of state variables. So the long-run equilibrium is unstable.

This leads to the following proposition.

Proposition 2 *If condition (A) is satisfied (not satisfied) then the long-run equilibrium point is saddle point stable (unstable).*

This long-run equilibrium point either satisfies saddle point stability with a unique transitional path converging to the equilibrium or is unstable. This result is conditional on the relative strength of two effects (i) the environmental effects on the demand for tourism; and (ii) the tourism development effect on environmental degradation.

4 Conclusion

A two sector dynamic model of a less developed economy is developed with one imported traded good sector and with a non-traded tourism service sector which serves only international tourists. Revenue earned from this tourism sector finances the expenditure on imports. The model takes care of the adverse effect of tourism development on environmental pollution. Environmental quality changes over time and so the negative environmental effect of tourism development is also spread over time. Capital accumulation is the only source of economic growth in this model; and it also takes place over time.

We use this dynamic model to derive interesting results related to the transitional dynamic properties of the unique long-run equilibrium. This long-run equilibrium point either satisfies saddle point stability with a unique transitional path converging to the equilibrium or is unstable. Dynamic models of Cerina (2007), Marsiglio (2015, 2016) who study the interactions between tourism development and environmental degradation also show that long-run equilibrium is either saddle point stable or unstable.

However, our model does not consider many important aspects of reality. Socio-cultural effects of international tourism are not introduced in this model. We assume full employment in the labour market; and thus we cannot analyse the effect of tourism development on the unemployment problem. The problem of financing abatement expenditure is not considered. We plan to remove all these difficulties of the present exercise in our future works.

Appendix (A)

Derivation of Equation (17)

The representative consumer maximizes $\int_0^\infty \frac{C^{1-\sigma}}{1-\sigma} e^{-\rho t} dt$ subject to the equation of motion given by

$$\dot{K} = WL + rK - C. \tag{A.1}$$

K(0) is given. K is the state variable; and C is the control variable satifying $0 \leq C \leq Y_S$.

The Current value Hamiltonian to be maximized at each point of time is given by

$$H = \frac{C^{1-\sigma}}{1-\sigma} e^{-\rho t} + q e^{-\rho t t} \dot{K}. \tag{A.2}$$

where, q is the co-state variable.

Using Eqs. (A.1) and (A.2), we have

$$H = \frac{C^{1-\sigma}}{1-\sigma} e^{-\rho t} + q e^{-\rho t} (WL + rK - C). \tag{A.3}$$

The first order optimality condition with respect to C is given by

$$\frac{\partial H}{\partial C} = C^{-\sigma} - q = 0. \tag{A.4}$$

Differentiating Eq. (A.4) with respect to time, we have

$$-\sigma \frac{\dot{C}}{C} = \frac{\dot{q}}{q}. \tag{A.5}$$

Optimum time path of the co-state variable satisfies the following differential equation.

$$\frac{\dot{q}}{q} = \rho - \frac{\partial H}{\partial K}$$

$$\Rightarrow \frac{\dot{q}}{q} = \rho - r. \tag{A.6}$$

Using Eqs. (A.5) and (A.6), we obtain

$$\frac{\dot{C}}{C} = \frac{1}{\sigma}(r - \rho). \tag{A.7}$$

Equation (A.7) is same as Eq. (17) in the body of the paper.

References

Ben-Gad, M. (2003). Fiscal policy and indeterminacy in models of endogenous growth. *Journal of Economic Theory, 108*, 322–344.

Benhabib, J., & Farmer, R. E. (1994). Indeterminacy and increasing returns. *Journal of Economic Theory, 63*, 19–41.

Benhabib, J., & Farmer, R. E. (1996). Indeterminacy and sector-specific externalities. *Journal of Monetary Economics, 37*, 421–443.

Benhabib, J., & Perli, R. (1994). Uniqueness and indeterminacy: On the dynamics of endogenous growth. *Journal of Economic Theory, 63*, 113–142.

Benhabib, J., Meng, Q., & Nishimura, K. (2000). Indeterminacy under constant returns to scale in multisector economies. *Econometrica, 68*, 1541–1548.

Brau, R., & Cao, D. (2005). *Uncovering the macrostructure of tourists' preferences. A choice experiment analysis of tourism demand to Sardinia* (CRENoS Working Paper 2005/14).

Cerina, F. (2007). Tourism specialization and environmental sustainability in a dynamic economy. *Tourism Economics, 13*, 553–582.

Chao, C., Hazari, B. H., & Sgro, P. M. (2004). Tourism, globalization, social externalities, and domestic welfare. *Research in International Business and Finance, 18*, 141–149.

Chao, C., Hazari, B. H., & Sgro, P. M. (2005). Tourism and economic development in a cash-in-advance economy. *Research in International Business and Finance, 19*, 365–373.

Copeland, B. R. (1991). Tourism, welfare and de-industrialization in a small open economy. *Economica, 58*, 515–529.

Crouch, G. I., & Louvière, J. J. (2001). A review of choice modelling research in tourism, hospitality and leisure. In J. A. Mazanec, G. I. Crouch, J. R. Ritchie, & A. G. Woodside (Eds.),*Consumer psychology of tourism, hospitality and leisure* (Vol. 2, pp. 67–86). CAB International.

Davies, T., & Cahill, S. (2000). *Environmental implications of the tourism industry* (Discussion Paper 00–14). Resources for the Future, Washington, DC.

Economides, G., & Philippopoulos, A. (2008). Growth enhancing policy is the means to sustain the environment. *Review of Economic Dynamics, 11*, 207–219.

Fernandez, E., Novales, A., & Ruiz, J. (2004). Indeterminacy under non-separability of public consumption and leisure in the utility function. *Economic Modelling, 21*, 409–428.

Gossling, S. (2002). Global environmental consequences of tourism. *Global Environmental Change, 12*, 283–302.

Gossling, S. (2000). Sustainable tourism development in developing countries: Some aspects of energy use. *Journal of Sustainable Tourism, 8*, 410–425.

Gray, H. P. (1970). *International tourism: International trade*. Lexington.

Gray, H. P. (1982). The contributions of economics to tourism. *Annals of Tourism Research, 9*, 105–125.

Greiner, A. (2005). Fiscal policy in an endogenous growth model with public capital and pollution. *Japanese Economic Review, 56*, 67–84.

Gupta, M. R., & Barman, T. R. (2009). Fiscal policies, environmental pollution and economic growth. *Economic Modelling, 26*, 1018–1028.

Gupta, M. R., & Barman, T. R. (2010). Health, infrastructure, environment and endogenous growth. *Journal of Macroeconomics, 32*, 657–673.

Gupta, M. R., & Chakraborty, B. (2007). Uniqueness and indeterminacy of the equilibrium growth path in the Uzawa-Lucas model with sector specific externalities. *The Japanese Economic Review, 58*, 400–406.

Gupta, M. R., & Dutta, P. B. (2017). Tourism development, environmental pollution and economic growth: A theoretical analysis. *The Journal of International Trade & Economic Development, 26*, 125–144.

Gupta, M. R., & Dutta, P. B. (2021). Taxation, capital accumulation, environment and unemployment in an efficiency wage model. *Journal of Economics, 135*, 151–198.

Hazari, B. R., & Sgro, P. M. (1995). Tourism and growth in a dynamic model of trade. *Journal of International Trade and Economic Development, 4*, 243–252.

Hazari, B. R., & Sgro, P. M. (2015). *Tourism, trade and national welfare.* Emerald.

Jim, C. Y. (2000). Environmental changes associated with mass urban tourism and nature tourism development in Hong Kong. *The Environmentalist, 20*, 233–247.

Jones, R. W. (1965). The structure of simple general equilibrium models. *Journal of Political Economy, 73*, 557–572.

Lahiri, A. (2001). Growth and equilibrium indeterminacy: The role of capital mobility. *Economic Theory, 17*, 197–208.

Lucas, R. E. (1988). On the mechanics of economic development. *Journal of Monetary Economics, 22*, 3–42.

Maddison, D. (2001). In search of warmer climates? The impact of climate. *Climatic Change, 49*, 193–208.

Marsiglio, S. (2015). Economic growth and environment: Tourism as a trigger for green growth. *Tourism Economics, 21*, 183–204.

Marsiglio, S. (2016). On the carrying capacity and the optimal number of visitors in tourism destinations. *Tourism Economics, 23*, 632–646.

Mathieson, A., & Wall, G. (1982). *Tourism: Economic, physical and social impacts.* Longman.

Mino, K. (2001). Indeterminacy and endogenous growth with social constant returns. *Journal of Economic Theory, 97*, 203–222.

Mino, K. (1999). Non-separable utility function and indeterminacy of equilibrium in a model with human capital. *Economic Letters, 62*, 311–317.

Nishimura, K., & Venditti, A. (2002). Intersectoral externalities and indeterminacy. *Journal of Economic Theory, 105*, 140–157.

Park, H., & Philippopoulos, A. (2004). Indeterminacy and fiscal policies in a growing economy. *Journal of Economic Dynamics and Control, 28*, 645–660.

Pearce, D. G. (1989). *Tourist development* (2nd ed.). Longman.

Perez, R., & Ruiz, J. (2007). Global and local indeterminacy and optimal environmental public policies in an economy with public abatement activities. *Economic Modelling, 24*, 431–452.

Rybczynski, T. M. (1955). Factor endowment and relative commodity prices. *Economica, 22*, 336–341.

Schubert, S., Brida, J. G., & Risso, W. A. (2011). The impacts of international tourism demand on economic growth of small economies dependent on tourism. *Tourism Management, 32*, 377–385.

Solow, R. M. (1956). A contribution to the theory of economic growth. *The Quarterly Journal of Economics, 70*, 65–94.

Stolper, W. F., & Samuelson, P. A. (1941). Protection and real wages. *The Review of Economic Studies, 9*, 58–73.

Sun, D., & Walsh, D. (1998). Review of studies on environmental impacts of recreation and tourism in Australia. *Journal of Environmental Management, 53*, 323–338.

Tisdell, C. A. (2001). *Tourism economics, the environment and development.* Edward Elgar.

Weder, M. (2001). Indeterminacy in a small open economy Ramsay growth model. *Journal of Economic Theory, 98*, 339–356.

A Holistic and Concrete Approach to Sustainable Development

Sampriti Sarkar and Siddhartha Mitra

Abstract The mainstream definition of sustainable development, which was put forward by the World Commission on Environment and Development (WCED), emphasizes the meeting of needs of the present generation without compromising the welfare of future generations. However, it is very difficult to connect this definition to the objectives of sustainable development put forward by the WCED. In this paper, we put forward a definition, objectives and strategies such that these are linked by a tight relationship. We define sustainable development as that which over time results in a non-decreasing proportion of the population meeting its basic needs: food, shelter, clothing, energy and the ability of each individual to enhance his/her well-being through human capital formation. The policies recommended by us include both adequate nutrition for children, and education which stresses on the development of comprehension, deductive powers, intuition and imagination as well as emotional intelligence, thereby giving an opportunity to an increasing proportion of the population to enhance their well-being. An adequate level of nutrition is needed for students to benefit through increases in human capital. Similarly, we recommend stress on health services so that the productivity of the human capital stock of adult workers remains intact. In emphasizing the meeting of basic needs, we target the alleviation of poverty and environmental conservation. We also recommend facilitating the expansion of those occupations which are intensive in human capital through policies which stimulate the demand and supply side in relevant product and labour markets. This helps to economize on the use of physical and natural capital while meeting the basic needs of an increasing proportion of the population.

S. Sarkar
Michigan State University, East Lansing, MI, USA

S. Mitra (✉)
Department of Economics, Jadavpur University, Kolkata, India
e-mail: mitsid@yahoo.com

B. Chatterjee and A. K. Karmakar (eds.), *Analytical Issues in Growth & Structural Change, Macroeconomy, Security, and Sustainability of India's Economic Development*, India Studies in Business and Economics,
https://doi.org/10.1007/978-981-95-5242-9_14

1 Introduction

Sustainable development has evolved as a trending keyword in modern literature. The scope of this concept has long escaped the boundaries of social sciences and has emerged as a common link connecting various different fields including modern science and modern literature. It has brought together staunch supporters from groups of conflicting interest by providing a common ground to them which does not involve compromising on self-interest. The importance of sustainability was further recognised with the UNDP's identification, in 2015, of 17 sustainable development objectives as global goals targeted for achievement by 2030.

Given the phenomenal attention received by the concept in the last few decades, the question that keeps policymakers all around the world engaged is "How can sustainable development be incorporated in our development policies?" and "How can we move towards a sustainable development approach?" However, certain nuances of the concept remain ambiguous even today. This in turn has affected comprehensive designing of policy strategies incorporating the concept.

The term "sustainability" originates from the French verb "soutenir," which means "to hold up or support" (Geissdoerfer et al., 2017). Geissdoerfer et al. (2017) identify that the term was later adopted in the ecological context "as a principle of respecting the nature to regenerate itself." If taken literally, sustainable development means development that can be sustained. Since often the distinction between objectives and means of development is not well-defined, the definition of SD also becomes ambiguous. Depending upon the character of development, the nature of sustainability also varies. Using sustainable development and sustainable growth interchangeably would also be inappropriate since that involves assuming development to be synonymous with growth.

Any definition of development must connect the objectives flowing from it and the necessary means and methods devised to meet those objectives. Failure to do this might result in lack of clarity in designing of policy. Therefore, it is necessary to establish a tight relationship between the objectives and strategies flowing from the definition.

This chapter starts with a critical review of the mainstream definition of sustainable development. Section 2 starts with the origin of the concept, the place of the concept in modern literature and various dimensions and scope of the concept. It identifies and addresses the requirements for removal of ambiguity from the definition and suggests a fine-tuned definition in Sect. 3. The objective is not to refute the present definition, but to build on it by adding the necessary rigour. A close relationship is established between the objectives and strategies of the definition. A comprehensive approach to sustainable development is provided by connecting the objectives with the necessary strategies required to attain those objectives. Section 4 highlights the importance of poverty alleviation and environmental conservation for a sustainable livelihood approach. It further emphasizes on the formation of human capital through appropriate mix of policies. Three mutually reinforcing synergies are identified that can help promote the cause. This paper recognises the limitations imposed by the state of technology and communications in various countries and thus calls for a progressive transformation of the society and high investment in these areas as illustrated in Sect. 5. The paper also calls for a cooperative and balanced approach towards sustainable development which involves all the economic agents in this process of transformation. Finally, in conclusion (Sect. 6), we reiterate the need for a concrete and holistic approach towards sustainable development and emphasize the development of the essential requirements needed to achieve the objectives. We conclude with some recommendations for the future.

2 Sustainable Development—A Multidimensional Concept

The word sustainability originated in the ecological context in regard to non-renewable resources. However, the scope of the term has widened to cover social and economic perspectives as well. Sustainable development is thus a multidimensional concept with diverse objectives. This multi-disciplinary nature inevitably invites trade-off between different objectives. As Böhringer and Löschel (2005) aptly commented, "Accomplishing one objective frequently means backpedaling on another."

According to Dixon and Fallon (1989), SD can be interpreted using three dimensions—

1. As a purely physical concept for a single resource: Here the sustainability is limited to sustainability of renewable resources where the usage of the resource is not greater than the annual increase in the resource.
2. As a physical concept for a group of resources, or an ecosystem
3. As a socio-economic physical concept

Environmentalists Ehrlich and Commoner in their equation "I = PxAxT" link the Environmental impact (I) through a function to its three primary determinants-population (P); affluence, which is a proxy for consumption (A); and technologies (T) (Geissdoerfer et al., 2017). However, the simplicity of this approach does not do justice to the complex dynamics between the different factors.

Markulev and Long (2013) are quite right in emphasizing that sustainable development can only be achieved when each pillar on which the term rests is promoted in concert with the others. Before the mainstream definition of the concept came into vogue, there were many definitions which were being used actively in the literature. This often resulted in a break-down of communication among policymakers as the term "sustainable development" was seen to imply different objectives by various policymakers. With the introduction of the mainstream definition, the confusion regarding the meaning of this concept has been alleviated considerably. However, there is still a lack of clarity in regard to how the mainstream definition translates into the various objectives flowing from it. It is in this regard that this paper tries to make a significant contribution: it fine-tunes the mainstream definition to give it more clarity and then links the definition to clear objectives through well-defined strategies.

3 Mainstream Idea

Sustainable development as a concept was first placed in the international agenda in 1980, when the International Union for the Conservation of nature and Natural Resources (IUCN) presented the World Conservation Strategy (WCS). Sustainable development was acknowledged as the basic goal of development for the first time. However, the WCS definition was rendered wanting as it was deemed to be supply sided and assumed demand to be independent and autonomous, i.e. the demand for resources was assumed to remain constant (Lele, 1991).

3.1 Mainstream Definition

This definition of sustainable development was put forward by the Brundtland Report (1987), popularly known as "Our Common Future." According to the report, "Sustainable development is development that meets the needs of the present without compromising the ability of future generations to meet their own needs."

As illustrated by the Brundtland report (1987), this core definition is built on two major concepts—

- The concept of "needs," in particular the essential needs of the world's poor, to which overriding priority should be given
- The idea of limitations imposed by the state of technology and social organisation on the environment's ability to meet present and future needs.

3.2 Criticism of the Mainstream Definition and Objectives

Ever since its introduction, the definition has invited criticisms from various disciplines. Böhringer and Löschel (2005) criticise this definition because its normative nature does not take into account practicalities and because strategies to meet the objectives flowing out of this definition have not been spelled out by those formulating the definition.

The critical objectives that stem down from the mainstream definition as highlighted by the Brundtland report (1987) are—

1. Reviving growth.
2. Changing the quality of growth.
3. Meeting essential needs for jobs, food, energy, water and sanitation.

4. Ensuring a sustainable level of population.
5. Conserving and enhancing the resource base.
6. Reorienting technology and managing resource risk.
7. Merging environment and economics in decision-making.
8. Reorienting economic relations.
9. Making development more participatory.

While the definition is simple, no clear linkage between the definition and the stated objectives has been provided in the Brundtland Report. According to the Brundtland Report (1987), "Far from requiring the cessation of economic growth, it (the definition) recognizes that the problems of poverty and underdevelopment cannot be solved unless we have a new era of growth in which developing countries play a large role and reap large benefits." However, one should keep in mind that ceaseless economic growth can bring about environmental stress by using scarce resources more intensively. Moreover, mere economic growth is not enough to ensure long-term sustainability of various developmental indicators. In fact, high rates of economic growth and widespread poverty can and have been seen to co-exist. For instance, Dauda (2016) highlights the case of Nigeria which has recorded unabated poverty even in the presence of substantial economic growth.

As pointed out by Lele (1991), neoclassical economists denote increase in social welfare to be the objective behind development. Social welfare is then measured in terms of growth in economic output and they implicitly assume that this growth "does not necessarily mean growth in physical throughput of materials and energy." This view perpetuates the thought that there are no apparent contradictions between sustainability and development. The process of increase in social welfare can go on indefinitely. According to Lele (1991), "to achieve continuous increases in social welfare one actually needs to know what constitutes social welfare, in which case one might as well explicitly state these constituents to be the objectives of development."

In the definition, it was not elaborated what constitutes "needs," and how these needs will change and evolve over time. The needs of humans are unlimited, variable and non-decreasing over time. The lack of specification of needs in the definition gives rise to ambiguities in addressing the issue. As preferences and requirements change over time, the composition of needs is also subject to change. Therefore, without clearly defining the needs and how the composition of needs will change in future, any objective based on sustainable development will not be comprehensive.

The definition also implies change in our consumption pattern to accommodate choices that are less resource-intensive. However, it fails to clarify how these choices will become popular among policy makers.

The operational aspects of sustainable development were also not clearly brought out. In emphasizing needs, the worry was that society may be enjoying high and increasing welfare at the expense of running down its capital, particularly its natural capital. To address this issue, economists have turned to looking at changes in the stock of wealth, where weal this defined to include natural, human, physical and social capital. If society's wealth per capita is declining, then it is leaving future generations with less with which to sustain present levels of consumption (Markandya, 2001). These aspects reflect a mixing of goals and means.

3.3 Fine Tuning the Definition

To get rid of the ambiguity in the definition, it is necessary to fine tune it by addressing the required changes.

1. First, it is necessary to specify what constitutes "needs." Complete specification of needs and how those needs will change over time is necessary to avoid any ambiguity. The lack of specification of "needs" leads Nayar (1994) to point out that "The 'need' with reference to sustainable development is affluence rather than basic, or opulence rather than squalor. Because, when basic needs become an integral component of a developmental model, the question of unsustainability does not arise."

2. The idea of growth as an integral part of sustainable development needs to be dropped and instead there should be a higher emphasis on specific needs. As reflected by the popular American author Edward Abbey, "Growth for the sake of growth is the ideology of the cancer cell." Ceaseless growth does not need to be an integral part of sustainable development. It should be noted that there are limits to material consumption. To achieve the objectives above, it is necessary to change the nature of our material consumption. Low resource-intensive goods should be consumed in higher quantities in place of high resource-intensive goods. Consumption of resources in excess of basic minimum needs is sustainable only when consumption standards have regard for long-term sustainability. It requires encouragement of values and views that encourage sustainable consumption standards.

3. The fact that the ability to meet finite number of needs for all future generations involves environmental conservation should be identified and utilised. Along with intergenerational equity aspect, intragenerational aspect should also be highlighted so that an individual is capable of maintaining at least the same level of well-being throughout his lifespan. As defined by Geissdoerfer and rest (2017), the term sustainability can be framed as "the balanced and systemic integration of intra and intergenerational economic, social, and environmental performance." This requires a shift in the preference of consumption towards less resource-intensive goods and services.

4. The importance of environmental conservation should be promoted. Inherent trade-off between economic growth and ecological stress should be recognised and environmental conservation should be of prime importance as opposed to ceaseless economic growth. Thus, an increase in productive potential, transformation in the nature of growth and consumption demand and provision of equitable opportunities for all are imperative to attain the goal of sustainable development. As the World Economic and Social Survey (2013) emphasize, "Achieving sustainable development will require global actions to deliver on the legitimate aspiration towards further economic and social progress, requiring growth and employment and, at the same time, strengthening environmental protection."

5. There should be an endeavour to suggest a definition and objectives/needs such that the ambiguity in links between the definition and specified objectives is removed.

6. It is also essential to specify the broad contours of a strategy that can achieve sustainable development as specified. Nayar (1994) highlights that the concept does not give a well-defined strategy required to attain the objectives and thus "remains an accepted philosophical approach but in vacuum."

3.4 *Fine-Tuning the Mainstream Definition to Arrive at a Robust Alternative*

Keeping in mind the above points, this paper provides an alternative to the mainstream definition which however retains the strengths of the latter:

> Augmenting the satisfaction of essential needs of the present generation and the ability of future generations to meet their essential needs

To understand the definition properly, we need to first address what is meant by essential needs. Satisfaction of human needs is one of the primary goals of development. Essential needs consist of the following:

- Adequate and nourishing food, clothing, shelter, energy, water, livelihood and sanitation for the present generation as well as future generations.
- Provision of access to ways and means to all individuals in present and future generations so that each individual can improve his/her well-being and be insured against significant declines in well-being.
- The above implies that poverty in satisfaction of essential needs as well as in opportunity to improve well-being should go down over time.

It should be noted that the above reflects the basic needs of the poor and beyond their basic needs these people have legitimate aspirations for an improved quality of life.

3.5 *A Holistic and Concrete Approach*

Over time, a non-decreasing proportion of the population should be able to meet their basic needs. This requires capital to be non-decreasing. In this context, the distinction between strong and weak sustainability becomes important. Weak sustainability assumes that human or manufactured capital is substitutable with natural capital and that both can have the same effect in promoting well-being. According to proponents of weak sustainability, only the aggregate level of capital needs to be maintained for sustaining the future demands. Such a view encourages pecuniary motives without taking any account of environmental degradation. Strong sustainability on the other hand demonstrates that both are complements rather than substitutes. Interaction between the two determines the capacity of the ecosystem.

GDP growth cannot be taken as an indicator of attainment of the objective of sustainable development. It takes into account marketed goods and services and not services of natural capital. Moreover, in the new definition, unbridled growth is dropped as an objective, reducing the importance of GDP. Given that the nature of our preferences and demand are required to change towards less-resource-intensive goods, the idea of measurable economic growth, based on a consumption basket that does not vary over time, loses its importance. Therefore, long-term growth in GDP as an objective becomes vacuous.

According to the strategy implied by the alternative definition, there should be a global consensus to move towards a sustainable livelihood approach, i.e. the proportion of poor able to get a basic livelihood meeting all the essential needs should be non-decreasing. Poverty (income or multidimensional) alleviation and environmental conservation are of fundamental importance for a sustainable livelihood approach. There are two standards that needs to be pursued in this regard—

1. Conserve natural capital unless the foregone benefits are huge
2. Precautionary principle: Avoid degradation if the probability of irreversibility is high

Conserving natural capital not only encourages use of renewable resources, but also helps promote food security and sustainable livelihood. The objectives should be based on the following operating principles:

1. Checking market factors: It is necessary to gauge and inspect the market factors on both the production side and the consumption side.
2. Regeneration rate should be greater than withdrawal rate for exhaustible resources to ensure that the resources can be sustained in future.
3. Technological change to be guided by indicative planning towards switching from non-renewable to renewable resources.

4 Towards a Sustainable Livelihood Approach

A society can compromise its ability to meet the basic needs of its people in the future in many ways such as overexploitation of resources, unequal access to existing resources, social conflicts leading to marginalisation of certain sections of the society and so on. Large sections of the population may be subjected to decrease in well-being through ill-designed developmental policies. The role of institutions and well-directed policies become highly significant in this regard. The Brundtland report (1987) highlights the statement of a speaker from WCED Public Hearing in this context: "if the desert is growing, forest disappearing, malnutrition increasing, and people in urban areas living in very bad conditions, it is not because we are lacking resources but the kind of policy implemented by our rulers, by the elite group."

To move towards a sustainable livelihood approach, fundamental changes in the outlook of development policies are required. There are often a number of threats, other than environmental problems, that hinders the provisioning of essential needs for the future generations, such as political, social, economic, technological and cultural constraints. The "triple bottom line" construct introduced by Elkington in 1997 gives the three pillars of sustainability—people, profit and planet (Geissdoerfer et al., 2017). It highlights the balanced integration of the three factors—environment, economy and the society. These factors act "as inter-dependent and mutually reinforcing pillars." Given the inherent trade-off between the different objectives of our definition, certain factors can mutually reinforce each other to promote the common objective of sustainability. Such mutually reinforcing synergies should be incorporated in our policies. We discuss three such strategies here.

4.1 Synergy 1: Nutrition/Health and Learning

Through the development process people get the benefits of development policies and that is reflected in their health, education and employment. In poorest countries, policies which accelerate income growth and reduce poverty make it possible for a large cluster of people to afford better diets, healthier living condition and better health care. Expanding educational opportunities bring people into the world of information and knowledge together and help them understand the importance of health and nutrition. World Bank identified this relationship as a "virtuous cycle" in which reduction of poverty and improvement in health reinforce each other (Akhter & Wohab, 2006).

Adequate nutrition has favourable impact on the learning potential of an individual. Alderman (2005) identifies six distinct economic benefits from improved nutrition: (a) Reduced infant and child mortality; (b) Reduced cost of health care for neonates, infants and children; (c) Productivity gain from reduced stunting; (d) Productivity gain from increased ability; (e) Reduction in costs of chronic diseases; (f) Intergenerational benefits through improved health.

Balanced nutrition can help to increase the learning capacity of the brain and improve cognitive power. Access to education along with good health will help people to learn, practice and improve their well-being in many ways. The process of learning in itself can promote well-being. Learning along with proper health and nutrition can provide ways and means to improve present and future well-being through (a) increase in the opportunities for productive employment and (b) enhancement of the ability to innovate. The ability to innovate helps in producing a sense of well-being enhancing achievement which in turn increases the social as well as individual productivity. (c) Learning also makes one conscious about one's surroundings. With increased provision for learning, there will be generation of awareness regarding environmental conservation. Curricula should also consist of ways and means for instilling emotional intelligence in humans so that they blend well with each other while enhancing their potential for invention and innovation. This will improve well-being for all.

The negative effects of malnutrition have also been documented in many studies. Malnutrition retards physical growth. If physical growth is suppressed for a long time in early years of development, it may produce irreversible mental and emotional changes (Eichenwald & Crooke Fry, 1969). Pertz and Putnam (1982) cites several studies to conclude that "poorly nourished children are less likely to achieve their academic potential than are their well-nourished peers." They further illustrate that there can be direct and indirect relationships between nutrition and learning. Nutrition from diet affects the body's capacity to learn, which can be considered as an indirect relationship. Nutrition through diet also affects the central nervous system which in turn affects learning. This can be considered as the direct effect.

Additionally, several studies demonstrate how malnutrition can negatively affect the development of cognitive abilities. For instance, Food and Agriculture Organization of the United Nations (2013) highlights that iron deficiency (anaemia) impacts negatively on cognitive development and academic performance in school-age children. World Economic and Social Survey (2013) reports that Vitamin A is a leading cause of blindness and corneal damage and "in developing countries, 163 million children were estimated to be vitamin A-deficient, with a prevalence of more than 30 per cent in 2007, down from approximately 36 per cent in 1990." However, even with significant evidence of the negative outcomes of poor nutrition, many governments have not assigned sufficient priority to this issue in their development agenda.

Even though economic growth has been seen to reduce malnutrition, it should not be seen as the sole determinant of improved nutrition. As highlighted by Alderman (2005), economic growth clearly reduces malnutrition as evidenced by various cross-country studies, but the percentage decline in malnutrition has been found to be half the rate at which GNP per capita grows. This calls for active intervention from the government in the form of well-designed policies recognising the synergy between nutrition and learning.

To get the right combination of both the inputs in their policies, the planner can experiment with nutrition and income supplements for the poor. Nutrition supplements can produce a direct positive leakage free impact on human capital formation as opposed to cash supplements, which are subject to leakages through alternative channels. However, though cash supplements have leakages, there can be additional benefits associated with it such as more security and better self-esteem that have been shown to have positive impact on the brain. Policymakers can also introduce a conditional cash transfer (CCT) programme which transfers cash to targeted households that have demonstrated their participation in health, nutrition and educational services. As illustrated by Adato and Hoddinott (2008), many of these CCT programmes, often called "a magic bullet in development," have been successful in improving the condition of human capital. Therefore, extensive research is required to arrive at the right mix of income and nutrition supplements.

For a child to learn, he/she needs proper nutrition and health. Learning itself augments our capacity to seek better nutrition and employment. Better learning makes one more conscious and thus allows him/her to adopt better health practices and better nutrition. To leverage the benefits of this synergy between nutrition and learning, it is necessary to improve infrastructure that facilitates the atmosphere for learning. There should be higher emphasis on educational policies that underscore the development of emotional intelligence as well as imaginative powers. This will allow the beneficiaries to tackle practicalities of the world and also design solutions through innovation. Further it gives an increasing proportion of population an opportunity to increase their welfare. Alvi and Ahmed (2014), in their cross-country study of 37 countries examining the impact of health and education on Total Factor Productivity (TFP), found significant impact of both the factors on TFP. Based on their findings, they reiterate "the need for improving health and education of the general populace to ensure sustainable growth and economic development."

4.2 Synergy 2: Health/Nutrition and Productivity of Human Capital Stock

The capacity and quality of work done by an individual depends directly on health and nutrition. It is one of the most important components of building productive human resources. Formation of productive human capital can improve well-being of the workers since they will get more employment opportunities owing to their higher productivity. Thus, generation of human capital allows people to access appropriate employment and income, which in turn, helps them to maintain good health, nutrition and also enhances poverty alleviation. Several studies have confirmed the strong linkages between nutrition and labour productivity. Strauss (1986) in his analysis of household data from Sierra Leone found significant effect of nutrition on farm level productivity. Croppenstedt and Muller (2000) in their study of the impact of nutrition on productivity of farm workers in Ethiopia found that elasticity of labour productivity with respect to nutritional status is quite strong. These studies lend support to the significant role of nutrition in developing productive human capital. However, it should be noted that freedom from hunger is a basic need and a human right. Therefore, all these should be promoted in addition to policies eradicating hunger.

Impact of health and nutrition on economic activities of workers can be understood in three different phases; current working capacity of workers, children's working capacity in future, intergenerational working capacity, particularly for female labour force (Akhter & Wohab, 2006). Workers with better nutrition will have higher strength and ability to concentrate on the job. It also decreases the probability of getting sick and thus reduces absence from work. Ill health and malnutrition decrease the probability of participation in the labour force and the zeal of actively seeking jobs. This becomes more arduous for daily wage labourers. Better productivity not only adds to a country's economic development, it adds to the well-being of the individuals as well. A balanced nutrition ensures that human capital is able to achieve or approach its potential productivity through adequate generation of human energy and development of immunity.

As pointed out by Akhter and Wohab (2006), apart from the lifelong effect, ill health and malnutrition (particularly of female) also produce intergenerational incapability in regard to work, since malnourished and ill health mothers are more likely to produce malnourished children. Their study in this context shows the effect of mothers' ill health on children in Bangladesh, where 33% anaemic mothers, among others, contributed to the 47% anaemic children. This reflects that the noxious effect of ill health on human productivity extends from generation to generation.

Ill health and nutrition also affect learning and education adversely by hindering the cognitive development of children. Healthier people are able to transform their energy into productivity, both mental and physical, more efficiently than people with ill health and malnutrition. Good health services ensure that the flow of human capital services to the production process is not interrupted. Strict emphasis should be given to preventive health measures since it prevents loss of productivity and is also more economical. Preventive measures may include sanitation facilities, cheap water treatment, popularisation and promotion of healthy practices such as cleanliness and washing of hands before eating. Some endemic disease can have disastrous effect on human resources. For example, AIDS affect adults in most of their productive lives. In some sub-Saharan countries, particularly in Zambia, Zimbabwe, Rwanda and Ethiopia, the percentage of people infected by HIV are 33.8, 47.4, 17.9 and 16.4 respectively (Akhter & Wohab, 2006). Strict preventive measures and increased awareness can alter this situation drastically.

Note that a higher productivity of human capital leads to higher real incomes and thus helps in the purchase of ways and means benefitting health and nutrition which in turn provides for improved human capital formation subsequently.

4.3 Synergy 3: Poverty Alleviation and Environmental Conservation

There are limitations imposed by the technological feasibility and social structure on the environment's ability to meet present and future requirements. Moreover, environmental challenges are emerging at an unprecedented rate owing to the consequences of past human activities. Therefore, it becomes necessary to conserve our resources.

In many countries there has been a failure to lift a significant proportion of the population out of poverty. Poverty and environmental stress are interlinked: avicious downward spiralis characterized by the poor people degrading the environment and the degraded environment increasing the incidence of poverty. As illustrated in the following example by Basiago (1999), "If a man in a rural area lacks a job, he is likely to be poor and disenfranchised. If he is poor and disenfranchised, he has an incentive to engage in practices that harm ecology, for example, by cutting down trees for firewood to cook his meals and warm his home." "The cumulative effect of these changes is so far-reaching as to make poverty itself a major global scourge" (World Commission on Environment and Development, 1987). On the other hand, growing demand for scarce resources due to increase in living standards of the relatively affluent has further aggravated the pressure on the environment. Therefore, it must be remembered that growth of incomes might also threaten the environment by increasing the demand for fuels and processed products with significant resource intensity.

Another important term that is gaining traction in this context is the term "Circular Economy." Circularity of an economic system assumes the economy to be a "closed loop" and advocates minimisation of wastes. Circular economy as defined by Geissdoerfer et al. (2017) is "a regenerative system in which resource input and waste, emission, and energy leakages are minimised by slowing, closing, and narrowing material and energy loops. This can be achieved through long-lasting design, maintenance, repair, reuse, remanufacturing, refurbishing, and recycling." The concept of a circular economy not only economises the use of resources but also promotes conservation of the environment. Therefore, integrating such ideas into policymaking will help the cause of sustainable development. Pressure on existing resources increases when there is lack of alternatives. So, developmental policies must introduce alternate sustainable career options particularly in areas under ecological stress. Conservation of agricultural resources are of utmost importance to meet the needs of a growing population. Improvement in productivity and productive capacity is required to deal with this. Depletion of resources should not be greater than the rate of regeneration. The capacity of land devoted to agricultural and forestry should be scientifically assessed. The rate of usage of water, agrochemicals and pesticides should be brought down through other alternatives. Conscious economic policy based on ecological reality is needed. Air and water pollution should be controlled to preserve the quality of air and water. For all this to happen, strong technological innovation capacity needs to be built. Technology needs to be directed more towards solving environmental conservation issues.

Efforts and policies that induce conservation of the environment through promotion of employment opportunities involving less intensive use of resources are required. Working on the supply side is not enough. There should be policies and measures to work on the demand side as well. The demand side is mainly concerned with the decrease in demand for high resource-intensive goods.

It should be noted that ecological and economic prosperity are not always at opposing ends. Policies conserving agricultural land and protecting forest increases the long-term scope for agricultural development, which in turn helps in prosperity of the economy. Hence poverty alleviation and economic betterment should mainly be associated with a process such that demand for resource-intensive products (heavy furniture, sugar, fuels for transport) declines. This can be achieved through higher taxation of such products and through change in preferences induced by enhancement of environmental awareness, especially among the youth. In Thaler and Sunstein (2008) it is discussed as to how a "nudge" in the right direction can promote behavioural changes reflected in choices that are favourable for the individual citizens as well as for the society. Policymakers can experiment with such aspects in their policies to solve the demand side of the issue through elicitation of moral consciousness. Productive human capital generation through soft skill development and vocational training is essential. This will qualify individuals for soft skill based human capital-intensive jobs which make low use of natural or physical capital, such as tourism, education, hospitality and health care.

As livelihood is identified as an essential need, sustainable and less resource-intensive work opportunities need to be created to ensure that poor households can increase their well-being. Different environmental regulations that promote efficiency and innovation can also be introduced. According to Porter and Linde (1995) hypothesis, the cost of compliance with strict environmental regulations can be offset by the increase in innovations that are triggered (Kriechel & Ziesemer, 2009). Kriechel and Ziesemer (2009) in their empirical analysis found that "Porter hypothesis will hold even for profit-maximizing firms under multiple market imperfections such as imperfect competition, X-inefficiency, and agency costs." There is no one successful formula for achieving sustainable development. Based on the nature of the country and its socio-economic aspects, policymakers need to try out different combinations of strategies with the aim of promoting poverty alleviation and environmental conservation.

5 Essential Requirements

5.1 Development of Physical Infrastructure and ICT

To facilitate the implementation of the policies discussed above, it is essential that proper development of physical infrastructure and ICT takes place. Though, some of the policies for developing infrastructure and ICT might be heavily resource-intensive, it should be kept in mind that it facilitates uses of less resource-intensive methods of production. It provides quick physical access to urban centres and places of work for employment. This encourages people to look more actively for employment in different urban areas. It effectively minimises barriers of transportation and communication. With the right infrastructure and policies in place, people begin to depend less on the natural resource base for generation of incomes. Even here there is a scope for resource conservation through taxing automobile purchases and fuel consumption while developing better public transport systems; using online systems of education and so on. Investment in ICT infrastructure, such as broadband rollout, is an important step to facilitate economic development, social integration and developmental policies.

Such investment in physical infrastructure must be complemented by initiatives to develop the skills that will be needed to extract value from this investment. Training and learning programmes, including certification schemes, must be a key component of initiatives that will assist in maximising the potential offered by enhanced broadband provision in rural areas (ECDL Foundation, 2009). Vocational education and training programmes can be introduced for people lacking formal education. Such policies are explicit drivers of productivity, innovation and social inclusion. ICT can also be used "to inform smallholders about new farming techniques and market prices (World Bank, 2008a), as well as to improve livestock traceability (Deloitte, 2012), maximizing output, while minimizing negative impacts on the environment" (World Economic & Social Survey, 2013). The accumulation of knowledge and technological development can lead to greater carrying capacity of the resource base. There are limits to this as well, but, before such limiting point is reached, sustainability requires more equitable access to consumption, opportunities and limited resource. Investment in research and development (R&D) can play a significant role in regard to better adaptation of existing technologies. A broader rural development strategy should also be formulated that can incorporate infrastructural linkages to ease the rural–urban linkages.

5.2 A General Equilibrium Approach Towards Sustainability

The goal towards sustainability requires the ability to meet human needs while reducing poverty and hunger and preserving our environmental balance system. The approach to this goal is constrained by the amount of resources available. Therefore, a mix of both demand and supply side policies are required to achieve the goals. There should be investment in regard to health, education and environmental conservation policies. This will help in creating productive human capital. At the same time, a greater number of less resource-intensive jobs should be created to absorb the surplus human capital. Thus, the approach should be a balanced one. The move should be towards a general equilibrium framework.

The focus should also be on poverty alleviation and equal opportunities for all by reducing social conflicts. Basiago (1999) highlights how the state of Kerala in India has become resource efficient and increased the quality of life. He illustrates that, "Kerala strives for low rates of reproduction and consumption, manufactures only that which is necessary and does so in a deliberate manner, and has tried to eliminate discrimination based upon race, caste, religion, and gender." Thus, through proper planning and strong political will, it is possible to increase the well-being of the society.

The capacity for technological innovation should be enhanced. Public policy should ensure through incentives and penalties that commercial organisations account for environmental factors in their decision-making. A balanced path is required towards sustainable development. Along with the supply, the nature of our demand also needs to change. With increased international interaction and technological knowhow, the complexity of our requirements also has increased greatly. We have to be careful of the thresholds limits to maintain the natural balance of the system.

Thus, essentially a general equilibrium approach to sustainable development should be promoted. Less resource-intensive ways of life have to be encouraged through a simultaneous boost to human capital generation and entrepreneurship. For example, promotion of tourism would require development of human capital (tourist guides and hotel management specialists), more entrepreneurship (subsidies, loans and facilitation of information for budding hoteliers and transporters); provision of better information regarding tourist sites to potential domestic and foreign tourists; and lowering of transaction costs to undertake tourism. As various low resource intensity sectors are developed simultaneously, the necessary and simultaneous generation of demand and supply is achieved.

6 Conclusion

Sustainable development requires that problems of the poorest strata of population are identified. Sustainable policies ensuring effective, efficient and equitable use of resources and economic growth without massive release of untoward environmental pollutants is required. A sustainable rate of growth needs to be maintained to attain the objectives. Changing the quality of growth requires changing our approach to development efforts to take account of all of their effects.

With globalisation and decreased international hegemony of developed countries, the consequences of national decisions of both developed and developing countries have far-reaching implications across all the nations. Therefore, an international consensus should be arrived at in regard to environmental and economic policies to address the global target of sustainable development. Even if the activities leading to environmental stress and dangers are concentrated in some countries, the risks and consequences of such actions are shared by all. Thus, it is in the common interest of every nation in the world to prioritize the design of such actions through mutual cooperation and interaction.

A sustainable society supports the meeting of basic needs with the extensive opportunity to aspire satisfactorily to a better life in the present and the future (Chukwuma, 1996). To achieve sustainability, developmental action must be supported with available resource in the society. According to the Brundtland report (1987), the pursuit of sustainable development requires:

- A political system that secures effective citizen participation in decision-making,
- An economic system that is able to generate surpluses and technical knowledge on a self-reliant and sustained basis,
- A social system that provides for solutions for the tensions arising from disharmonious development.
- A production system that respects the obligation to preserve the ecological base for development,
- A technological system that can search continuously for new solutions.
- An international system that fosters sustainable patterns of trade and finance. and

- An administrative system that is flexible and has the capacity for self-correction.

The current model of production and consumption of goods and services with higher emphasis on present consumption is unsustainable. The progress we have made so far has been uneven and inadequate. This should be recognised by policymakers as well as consumers all around the world. A progressive ecological, social and economic transformation requires participation from all corners of the society. To move towards a sustainable livelihood approach, we must first acknowledge the mistakes made so far and realise that a well thought out move will benefit us all. All the nations should put aside their differences and join hands in promoting this objective.

There should be an inclusive approach. All sections of the society should be involved in the process. Poverty alleviation, meeting the essential needs of the poor and more equitable access to resources is a precondition for the poor people to actively participate in this transformation. As highlighted by the book Sustainable Development Challenges (2013) published by United Nations, "Inequality undermines prospects for inclusive growth, equal access to social protection, and broader sustainable development by negatively affecting aggregate demand, investments in health care and education, and socio-political and economic stability." The literature emphasizes that protecting the rights of the local people to access and control their local resources in an increasingly competitive global economy is of primary importance in achieving sustainable development. In this context, the role of NGOs can be of paramount importance. NGOs can help in integrating global and local dimensions that are more difficult to implement for international agencies. There should be a conscious effort and commitment to move towards a better future. The conceptual clarity of sustainable development and a tightly bounded relationship between its objectives and strategies will help policymakers to design a new approach to development that will increase the general welfare of the society.

References

Adato, M., & Hoddinott, J. (2008). Conditional cash transfer programs: A "magic bullet" for reducing poverty? *The poorest and hungry* (pp. 299–306). International Food Policy Research Institute.

Akhter, S., & Wohab, M. A. (2006). Health, nutrition and human resource development: A crucial link. *BRAC University Journal, III*(2), 125–132.

Alderman, H. (2005, November). Linkages between poverty reduction strategies and child nutrition: An Asian perspective. *Economic and Political Weekly, 40*(46), 4837–4842. https://www.jstor.org/stable/4417394

Alvi, S., & Ahmed, A. M. (2014). Analyzing the impact of health and education on total factor productivity: A panel data approach. *Indian Economic Review, 49*(1), 109–123. http://www.jstor.org/stable/24583409

Basiago, A. (1999). Economic, social, and environmental sustainability in development theory and urban planning practice. *The Environmentalist*, 145–161.

Böhringer, C., & Löschel, A. (2005, August). *Measuring sustainable development: The use of computable general equilibrium models* (ZEW—Centre for European Economic Research Discussion, Paper No. 04-014). https://doi.org/10.2139/ssrn.581381

Chukwuma, C. (1996, December 1). Perspectives for a sustainable society. *Environmental Management and Health, 7*(5), 5–20. https://doi.org/10.1108/09566169610130377

Croppenstedt, A., & Muller, C. (2000, April). The impact of farmers' health and nutritional status on their productivity and efficiency: Evidence from Ethiopia. *Economic Development and Cultural Change, 48*(3), 475–502. http://www.jstor.org/stable/10.1086/452607?origin=JSTOR-pdf

Dauda, R. S. (2016). Poverty and economic growth in Nigeria: Issues. *Journal of Poverty, 21*(1), 61–79. https://doi.org/10.1080/10875549.2016.1141383

Dixon, J. A., & Fallon, L. A. (1989). The concept of sustainability: Origins, extensions and usefulness for policy. *Society and Natural Resources, 2*(1), 73–84. https://doi.org/10.1080/08941928909380675

ECDL Foundation. (2009). *Maximising the impact of ICT infrastructure investment*. ECDL Foundation.

Eichenwald, H. F., & Crooke Fry, P. (1969, February 14). Nutrition and learning. *American Association for the Advancement of Science, 163*(3868), 644–648. https://www.jstor.org/stable/1726319

Geissdoerfer, M., Savaget, P., Bocken, N., & Hultink, E. (2017). The circular economy—A new sustainability paradigm? *Journal of Cleaner Production*, 757–768.

Kriechel, B., & Ziesemer, T. (2009, April). The environmental Porter hypothesis: Theory, evidence, and a model of timing of adoption. *Economics of Innovation and New Technology, 18*(3), 267–294. https://doi.org/10.1080/10438590801943235

Lele, S. (1991). Sustainable development: A critical review. *World Development, 19*, 607–621. https://doi.org/10.1016/0305-750X(91)90197-P

Markandya, A. (2001). *Poverty alleviation and sustainable development*. https://www.iisd.org/pdf/pe_markandya_presentation.pdf

Markulev, A., & Long, A. (2013). *On sustainability: An economic approach*. Productivity Commission.

Nayar, K. (1994, May 28). Politics of 'sustainable development'. *Economic & Political Weekly, 29*(22), 1327–1329. http://www.jstor.org/stable/4401259

Pertz, D. L., & Putnam, L. R. (1982, March). An examination of the relationship between nutrition and learning. *The Reading Teacher, 35*(6), 702–706. https://www.jstor.org/stable/20198075

Porter, M. E., & Linde, C. V. D. (1995). Toward a new conception of the environment-competitiveness relationship. *Journal of economic perspectives, 9*(4), 97–118.

Strauss, J. (1986). Does better nutrition raise farm productivity? *Journal of Political Economy, 94*(2), 297–320. https://doi.org/10.1086/261375

Thaler, R. H., & Sunstein, C. R. (2008). *Nudge: Improving decisions about health, wealth, and happiness*. Yale University Press.

UN, Department of Economic and Social Affairs. (2013). *World economic and social survey 2013: Sustainable development challenges*. E/2013/50/Rev. 1, ST/ESA/344.

World Commission on Environment and Development (WCED). (1987). *Our common future*. Oxford University Press.

World Economic and Social Survey. (2013). *World economic and social survey—Sustainable development challenges*. Department of Economic and Social Affairs. United Nations.

Access to Irrigation and Socioeconomic Status of Farm Households: A Study in a Saline Zone in India

Sebak Kumar Jana and Shailendra N. Gajanan

Abstract The paper empirically investigates whether adequate access to irrigation improves the Socioeconomic Status (SES) of poor and marginal rural farmers. The study is based on primary data from a sample of 440 rural farming households located in a saline zone, in the state of West Bengal, India. First, a multidimensional index of SES for each household has been derived, using factor analysis. Then the relationship has been characterized between the SES-index and various independent variables that affect livelihood, including access to irrigation, through quantile regression analysis. Quantile regression results show that while access to irrigation does improve SES, the marginal effects of access differ substantially between low-versus-high income quantiles, and that access to irrigation has larger marginal effects at the lower end of the distribution. The results are useful for targeted irrigation-intervention policy programs.

Keywords Irrigation · Water body · Socioeconomic status index · PCA · Quantile regression

1 Introduction

Nearly 60% of India's cultivation depends upon rains, and covers majority of rural poor and marginal farmers. Naturally, adverse climatic conditions severely affect the livelihood of rural farm households (Palanisami et al., 2010). There is substantial research consensus in Development and Agriculture Economics that irrigation-intervention programs have a positive impact on rural standard of living (Jana and

S. K. Jana (✉)
Department of Economics, Vidyasagar University, Midnapore, West Bengal, India
e-mail: sebakjana@mail.vidyasagar.ac.in

S. N. Gajanan
Division of Business Management, University of Pittsburgh, Bradford, PA, USA
e-mail: Sng1@pitt.edu

B. Chatterjee and A. K. Karmakar (eds.), *Analytical Issues in Growth & Structural Change, Macroeconomy, Security, and Sustainability of India's Economic Development*, India Studies in Business and Economics,
https://doi.org/10.1007/978-981-95-5242-9_15

Tamang, 2023). Access to irrigation has positive externalities on nutrition, health, income, and women empowerment, as shown by Domenech and Ringler (2013) and Domènech (2015) for Africa. Similar results are also obtained by Mekonnen et al. (2016) and Jehangir et al. (2003) for Pakistan, and by Nkhata (2014) for Malawi. Agarwal et al (2001), and Vaidyanathan (2006) also establish the link between access to irrigation and Socioeconomic Status (SES), for India. Further, Shah and Singh (2004), Chand et al. (2011), Bhattarai and Narayanamoorthy (2003), Saleth et al. (2003), Hussain and Hanjra (2004) are examples of supporting empirical evidence that links rural poverty alleviation to irrigation in India. Bell et al. (2015) demonstrate that access to irrigation has the greatest influence on boro rice yield during the dry season, particularly for the coastal south of Bangladesh. Similar observations are also made by Ricart and Gandolfi (2017) for Italy, and Baskaran et al (2013) for New Zealand. Adequate access to irrigation hinges crucially on the location and availability of sufficient water bodies as noted by ADB (2006), Narayanamoorthy and Deshpande (2005), Tiwary (2009) and Pant and Verma (2010). As Pandey and Suganthi (2015), Awasthi (2014), Asthana and Shukla (2014), Lise et al. (2019) point out, the under-provision of waterbodies is of particular concern, as in the case of India, where agriculture underperforms frequently. Consequently, the issue of access to alternative irrigation systems for farmers' livelihood becomes a key concern for irrigation-intervention programs, particularly, if much of farming is constrained within saline zones. Previous researchers like Jana (2016), Jana et al. (2018), and Mandal et al. (2005) have noted the presence of saline zones in the farm sector of India, and have listed coping strategies through optimal water management.

The present chapter attempts to find whether the access to irrigation help poor and marginal rural farmers improve their Socioeconomic Status (SES). The main objective of the paper is to empirically verify the link between access to irrigation and SES to a sample of 440 rural farming households located in a saline zone, in the state of West Bengal, India. Our primary sample data is ideally suited for this purpose, because we have information on two types of households, those with and those without access to irrigation.

Based on the above considerations, and following Acharya (2006), livelihood has been defined here as adequate stock and flow of food and cash with an individual or a family to meet its basic needs. We use this broad definition to construct a multidimensional SES-index, for farmers residing in a saline zone, and characterize the behavior of SES-index, based on access to irrigation, and other independent variables. We have selected the district of South 24-Parganas (also called South 24-Pgs) in the saline zone in the state of West Bengal, India, where surface irrigation consisting of irrigation from tanks and water bodies is predominant. The district is located in the mature tract of lower Ganga sub-basin, where rice, wheat, and pulses are the major crops. In order to test the link between access to irrigation and SES, we first derive a multidimensional index of SES for each household, using factor analysis. We then characterize the relationship between the SES-index to various independent variables that affect livelihood, including access to irrigation, through quantile regression analysis.

The rest of the chapter is organized as follows. Section 2 presents the background of the research, details of the current study area and the sample survey methodology. Section 3.1 presents the details of computing an index of Socioeconomic Status (SES), using factor analysis. Section 3.2 investigates the characteristics of the index based on quantile regression analysis, where we demonstrate the differential effects of income and access to irrigation. Section 8 provides a brief summary and conclusions.

2 Materials and Methods

2.1 Data and Study Area

Table 1 presents the villages in the district of South 24-Pgs in the state of West Bengal in India from which the water bodies have been selected. Out of the 22 water bodies surveyed, the number of tanks is 10 and the number of *khals* (elongated water bodies) is 12. The renovation works for the selected 19 schemes under National Project were carried out in 2006–07. The rest 3 projects under survey were renovated under NABARD, RIDF scheme during 2013–14.

The Fig. 1 shows the study area.

2.2 Methodology

We first develop an index of Socioeconomic Status (SES), derived from primary data collected for many factors that affect livelihood, such as income, education, housing, family size, and most importantly access to irrigation. Various socioeconomic and demographic features have been included to ensure a multidimensional approach in understanding socioeconomic differentiation, reflecting the patterned unequal distribution of resources, opportunities, advantages, and power among subgroups of a population. Based on extant research, 32 theoretically important and policy-relevant variables are chosen for the present study. Multidimensional index construction has been used by various authors like Krishnan (2010), Fukuda et al. (2007), Antony and Rao (2007), Vyas and Kumaranayake (2006), Harvard et al. (2008), Messer et al. (2008), Pampalon et al. (2009), Singh et al. (2002) and Zagorski (1985).

In the first part of our estimation, we apply factor analysis to identify the important variables that determine socioeconomic status, so as to reduce the dimensionality of the problem. Factor analysis enables us to obtain the reduced subset of the important variables, because it exploits the inherent pattern in the correlation between these variables. Additionally, we also use the relevant factors to derive a composite index of socioeconomic status (SES).

Factor analysis is a useful technique to reduce the dimensionality of the problem, and allows us to express each variable as a linear combination of uncorrelated factors.

Table 1 Survey data: selected blocks, gram panchayats, villages, water bodies, and household-types in the district of south 24-Pgs in the state of West Bengal

Blocks selected	Number of *Gram Panchayats*[a]	Number of villages[b]	Number of water bodies selected	Renovation scheme[c]	Households with irrigation (treated)[d]	Households without irrigation (untreated)
Sagar	5	5	Tank:6, *Khal*:1	NP: 6 & RIDF:1	80	60
Kakdwip	2	3	*Khal*:7	NP: 7	60	80
Patharpratima	3	3	Tank:4	NP: 4	40	40
Kulpi	2	2	*Khal*:2	NP: 2	20	20
Bishnupur-I	1	2	*Khal*:1	RIDF:1	20	0
Mandirbazar	1	2	*Khal*:1	RIDF:1	20	0
Total Sample	15	17	18		240	200

Notes [a]A *Gram Panchayat* is a local self-government institution at the village level in India. The specific Gram Panchayats selected are Muriganga, Ramkarchar, Gangasagar, Dhoblat, Dash (under Sagar), Bapuji and Rabindra (under Kakdwip), Dakshin Gangadharpur, Brajaballavpur and Lakshidanardan (under Patharpratima), Koratala and Dhola (under Kulpi), Pankua (under Bishnupur-I), and Chandpur-Chatyannapur (under Mandirbazar)

[b]Villages within each block are Mandirtala, Khan Saheber Abad, Beguakhali, Purusatyampur, and Haradhanpur (under Sagar), Taktipur Abad, Jaharpur, and Hesamabad (under Kakdwip), Dakshin Madhusudanpur, Gonidapur Abad, and Purba Chintamanipur (under Patharpratima), Lakshmipur and Lakshminarayanpur (under Kulpi), RammakhalerChak and Jhanjhra (under Bishnupur-I), and Bhabanipur–Muldia and Alemaheshpur (under Mandirbazar)

[c]NP stands for National Project. RIDF represents Rural Infrastructure Development Fund

[d]Households have been selected randomly such that every irrigation scheme is covered by a minimum of 20 households

The results from factor analysis can be used to develop an SES-index for each household in the sample. As noted in the previous section, the factor loadings indicate those variables associated with the first seven factors which account for the maximum variation in the dataset. The first step in this process is to compute the factor score coefficients. The factor score coefficients are estimated using regression, and each predicted f_i is computed for each observation. This score measures the position of the ith household in relation to other households, with respect to the k-th factor. The importance, or the weight of each factor is different, as the percentage of explained variation is different across factors. A composite SES-index is developed for each observation, as a weighted sum of scores corresponding to that particular observation. Suppose $[X_1, X_2, \ldots, X_n]$ are different indicators observed for each household in the sample. As a first step toward data diagnostics, we perform the Bartelett's test of sphericity and also the Kaiser–Meyer–Olkin (KMO) test. These tests check for for the strength of correlation, between these variables, and also indicate, whether factor analysis is suitable for the given data.

A standard approach using OLS to investigate whether access to irrigation affects SES might have been satisfactory if the marginal effects of the population characteristics were the same over the entire range of the dependent variable's (SES)

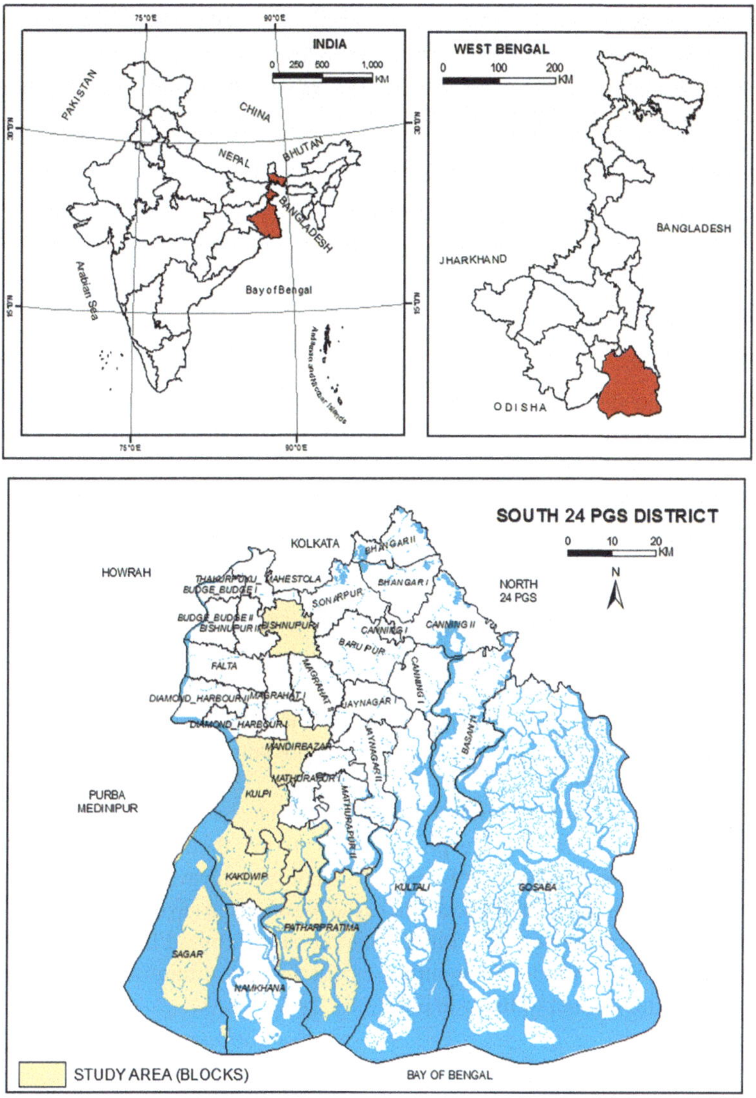

Fig. 1 Map showing details of the study area of six block levels: (Bishnupu-I, Mandirbazar, Kulpi, Kakdwip, Patharpratima, and Sagar)

conditional distribution. This assumption may not be valid under certain circumstances, if say, variables such as Education, Food share exhibit a different effect at the tails of the distribution compared to the mean. Consequently, whether there is any evidence that access to irrigation affects SES differently depending upon the location of the distribution becomes an empirical question. So, following Variyam et al. (2002), we employ quantile regression technique to characterize SES levels among farmers by including sections the conditional distribution of SES, other than the conditional mean. The quantile regression approach allows the influence of the exogenous variables to vary over the entire range of SES levels. The estimation procedure allows us to estimate SES differences of population subgroups, at special points in the conditional distribution, such as the 10th or the 90th percentile.

The empirical estimation is based on the household production model following Becker (1965), Grossman (2006), Strauss and Thomas (1995), and also adopted by Variyam et al. (2002). The quantile regression equation can be viewed as an approximation to production function specification:

$$\text{SES} = f\,(X_1, X_{2.})$$

where the independent variables capture farmers' characteristics including socioeconomic features, and most importantly access to irrigation. Information on farmers' characteristics should be considered as intermediate pathways that influence SES. The quantile estimation procedure allows us to capture the net benefits to SES from the various inputs at different points along the SES distribution.

Koenker and Bassett (1978) on quantile regression analysis has been a major influence in econometric estimation, spanning several research areas, and leading to many extensions.[6] For example, Variyam et al. (2002) note that the fat intake for men at the 90th percentile is considerably higher than the recommended level, and the cholesterol intake at the 7th percentile for women is 273 mg, much below the recommended level. Essentially, researchers have begun to look at the standard relation between the outcome variable y and the independent variables x at different points of in the distribution of y.

The standard regression estimation provides estimates at the average of the distribution E(y|x). Quantile regressions provide information about the intergroup difference along the whole distribution of y rather than only at the average locations. From a policy angle, it is important to know where the between-group difference is located, so as to make informed decisions, rather than pursuing a broad-based approach.

The qth quintile regression estimator $\beta_{!}$ is obtained by minimizing the following loss function with respect to the true $\beta_{!}$:

$$Q(\beta_q) = \sum_{i:y>x'\beta}^{N} q\left|y - x'\beta_q\right| + \sum_{i:y<x'\beta}^{N} (1-q)\left|y - x'\beta_q\right|$$

where q is a parameter which lies between (0,1), and where $Q(\beta_q)$ achieves symmetry when $q = 0.5$ and because asymmetrical when q approaches 0 or 1. Cameron and Trivedi (2010, p. 212) note that the quantile regression estimates are robust to the presence of outliers in the data, and can capture special features of the data at the extremes. Further, the technique has become widely applicable to many research fields including nutrition economics.

3 Results and Discussion

3.1 Socioeconomic Index

The unique contribution of the present study is the incorporation of a livelihood-framework in the context of irrigation infrastructure. A description of the variables used in the present study is provided in Table 2. Average values of the farmer households for the two groups on the basis of the access to irrigation.

The results of KMO and Bartlettt's sphericity are given in Table 3.

Bartlett's test results indicate that we can reject the null hypothesis that the correlation matrix is an identity matrix, or that the variables are uncorrelated, and that there are no common factors. The Bartlett's test statistic is computed from the determinant of correlation matrix, and is based on a chi-square test. The results indicate that the correlation matrix is not generated from a population in which the correlation matrix is an identity matrix. Table 3 also presents the KMO test, which computes the ratio between partial correlation to total correlation coefficient. The value of KMO is 0.61, and this suggests that the data is suitable for factor analysis. We note from the scree plot (Fig. 2) and also from Table 4 that the first seven factors account for more than 90% of the data. While the first 10 factors account for all of the variation, we note that the proportion of variation accounted by factors 8, 9, and 10 is marginal. Consequently, supported by the evidence from the scree plot, we retain 7 factors for further analysis, and for the derivation of the SES-index. We apply Dinno's (2009) implementation of Horn's parallel analysis to our data. The scree plot showing the results is provided in Fig. 2. The parallel analysis in Fig. 3 indicates that the original number of seven principal factors provides a satisfactory account of the variation in the data.

The next step in the analysis is to examine the factor loadings that indicate which variables to retain, and which groups of variables reflect an underlying similarity in the variation in the data. The factor loadings for all the variables under varimax rotation are in Table 4. The motivation in this computational process is to get a sense of the underlying correlation across all the variables in our data from Table 4 we note that seven factors account for 90.52% of total variation in the data, very similar to the results obtained under primary loadings.

We note from Table 5 that under varimax rotation, the first factor loads heavily and positively for the following variables related to the educational status of the household: Education of the Head of the Household, and Average Years of Schooling in the Family, Wife's Education, Highest Education Level in the Family, Average Schooling years of Male and Females in the Family. Higher values of these variables in the original data indicate better social circumstances. The first factor accounts for 25.15% of total variation and can be considered as a reasonable representation of the agriculture data generation process. Better economic outcomes are associated with higher values of educational status. For the second factor, Farmer's Income and Annual Agricultural Profits show strong positive loadings. We can interpret the second factor as a measure of household income status, and we note that this factor

Table 2 Data description: variables and mean values for the treated (irrigators) and untreated groups (non-irrigators)

No	Variables	Mean (irrigators)	Mean (non-irrigators)
1	Annual Off-farm income (Rs.)	58686.4	54015.0
2	Annual Farm income (Rs.)	115307.8	28564.4
3	Annual Livestock income (Rs.)	24158.3	22683.8
4	Annual agricultural profit (Rs.)	87292.1	3759.4
5	Migration income (Rs.)	13874.2	20542.3
6	Education of the head of the household (Years)	6.2	6.2
7	Household average schooling (Years)	7.0	6.7
8	Education of the head's wife (Years)	5.7	5.2
9	Highest education of the household (Years)	10.6	10.5
10	Illiteracy (Number of illiterates in the household)	0.4	0.4
11	Household male average schooling (Years)	7.5	7.3
12	Household female average schooling (Years)	6.6	6.0
13	Household health (Presence of Diarrhea =1, No =1)	0.3	0.5
14	Distance from drinking water sources (Kms.)	0.9	0.7
15	Distance from Hospital (Kms.)	12.4	12.3
16	Overall food security (Food secured =1, No = 0)	0.6	0.2
17	Food security in the last month (Number)	1.8	3.2
18	Poverty (Poor =1, Non Poor =0)	0.4	0.4
19	Food expenditure per adult/annum (Rs.)	8688.9	8760.3
20	Non-food expenditure per adult/annum (Rs.)	6837.3	5689.2
21	Share of food expenditure (%)	57.6	62.2
22	Household expenditure per adult (Rs.)	15526.2	14449.5
23	Job card (Yes =1, No =0)	0.9	0.8
24	Agricultural skills training (Yes =1, No =0)	0.6	0.2
25	Access to extension service (Yes =1, No =0)	0.7	0.4
26	Access to credit (Yes =1, No =0)	0.7	0.7
27	Formal credit (Yes =1, No =0)	0.4	0.4
28	Informal credit (Yes =1, No =0)	0.2	0.3
29	Formal and informal credit both (Yes =1, No =0)	0.0	0.0
30	Hired labor (Number)	17.2	9.4
31	Value of assets (Rs.)	33065.8	19299.0
32	Value of agricultural assets (Rs.)	12416.7	5074.0

Table 3 Diagnostics with Bartlett's test of sphericity and KMO sampling adequacy

Bartlett test of sphericity:
Chi-square = 7439.578
Degrees of freedom = 435
p-value = 0.000
H_0: Variables are not intercorrelated, and there are no common factors H_A: There is atleast one common factor
Kaiser-Meyer-Olkin measure of sampling adequacy:
KMO = 0.613

Source Authors' own estimation

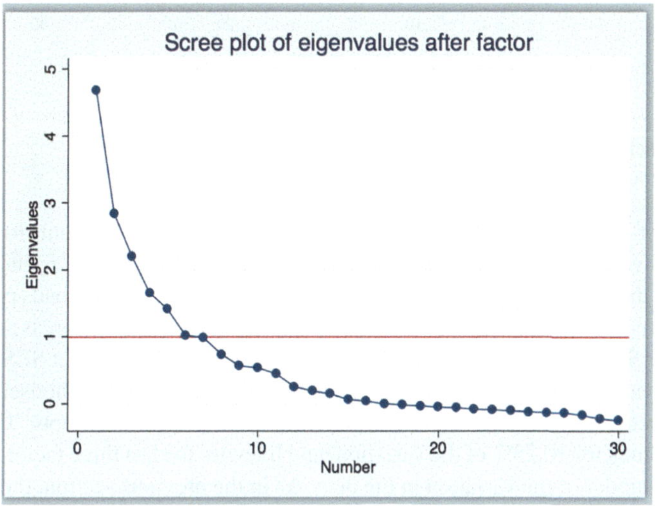

Fig. 2 Scree plot for the farmers' data

Table 4 Eigenvalues and variation under varimax rotation

Factor	Eigenvalue	Difference	Proportion	Cumulative
Factor1	4.11098	1.39621	0.2515	0.2515
Factor2	2.71477	0.53146	0.1661	0.4176
Factor3	2.18331	0.51199	0.1336	0.5512
Factor4	1.67133	0.17417	0.1023	0.6535
Factor5	1.49715	0.14523	0.0916	0.7451
Factor6	1.35192	0.08652	0.0827	0.8278
Factor7	1.2654	0.00541	0.0774	0.9052

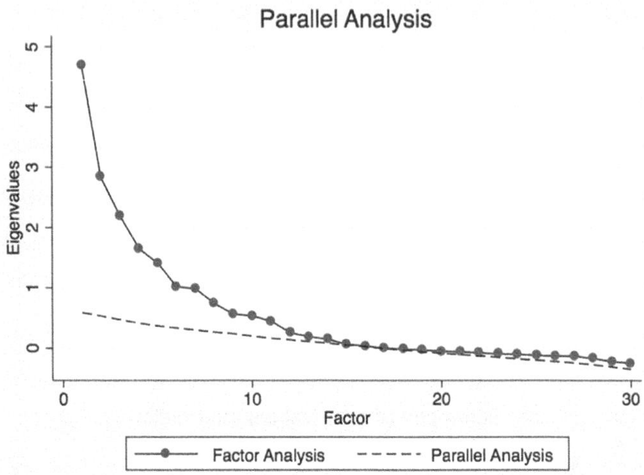

Fig. 3 Parallel analysis versus factor analysis

accounts for 16.6% of total variation in the data. The third factor accounts for 13.36% of the total variation and is closely associated to Annual Non-Food Expenditure per Adult, and the Expenditure-HH ratio. While Non-Food Expenditure loads positively, Expenditure-HH loads negatively. A variable with a positive factor score is associated with higher SES, while a negative factor score is associated with a lower SES (Vyas & Kumaranayake, 2006). This implies that, other things being equal, a household with higher Expenditure-HH equivalent will be ranked with a lower SES score. The fourth factor accounts for 10.23% of the variation, and likewise the last three factors account for the remainder of the variation in the data. As in the previous section, the varimax rotation allows us to group selected variables closely to factor loadings.

The weight is the percentage of the variation that is explained by the factors, and the SES-Index is derived by using the predicted factor scores from Table 6, and the weights, based on the information from Table 5. For the agricultural data, a total of seven factors, which explains 90% of total variation has been used. Following Antony and Rao (2007), Vyas and Kumaranayake (2006), a non-standardized index S_i is developed for each observation, using the proportion of these percentages from each factor as weights (w_i), on the factor score coefficients (f_i):

$$S_i = \sum_{i=1}^{7} w_i f_i$$

The summary statistics of the non-standardized index S_i are presented in Table 6.

The weights indicate that the importance of the factors in measuring SES is not the same. Following Antony and Rao (2007), Vyas and Kumaranayake (2006), the composite SES_i has been computed for all 440 observations, using the weights (w_i),

Table 5 Factor loadings, pattern matrix, and uniqueness under varimax rotation

Household characteristics	Factor 1	Factor 2	Factor 3	Factor 4	Factor 5	Factor 6	Factor 7	Uniqueness
Off-farm income								0.8248
Farm income		0.9329						0.1256
Livestock income								0.9537
Annual agriculture profit		0.9172						0.1496
Migration income								0.9267
Education of the head	0.7293							0.4284
Average schooling year of the family	0.9527							0.0663
Education of the head's wife	0.6658							0.4153
Highest education of the family	0.7348							0.3631
Illiterate				0.4151				0.6483
Male average schooling	0.86							0.2201
Female average schooling	0.7469							0.3998
Family health								0.8077
Distance from drinking water sources								0.9307
Distance from hospital								0.8536
Food secure		0.5372						0.6419
Food security (month)		−0.5497						0.622
Poverty			−0.5351	0.4131				0.4994
Food expenditure per adult/annum				−0.7644				0.3274

(continued)

Table 5 (continued)

Household characteristics	Factor 1	Factor 2	Factor 3	Factor 4	Factor 5	Factor 6	Factor 7	Uniqueness
Non-food expenditure per adult/annum			0.9177					0.0947
Share of food expenditure			−0.9256					0.0965
Job card								0.9644
Agricultural skills training								0.8904
Access to extension service								0.9375
Access to credit					0.8773			0.1364
Formal credit					0.7499		−0.5518	0.121
Informal credit							0.8974	0.1716
Hired labor (No./Year)								0.8283
Value of asset						0.7851		0.3588
Value of agricultural assets						0.7607		0.4011

Note Variables with loadings less than 0.4 have been omitted from the table

Table 6 Summary statistics of the non-standardized index S_i

Variable	*n*	Mean	Std deviation	Minimum	Maximum
S_i index	440	0.00012	0.42395	−1.045066	1.761969

and for the ease of comparison, the index is standardized to a scale of 0 to 100, as follows:

$$\text{SES}_i = \frac{S_i - S_{\text{Minimum}}}{S_{\text{Maximum}} - S_{\text{Minimum}}}$$

or,

$$\text{SES}_i = \frac{S_i - (-1.045066)}{1.761969 - (-1.045066)}$$

3.2 *Quantile Regression*

The importance of access to irrigation to farmers' well-being has been well established in agricultural economics (Smith, 2004, Senaratna et al., 2014). While irrigation and technical capabilities are important for SES, the risk or a lack of such resources is greater at the tails of the access distribution than at the mean. This aspect is illustrated in Table 7, which reports the mean and selected percentiles of all key variables, used in the analysis thus far. Note that the values of SES, Education, and Food share are much larger at the upper end of the distribution. The relation between SES and U also gains credibility at the upper end of the distribution (at 50th, 75th, and 90th percentiles). From a public policy perspective, the production function relation is of greater importance at the tailes of the SES distribution than those around the mean. As noted by Variyam et al. (2002), the *location* of the intergroup differences along the whole distribution is more important than the average between-group differences. For example, policymakers interested in improving farmers' SES via access to irrigation should be more concerned if the between-group difference is located mainly at the lower end of the distribution.

The quantile regression estimates are presented in Table 8. The conditional quantile regressions for have been estimated for five selected quantiles ($P = 5$). For the purpose of comparison, the second column presents the OLS estimates, with their robust standard errors. The standard errors for the quantile regression estimates were generated using the bootstrap method with 500 replications.

Table 7 Mean values of farmers' characteristics within percentiles

Variables	10th	25th	50th	75th	90th	Overall mean
SES	0.195	0.260	0.358	0.465	0.575	0.372
Log (income)	11.161	11.578	12.022	12.521	12.996	12.060
Education	4.185	5.25	6.5	8.4	10	6.890
Diarrhea	0	0	0	1	1	0.406
Water	0	1	1	1	1	0.820
Hospital	6	8	12	15	20.2	12.373
Food security	0	0	0	1	1	0.390
Poverty	0	0	0	1	1	0.395
Food share	0.479	0.555	0.610	0.655	0.699	0.596
Log (HH expenditure)	9.308	9.429	9.560	9.746	9.903	9.588
Job card	0	1	1	1	1	0.854
Training	0	0	0	1	1	0.411
Extension	0	0	1	1	1	0.568
Hired Labor	2	6	11	18	28	13.667
Log (assets)	6.907	9.268	9.268	9.305	9.441	8.989
U (Access to irrigation)	0	0	1	1	1	0.547

Table 8 OLS and quantile regression estimates: determinants of socioeconomic status (SES) of farm households

Regressors	OLS	10	25	50	75	90
Intercept	0.794** (0.315)	0.917** (0.512)	0.750 (0.684)	1.025*** (0.391)	1.088*** (0.383)	0.424 (0.515)
Log (income)	0.042*** (0.008)	0.020** (0.013)	0.033*** (0.009)	0.036*** (0.009)	0.044*** (0.002)	0.070*** (0.010)
Education	0.041*** (0.001)	0.044*** (0.003)	0.042*** (0.003)	0.040*** (0.002)	0.004*** (0.002)	0.041*** (0.003)
Diarrhea	0.005 (0.008)	0.004 (0.014)	-0.003 (0.018)	0.003 (0.010)	0.005 (0.009)	0.013 (0.011)
Water	0.006 (0.008)	-0.021 (0.016)	0.000 (0.014)	0.003 (0.009)	0.016 (0.010)	0.015 (0.012)
Hospital	0.000 (0.001)	0.000 (0.001)	-0.001 (0.001)	0.001 (0.001)	0.001 (0.001)	0.001 (0.001)
Food security	0.022*** (0.007)	0.023 (0.015)	0.019 (0.011)	0.023*** (0.007)	0.015* (0.010)	0.024** (0.011)
Poverty	0.022*** (0.007)	0.018 (0.015)	0.008 (0.017)	0.012 (0.013)	0.018 (0.015)	0.018 (0.011)
Food share	−0.624*** (0.063)	−0.540*** (0.125)	−0.589*** (0.101)	−0.690*** (0.083)	−0.694*** (0.079)	−0.643*** (0.096)
Log (HH expenditure)	−0.098*** (0.026)	−0.096** (0.044)	−0.088 (0.059)	−0.107*** (0.033)	−0.122*** (0.035)	−0.090** (0.044)
Job card	−0.002 (0.009)	−0.005 (0.017)	−0.018 (0.015)	0.003 (0.011)	−0.005 (0.013)	−0.000 (0.015)
Training	−0.004 (0.007)	−0.007 (0.013)	−0.013 (0.011)	−0.005 (0.009)	0.002 (0.009)	0.005 (0.011)
Extension	−0.008 (0.007)	−0.017 (0.014)	−0.010 (0.010)	−0.003 (0.009)	0.002 (0.010)	0.014 (0.001)
Hired Labor	0.001*** (0.000)[a]	0.001 (0.001)	0.001 (0.001)	0.003 (0.009)	0.001 (0.001)	0.001 (0.001)
Log (Assets)	0.007** (0.003)	0.007 (0.006)	0.009** (0.003)	0.004 (0.004)	0.005 (0.004)	0.001 (0.006)
U (Access to irrigation)	0.029*** (0.009)	0.054*** (0.016)	0.053*** (0.016)	0.029*** (0.012)	0.006 (0.010)	−0.017 (0.010)
R-sq	0.92	0.91	0.92	0.92	0.91	0.89

Note: Standard-errors are given in parenthesis. Statistical significance (* at 0.1 level, ** at 0.05 level and *** at 0.01 level)

A crucial result from Table 8 for our purposes in this paper that variable U, or the access to irrigation, which is significant under OLS and across all quantiles, except at $0.9q$. The important observation here is the additional information revealed by quantile estimation as compared with OLS. While the OLS estimate shows that U has a positive effect on SSI, the quantile estimates show that much of the beneficial effect occurs at lower quantiles. For farmers at $0.1q$ and 0.25q, the effect of U on SSI is roughly *86%* larger than the OLS estimate. This implies that, as access to irrigation increases across upper tails, the upper conditional quantiles of SSI decrease, when compared to the conditional mean estimate.

We also note that the estimate of *U* at *0.5q* matches the OLS estimate, while the estimate at *0.75q* is smaller than the OLS estimate. Further, at the topmost *0.9q*, the estimate of *U* is negative, albeit insignificant. The positive and significant relation between *U* and SSI at lower quantiles becomes more evident, when we compare the OLS estimates of *Income* with the corresponding conditional quantile estimates. We note that *Income* has a predictable positive effect on SSI, and the effect is significant under OLS and across all quintiles. However, the largest marginal effect is for farmers who are at *0.9q*. Further, the marginal effect *Income* on SSI is smaller than the effect of *U*, for lower quintiles *0.1q* and *0.25q*. The *U-Income* differential impact, switches at the mean and at higher quintiles, which stresses the idea that access to irrigation for the lower quintiles is a strong factor of SSI. On the other hand, it is *Income* and not *U* that acts as a relatively more important determinant of SSI at the upper end of the distribution.

The difference between QR and OLS estimates are highlighted in Figs. 4 and 5 which display the coefficients of *Income* and *U* along with their confidence intervals. The horizontal lines in Figs. 4 and 5 represent the OLS estimates and confidence intervals, which remain constant across quintiles. Figure 4 shows that the coefficient of *Income* is positive over most of the range of *q*, with much larger effect at the both tail-ends. Figure 5 indicates that the coefficient of *U* falls after crossing the mean, stressing the *Income-U* relation on SES, corroborating the Quantile Regression estimates in Table 8.

To further examine the differences in estimates across different subgroups, Table 9 presents four sets of statistics, for testing the equality of the slope coefficients across the quantiles. The first three sets give F-statistics and their associated p-values for the test that, for a given independent variable (*Income* or *U*), its slope at 0.10 quantile is equal to its slope at 0.75 quantile (or $q_{10} = q_{75}$), and its slope at 0.9 quantile (or $q_{10} = q_{90}$), and its slope at 0.25 quantile is equal to its slope at 0.75 quantile (or $q_{25} = q_{75}$). The last column presents the F-statistics to test the equality of the slope coefficients of an independent variable (*Income* or *U*) across all quintiles ($q_{10} = q_{25} = q_{75} =$

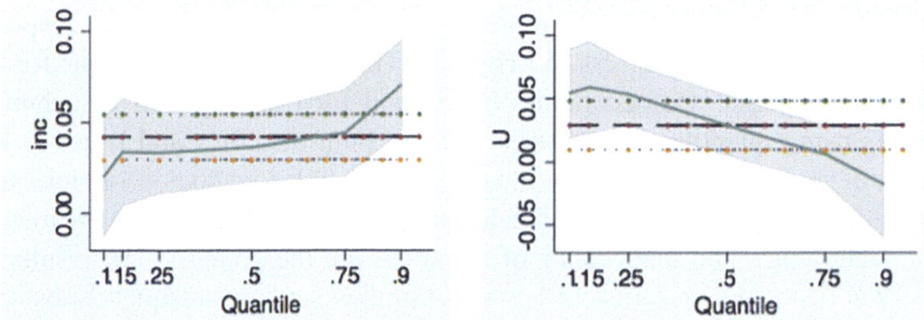

Figs. 4 and 5 QR and OLS coefficients and confidence intervals for *Income* (Fig. 4) and *U* (Fig. 5) as *q* varies from 0 to 1

Table 9 Tests of equality of slope parameters across quintiles

Variable	$q_{10} = q_{75}$	$q_{10} = q_{90}$	$q_{25} = q_{75}$	$q_{10} = q_{25} = q_{75} = q_{90}$
U	6.87 (0.0093)*	13.14 (0.0003)*	7.64 (0.0061)*	4.79 (0.0009)*
Income	2.89 (0.0903)*	10.96 (0.0011)*	0.65 (0.4276)	3.78 (0.0052)*

q_{90}). If the null hypothesis of equal slopes is rejected, then the F-test implies that the restricted conditional quantile estimates yield the optimal combination of the five quantile slope coefficients. Table 9 indicates that in 7 out of 8 cases, the equalities of slope parameters are rejected across the five quantiles at $p < 0.001$. The chi-square tests, therefore, suggest the presence of heteroscedasticity in the farmers' irrigation data set.

There is also less evidence of differing, or increasing marginal effects of *Education, Food Security, Food Share,* and *HH measure.* While all these factors are significant and have the correct signs, their effects on SSI are not statistically different at the tails of the distribution, and corresponding F-tests also reveal this tendency.

4 Summary and Conclusions

Deriving an aggregate index of farmers' socioeconomic status, and linking this index to related exogenous factors, is important for developing useful agricultural policies. The purpose of this paper is to develop a logical index of Socioeconomic Status (SES) using factor analysis. Additionally, the paper uses quantile regression analysis to characterize the determinants of SSI, and its distributional implications. The nature of SSI distribution in the present study is such that access to irrigation and income has larger effects at lower end of the distribution than at the mean. Hence, whether the marginal effects of population characteristics remain constant along the entire distribution of SSI, remains an empirical question and cannot be assumed to be true, *apriori.*

Findings of the present study suggest that the marginal effects at the tails of SSI distribution are different than those at the mean, particularly with respect to farmers' income and their access to irrigation. The study has implications for both deriving an aggregate socioeconomic index, and for evaluating its distributional properties, using quantile regression technique. Future studies and research must uncover effects beyond conditional mean, so as to link low socioeconomic status to population features inherent at the lower tails, where lack of access to information, technology, and inadequacy of resources are the greatest. The results also suggest that access to irrigation to low-end families serve as adequate substitutes, particularly when straightforward income-transfer policies are not possible. Consequently, successful irrigation-intervention programs must call for complementary schemes (Turner, 1994), that emphasize optimal water management and governance

(Das et al., 2015), crop rotation, transportation and storage facilities, and institutional credit (Guijt & Thompson, 1994; Singh, 2015). As demonstrated by Kam et al. (2006), for Vietnam, holistic approaches through optimal Resource Management Domain (RMD) constructs are excellent starting points for mapping farmers' needs to overall collective good. Sustainable watershed policies have also proven successful, as in rural Andhra Pradesh in South India, as evidenced by Reddy et al. (2004).

Acknowledgements The Primary data for the work have been collected under research project 'Impact of Public Investment on Water Bodies in Improving Rural Livelihood—a Study in the Saline Zone in West Bengal India', supported by National Bank for Agriculture and Rural Development (NABARD), Mumbai, India (Principal Investigator: Professor Sebak Kumar Jana, Department of Economics, Vidyasagar University, Midnapore).

References

Acharya, S. S. (2006). Sustainable agriculture and rural livelihoods. *Agricultural Economics Research Review, 19*, 205–217.

ADB. (2006). *Rehabilitation and management of tanks in India*. Asian Development Bank. http://www.adb.org/documents/studies/tanks-india/rehabilitation-management-tanks.pdf

Agarwal, A., et al. (Eds). (2001). *Making water everybody's business*. Centre for Science and Environment.

Antony, G. M., & Rao, K. V. (2007). A composite index to explain variations in poverty, health, nutritional status and standard of living: Use of multivariate statistical methods. *Public Health, 121*, 578–587.

Asthana, V., & Shukla, A. C. (2014). *Water security in India: hope, despair, and the challenges of human development*. Bloomsbury Publishing.

Awasthi, M. K. (2014). Socioeconomic determinants of farmland value in India. *Land Use Policy, 39*, 78–83.

Baskaran, R., Colombo, S., & Cullen, R. (2013). Public preferences in irrigation and conservation development projects: Does simultaneous consideration of substitutes in choice sets matter? *Land Use Policy, 33*, 214–226.

Becker, G. S. (1965). A theory of the allocation of time. *The Economic Journal*, 493–517.

Bell, A. R., Bryan, E., Ringler, C., & Ahmed, A. (2015). Rice productivity in Bangladesh: What are the benefits of irrigation? *Land Use Policy, 48*, 1–12.

Bhattarai, M., & Narayanamoorthy, A. (2003). Impact of irrigation on rural poverty in India: An aggregate panel-data analysis. *Water Policy, 5*(5–6), 443–458.

Cameron, C., & Trivedi, P. (2010). *Microeconometric using Stata*. A Stata Press Publication, StataCorp LP.

Chand, R., Prasanna, P. L., & Singh, A. (2011). Farm size and productivity: Understanding the strengths of smallholders and improving their livelihoods. *Economic and Political Weekly*, 5–11.

Das, B., Singh, A., Panda, S. N., & Yasuda, H. (2015). Optimal land and water resources allocation policies for sustainable irrigated agriculture. *Land Use Policy, 42*, 527–537.

Dinno, A. (2009). Implementing Horn's parallel analysis for principal component analysis and factor analysis. *The Stata Journal, 9*, 2, 291–298.

Domènech, L. (2015). Improving irrigation access to combat food insecurity and undernutrition: A review. *Global Food Security, 6*, 24–33.

Domenech, L., & Ringler, C. (2013). The impact of irrigation on nutrition, health, and gender: A review paper with insights for Africa south of the Sahara. International food policy research institute (IFPRI). Discussion Paper 01259. 13pp.

Fukuda, Y., Nakamura, K., & Takano, T. (2007). Higher mortality in areas of lower socioeconomic position measured by a single index of deprivation in Japan. *Public Health, 121*(3), 163–173.

Grossman, M. (2006). Household production and health. In S. Grossbard (Ed.), *Jacob Mincer: A pioneer of modern labor economics* (pp. 161–180). Springer.

Guijt, I., & Thompson, J. (1994). Landscapes and livelihoods: Environmental and socioeconomic dimensions of small-scale irrigation. *Land Use Policy, 11*(4), 294–308.

Hussain, I., & Hanjra, M. A. (2004). Irrigation and poverty alleviation: Review of the empirical evidence. *Irrigation and drainage, 53*(1), 1–15.

Jana, S. K., & Tamang, P. (2023). Prospects of rehabilitation of ancient irrigation systems in India–A case study from coastal saline zone of West Bengal. *Agricultural Systems, 207*, 103638.

Jana, S. K., Palanisami, K., & Manna, S. S. (2018). Economics of public investment in rehabilitation of water bodies in the saline zone of West Bengal, India. *International Journal of Agricultural Resources, Governance and Ecology, 14*(2), 165–180.

Jana, S. K. (2016). *Impact of public investment on water bodies in improving the rural livelihood—A study in the saline zone in West Bengal in India, Research project submitted to National Bank for Agriculture and Rural Development (NABARD)*. Mumbai.

Jehangir, W. A., Ashfaq, M., & Christen, E. (2003). Alternate modes of irrigation and farmer returns under conjunctive water management in Pakistan. *Australasian Agribusiness Review, 11.*

Kam, S. P., Nhan, N. V., Tuong, T. P., Hoanh, C. T., Nam, V. B., & Maunahan, A. (2006). 15 Applying the Resource Management Domain (RMD) concept to land and water use and management in the coastal zone: Case study of Bac Lieu Province, Vietnam. *Environment and Livelihoods in Tropical Coastal Zones, 193.*

Krishnan, V. (2010). *Constructing an area-based socioeconomic index: A principal components analysis approach.* Edmonton, Alberta: Early Child Development Mapping Project. https://www.ualberta.ca/en/community-university-partnership/media-library/community-university-partnership/research/ecmap-reports/seicupwebsite10april13-1.pdf

Lise, W., Jana, S. K., & Manna, S. (2019). Participation in the water body irrigation management in Saline Zone in West Bengal in India. *Water Economics and Policy, 5*(01), 1850004.

Mandal, K. G., Hati, K. M., Misra, A. K., Bandyopadhyay, K. K., & Mohanty, M. (2005). Irrigation and nutrient effects on growth and water–yield relationship of wheat (Triticum aestivum L.) in central India. *Journal of Agronomy and Crop Science, 191*(6), 416–425.

Mekonnen, D., Hira, C., Claudia, R., Mekonnen, D., Hira, C., & Claudia, R. (2016). Where to invest in the Indus Basin Irrigation System in Pakistan to improve land and water productivity? Insights from a hierarchical model. https://doi.org/10.22004/AG.ECON.235977

Narayanamoorthy, A., & Deshpande, R. S. (2005). *Where water seeps!: Towards a new phase in India's irrigation reforms.* Academic Foundation.

Nkhata, R. (2014). *Does irrigation have an impact on food security and poverty: Evidence from Bwanje Valley Irrigation Scheme in Malawi* (Vol. 4). Intl Food Policy Res Inst.

Palanisami, K., Meinzen-Dick, R., & Giordano, M. (2010). Climate change and water supplies: Options for sustaining tank irrigation potential in India. *Economic and Political Weekly,* 183–190.

Pampalon, R., Hamel, D., &Gamache, P. (2009). A comparison of individual and area-based socioeconomic data for monitoring social inequalities in health (Statistics Canada, Catalogue no. 82-003-XPE). *Health Reports, 20*(3) (September), 85–94.

Pandey, V. L., & Suganthi, D. (2015). Fueling agricultural growth in India: Some reflections. *Land Use Policy, 42*, 227–232.

Pant, N., & Verma, R. K. (2010). *Tanks in Eastern India: A study in exploration.* IWMI.

Reddy. R., Gopinath, R. V., Galab, M., Soussan, S., & Springate-Baginski, O. (2004). Participatory watershed development in India: Can it sustain rural livelihoods?. *Development and Change, 35*(2), 297–326.

Ricart, S., & Gandolfi, C. (2017). Balancing irrigation multifunctionality based on key stakeholders' attitudes: Lessons learned from the Muzza system, Italy. *Land Use Policy, 69*, 461–473.

Saleth, R. M., Namara, R. E., & Samad, M. (2003). Dynamics of irrigation-poverty linkages in rural India: Analytical framework and empirical analysis. *Water Policy, 5*(5–6), 459–473.

Senaratna Sellamuttu, S., Aida, T., Kasahara, R., Sawada, Y., & Wijerathna, D. (2014). How access to irrigation influences poverty and livelihoods: A case study from Sri Lanka. *Journal of Development Studies, 50*(5), 748–768.

Shah, T., & Singh, O. P. (2004). Irrigation development and rural poverty in Gujarat, India: A disaggregated analysis. *Water International, 29*(2), 167–177.

Singh, A. (2015). Land and water management planning for increasing farm income in irrigated dry areas. *Land Use Policy, 42*, 244–250.

Singh, G. K., Miller, B. A., Hankey, B. F., Feuer, E. J., & Pickle, L. W. (2002). Changing area socioeconomic patterns in US cancer mortality, 1950–1998: part I—all cancers among men. *Journal of the National Cancer Institute, 94*(12), 904–915.

Smith, L. E. (2004). Assessment of the contribution of irrigation to poverty reduction and sustainable livelihoods. *International Journal of Water Resources Development, 20*(2), 243–257.

Strauss, J., & Thomas, D. (1995). Human resources: Empirical modeling of household and family decisions. *Handbook of Development Economics, 3*, 1883–2023.

Tiwary, R. (2009). Water bodies, multiple uses and their political ecologies in West Bengal. *International Journal of Rural Management, 5*(1), 21–48.

Turner, B. (1994). Small-scale irrigation in developing countries. *Land Use Policy, 11*(4), 251–261.

Vaidyanathan, A. (2006). *India's water resources*. Contemporary Issues of Irrigation, Oxford India Paperbacks.

Variyam Jayachandran, N., Blaylock, J. & Smallwood, D. (2002). Characterizing the distribution of macronutrient intake among U.S. adults: A quantile regression approach. *American Journal of Agricultural Economics, 84*(2), 454–466.

Vyas, S., & Kumaranayake, L. (2006). Constructing socioeconomic status indices: How to use principal components analysis. *Advance Access Publication, 9*, 459–468.

Zagorski, K. (1985). Composite measures of social, economic, and demographic regional differentiation in Australia: application of multi-stage principal component methods to aggregate data analysis. *Social Indicators Research, 16*, 131–156.

Measurement and Determinants of Climate Change Vulnerability: A Household-Level Study in the Drought-Prone District of West Bengal, India

Jyotish Prakash Basu and Aishwarya Basu

Abstract The paper attempts to evaluate household's climate change vulnerability and identify its determinants in Purulia, a drought-prone district in West Bengal. For vulnerability assessment, we have followed Livelihood Vulnerability Index along with its modified versions. Primary data was gathered in 2018 from 150 households across four villages in Purulia through structured surveys. The resulting vulnerability index for the sampled households averaged at 0.6987, highlighting substantial variation in vulnerability across households: approximately half of the sample exhibited high vulnerability, 47% moderate, and only 3% low. Using an ordered logit model, socio-economic and environmental factors were identified as significant contributors to household vulnerability. The findings suggest vital policy implications for reducing poverty and vulnerability and enhancing livelihood resilience.

Keywords Livelihood vulnerability index · Ordered Logit model · Socio-economic · Climate · adaptation and perception

1 Introduction

Research on climate change vulnerability gained significant momentum in the 1990s when globalization and climate change began to dominate discourse. The research on vulnerability traces back to development discourse like poverty (Dercon & Krishnan, 2000). Again, vulnerability is treated as deprivation resulting from entitlement failures (Sen, 1984). Various methods are available for assessing vulnerability, including

J. P. Basu (✉)
Department of Economics, West Bengal State University, Kolkata, India
e-mail: bjyotish@yahoo.com

A. Basu
Department of Economics, Sister Nivedita University (SNU), Newtown Kolkata, India

B. Chatterjee and A. K. Karmakar (eds.), *Analytical Issues in Growth & Structural Change, Macroeconomy, Security, and Sustainability of India's Economic Development*, India Studies in Business and Economics,
https://doi.org/10.1007/978-981-95-5242-9_16

indicator-based and econometric approaches. Indicator-based assessments are widely used for simplicity (Adger et al., 2004; Tonmoy et al., 2014). Econometric methods are also employed to analyze vulnerability (Hoddinott & Quisumbing, 2003). The indicator-based method is often preferred to consider social, economic, and environmental factors, unlike econometric models, which focus primarily on socio-economic factors. Studies on vulnerability measurement span various geographic regions, including the Himalayas, Africa, and South America. Due to the multi-dimensional nature of vulnerability, there is no universally accepted methodology (Adger, 2006; Alwang et al., 2001).

This study adopts two methodologies regarding the measurement of vulnerability. One is based on the livelihood vulnerability index measured by Hahn et al. (2009) and the other is a modified version framework (Sisay, 2016). Many researchers developed composite indices using weighted averages (Opiyo et al., 2014; Piya, 2012).

Despite the importance of household-level studies, few empirical studies focus on household vulnerability, which plays a significant role in community-level adaptation decisions (Koirala, 2015). The aims of the paper are twofold. One is to examine the degree of vulnerability and to estimate the key factors influencing it.

2 Materials and Methods

2.1 Study Area

The district Purulia is the study area, which is one of the drought-prone districts in West Bengal, India. Its boundaries include Bankura and West Midnapore districts to the east, Burdwan district to the north, and several Jharkhand districts to the west and south. Within Purulia, the Bagmundi block, known for its drought vulnerability, was selected as the study area.

Purulia experiences a tropical climate, with high temperatures reaching 43.67 °C in summer (April and May) and lows around 9 °C in winter (December). The average annual rainfall of the district is 1309.6 mm during the southwest monsoon, though it remains rainfall-deficient. This region falls within West Bengal's red laterite soil zone and is one of its poorer and less developed areas. Forests cover 14% of the district, and local livelihoods primarily depend on forestry, agriculture, livestock rearing, and wage labor.

2.2 Sampling Techniques

This study is based on primary data collected from four villages in Bagmundi block—Ajodhya, Banduri, Ebildi, and Matha. In 2018, 20% of households in each village were randomly sampled, totalling 150 households. Household heads were surveyed using structured questionnaires addressing socio-economic and demographic factors, climate perception, and local adaptive strategies.

2.3 Data

Socio-economic data included variables like age, gender, marital status, housing quality, sanitation, livelihood, migration, self-help group participation, income, livestock, climate change perception, and adaptation strategies.

2.4 Analytical Method

An ordered logistic model is utilized for identifying the factors influencing household vulnerability. According to the equation for the ordered logistic equation (Greene, 1997) is given as follows:

$$Y_j^* = X_{ij}\beta + U_{ij} \tag{1}$$

Y_j^* is the latent variable showing three types of outcomes. Households are categorized into these levels of vulnerability based on their vulnerability index. Households with an index below 0.5 are classified as low vulnerability ($Y = 1$). Those with an index between 0.5 and 0.7 are considered moderately vulnerable ($Y = 2$). An index above 0.7 signifies high vulnerability ($Y = 3$). X_{ij} shows 13 explanatory variables shown in Table 6. U_{ij} is the random disturbance term.

2.4.1 Livelihood Vulnerability Index (LVI)

The LVI, following Hahn et al. (2009), is a composite index derived from eight subcomponents: Socio-Demographic Profile (SDP), Livelihood Strategies (LS), Food, Social Network (SN), Natural Capital (NC), Water, Health, and Climate Variables (CV). Each sub-component includes multiple indicators, which were normalized to a scale from 0 to 1, where "0" indicates the lowest vulnerability and "1" is the highest. Weighted averages were applied to create a unit-free composite index.

2.4.2 LVI-IPCC Index

Based on IPCC (2001), this index assesses three main factors—exposure, sensitivity, and adaptive capacity. There are four sub-components of adaptive capacity, which comprise Socio-Demographic Profile, Livelihood Strategies, Food, and Social

Network, while sensitivity incorporates Water, Health sub-components, and Natural Capital.

3 Results and Discussions

The socio-demographic profile comprises four indicators: the percentage of dependent individuals, the proportion of female-headed households, the illiteracy rate among household heads, and the percentage of female family earners. The calculated socio-demographic profile index is 0.473 (Table 1).The livelihood strategy index includes five indicators: the percentage of households with members engaged in temporary migration, the percentage of households altering sowing and cropping schedules due to climate change, the livelihood diversification index, the livestock diversification index, and monthly per capita income. The livelihood strategy index for these indicators is 0.837. Crop diversity serves as a proxy for food access and is measured by whether a household grows at least one additional crop (e.g., vegetables or pulses) alongside traditional crops. Households cultivating multiple crops are more resilient to vulnerability. The food access index is calculated at 0.986.

The social network index considers four aspects: the percentage of households aware of the Indira Awas Yojana, the percentage lacking access to communication media like television, and the percentage of households with no members participating in MGNREGA or Self-Help Groups (SHGs). These indicators together yield a social network index of 0.495 (Table 1).

Natural capital is assessed using two indicators: dependence on forest resources for cooking and land ownership. In the study area, 86% of households rely on resources like fuelwood, dry tree branches, and cow dung collected from grazing lands for cooking. Additionally, 74% of households are small or marginal farmers. The natural capital index is calculated at 0.912.

The water index is derived from three factors: irregular availability of drinking water (reported by 84% of households), the use of natural water sources such as wells

Table 1 Livelihood vulnerability index in Purulia

Components	Weighted Index
Social demographic profile index	0.473
Livelihood strategies index	0.837
Social network index	0.495
Natural capital index	0.912
Food index	0.986
Water index	0.55
Health index	0.614
Climate variable index	0.723
Livelihood vulnerability index	**0.6987**

and ponds (reported by 41% of households), and the need to travel at least 1 km for water (reported by 63%). These indicators result in a water index of 0.55.

The health index is based on three indicators: households reporting at least one member suffering from chronic illness (23%), households accessing treatment from local health centers (90%), and households without toilet facilities (79%). A lack of sanitation increases vulnerability to waterborne diseases. The health index stands at 0.614.

Climate variables include four indicators: households noticing reduced rainfall over five years (65%), increased drought (11%), increased storms (67%), and a lack of disaster warnings from authorities (69%). As the study area is drought-prone, these climate variables significantly affect vulnerability. The climate variable index (CVI) is 0.723.

The proportion of households falling into different types of vulnerability is shown in Table 2. 50% are highly vulnerable, 47% are moderately vulnerable, and 3% belong to less vulnerable. The LVI underscores that climate variability intensifies household vulnerability in Purulia. Figure 1 illustrates the distribution of vulnerable households.

The modified Livelihood Vulnerability Index for Purulia district is detailed in Table 3, with an overall value of 0.7041. The exposure component seems to be the highest contributor to climate change vulnerability (Table 3). The exposure index, derived from climate indicators, is valued at 0.7225 (Table 3). Sensitivity is measured using the natural capital, health, and water indices, with a composite score of 0.6919. The adaptive capacity index is found to have a value of 0.6978. Vulnerability spider diagrams for sample households in Purulia are depicted in Figs. 2 and 3.

Table 2 Percentage of households by category of vulnerability

Vulnerability index	No. of households	% of households
<0.500	5	3.33
0.50–0.700	71	47.33
>0.7000	74	49.33

Source Computed from primary data

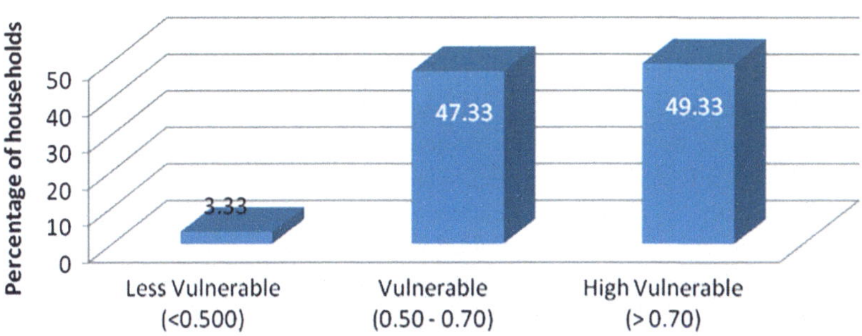

Fig. 1 Percentage of vulnerable households

Table 3 Modified Vulnerability Index (LVI-IPCC) in the District of Purulia

Components	Weighted Index
Exposure	0.7225
Sensitivity	0.6919
Adaptive capacity	0.6978
LVI-IPCC	**0.7041**

Fig. 2 LVI of households

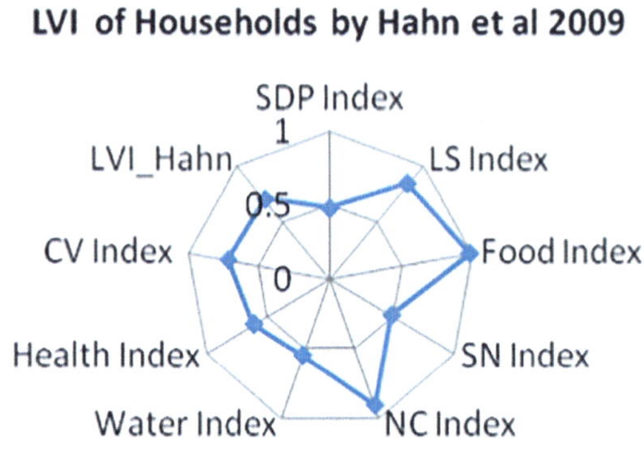

Fig. 3 Vulnerability of households by LVI-IPCC

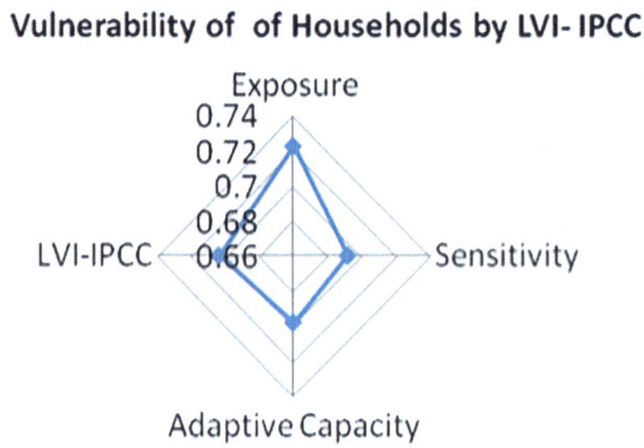

The ordered logistic regression analysis presented in Table 6 identified factors influencing household vulnerability. Household size and forest degradation had significant positive associations with vulnerability, meaning that larger households and those more affected by forest degradation tend to experience higher vulnerability. Conversely, factors like education, non-farm income, sanitation, landholdings, drought awareness, housing conditions, and adaptive behaviors were negatively associated with vulnerability, implying that higher levels of these factors tend to lower vulnerability. The definition of different explanatory variables along with their expected relationship with the vulnerability is shown in Table 4.

The descriptive statistics are displayed in Table 5.

Table 4 Definition of explanatory variables and expected relation with vulnerability

Name of variables	Definition	Expected relationship
Marital status	Married = 1, unmarried = 0	+
Age	Years	−
Non-farm income	Total income minus income from agriculture and allied	+
Caste	SC = 1,ST = 2, Gen = 3, OBC = 4	+
Education	Years of schooling	−
Sex	Male = 1, Female = 0	+
Household size	Number of family members	−
Land holdings	Operational holdings = own + leased in-leased out	−
Sanitation	Having toilet facility Yes = 1, No = 0	+
Drought perception	Having perception about drought Yes = 1,No = 2	−
Housing condition	Pucca = 1,Semipucca = 2, kuchha = 3	+
Adaptation	At least 2 adaptive strategies = 1, no = 0	−
Forest degradation	Collected values of fuel woods over and above the own family consumption	+

Table 5 Descriptive statistics of explanatory variables

Variable	Mean	Std. Dev.	Min	Max	Skewness	Kurtosis
Sex	0.780	0.416	0	1	−1.352	2.828
Age	43.580	14.638	17	85	0.441	2.726
Household size	4.800	1.699	1	11	0.801	4.338
Caste	2.160	0.860	1	4	0.768	3.147
Education	4.527	4.587	0	14	0.408	1.710
Marital status	0.973	0.162	0	1	1.276	5.163
Non-farm income	55.087	55.911	0	291.667	1.400	2.959
Land holdings	0.801	0.941	0	4.806	2.124	7.704
Sanitation	0.213	0.411	0	1	1.400	2.959
Drought perception	2.207	1.119	0	3	−0.990	2.392
Housing condition	1.953	0.241	1	3	−2.767	15.571
Adaptation	0.407	0.493	0	1	0.380	1.144
Forest degradation	15.300	38.312	0	400	7.250	69.691

Source Computed from primary data

Table 6 examines 13 explanatory variables representing socio-economic and environmental factors to determine how they influence the level of household vulnerability to climate change in Purulia. Each variable's impact is assessed based on its coefficient, significance level, and practical implications for vulnerability.

The coefficient for household size is positive (0.18934) and statistically significant at the 10% level ($p < 0.1$). This indicates a direct association between household size and vulnerability: larger households are more likely to be vulnerable to climate-related risks. This means that larger households have more members to support, leading to higher resource demands and potential economic strain, especially during droughts or climate stress events. Larger families may struggle with resource allocation, potentially lacking adequate food, water, or income security. Consequently, family size management and resource allocation strategies could be focal points for reducing vulnerability.

Table 6 Estimates of ordered logistic model

	Coef.	Std. Err.	z	$P > \|z\|$	[95% Conf.	Interval]
Sex	−0.46505+	0.475906	−0.98	0.328	−0.46771	1.397812
Age	−0.01714+	0.015264	−1.12	0.261	−0.01278	0.047059
hhsize	0.18934***	0.099919	1.89	0.058*	−0.0065	0.385178
Caste	0.109581+	0.231248	0.47	0.636	−0.34366	0.562818
Edu	−0.06066+	0.047326	−1.28	0.02**	−0.15342	0.032097
Marital status	−1.27908+	1.31709	−0.97	0.331	−3.86053	1.302366
Non-farm income	−0.00528**	0.003167	−1.67	0.096*	−0.01148	0.000931
Sanitation facility	−1.71028*	0.543384	−3.15	0.002**	0.645265	2.775293
Land holdings	−0.85259*	0.22441	−3.8	0.000***	−1.29243	−0.41275
Drought perception	−1.22625*	0.249177	−4.92	0.000***	−1.71463	−0.73787
Housing condition	−0.460462+	0.444582	1.04	0.039**	−0.4109	1.331826
Adaptation	−0.2874+	0.425478	−0.68	0.099*	−1.12132	0.546524
Forest degradation	0.007451+	0.005203	1.43	0.102	−0.00275	0.017647

Note *, **, *** show significant at 1%, 5%, and 10%. + shows insignificant
Source Computed from primary data
Number of observations = 150
LR $chi^2(12) = 58.75$
Prob > $chi^2 = 0.0000$
Log likelihood = −78.020414; Pseudo $R^2 = 0.3809$

Education has a negative coefficient (−0.06066), indicating that higher educational attainment reduces household vulnerability. This effect is statistically significant at the 5% level ($p < 0.05$) (Table 6). This means that educated households may have better access to knowledge about climate risks and adaptation techniques, allowing them to make informed decisions that enhance resilience. Education also improves economic prospects, enabling households to diversify income sources or adopt more resilient agricultural practices. Promoting education could thus be a key strategy for reducing vulnerability in climate-sensitive regions like Purulia.

Non-farm income has a negative coefficient (−0.00528) and is significant at the 10% level ($p < 0.1$), suggesting that households with income sources outside agriculture are less vulnerable (Table 6). This implies that income from non-agricultural sources provides a buffer against agricultural losses due to climate impacts, offering financial security during adverse conditions. Diversifying income sources can reduce households' dependence on climate-sensitive agriculture, thereby lowering overall vulnerability. Policy interventions to promote non-farm income opportunities could be beneficial, especially in drought-prone districts.

Sanitation access has a large negative coefficient (−1.71028) and is highly significant ($p < 0.01$). This strong relationship suggests that households with proper sanitation facilities are significantly less vulnerable.

This means that the access to sanitation reduces health-related vulnerabilities, particularly in areas exposed to waterborne diseases. Improved sanitation can prevent disease outbreaks, which otherwise increase household vulnerability by imposing health and economic burdens. Enhancing sanitation infrastructure in rural areas should be a priority for reducing vulnerability to climate change.

Land holdings have a negative coefficient (−0.85259) and are highly significant ($p < 0.01$), indicating that larger land holdings correlate with reduced vulnerability. Larger land holdings enable households to produce more food and possibly diversify crop types, enhancing food security and economic stability. Households with more land may also be able to allocate land for drought-resistant crops or other adaptive measures, thus lowering vulnerability. Support for land access or improvement of smallholder productivity could be effective in reducing vulnerability.

Households with a clear perception of drought risks have a significantly lower vulnerability level (coefficient = −1.22625, $p < 0.01$). This further implies that awareness of drought risks encourages proactive adaptation behaviors, such as water conservation, early crop planting, or other risk-reducing strategies. Households informed about drought risks are better equipped to prepare and respond effectively. Public awareness campaigns and education on climate risks could thus play an essential role in fostering resilience.

The negative coefficient of housing condition (−0.460462) and statistical significance at the 5% level ($p < 0.05$) suggest that better housing conditions reduce vulnerability. Quality housing provides better protection against extreme weather, safeguarding lives and property. For vulnerable households, structural improvements (e.g., weather-proofing) could reduce exposure to climate risks. Investment in housing quality improvement, particularly for marginalized households, could be instrumental in reducing vulnerability.

Households employing adaptive measures have a lower vulnerability level (coefficient = −0.2874, $p < 0.1$), indicating that proactive adaptation efforts contribute to resilience. Households engaging in adaptation strategies—such as diversifying income, adjusting agricultural practices, or joining self-help groups—are better prepared to handle climate stresses. Policies supporting adaptation initiatives, such as microfinance for adaptive technologies or training on climate-resilient practices could help reduce vulnerability across households.

Although forest degradation is positively associated with vulnerability (coefficient = 0.007451), this relationship is not statistically significant ($p > 0.1$). This means that despite the lack of statistical significance, the positive trend suggests that forest degradation might increase vulnerability, particularly for households dependent on forest resources for fuel, fodder, and other needs. Conservation efforts to prevent forest degradation could help protect household resources and reduce vulnerability, though further research might be needed to confirm this effect.

4 Conclusions and Policy Suggestions

From the above analysis, the following conclusions have emerged.

Firstly, larger household sizes and potential forest degradation appear to increase vulnerability. Large households face greater resource demands, while forest degradation affects households reliant on forest resources for their livelihoods.

Secondly, education, non-farm income, sanitation, larger land holdings, drought perception, better housing, and adaptation efforts all reduce vulnerability. These factors represent various forms of resilience—economic stability, improved health, resource access, proactive awareness, and infrastructure—all of which equip households to better manage climate stresses.

The study has policy implications. The priority should be given to education, income diversification, sanitation improvement, climate awareness, and infrastructure development.

Bibliography

Adger, W. N. (2006). Vulnerability. *Global Environmental Change, 16*, 268–281. https://doi.org/10.1016/j.gloenvcha.2006.02.006

Adger, W. N., Brooks, N., Bentham, G., Agnew, M., & Eriksen, S., (2004). *New indicators of vulnerability and adaptive capacity* (Technical Report 7, pp. 1–122). Tyndall Centre for Climate Change Research.

Alwang, J., Siegel, P. B., & Jorgensen, S. L. (2001). *Vulnerability: A view from different disciplines* (Discussion paper). Social Protection Unit, World Bank.

Dercon, S., & Krishnan, P. (2000).Vulnerability, seasonality and poverty in Ethiopia. *Journal of Development Studies, 36*(6), 25–53.

Greene, W. H. (1997). *Econometric analysis*. Prentice Hall.

Hahn, M. B., Riederer, A. M., & Foster, S. O. (2009). The livelihood vulnerability index: A pragmatic approach to assessing risks from climate variability and change—A case study in Mozambique. *Global Environmental Change, 19*(1), 74–88. https://doi.org/10.1016/j.gloenvcha.2008.11.002

Hoddinott, J., & Quisumbing, A. (2003). *Methods for micro econometric risk and vulnerability assessments* (Social Protection Discussion Paper Series 0324). Human Development Network, The World Bank.

Koirala, S. (2015). *Livelihood vulnerability assessment to the impacts of socio-environmental stressors in Raksirang VDC of Makwanpur District Nepal* (Master thesis). The Department of International Environment and Development Studies, Noragric, Norwegian University of Life Sciences.

Opiyo, F. E., Wasonga, O. V., Nyangito. M. M., et al. (2014). Measuring household vulnerability to climate-induced stresses in pastoral rangelands of Kenya: Implications for resilience programming. *Pastoralism: Research, Policy and Practice, 4*(10).

Piya, L. (2012). *Vulnerability of rural households to climate change and extremes: Analysis of Chepang households in the Mid-Hills of Nepal* (PhD thesis). Graduate School for International Development and Cooperation (IDEC) Hiroshima University, Japan

Sen, A. K. (1984). *Resources, values and development* (p. 497). Blackwell.

Sisay, T. (2016). Vulnerability of smallholder farmers to climate change at Dabat and West Belesa Districts, North Gondar, Ethiopia. *Journal of Earth Science & Climatic Change, 7*, 8. https://doi.org/10.4172/2157-7617.1000365

Tonmoy, F. N., El-Zein, A., & Hinkle, J. (2014). Assessment of vulnerability to climate change using Indicators: A meta-analysis of the literature. *Wiley Interdisciplinary Review of Climate Change, 5*, 775–792. https://doi.org/10.1002/wcc.314

The manufacturer's authorised representative in the EU is Springer Nature Customer Service Centre GmbH, Europaplatz 3, 69115 Heidelberg, Germany. If you have any concerns regarding our products, please contact ProductSafety@springernature.com

Printed and bound by CPI Group (UK) Ltd, Croydon, CR0 4YY

21/09/2026

02219990-0010